Economics and Jewish Law

THE LIBRARY OF JEWISH LAW AND ETHICS

EDITED BY NORMAN LAMM

Jakob and Erna Michael professor of Jewish philosophy
Yeshiva University

Economics and Jewish Law

by

AARON LEVINE

KTAV PUBLISHING HOUSE, INC.
HOBOKEN
YESHIVA UNIVERSITY PRESS
NEW YORK
1987

Library of Congress Cataloging-in-Publication Data

Levine, Aaron.
Economics and Jewish law.

(The Library of Jewish law and ethics; v. 13)
Bibliography: p.
Includes index.
1. Economics—Religious aspects—Judaism.
2. Judaism—Doctrines. I. Title. II. Series.
BM509.E27L48 1987 296.3'8785 86-15250
ISBN 0-88125-106-2

Manufactured in the United States of America

For my dear parents

Dedicated to one of the distinguished philanthropists of our generation

MR. LUDWIG JESSELSON
Chairman of the Executive Committee, Yeshiva University Board of Trustees
who has combined lifelong devotion to Jewish Education with an outstanding career in business.

Contents

Foreword, by Dr. Norman Lamm xiii
Acknowledgments xv
Introduction xvii

1. **Jewish Business Ethics and Market Ethics Compared** 1
Introduction 3
Market Ethics 3
Jewish Business Ethics 5
The Self-Interest Motive in Jewish Law 5
Hin Ẓedek 6
VeYareta Me'elohekha 7
Lifnei Ivver 8
Ona'at Devarim 8
Idealized Market Conduct in Jewish Ethics 9
Genevat Da'at 11
Undeserved Good Will 12
Revealing a Secondary Motive and Concealing the Primary Motive 12
Genevat Da'at: The Passive Case 14
Above Suspicion 16
Limits to the Openness Responsibility 17
The Right to Know and the *Genevat Da'at* Interdict 17
Bilateral Monopoly and the Disclosure Obligation 20
Bluffing 21
The Corrective Obligation in the Case of Self-Deception 22
Creating a False Impression to Remove an Unwarranted Bias 24
Waiving of Rights and Forced Generosity in Market Behavior 26
Li-fenim Mi-shurat ha-Din 26
Li-fenim Mi-shurat ha-Din and Judicial Coercion 30
The Law of the Abutter 31
The Law of the Abutter and the Welfare of the Seller and Other Interested Buyers 32
Protection of the Seller's Rights 32

Protection of the Rights of Nonabutting Prospective Buyers 33
Intended Use and the Law of the Abutter 35
Suspension of the Law of the Abutter When the Buyer Is an Out-of-Town Resident 36
Kofin al Midat Sedom 36
The Lessee's Right to Make Improvements in His Rented Apartment 38
Intruding Upon the Air Space of a Neighbor's Property 38
Limitations on the Operational Significance of the *Kofin* Principle 38
Elastic Definition of Loss 39
Rights the *Kofin* Principle May Not Infringe Upon 39

2. **Advertising and Promotional Activities as Regulated in Jewish Law** 43
Bait and Switch 45
Undeserved Good Will 47
Disparagement of a Competitor's Product 49
The Comparative Merit Stratagem 49
Exclusivity Claims 51
Superiority Claims 51
Puffery 51
Puffery in the Performance Domain 54
Puffery as Treated in American Law: A Critique 54
The Testimonial Technique 57
Installments Plans Allowing the Buyer to Live Beyond His Means 59
Advertising that Incites Envy 62
Dissuading a Customer from Making a Purchase 63
Ona'ah 63
Ona'ah and Shadow Prices 67
Financial Ruination and the *Ona'ah* Interdict 68
Lifnei Ivver and the Dissuasion Responsibility 68
Lo Ta'amod al Dam Rei'akha and the Dissuasion Responsibility 69

3. **Supply-Side Economics: A Jewish Perspective** 73
Introduction 75
Supply-Side Economics 75
Preventing Excessive Competition 76
Regulation to Provide Better Information to Market Participants 77
Product Safety 78

Certification 79
Il-Defined Property Rights 79
Natural Monopoly 80
Supply-Side Economics: A Halakhic Perspective 80
Economic Incentives and Efficient Work Effort in the Rabbinic Literature 81
The Subsidiary Role of Livelihood Activities 86
Economic Incentives and the Humane Impulse 86
Economic Disincentives for Idleness and Halakhah 87
Regulation of the Marketplace and Jewish Law 87
The Nature of the Information Channels and Halakhah 88
Disclosure Obligations in Jewish Law 89
Forthright Disclosure 90
Seller Rights in the Defective Product Case 91
The Seller's Testing Obligation 92
Safe Working Conditions 94
The Enforcement Mechanism for Judaism's Disclosure and Testing Obligations 94
Certification and Regulation in Jewish Law 94
Elimination of Unnecessary Risks 96
Ill-Defined Property Rights and Jewish Law 97
The Reciprocal Nature of the Externality Problem 97
Economic Regulation of the Marketplace and Halakhah 101
Natural Monopoly in Jewish Law 102

4. **Social Welfare in Jewish Law** 105
Social Welfare Rooted in Self-Interest 107
Judaism's Social Welfare Program 113
Dei Maḥsoro 116
Dei Maḥsoro: A Collective Responsibility 116
Rate Limitations 116
Priorities in Charity-Giving 117
Eligibility for Public Assistance in Talmudic Times 118
Eligibility for Public Assistance Today 119
The Halakhic Definition of Subsistence 122
Eligibility for Private Assistance 124
Public Social Welfare 125
The Public Sector's Obligation to Uphold the Dignity of the Poor 131
The Public Sector and a Humane Environment 132
Obligations of the Recipient 133
Distributive Justice in Jewish Law 135
Profit Regulation in the Necessity Sector 136
Medical Fees 136

5. **Issues Involving Inflation in Jewish Law** 139
Introduction 141
Real vs. Nominal Interest Rates and the *Ribbit* Interdict 141
Commodity Loans 147
Denominating Loans in a Foreign Currency 150
Small Commodity Loans from a Neighbor 151
Reciprocal Labor Agreements 152
The Charity Obligation and Inflation 153
Religious Functionaries and Inflation 154
Delinquency in the Payment of Wages and Inflation 154
Theft Liability and Price Changes 155

6. **Efficiency as Treated in Jewish Law** 157
Introduction 159
Efficiency in Economic Theory 159
Efficiency as Treated in Jewish Law 160
Subsidizing Farm Income by Destroying Crops 167
Allocational Efficiency and Jewish Law 169
Efficiency Obligations Halakhah Imposes on a Businessman in a Competitive Environment 171
Technological Innovation: A Halakhic Perspective 172
Efficiency Obligations Halakhah Imposes on the Worker 177
Labor Productivity and Halakhah 178
Limits on the Employer's Right to Impose Productivity Standards 181

7. **Speculation as Treated in Jewish Law** 183
Investment Vehicles and Jewish Law 185
Corporate Bonds 185
Preferred Stock 185
Hetter Iska 188
Margin Agreements 191
Asmakhta 194
Maintenance of Margin and *Asmakhta* 197
Selling Short and *Asmakhta* 198
Remedy for *Asmakhta* 199
Selling Short and the *Ribbit* Interdict 200
Yaẓa ha-Sha'ar 202
Yesh Lo 204
Speculative Activity as Treated in Jewish Law 205
The Prohibition Against Hoarding 205
Speculation and Gambling 207
The Social Usefulness of the Stock and Bond Markets 207

The Social Usefulness of the Futures Markets 208
Stock Index Futures and Options 210
Options 212
Conclusion 212

Glossary of Economic and Legal Terms 215
Glossary of Hebrew and Aramaic Terms 221
Notes 225
Indexes 253

Foreword

Professor Aaron Levine's *Free Enterprise and Jewish Law,* published in 1980 as part of The Library of Jewish Law and Ethics, was by its very nature a pioneering work. He had to bring together two disciplines—economics and Halakhah—that had never been formally introduced in the scholarly literature, and focus both of them on the issue of free enterprise in its many ramifications. It was a superb accomplishment, and demanded of the reader a rather sophisticated level of knowledge of both economics and Talmudic law.

In the present volume, our author casts a wider net, touching on a variety of topics and analyzing the ethical and legal views of Jewish law on these multifaceted issues. He has made a conscious attempt to facilitate comprehension of the subject matter by the non-specialist. The nature of the material is such that it can never compete with a paperback thriller for light reading. But it certainly will satisfy the reader who, though neither a professional economist nor a halakhic scholar, is willing to invest a little time and somewhat more intellectual energy in order to follow Professor Levine's fascinating description of how an ethico-legal system that stems from biblical origins deals with complex economic realities of the late twentieth century.

August 29, 1986

NORMAN LAMM
Editor

Acknowledgments

The present volume is the product of research I began under a grant from the Memorial Foundation for Jewish Culture (1982–1983) and a Mellon grant from Yeshiva University (1982).

Portions of chapters 1 and 2 of this volume expand and elaborate upon my chapter "Jewish Business Ethics in Contemporary Society," in Leo Jung and Aaron Levine, *Business Ethics in Jewish Law* (New York: Hebrew Publishing Co., 1987).

With slight variation, chapter 5 of this work originally appeared in the *Journal of Halacha and Contemporary Society* (vol. 5, April, 1983, pp. 25–45).

My heartfelt appreciation to the editor of this volume, Rabbi Dr. Norman Lamm, president Yeshiva University, for his stimulating critique of my manuscript as well as for the warm encouragement he offered me throughout this project.

Dr. Yaakov Elman, associate editor at Ktav Publishing House, Inc., scrupulously read the entire manuscript and offered many valuable suggestions, both substantive and stylistic. My debt of thanks to him.

Chapter 2 benefited from the editorial assistance of my dear friend, Yaakov Kornreich. Many thanks to him.

My appreciation to Rabbi Jacob Mandlebaum, librarian at the Mendel Gottesman Library at Yeshiva University, for the very patient assistance and direction he provided me in tracking down the biographical vignettes appearing in this work.

The name index of this volume was compiled by my dear daughters, Bat-Sheva and Aliza. My heartfelt thanks to them for their labor of love, which they carried out with skill, alacrity, and extreme patience.

Ira Goldklang and David Wasserman, two very able and devoted students, assisted in the preparation of the subject index of this volume.

On the occasion of the publication of this volume, I would like to express an appreciation to my beloved wife and life companion, Sarah. As wife, mother, and unique person, she is an ever-increasing source of blessing, ennoblement, and endearment. Personifying the golden bell of the high priest's robe, she gently inspires me and our cherished children toward Torah idealism and high purpose.

I would also like to express an appreciation for my dear father-in-law and revered rebbe, Rabbi Shmuel Dovid Warshavchik. His abiding love, warm companionship, and brilliant and inspiring Torah teaching have sublimely uplifted me.

The selfless devotion and warmth showed me by my mother-in-law, Nachama Warshavchik, of blessed memory, remains indelibly impressed in my heart and mind.

To my dear parents, Rabbi Dr. Mordecai and Esther Levine, a special note of appreciation. Their deep affection, steadfast devotion, and constant encouragement have immeasurably enriched my life. My eternal debt to my father for so beautifully embodying and transmitting to our family the Torah majesty of my grandfather, *ha-Gaon meReisha z'l*. To my parents this book is dedicated.

New York — Aaron Levine
30 Sivan 5746

Introduction

The present study will analyze contemporary economic issues from the standpoint of Jewish law. Our underlying purpose will also be to demonstrate that economic analysis both sharpens the focus of halakhic study and serves it well as a tool which enhances its goals.

Chapter 1 compares Jewish business ethics and market ethics. Our thesis here is that Halakhah urges a degree of openness in market conduct beyond what the profit motive dictates. The halakhic ideal for the marketplace, we will contend, is to require market participants to deliberately expose themselves to objectively verifiable standards of conduct.

Chapter 2 will analyze modern advertising and promotional techniques from the perspective of Jewish law. Besides providing a fertile setting for the application of the moral principles developed in Chapter 1, the ethics of persuasion will be explored in more general terms. The advertising and promotional techniques we will explore include: the disparagement of a competitor's product, exorbitant claims regarding both performance and less objectively verifiable aspects of a product, the testimonial technique, installment plans allowing the buyer to live beyond his means, and finally, the incitement of envy through advertising.

One final issue of concern in this chapter will be the question of compelling a salesperson to discourage a potential buyer when it becomes evident to him that the latter's interest would best be served by the competition.

Ronald Reagan's inauguration in 1980 marked the adoption of many of the tenets of the supply-side school of economics. One of its prescriptions is the call for the government in both its tax and welfare programs to promote the operation of economic incentives in the marketplace. Another proposal is its general opposition to government regulation of industry. To the supply-sider, government regulation should only be carried to the point where the incremental costs equal the incremental benefits. In Chapter 3 we will analyze these two prescriptions from the perspective of Jewish law. In respect to the first proposition, we will demonstrate that while Judaism regards the efficiency aspect of economic incentives as a positive good, an economic system which *maximally* encourages people to increase time spent in the marketplace is not desirable from a halakhic point of view. In respect to the second proposition, Judaism is decidedly opposed to a system of unbridled capitalism. Jewish law calls for government regulation of the marketplace to protect the consumer against defective and harmful products as well as against false and misleading advertising claims. Government intervention to protect the laborer against unsafe working conditions is also necessary. Finally, a "halakhic society" demands government regulation of environmental pollution.

Government intervention in the marketplace to protect the consumer in the area of product safety can take the form of regulation or certification. Regulation thrusts the government into the role of acting in the interests of the typical consumer. If premarket testing of a product determines that it poses a threat to either the health or the safety of the consumer, the product would be banned. Certification, on the other hand, removes government from a paternalistic role; full public disclosure of the relevant risks is made, but the final decision of whether or not to buy the product is left as a matter of individual choice. Supply-siders favor certification. We will demonstrate that certification, as a means of promoting product safety in the halakhic society, is valid only when the risk the consumer will likely be exposed to is both reasonable and not immediate. Notwithstanding the validity of the certification method under certain circumstances, the product safety commission of the halakhic society would be charged with the responsibility for eliminating unnecessary risks to consumers. This duty translates into a responsibility for mandatory product design features when a presumption exists that consumers, when given all the facts, would willingly spend money to secure safety features.

While calling for deregulation of the marketplace, supply-siders recognize the need for government intervention to protect the environment. Cost-benefit analysis provides the essential element of the supply-siders' approach to the issue. In our opinion Halakhah favors instead the cost-effective approach. This method sets goals in the area of pollution abatement and facilitates the efficient pursuit of these goals without discriminating against any particular group.

Despite this particular difference in approach, Halakhah and supply-side economics are in general ageement regarding the issue of freedom of entry into the marketplace.

Chapter 4 takes up the issue of social welfare from the perspective of Jewish law. Our task here will be to delineate Judaism's social welfare philosophy and to draw out its implications both for the individual's responsibility to the poor and for governmental policy. Our major theme is that the principle of *imitatio Dei* forms the basic model for Jewish social welfare philosophy. Judaism hence rejects social welfare philosophies rooted in some form of self-interest.

The obligation to give charity includes for the public sector a duty to foster a favorable economic environment as well as an obligation to encourage a humane spirit on both a personal and an institutional level. In addition, measures to prevent poverty must take primacy over measures to relieve poverty.

Limiting the public sector's involvement in poverty relief out of concern that it not be at the expense of economic growth is a clear-cut *abdication* of society's charitable obligation. Nonetheless, once society has already devoted 10 percent or more of its income to the prevention and relief of poverty, the possible conflict between these two objectives must be taken into account. To illustrate, suppose conventional economic wisdom insists that any further substantial increase in government spending, regardless of how it is financed, threatens the economic viability of the economy. Increasing the tax burden would act as a work disincentive. On the other hand, financing increased spending by means of money-supply creation and/or borrowing runs the risk of both increasing inflationary expectations and causing a surge in interest rates. Within the context of this assessment, unless the federal government is willing to restructure its priorities, further poverty *relief* efforts must be shifted to the private sector, while the public sector fulfills its primary responsibility in the area of poverty prevention.

Judaism does not subscribe to the ethical principle of distributive justice. The Torah prescribes responsibilities to the poor, not income redistribution. It makes no judgment as to what constitutes equity in income distribution. But, while Judaism does not subscribe to the notion of income redistribution, many other factors work to enhance the economic well-being of the poor and lower-income brackets in the Torah society. These advantages include the amenities beyond merely physiological subsistence to which Halakhah entitles those who qualify for public and private assistance, the tax-exempt status of the poor, the use of a progressive income tax, and the restraint imposed on both the price of necessities and medical fees.

Alternative economic policies often present themselves as a means of achieving a particular macroeconomic goal, e.g., reducing runaway inflation. Our research will indicate that poverty reduction in the halakhic society is not a responsibility which falls equally on all, but rather is an obligation proportional to wealth. Since the creation of a favorable economic environment is of highest priority, it follows that the burden of achieving any macroeconomic social goal must be borne disproportionately by the wealthy. As a corrollary of the above, the government's responsibility is to explore alternative means of achieving macroeconomic goals with consideration of their impact on both the overall wealth and the income distribution of society. Preference must be given to those policies which offer the least prospect of increasing inequality of wealth and income in society.

In Chapter 5 we discuss inflation issues in Jewish law. One major topic is the real-nominal interest rate as it relates to Judaism's prohibition against interest payments (*ribbit* law): Does *ribbit* law merely prohibit the lender from realizing a *real* return on his loan, or is he interdicted from even earning a *nominal* return on his loan? Resolution of this dilemma involves us in an economic analysis of talmudic and rishonic sources. The real-nominal interest rate issue hence provides an example of an interface between economic analysis and Jewish law.

Other issues related to inflation in Jewish law are also taken up in Chapter 5: commodity loans; denominating a loan in a foreign currency; small commodity loans from a neighbor; reciprocal labor agreements; the real-nominal issue as it relates to the charity obligation; automatic escalator clauses for communally hired religious ministrants; delinquency in the payment of wages; and theft liability.

Providing a major example of how economic analysis can serve as a tool to sharpen the halakhic focus on an economic issue is the concept of *efficiency*. In Chapter 6 we will begin by defining efficiency as it is discussed in the economic literature. Two aspects of efficiency, one called *allocational*, and the other, *x-efficiency*, will be explored. We will then examine the extent to which Halakhah mandates the achievement of efficiency as a *religious* duty. We will find that, while not mandating general efficiency, Halakhah nevertheless imposes a measure of both allocational and X-efficiency as a religious duty.

In this chapter we will also explore the halakhic approach to technological advance as it affects the marketplace. Specifically, what protection does Halakhah afford the firm that becomes noncompetitive as a result of its failure or inability to adopt the available technology? Our contention here will be that, aside from cases of ruinous competition, Halakhah adopts a laissez-faire attitude regarding the issue of protecting firms against competitive pressures. In addition, few impediments are placed in the path of innovation and advancing technology in the halakhic society.

One final topic dealt with in this chapter concerns the issue of labor productivity. The halakhic standard of productivity, as we will show, not only requires the worker to exert himself to the utmost on behalf of his employer, but, in addition, prohibits him from engaging in actions which will have an adverse impact upon his efficiency during working hours. Prevailing practice, it will be shown, nevertheless plays a role in determining the worker's right to certain privileges outside his working schedule when the labor contract is silent on these matters. The ethics of assigning an employee useless work for the sake of keeping him busy will also be discussed.

Finally, our task in Chapter 7 will be to discuss speculation as it is treated in Jewish law. One concern is that certain investment vehicles may violate aspects of Jewish *ribbit* law. Investment in bonds and a certain type of preferred stock in a corporation a majority of whose stockholders are Jewish is a case in point. Another issue for Jewish law is that margin agreements may constitute an agreement concluded without the presumptions of perfect resolve and mutual reliance *(asmakhta)* and hence may not be legally binding. It will be our task to identify these problems and suggest halakhic means of overcoming them.

Still another issue that speculation raises for Jewish law is the question of its legitimacy as a profession. Should speculation be equated with gambling, with all the disabilities that equation brings? To avoid this we must demonstrate the social usefulness of financial markets. Economic analysis will be offered as a means of making this assessment.

· 1
Jewish Business Ethics and Market Ethics Compared

Introduction

Our task in this chapter will be to identify the distinctive features of Jewish business ethics. We will begin by describing the type of moral conduct a competitive business environment imposes on market participants. The morality imposed by the marketplace, as we will demonstrate, is, in the final analysis, rooted in self-interest. Relying on competitive pressures to produce morality reduces the *ideal* of business ethics both to the degree man fears discovery of his wrongdoing and to the intensity with which he desires to secure social approbation through his market activities.

Instead of appealing to self-interest, Judaism appeals to man's fear of God and to his sense of dignity. It makes specific demands on his market conduct. Taken together, Judaism's prescriptions for the marketplace, we will argue, have the effect of urging man to demonstrate his commitment by formulating his business policies with a degree of integrity, openness, precision, and magnanimity beyond what profit considerations would dictate.

Market Ethics

Classical economic theory rejected the widely held eighteenth-century idea that every action motivated by private gain is intrinsically antisocial. Instead, the self-interest motive was elevated to the category of virtue. Admiration for this impulse of human nature took on several dimensions. Most basically, it was recognized that only by appealing to man's self-interest can we hope for the satisfaction of our material wants. As the father of classical economics, Adam Smith, put it: "It is not from the benevolence of the butcher, the brewer, or the baker, that we expect our dinner, but from their regard to their own interest. We address ourselves, not to their humanity but to their self-love; and never talk to them of our own necessities but of their advantages."[1] In a broader sense, it is the profit motive that assures us that production decisions and occupational choices are made on the basis of the individual's assessment of society's hierarchy of preferences.

The doctrine of "spontaneous harmony" represents another dimension of classical economic theory's admiration for the self-interest motive. This doctrine teaches that private interests are essentially consistent and harmonious with social welfare. Intending only their own good, men are led by an "invisible hand" to further social ends.

Adam Smith illustrated the workings of this doctrine in his critique of eighteenth-century English university education. Universities in his time were heavily endowed, and most teachers derived their incomes entirely from these endowments. The result was that the dons' income bore no relationship to their proficiency either as teachers or as scholars. What was necessary was a system of teacher compensation that would both promote pedagogical skill and scholarship and ferret out professional incompetency. Replacing the endowment scheme with a system which calls for teachers' salaries to be derived directly from student tuition payments would, according to Smith, accomplish this end. Hence, appealing to the self-interest motive accomplishes the socially desirable goal of improving education.[2]

The underlying thesis of the doctrine of spontaneous harmony is that the interest of the community is simply the sum of the interests of the members who compose it: Each man, if left alone, will seek to maximize his own wealth; therefore, all men, if unimpeded, will maximize aggregate wealth.

Economic freedom is the essential feature of the free enterprise ethic: Consumers buy what they want, businessmen produce what they can sell, and laborers work for whoever pays most.

Why don't economic freedom and decentralized decision-making produce chaos in the allocation of society's resources? This is explained by the workings of the price mechanism. In the unregulated marketplace, price will rise when demand exceeds supply at the prevailing norm. This is the result of competitive bidding among demanders to secure the available supply. Similarly, when supply exceeds demand at the prevailing norm, competition among sellers to liquidate their inventories will depress market price.

Differences in prices act as a powerful stimulus for resource owners to expand output in those areas where supply is scarce relative to demand, and to limit output where the situation is in the reverse.

Within the free enterprise model, abnormal profits in any particular industry would be a transient phenomenon. Alert resource owners would switch to the more profitable industry. With supply increasing relative to demand, prices and profit margins would be expected to fall in the advantaged area. Simultaneously, the decrease in supply, other things being equal, in the disadvantaged sectors would tend to increase prices and profit margins there. These adjustments thus tend to narrow the original differential.

Though the free enterprise model allows man's selfish nature full expression, market forces, paradoxically, harness the selfish motive to serve the social interest. Business establishments are deterred from furnishing adulterated or shoddy goods by the fear that customers may shift their patronage to rivals. Likewise, enterprises which fail to protect their labor force against accidents or industrial disease or which work them unusually hard are penalized by the refusal of workers to work for them except at a higher wage than other employers pay.

The growing complexity of the products of the modern industrial economy has not dampened the faith of many proponents of free enterprise in the efficiency of the marketplace as a self-regulating mechanism against fraud. While individuals may not be capable of judging the quality of complex products, specialists capable of making such assessments, to be sure, exist. The success of these specialists, such as large retailers and other middlemen, hinges heavily upon the reputation of reliability they build up among their customers.

Undeniably, improvements in the information channels and increased competitive pressures work to *force* higher and higher ethical standards in business conduct. Nonetheless, a morality rooted in the fear that dishonesty may be discovered causes the level of integrity in business conduct to be dictated by profit considerations. To illustrate, let us suppose that A and B are rival vacuum cleaner manufacturers. A guarantees his product but hedges his warranty by attaching to it various caveats and disclaimers. B offers the *same* guarantee but formulates the warranty in precise, clear terms. What becomes evident is that in the event of product defect, it will be easier to obtain a refund from B than from A. Now, unless consumers are willing to pay a premium for the perceived increase advantage B offers in the event of product defect, the latter will be at a competitive disadvantage. Market ethics does not promote a level of honesty higher than profit considerations dictate.

Relying on the competitive environment and society's legal institutions to check fraud and deceit in the marketplace may at times produce very disappointing results. When competitive forces are weak and the information channels are poor, the automatic check of the marketplace against fraud and deceit becomes ineffectual. Moreover, man's avarice may convince him that artful cunning and sophisticated deceit will go undetected and offer him the best route to higher profits.

Jewish Business Ethics

In this section we will demonstrate that while Judaism fully appreciates the social usefulness of the self-interest motive, it rejects the notion that the marketplace is a self-regulating mechanism.

The Self-Interest Motive in Jewish Law

Man, according to Jewish tradition, is endowed by the Creator with two diametrically opposite inclinations, i.e., the evil impulse and the good impulse.[3] While the evil impulse impels man to behave in an acquisitive, covetous manner, the good impulse directs him toward selfless and righteous conduct.[4]

Divinely approved behavioral standards can be achieved, Judaism teaches, only by constantly encouraging the good inclination against the evil impulse.[5]

Notwithstanding its characterization of the acquisitive motive as an intrinsically debasing force, Judaism neither denies the selfish impulse a useful purpose in society nor places this proclivity completely outside the category of virtue.

Talmudic recognition that the acquisitive motive contributes in some measure to the material advancement of society is evidenced by the observation that were it not for the evil impulse, no man would procreate, build, or engage in business enterprise.[6]

Similarly, *Midrash Tanḥuma* teaches that God concealed death from man's heart in order to delude him into thinking that whatever his labor produced would be his to enjoy. If man were weighed down by thoughts of his own mortality, civilization would never thrive. Man would neither build nor plant, claiming, "Tomorrow I will die. Why should I toil for others?"[7]

Since society's physical survival would be in question without expression of the acquisitive motive, man's duty is not to *suppress* the evil impulse *entirely,* but rather, to *sublimate* it into acceptable channels.

Besides appreciating the social value of the self-interest motive, Judaism, as discussed in Chapter 6, subscribes to the notion that efficiency in work effort is best promoted by a system of economic incentives. Nonetheless, as is evident from the many instances in which Halakhah calls for intervention in the marketplace, Judaism rejects the model of unbridled capitalism. Specific instances of halakhic intervention in the marketplace will be taken up in Chapter 3. Here, we will be concerned with Judaism's moral prescriptions that force on market participants a higher ethical standard than the profit motive would dictate.

Hin Ẓedek

One of the central moral principles that Judaism prescribes for interpersonal relations is the good faith *(hin ẓedek)* imperative. In connection with the biblical prohibition against false weights and measures, the Torah writes: *Just* (ẓedek) *balances, just weights, a just ephah, and a just hin shall you have* (Leviticus 19:36). Since the *hin* is a measure of smaller capacity than the *ephah,* its mention is apparently superfluous. If accuracy is required in measures of large capacity, it is certainly required in measures of small capacity. This apparent superfluity leads Abaye (4th cent.) to connect *hin* with the Aramaic word for "yes," *hen*, giving the phrase the following interpretation: Be certain that your "yes" is *ẓedek* (sincere), and (by extension) be certain that your "no" is *ẓedek* (sincere). Hence, the phrase *hin ẓedek* forewarns against hypocritical behavior. If an individual makes a commitment or offer, he should fully intend to carry it out.[8]

Business commitments in contemporary society are often concluded through the medium of the standard contract. By supplying a set of normal terms, the standard contract covers the issues, circumstances, and contingencies that parties to the negotiations at hand would normally want to consider. Such contracts are usually written in legalistic jargon, not fully comprehensible to the layman. Some of the contractual clauses relate to minor and peripheral issues. Other clauses concern contingencies which either one or both parties regard as unlikely to occur.

To be sure, profit considerations may convince a party to a negotiation deliberately to formulate certain aspects of his commitment in vague terms. Vagueness allows room for favorable interpretation of the original agreement should the need arise. Proceeding, however, from the "good faith" imperative is the responsibility for parties to a negotiation to understand fully every aspect of their proposed contract before concluding it. Without such clarification the agreement cannot be said to have been concluded in "good faith," as each party is not aware of *precisely* what he is obligating himself to do.

Conditional obligations, it should be noted, may fall under the rubric of *asmakhta* (discussed in further detail in Chapter 7) and hence may not be legally binding. The essential feature of *asmakhta* is the presumed attitude on the part of the obligator that the *triggering condition* he mentions will never occur. Given this presumed attitude, the commitment cannot be said to have been made with perfect resolve. Since *asmakhta intrinsically* lacks the element of perfect resolve, it violates, in our view, the "good faith" imperative, notwithstanding that such a commitment would, in any case, not be subject to enforcement by the Jewish court.

VeYareta Me'elohekha

Cunning and shrewdness can often camouflage deceitful and fraudulent conduct and avoid for the perpetrator both legal consequence and social outrage. With this possibility in mind, the Torah invokes the exhortation *And you shall fear your God* in connection with those of its moral prescriptions which are likely to be viewed as easy to violate without detection.[9] Two of these prescriptions, applicable to the marketplace, are the prohibitions against offering ill-suited advice *(lifnei ivver lo titen mikh'shol,* Leviticus 19:14)[10] and the injunction against causing someone needless mental anguish *(ona'at devarim,* Leviticus 25:17).[11] Both of these injunctions illustrate the inherent weakness of a system of ethics rooted in economic self-interest.

Lifnei Ivver

Realtors, stockbrokers, and salesmen frequently function in the role of counselor and adviser. Personal economic gain may tempt such individuals to offer their clients ill-suited advice. Given their professional standing and the relative naiveté of many of their clients, the automatic check against misleading may at times prove very weak. To illustrate, a shrewd realtor may be able to persuade a young, naive couple to buy an undesirable home. His ill-suited advice may never be detected, as his clients may come to accept the unexpected repairs and financial problems associated with their home as common to all homeowners.

Ona'at Devarim

Ona'at devarim in a commercial setting, cited in the Mishnah at *Bava Meẓia* 4:10, occurs when an individual prices an article he has no intention of buying. What is objectionable here, according to R. Menaḥem b. Solomon Meiri (Perpignan, 1249–1316), is that pricing an article creates an anticipation on the part of the seller that he will make a sale. This anticipation is dashed when the inquirer decides not to pursue the matter further.[12] While the prospective buyer need not concern himself with the disappointment a vendor may experience should his price inquiry not result in his making a purchase, pricing an article he has *no intention* of buying causes the vendor *needless distress* and is hence prohibited.[13]

Given the widespread phenomenon of comparison shopping, application of the *ona'at devarim* interdict to the modern commercial setting is a bit problematic. The setting for a clear-cut modern application of this interdict is provided by the market in durable goods. Modern retail outlets in this market fall essentially into either of two categories. One type of store offers an elaborate showroom displaying a variety of models, along with expert salesmen who demonstrate their proper use and maintenance. The other is typically small, and offers only a limited number of models, with no expert salesmen at hand. These establishments do, however, allow their customers to order from catalogues which display color photographs of the models not available in the store. Due to the savings effected by maintaining a skeletal sales force and a limited range of samples, the catalogue stores can often undersell the showroom outlets. Pricing an article, such as a piece of furniture, at the showroom establishment, and eliciting the service of its salespeople, and then ordering the same item at the catalogue store violates, in our view, Jewish business ethics. Since the consumer has *no intention* of purchasing the item at the showroom store, the disappointment the salesman experiences when the inquiry does not result in a purchase amounts to a violation of *ona'at devarim.*

Idealized Market Conduct in Jewish Ethics

Judaism enjoins a market participant to act in a manner that will make his integrity objectively evident. It aims at conduct that will sanctify the mundane, i.e., behavior that will contribute positively to the moral climate of society. This calls for behavior according to objectively verifiable standards and formulating commitments in precise and unequivocal terms.

In Jewish tradition it is the character of Jacob the Patriarch that personifies integrity in its highest form (Micah 7:20). Jacob's integrity is demonstrated in his dealings with his unscrupulous father-in-law, Laban. Tending Laban's flock for hire, Jacob exerts himself to the utmost for him and never idles on his time.[14] When a mishap occurs, Jacob never shifts the blame, but instead makes good the loss even when he is not legally required to do so.[15] After fourteen years in his employ, Jacob desires to take leave of Laban, leading to the following dialogue between them:

> *Laban said to him: "If I have found favor with you, stay. I have noted the omens and seen that the Lord has blessed me for your sake. Fix your own wage, and I will pay it." Jacob answered: "You know well how I have served you, and how your livestock fared under my care. Before I came you had little indeed, but now it has increased greatly; the Lord has blessed you wherever I have turned. But when am I to provide for my own household?"* (Genesis 30:27–30)

By ascribing his good fortune to Jacob's piety rather than to his diligence, Laban, notes R. Samson R. Hirsch (Germany, 1808–1888), fails to recognize Jacob's integrity.[16]

Laban's lack of appreciation for Jacob's integrity provides, in our view, an insight as to why Jacob decides to remain in Laban's employ, despite his exploited status until now. Jacob considered it his mission to perfect in himself the character trait of integrity. His failure to make an *impact* on Laban proved to Jacob that he had not yet achieved the highest level of integrity. Jacob therefore redoubled his efforts to display a level of honesty that would make his integrity *objectively evident*. Toward this end, he proposes a plan for compensation in which he deliberately exposes himself to an objectively verifiable standard: All the spotted and mottled lambs will be removed from Laban's flock, leaving in his (Jacob's) care only the single-colored lambs. Jacob's wage will consist of the mottled and spotted goats born from the single-colored herd.[17] Jacob proclaims: *Thus my honesty will tell, when you come to look into my wages with you: Any goat in my lot that is not speckled and spotted, any sheep that is not dark, you may consider to have been stolen* (Genesis 30:33).

Paradoxically, Jacob's grand display of honesty fails to make an impact on Laban. Laban, the personification of duplicity,[18] reads ambiguity into even the most objectively precise terms of agreement. Accordingly, the exact definition of Jacob's wage is unilaterally changed by Laban no less than ten times in five years.[19] Jacob's miraculous success, with the aid of the striped rods, in producing spotted animals from the herd of single-colored ones is nevertheless taken by Laban's coterie as outright theft![20] However, persistence in displaying his honesty in an objectively evident manner does finally bring success to Jacob. His integrity makes its impact on Laban at their encounter at the mountain of Gilead. Jacob had stealthily fled with his family from Laban. When Laban overtakes him at Gilead, he is full of accusations and complaints.

> *Laban said to Jacob: "What have you done? You have deceived me and carried off my daughters as though they were captives taken in war. Why did you slip away secretly without telling me? I would have sent you off with rejoicing and song, with music and tambourines and harps. You did not even let me kiss my daughters and grandchildren; you have acted foolishly. It is in my power to do you harm; but last night the God of your father said to me, 'Beware of saying anything to Jacob, either good or bad.' If you had to leave because you longed so much for your father's home, why did you steal my gods?"* (Genesis 31:26–30)

In his reaction to Laban's outcry, Jacob once again adheres to an objective standard of honesty.

> *Jacob answered Laban, saying: "I was afraid, for I thought you would take away your daughters from me by force. If you find your gods in anyone's possession, he shall not live. In the presence of our kinsmen, identify whatever of yours I may have, and take it . . ."* (Genesis 31:31–32).

When Laban's search for his idols turns up nothing, (Genesis 31:33), Jacob unleashes a tirade against him. Jacob contrasts his own integrity with Laban's perfidy during their entire twenty-year relationship (Genesis 31:36–42). Only at this point is Laban moved to propose a covenant of peace between himself and Jacob (Genesis 31:44). Jacob's integrity has finally made its impact on Laban.

The encounter between Jacob and Laban at Gilead brings into sharp relief the contrast between authentic and false integrity. While Jacob adheres to an objectively verifiable standard of honesty, Laban's claims are not subject to verification. Masquerading as a doting father, Laban berates Jacob for depriving him of the opportunity to embrace his daughters and grandchildren before they took leave of him (Genesis 31:38). Laban's protest that he would have sent off Jacob amidst musical accompaniment amounts to nothing more than an unsubstantiated claim, bordering on mockery in the light of their previous relationship (Genesis 31:27). Finally, Laban's assertion that God commanded him to do Jacob neither good nor evil amounts to another unverifiable claim (Genesis 31:29).

The Gilead episode demonstrates that championing the cause of integrity often requires polemics with both attackers and evildoers. If integrity is to elevate the moral climate of society, its exponent must choose his battles carefully. The temptation to disprove the charges of an attacker must be resisted if such polemics would divert society's attention from one's own honesty. Jacob resists the temptation to explode Laban's masquerade as a doting father. To do this Jacob would have needed only to relate to Laban Rachel and Leah's reaction when Jacob asked them to flee with him. *Rachel and Leah answered him, saying: "Have we any share or heritage left in our father's house? Are we not regarded as strangers by him? He has sold us, and then used up our money."* (Genesis 31:14–15).

A lesser man surely would have seized the moment for sweet revenge by *setting the record straight*. Jacob, however, knows that his prime concern must be to establish his own integrity. The true feelings of Leah and Rachel toward their father are secondary. To avoid diverting Laban's attention from the central issue, i.e., Jacob's integrity, he allows Laban's self-serving pretense as a doting father to go undisputed. Jacob, who epitomizes integrity, chooses his battles carefully and is not obsessed with a need to set the record straight as regards his opponent's wrongdoing.

Genevat Da'at

One fundamental moral principle that Judaism prescribes for the marketplace is the prohibition against creating a false impression *(genevat da'at)*.[21]

An example of misleading conduct, discussed in the Mishnah, is the commercial practice of painting old utensils for the purpose of passing them off as new.[22]

The biblical source of the *genevat da'at* interdict is disputed by talmudic decisors. R. Yom Tov Ishbili (Seville, ca. 1250–1330) places such conduct under the rubric of theft.[23] R. Jonah b. Abraham Gerondi (ca. 1200–1264), however, regards *genevat da'at* as a form of falsehood *(sheker)*.[24]

Since violation of the *genevat da'at* interdict can only be avoided by making proper disclosure, this prohibition promotes objectively forthright behavior in the marketplace.

Undeserved Good Will

Good will in the form of a reputation for fine customer service, low prices, or a high-quality product is an important factor for business success and expansion. Generating good will on the basis of deception and illusion violates Jewish business ethics. Such conduct is prohibited under the *genevat da'at* interdict.

An illustration of generating undeserved good will, discussed in the Talmud, involves the sale to a non-Jew of meat originating from an organically defective animal. Duping the customer into believing he is getting a bargain by misrepresenting the meat as originating from a healthy animal constitutes *genevat da'at*. While price fraud may not be involved, as the non-Jew is charged a fair price for what he actually receives,[25] the transaction is, nonetheless, prohibited, since it leaves the customer with a feeling of obligation to the storekeeper which is undeserved. This sense of appreciation is undeserved, of course, because the bargain is imaginary.[26]

A variant of the above case occurs when the storekeeper offers the misrepresented meat as a gift to his non-Jewish friend. Authorities are in dispute as to whether this practice is objectionable.[27]

Violation of the *genevat da'at* interdict, according to Rabbi Joseph D. Epstein (contemporary), does not stand pending until the duped party actually performs an undeserved favor for the offender, but rather is transgressed immediately by dint of the "stolen" feeling of indebtedness the offender secures by means of his ploy.[28]

Revealing a Secondary Motive and Concealing the Primary Motive

Revealing to someone the secondary purpose behind one's action while concealing its primary purpose may entail infraction of *genevat da'at* law.

R. Natan's dictum, recorded in *Yevamot* 65b, states that altering the truth for the purpose of preserving peace constitutes meritorious conduct. He derives this from the Almighty's charge to Samuel when He dispatched him on the mission to anoint David as king of Israel. Initially, Samuel protested his mission: *How shall I go? For, if Saul hears, he will kill me* (I Samuel 16:2). To quiet Samuel's fear, the Almighty created a pretext for him to go: *And the Lord said, "You shall take a heifer with you, and you shall say, 'I have come to slaughter [a sacrifice] to the Lord' "* (I Samuel 16:2). When Samuel arrived at Bethlehem, the elders of the city trembled from fear, not knowing what had brought about Samuel's unexpected visit: . . . *and the elders of the city hurried toward him, and one said, "Is your coming peaceable?"* (I Samuel 16:4). Samuel now acts out the pretext and says: *Peaceable. I have come to slaughter [a sacrifice] to the Lord. Prepare yourselves, and you shall come with me to the sacrificial feast* (I Samuel 16:5).

Since Samuel actually offered the sacrifice and invited the elders to attend the sacrificial feast, why, asks R. Samuel Edels, (Poland, 1555–1631), does R. Natan regard Samuel's declaration of sacrificial intent as an untruth? Recall, however, that Samuel's primary mission in Bethlehem was to anoint David as king of Israel; his statement to the elders effectively concealed his primary purpose and therefore amounted to deceptive conduct. While such conduct would normally be prohibited, for the purpose of preserving peace it was permitted.[29]

Disclosing the secondary purpose behind one's action while concealing the primary purpose is common practice in the modern business setting. Shifting responsibility to act upon a subordinate's suggestions provides a case in point. To illustrate, Ẓemaḥ, a worker in the shipping department of a large publishing house, offers suggestions to improve the efficiency of his unit to Ḥai, his supervisor. Ḥai thinks highly of the ideas, but fears that acceptance of the plan might cast him in a poor light for not originating the plan himself. He therefore embarks upon a scheme to suppress Ẓemaḥ's ideas. Vetoing the plan outright would only run the risk of antagonizing Ẓemaḥ and drive him to pursue his plan with the president of the company. Instead, Ḥai decides to praise Ẓemaḥ for his insights but point out to him that any new plan must ultimately be approved by Medaber, the vice-president in charge of plant operations. So as not to ruffle Medaber's feelings, Ḥai directs Ẓemaḥ to submit to him a written report detailing his proposal. Knowing full well both Ẓemaḥ's difficulty in expressing himself in writing and his distaste for paperwork, Ḥai is quite confident that this course of action will effectively sabotage the threatening plan. Notwithstanding Ḥai's *legitimate concern for protocol,* by handling Ẓemaḥ's initiative in this manner, Ḥai effectively conceals both his opposition to the plan and his obstructionist scheme.

A variant of the above case provides us with another frequently encountered situation in personnel relations. Suppose Ḥai views Ẓemaḥ's ideas as being without merit, but does not want to antagonize him by assuming the onus of rejecting the suggestions himself. Instead of using his discretionary authority to reject the ideas outright, Ḥai insists that a report be submitted to vice-president Medaber. Notwithstanding Ḥai's legitimate concern for protocol, his approach is primarily rooted in a desire to shift the onus of decision-making to Medaber, rather than in a concern to involve the latter in the ideas of his subordinates. Since Ḥai's action effectively allows him to conceal his own opposition to Ẓemaḥ's plan, the conduct must be characterized as deceptive.

One may very well object to characterizing Ḥai's behavior in the latter instance as unethical. Since his motive is clearly to prevent a strain from developing in his relationship with Ẓemaḥ, concealing his opposition to the plan effectively preserves "peace," and by dint of R. Natan's dictum should be deemed permissible conduct. The legitimacy of Ḥai's conduct hinges, as it appears to us, on the consistency he displays in exercising his discretionary authority. Reacting to Ẓemaḥ's suggestion by insisting that a higher authority be involved in the decision, rather than by rejecting it outright, can be said to preserve "peace" only when Ḥai handles *all* subordinate suggestions of similar type, regardless of origin, in the same manner. Dissension and not peace, however, is fostered by a discriminatory policy. While concealment enables Ḥai to preserve his smooth relationship with Ẓemaḥ, dignifying the latter's plan by insisting that the vice-president consider its merits serves only to generate jealousy and resentment among those who are accustomed to having their equally important ideas shunted at the supervisory level.

Genevat Da'at: The Passive Case

Suppose A is aware that B harbors a false impression of him, but he has played no role, either through action or through word, in inspiring this false impression. Does A's passivity in the matter free him of an obligation to correct B's misconception about him? An analysis of a point of law dealing with the treatment of the unintentional murderer provides an insight into the attitude of Jewish law in such a case. The unintentional murderer is sentenced by the Jewish court to flee to one of the "cities of refuge." There he must remain until the death of the high priest (Numbers 34:9–34). In respect to the status of the manslayer during his stay in the city of refuge, the Mishnah at *Makkot* 2:11 states:

> Similarly, a manslayer, if on his arrival at his city of refuge, the men of that city wish to do him honor, he should say to them, "I am a manslayer!" And if they say to him, "Nevertheless [we wish it]," he should accept from them [the proffered honor], as it is said: *And this is the word of the manslayer* [Deuteronomy 19:14].

One critical element in identifying the circumstance of the Mishnah's case is the precise nature of the presumption the townspeople are operating under when they proffer the manslayer the honor. Does the Mishnah speak of a case where the townspeople are fully aware that their proposed honoree is a manslayer? Or is the Mishnah speaking of a simple case of mistaken identity (i.e., if the townspeople had known of his criminal status, the honor would not have been tendered)? The latter interpretation squarely places the manslayer within the framework of *genevat da'at* law.

A proof in support of the latter interpretation is the following point in *genevat da'at* law that the Jerusalem Talmud derives from the above Mishnah: Suppose the townspeople assess A to be proficient in two tractates, when, in fact, he is proficient in only one. Notwithstanding A's *passive role* in the community's bloated assessment of him, he is, nonetheless, obligated to correct their misconception. This lesson is derived by the Jerusalem Talmud from the refusal obligation of the manslayer discussed above.[30] Now, if the bloated-assessment ruling is derived from the manslayer case, then parallel structure requires the manslayer case to involve a mistaken offer of honor as well.

This approach to the above-cited passage from the Mishnah makes it abundantly clear why the manslayer's obligation to refuse the mistaken honor must be established by force of the verse *And this is the word of the manslayer.* Since the "refusal obligation" is rooted in *genevat da'at* law, it might be argued that given the *passive role* the manslayer assumed in inspiring the community's false impression, he is free of any obligation to correct their misconception of him. Interjection of *And this is the word of the manslayer* is therefore necessary to include even the passive case in the corrective obligation.

Broadening the corrective obligation to even the passive case apparently does not follow from R. Yom Tov Ishbili's discussion of the introductory clause of the above-cited Mishnah passage. The passage in question begins with the connecting word *similarly,* points out R. Ishbili, and this indicates a definite link with the preceding passage (*Makkot* 2:10). In this passage we are told that if the manslayer is a Levite already residing in an official city of refuge, he may not serve his punishment of "exile" in his own city of residence, but rather must be banished to another city of refuge. The underlying purpose of banishment, explains R. Ishbili, is to humble the manslayer by isolating him from his familiar surroundings. Allowing the Levite the convenience of serving his exile in his *own* place of residence would therefore defeat the whole purpose of banishment. Now, the link between *Makkot* 2:10 and 2:11 becomes abundantly clear. The point of law discussed in 2:11 is also rooted in a desire to humble the manslayer so as to effect his atonement. Accordingly, should the townspeople of his city of refuge offer to honor him, the manslayer must humble himself and initially refuse the honor, so as to say, "On account of the heinous crime I committed I am not worthy of honor."[31]

Since the manslayer's obligation to refuse the proffered honor stems from his need for atonement, extending the corrective responsibility to the bloated-assessment case discussed above would not appear valid. What follows from R. Ishbili's view is that a *compelling* case cannot be made for imposing corrective responsibility in the *passive* case.

Above Suspicion

Displaying honesty in an open fashion also has a passive component. This consists of the obligation to avoid behavior which, while intrinsically upright, arouses suspicion of wrongdoing. Admonition against such conduct is found in the biblical exhortation *And you shall be guiltless before the Lord and before Israel* (Numbers 32:22).

Applications of this moral imperative abound in the talmudic literature.[32] One application relates to the conduct prescribed for charity wardens.

In mishnaic and talmudic times, copper coins were considered unsuitable for extended storage because they were liable to tarnish and mold. Thus, when copper coins accumulated, they were typically exchanged for silver coins. To avoid suspicion, charity wardens were not permitted to exchange copper coins in their trust for their own silver coins. Instead, they were required to exchange the coins with outsiders only.

Similarly, when surplus food accumulated in the soup kitchen the overseers could not buy the food themselves, but instead had to sell it to others.[33]

The "above suspicion" imperative finds ready application in the modern business setting. An employee in a position of trust often can secure reimbursement of business expenses without submitting verifying receipts. The "above suspicion" imperative, however, requires the employee to submit appropriate documentation and verification data, instead of taking advantage of his position of trust by securing reimbursement by means of self-declaration alone.

Limits to the Openness Responsibility

The preceding discussion has demonstrated that the *genevat da'at* interdict as well as the "above suspicion" imperative work to force market participants to display an openness beyond what may be dictated by profit considerations. The openness responsibility, however, has its limits. First, forthright and complete disclosure extends only to matters a negotiating party has a right to know. Second, correcting a false impression applies only when the inference was an objectively reasonable judgment or assessment. The corrective responsibility is, however, not morally expected when the false impression is the result of self-delusion. Finally, for the purpose of counteracting an unwarranted bias, the creation of a false impression is permissible under limited circumstances. In this section we will take up each of these points of leniency in *genevat da'at* law.

The Right to Know and the Genevat Da'at Interdict

Contrary expectations and entrepreneurial intent, especially in the real estate and financial securities sectors, provide the basis for numerous market transactions in the modern business setting. Any ethical prescription calling for the sharing of *all* information in the marketplace would not only eliminate a good deal of speculative profit but also would generate a disincentive to engage in entrepreneurial activity. Concealment of information, as it appears to us, can only be viewed as deceptive if it in *some way misrepresents the nature of the property right being transferred.* When the information, however, relates only to either the motives or the entrepreneurial intent of the parties involved, full disclosure of the information becomes a moral obligation only when the other party explicitly *requests* its disclosure. In the absence of such an explicit request, engaging in tactics to *distract* one's opposite number from pursuing certain lines of inquiry is permissible.

Identity disclosure provides a case in point: Tower, the head of a multibillion-dollar real estate development conglomerate, desires to build a Disneyland-like project in Seattle. Realizing that his open entry into the real estate market would have the effect of enormously bidding up the value of the desired parcels of land, Tower uses several of his less-known subsidiaries to negotiate the real estate deals. Alternatively, Tower creates a new corporation for the purpose of acquiring the desired parcels. With obscurity thereby achieved,

Tower secures the desired parcels at relatively low prices. Since the use of one or the other of these ploys has merely enabled Tower to capture entirely for *himself* the market value of his entrepreneurial effort, his subterfuge for concealing his identity does not, in our view, violate *genevat da'at* law.

Supporting the above thesis, in our view, is the mainstream rabbinic interpretation of the first two commercial transactions recorded in the Pentateuch.

In the first recorded transaction, Abraham acquires the Cave of Machpelah from Ephron the Hittite as a burial plot for his wife, Sarah (Genesis 23:1–20). Midrashic tradition teaches that Abraham was acutely anxious to acquire this particular cave because he knew that Adam and Eve were buried there. This circumstance imparted inestimable spiritual significance to the cave, making it priceless as far as Abraham was concerned. From Ephron's standpoint, however, the cave was no more than a dark, desolate place, having no value whatsoever. In fact, tradition has it that whenever Ephron tried to enter the cave, he saw a man who appeared ready to kill him. Ephron's lowly spiritual status made him unworthy of learning the secret of the cave and deriving any personal benefit from it. Notwithstanding the cave's negative value to him, had Ephron only known its great value to Abraham, he probably would have spared no effort to extract the highest possible price for its sale. Here, Abraham demonstrated his business acumen. Instead of revealing his interest in the cave immediately, which would put him at a commercial disadvantage, Abraham initiates his discussion with the Hittites with a neutral statement: *Give me property for a burial site with you* (Genesis 23:4). Taking this statement as a gesture of warmth and endearment, the Hittites understand Abraham as saying: "I do not wish to be separated from you even after death. Therefore I wish to bury my dead among yours." Abraham now pauses and waits for the opportune moment to express his interest in the Cave of Machpelah. This moment arrives immediately, as the Hittites respond glowingly: *You are a prince of God in our midst, bury your dead in the choicest of our burial sites* (Genesis 23:6). By expressing his interest in the cave in an incidental manner, Abraham conceals his eagerness and strikes the best possible deal for the cave.[34]

Another indication of the permissibility of the buyer's engaging in tactics designed to distract the seller from his entrepreneurial intent is provided by an analysis of Jacob's purchase of the birthright from Esau.

> *Once when Jacob was making a stew, Esau came in from the fields famished. Whereupon Esau said to Jacob: "Let me swallow some of that red*

> *pottage, for I am famished!" . . . Said Jacob: "First sell me your birthright." Said Esau: "I am about to die; of what use is a birthright to me?" Said Jacob: "First give me your oath." So he gave him his oath, and sold his birthright to Jacob. Jacob then gave Esau bread and stewed lentils. He ate and drank, then rose and went away. Thus did Esau disdain the birthright* (Genesis 25:29–34).

A superficial reading of the biblical account of the sale of the birthright leaves the impression that Jacob secured the birthright for a nominal sum by means of exploiting Esau's famished condition. Far from finding fault with Jacob's conduct, the sages defend him. The key to the defense is Scripture's characterization of Esau's attitude toward the birthright as one of disdain *(ve-yivez et ha-bekhorah)*.[35] Since we are already informed that it was Esau's famished condition which led him to sell his birthright, mention of his disdainful attitude toward the birthright at the conclusion of the transaction implies, according to Naḥmanides (Spain, 1194–1270), that it was not desperation which drove him to accept a pittance for his birthright. Even without his feelings of desperation, Esau would still have regarded the pot of lentils as a fair price for the birthright.[36]

Esau's contempt for the birthright stemmed from his assessment that it entailed no material benefit for him, according to R. Abraham Ibn Ezra (Spain, 1089–ca. 1164). Since his father, Isaac, was destitute, the double-portion inheritance right of the firstborn offered no prospect of material advantage.[37]

Strenuously objecting to R. Abraham Ibn Ezra's pauperization of Isaac, Naḥmanides avers that Isaac, along with the other Patriarchs, was an individual of prodigious wealth. The double-portion right of the firstborn was, however, not instituted until the Sinaitic Covenant. Before Sinai, the advantage of the firstborn consisted of inheriting the authority of the father. This conferred the firstborn with honor and distinction in relation to the younger brothers. Since the birthright carried with it no distinction except after the passing of the father, it had no value to a man like Esau, who was in constant mortal danger from the animals he hunted. His brutal lifestyle convinced him that in all likelihood he would not outlive his father.[38]

We should note that one aspect of the distinction the firstborn enjoyed at the time Esau sold his birthright was the privilege of being the family priest in offering sacrifices to the Almighty. The negotiation between Jacob and Esau focused, according to R. Solomon b. Isaac (Troyes, 1040–1105), around this aspect of the birthright. When Jacob informs Esau of the various stringences in law surrounding this privilege, Esau regards it as a burden, exclaiming, *I am about to die; of what use is a birthright to me?* (Genesis 25:32)—"I will surely deserve death on account of it." Regarding Esau as a wicked man, unworthy of representing the family in offering sacrifices, Jacob eagerly seeks to acquire the birthright, thereby preventing Esau from performing the priestly service.[39]

Esau's contempt for the birthright makes it of little value in his own eyes, but Jacob's keen interest in it creates a lucrative commercial opportunity for him. Seizing the moment of Esau's famished condition to initiate negotiations for the birthright represented an opportune time for Jacob to secure it. Since Esau *intrinsically* valued the birthright as worth no more than a pot of lentils, the tactic amounted to nothing more than a diversionary maneuver. In his weakened state Esau would be quite amenable to thinking of the birthright in terms of what it meant to him rather than in terms of its significance to Jacob. Since the birthright could not theoretically be transferred to anyone other than Jacob, the latter's tactic did not deprive Esau of the opportunity to secure a higher price for the right from another party.

Supporting our assertion is R. Ephraim Solomon b. Aaron of Lenczycza's (d. 1619) interpretation of the birthright sale. It was no mere coincidence that upon his return from a hunting expedition, Esau encountered Jacob while the latter was preparing a lentil stew. Rather, this encounter was carefully planned by Jacob. Noting that lentils is the food of mourners, R. Ephraim suggests that Jacob's intent was to reproach Esau immediately upon his return from his dangerous adventure, in effect saying, "Esau, your brutal style of living will result in imminent death for you. Soon, I will be sitting in *mourning* for you."[40] This, he hoped, would drive Esau into an amenable state of mind for the purpose of conducting the sale of the birthright. Instead of fixing on the significance of the birthright to Jacob, Esau is made to reflect upon his own precarious existence, which, in turn, makes him realize that the birthright is worthless to him.

Bilaterial Monopoly and the Disclosure Obligation

The Machpelah and birthright transactions, as it appears to us, share one important characteristic: Both pit a single buyer against a single seller. Alternative sources of supply are not available to the buyer. Likewise, the seller does not enjoy the benefit of having bidders compete for his product or service. The article of transfer hence has no objective value; its value is, rather, determined by the negotiating process itself. The above circumstance is referred to by economists as the *bilateral monopoly model*. It is within this context that some measure of diversionary tactics is halakhically countenanced.

Conceptualizing the birthright-sale case into the mold of the bilateral monopoly model puts to question a halakhic ruling which is based on this biblical narrative. The ruling involves the ethics of duping a *rasha* (wicked person) into selling a *Sefer Torah* (holy scroll) or other religious article below its market price. Since the *rasha* derives no personal use from the *essence* of the religious article, i.e., its spiritual dimension, it is not unethical, according to R. Judah b. Samuel He-ḥasid of Regensburg (ca. 1150–1217), to take advantage of his ignorance of its commercial value.[41] The ruling is apparently astonishing, since it bears no resemblance to the bilateral monopoly model. A religious article has commercial value *independent* of the transaction at hand, and its sale should be subject to the law of *ona'ah* (price fraud), discussed at length in Chapter 3. The Talmud, in fact, specifically mentions the operational significance of the law of *ona'ah* in connection with a *Sefer Torah.*[42]

One of the most important applications of the bilateral monopoly model in contemporary society is the collective bargaining process. Within the framework of this process, labor seeks to strike a deal above the minimum level its members would accept and management seeks to impose a settlement below the maximum level the company would tolerate. The outcome of the negotiation is not predictable, since its final shape will be determined by the negotiating skills of the parties involved. Neither management nor labor has a legitimate right to know each other's minimum acceptable position. What the threat of a strike or plant closure represents, hence, is no more than the ultimate means available to labor and management, respectively, to protect the privacy of their minimum acceptable positions. Consequently, if, say, the labor negotiator feels that management has not yet come forward with its best offer, no objection would be found to his reacting to management's proposal at hand with the prediction that it would trigger a strike. Though the negotiator has no direct handle on the sentiments of the membership, legitimacy would be given to his expressing the above threat. Given both the confidence and the discretion entrusted to him, the negotiator may well rely on his own judgment that the membership would follow his recommendation.

Bluffing

A threat amounts to no more than a bluff, however, when the negotiator is aware, at the time he makes his representations, that they run counter to the explicit instructions of his principals. Despite the intent of pushing management toward further concessions, such conduct clearly violates his agency relationship and hence is unethical. In a similar vein, it is unethical for a principal in a negotiating process to engage in bluffing tactics. Expressing an intent with no resolve to carry it out violates Judaism's good faith *(hin ẓedek)* imperative.

Bluffing is legitimate in Jewish law, however, when it is resorted to as a means of averting loss in a breach-of-contract setting. Illustrating this is the recourse Halakhah offers an employer who stands to suffer a *material* loss as a result of a work stoppage by his day-laborer *(po'el)*. While the right of the *po'el* to withdraw without incurring penalty for the unfulfilled portion of his contract is generally recognized,[43] this right is suspended when the employer would suffer a *material* loss if the work is not given immediate attention. Faced with the prospect of a work stoppage here, the employer may promise the recalcitrant worker a raise as an inducement to complete the work. Should the tactic succeed, the employer bears no responsibility to pay the differential,[44] and is entitled to recovery of the "extra wage" in the event he paid it out.[45]

The Corrective Obligation in the Case of Self-Deception

While misleading someone by word or action is prohibited, an individual is not obligated to correct an erroneous impression when it is the result of self-deception. The following episode, recorded in *Ḥullin* 94b, illustrates this point:

> Mar Zutra, the son of R. Naḥman, was once going from Sikara to Maḥuza, while Rava and R. Safra were going to Sikara, and they met on the way. Believing that they had come to meet him he said, "Why did the rabbis take this trouble to come so far [to meet me]?" R. Safra replied, "We did not know that the master was coming; had we known of it we should have put ourselves out more than this." Rava said to him, "Why did you tell him this? You have now upset him." He replied, "But we would be deceiving him otherwise." "No. He would be deceiving himself."

Talmudic decisors regard Rava's reaction as appropriate. Since Mar Zutra had no basis for presuming that his fortuitous meeting with his colleagues constituted a welcoming party, Mar Zutra was guilty of self-deception. Consequently, the group was not under obligation to correct the erroneous impression.[46]

While the judgment that Mar Zutra was a victim of self-deception provides the rationale for relieving R. Safra and Rava of an obligation to divulge to him the fortuitous nature of their encounter, the appropriateness of this course of action apparently follows from a different standpoint as well. Examination of the details of the incident reveal that had R. Safra and Rava only known of Mar Zutra's impending arrival, they would have gladly formed a greeting party in his honor. Why, then, would their failure to correct Mar Zutra's misconception be a violation of the *genevat da'at* interdict? This incident is apparently analogous to the wine-barrel hospitality case discussed in *Ḥullin* 94a. Here, we are told that a host should not delude his guest into believing that he had acted toward him with magnanimous hospitality when in fact he had not done so. Opening a barrel of wine in honor of a guest usually constitutes a gesture of magnanimous hospitality, as the wine remaining in the barrel may deteriorate as a result of its exposure to the air. The magnanimity of the gesture is, however, considerably reduced when the host happened to have sold the barrel of wine to a retailer just prior to the arrival of his guest. Opening a barrel of wine for a guest without informing him of the sale violates the *genevat da'at* interdict, as the nondisclosure generates an undeserved sense of indebtedness to the host. Nonetheless, the Talmud relates that R. Judah (second half of 3d cent.) opened a barrel of presold wine for his guest, Ulla. While one version of the incident reports that R. Judah made disclosure of the sale to his guest, another version insists that he did not. The second version is defended by the Talmud on the grounds that Ulla was very dear to R. Judah, and consequently he would have extended him the hospitality gesture even if it entailed considerable expense.

The Tosafot reject the above analogy. In the wine-barrel hospitality case, R. Judah's *action,* i.e., the opening of the barrel, involved no element of deception, as it was clearly done to honor Ulla. The only element of possible infringement of *genevat da'at* consists of the false impression conveyed that the act of hospitality entailed considerable expense. Since R. Judah was quite certain that he would have honored his guest Ulla by opening a barrel of wine for him even if it entailed considerable expense, nondisclosure does not amount to *geneva da'at*. In sharp contrast, R. Safra and Rava's journey to Sikara was clearly *not* undertaken for the purpose of honoring Mar Zutra. Given the fortuitous nature of the encounter, relieving R. Safra and Rava of an obligation to correct Mar Zutra's false impression of tribute cannot be defended on the basis of the certainty that these scholars would have formed a greeting party for Mar Zutra had they only known of his arrival.[47]

It should be noted that the point of leniency in *genevat da'at* law which emerges from the R. Judah–Ulla incident is conspicuously omitted by Maimonides and R. Jacob b. Asher in their treatments of the wine-barrel hospitality case. Noting the curious omission, R. Aryeh Judah b. Akiba (Galicia, 1759–1819) posits that the aforementioned codifiers regard the talmudic incident as lacking general applicability. Vicarious assessment of a selfless devotion toward a guest frees the host of an obligation to correct the latter's false impression of magnanimous hospitality only when the host is a man like R. Judah, i.e., an individual of exceptional moral character. Here, the host's self-assessment that he would confer a generous gesture of hospitality upon his guest even if it entailed a considerable expense is completely reliable. Such an assessment would not, however, free an individual of ordinary moral character from the disclosure obligation. For an ordinary person such an assessment amounts to *self-delusion*. Confronted with an *actual* opportunity to confer a generous gesture of hospitality on his friend only at a considerable expense, the average person would find many convenient excuses not to do so. Since the point of leniency in *genevat da'at* inferred from the R. Judah–Ulla incident does not have general applicability, Maimonides and R. Jacob b. Asher omit mention of it.[48]

In our view, a host who assesses himself as ready to incur the necessary expense to provide a guest with whatever the guest imagines himself to be bestowed is free from the obligation to correct the guest's false impression only if the *genevat da'at* interdict is regarded as pertaining to a form of falsehood. Should the *genevat da'at* interdict be regarded as a form of theft, however, it is difficult to see why an assessment of selfless devotion toward the guest frees the host from the obligation to correct the latter's false impression of lavish hospitality. Since the sense of indebtedness a guest feels toward his host is based on what he *perceives* the host as actually doing for him and not on what the host is certain in his *own* heart he would do for him, the failure of the host to correct his guest's false impression of hospitality would cause the guest to feel an undeserved sense of indebtedness to the host.

Proceeding as a corollary from the above analysis is that the two versions of the R. Judah–Ulla incident are rooted in the source of the *genevat da'at* interdict. Following the line that *genevat da'at* is a form of theft, Maimonides and R. Jacob b. Asher rule according to the version which held that R. Judah did correct Ulla's false impression of hospitality.

Creating a False Impression to Remove an Unwarranted Bias

In today's labor market, job seekers often encounter unwarranted biases against them. Is it permissible for the job seeker to create a false impression to neutralize the unwarranted bias?

One specific example is the question of whether an individual is permitted to sham a youthful appearance by dyeing his beard, for the purpose of enhancing his chances to secure employment. Addressing himself to this question, Rabbi Mosheh Mordecai Epstein (Israel, 1866–1933) permits the conduct, provided that the employer's expectations of the employee's performance will be met. Realizing that productivity could decline sharply with advancing age, Rabbi Epstein points out that, in the final analysis, the legitimacy of the conduct rests on the accuracy of the self-assessment of the job seeker.[49] Advancing a similar analysis, Rabbi Eliezer Meir Preil (New Jersey, 1881–1934) arrives at the same conclusion.[50] Concurring with the above rulings is Rabbi Mosheh Feinstein.[51]

R. Aryeh Judah b. Akiba's conclusion regarding the unreliability of self-assessment, cited earlier, apparently places him at odds with these lenient rulings. It is possible to reconcile them, however, by dividing instances of self-assessment into two categories: those relating to routine circumstances, and those relating to extraordinary, hypothetical situations. Self-assessment may very well be reliable when it relates to ordinary, predictable life situations. While productivity may drop off with advancing age, honest self-appraisal can indicate to the senior job seeker whether or not he can meet the employer's performance standards.

The reliability of self-assessment when it relates to the realm of the hypothetical is another matter. Individuals of ordinary moral character cannot extrapolate with any degree of certainty how they would react to a hypothetical situation requiring extraordinary effort on their part.

Let us apply this distinction to another case involving the bias a job seeker often encounters. Suppose, in the course of Strulowitz's interview for a computer programming job, Perach, his interviewer, makes note of the fact that Strulowitz lives a good two-hour ride from the prospective work site. Perach then launches a tirade against plant workers who live similar distances away from work, complaining that every time the area is hit with inclement weather, these workers arrive several hours late. Perach's attack ends with the stern admonition that the firm expects workers to report on time regardless of weather conditions. Strulowitz has no intention of moving, but realizes that unless he gives the impression of such an intent, he has no chance of landing the job. Rationalizing that in the event of inclement weather he would set out from his home several hours earlier than usual to ensure punctual arrival, Strulowitz proceeds to bemoan the various inconveniences he must endure by living so far from the city. Strulowitz's grumbling creates the impression that he is amenable to moving. Given the unreliability of self-assessment when it relates to willingness to undertake an extraordinary effort in a hypothetical situation, Strulowitz's maneuver amounts to deceptive conduct.

It should be noted that what appears to the job seeker as unwarranted bias may, in fact, be reasonable, given all the facts. For instance, a firm may desire to fill a position with an individual who would blend well into the personality mix and socioeconomic background of the existing work force. Selection according to such criteria promotes the efficiency of the entire team of which the new employee will become part. Given the job seeker's limited knowledge regarding the *needs* of his prospective employer, deliberately deceptive maneuvers to counteract "perceived" bias can be permitted only in very limited and clear-cut circumstances.

Waiving of Rights and Forced Generosity in Market Behavior

The responsibility for openness in business dealings, described above, represents but one aspect of Jewish business ethics. Another aspect of Jewish business ethics is the degree of altruism and decency it requires of man in all his interpersonal relations. The effect of this latter moral imperative, as we will demonstrate, is to prescribe for market participants a level of magnanimity the profit motive would not be likely to force on them. Two of these principles are the *li-fenim mi-shurat ha-din* imperative and the *kofin al midat sedom* principle. In this section we will discuss, in turn, each of these two principles.

Li-fenim Mi-shurat ha-Din

One aspect of Judaism's requirement to act magnanimously in interpersonal relations is its *li-fenim mi-shurat ha-din* imperative. This dictum requires that one conduct himself beyond the strict letter of the law as both claimant and defendant. R. Joseph derives this code of conduct from the verse *and make them know the way wherein they must go, and the deeds that they must do* (Exodus 18:20)—*the deeds* refers to strict law; *that they must do* refers to *li-fenim mi-shurat ha-din.*[52]

Underscoring the importance Judaism attaches to the *li-fenim mi-shurat ha-din* behavioral expectation is R. Yoḥanan's dictum, "Jerusalem was destroyed only because they gave judgment therein in accordance with the law of the Torah . . . and did not act *li-fenim mi-shurat ha-din.*"[53]

The Tosafot offer an operational guideline as to the extent of the obligation to act *li-fenim mi-shurat ha-din.*[54] Sorting out the various talmudic cases dealing with the *li-fenim mi-shurat ha-din* concept, the Tosafot divide the cases into three separate categories.

The first category deals with cases where Halakhah prescribes a general behavioral norm for a particular circumstance, but exempts certain people from this norm. Here, *li-fenim mi-shurat ha-din* requires the person exempted to waive his privileged status and conform to the general legal norm, even if so doing would involve him in a monetary loss.

Illustrating the above rule is R. Ḥiyya's behavior in a currency-validation case, discussed in *Bava Kamma* 99b. The following background information will clarify the point at issue. In talmudic times, merchants were sometimes offered for payment coins which they were uncertain would circulate in the marketplace. Money changers were frequently approached for advice in this regard. Determining whether a particular coin would be accepted as a medium of exchange was regarded by the sages as a very precise art. Only an authoritative expert, i.e., one who needed no further instruction in the art, was therefore really qualified to make such judgments. Consequently, money changers who had not attained authoritative status were responsible for replacing coins they erroneously determined would circulate.[55] To be sure, the authoritative expert, too, was responsible for his error, in the event he stipulated a fee for his service.[56] While his judgment cannot be viewed as a form of negligence, the fee arrangement makes it clear that the client relied on his judgment. Since the damage resulted directly from relying on the expert's advice, the latter's action was regarded as a form of *garme*.[57]

Against the above background, the Talmud relates that R. Ḥiyya, who was an authoritative money changer, once erroneously advised a woman gratis that the coin she was offered would circulate. Upon learning of his mistake, R. Ḥiyya, acting *li-fenim mi-shurat ha-din*, chose to reimburse the woman for her loss. Since a professional nonexpert money changer was usually liable in this case, R. Ḥiyya chose to waive the special privilege proceeding from his status as an authoritative money changer, even though in so doing he incurred a monetary loss.[58]

Li-fenim mi-shurat ha-din conduct of a less demanding nature is expected of man when Halakhah generally exempts everyone from a particular duty, but waiving the privilege and performing the duty does not generate a monetary loss for the exempted party. An illustration of this is a case in which Samuel's father restored lost donkeys to their owner. By the strict letter of the law, the finder of a lost animal must make a public announcement of his find. If the animal is capable of working to earn its keep, the finder is not obligated to hold it more than twelve months—even if the owner has not made his claim. After this period, the finder may sell the animal and hold the proceeds for the owner. Acting *li-fenim mi-shurat ha-din*,

Samuel's father held the donkeys for more than twelve months until they were claimed.[59] Since holding on to the donkeys instead of selling them involved no monetary loss for Samuel's father, *li-fenim mi-shurat ha-din* conduct required him to hold on to them until they were claimed.[60]

When the legal right consists of a damage claim against an employee, *li-fenim mi-shurat ha-din* conduct, according to the Tosafot, does not require the employer to waive his claim. Another moral principle of special piety, as discussed in the following talmudic text in *Bava Meẓia* 83a, may, however, at least recommend that he do so.

> Some porters broke a barrel of wine belonging to Rabbah b. Bar Ḥannan. Thereupon he seized their garment; so they went and complained to Rav. "Return them their garment," he ordered. "Is that the law?" he inquired. "Yes," he rejoined, *"that you shall walk in the way of good men* [Proverbs 2:20]." Their garments having been returned, they observed, "We are poor men, have worked all day, and are hungry. Are we to get nothing?" "Go and pay them," he ordered. "Is that the law?" he asked. "Yes," he rejoined, *"and keep the path of the righteous* [Proverbs 2:20]."

Under the assumption that the wine barrels were broken through the negligence of the porters,[61] Rabbah b. Bar Ḥannan had a legitimate damage claim against them. While the behavioral expectation to act *li-fenim mi-shurat ha-din* did not require Rabbah b. Bar Ḥannan to forgo his damage claim, Rav urged him to do so on the basis of the moral principle *that you shall walk in the way of good men.* Upon learning that the porters were indigent, Rav even urged Rabbah b. Bar Ḥannan to pay them their wages on the basis of the ethical imperative *and keep the path of the righteous.*[62] These latter ethical teachings evidently demand of man an even more generous and selfless nature than the *li-fenim mi-shurat ha-din* imperative.

While the Tosafot understand the ethical principles proceeding from the verse in Proverbs as constituting a moral principle distinct from the *li-fenim mi-shurat ha-din* behavioral expectation, R. Solomon b. Isaac and others regard these teachings as forming an integral part of the latter concept.[63]

The operational significance of the *li-fenim mi-shurat ha-din* concept is a matter of dispute among the Rishonim.

One aspect of the dispute concerns the question of whether the *li-fenim mi-shurat ha-din* behavioral imperative is directed only to the ethical elite of society or is prescribed even for the ordinary man.

Adopting the former view, Maimonides teaches that *li-fenim mi-*

shurat ha-din conduct is expected only of the *ḥassid*, i.e., the individual of extraordinary piety. What God requires of the ordinary man is not to be a *ḥassid*, but merely to "walk in His ways"—meaning, the middle way, not the extremes even in piety and goodness. Man, according to Maimonides, is not bidden to waive his legal rights and act *li-fenim mi-shurat ha-din*, but if he voluntarily does so, his conduct is regarded as commendable.[64] Illustrating Maimonides' voluntaristic approach to the *li-fenim mi-shurat ha-din* behavioral expectation is his treatment of the lost property case.

> If the majority of the inhabitants are heathen, the rule is that if one finds lost property in a part of town which is chiefly frequented by Israelites, he must advertise it. But if he finds it in a public highway or in a large square, or in assembly halls or lecture halls frequented regularly by heathens or in any other place frequented by the general public, whatever he finds belongs to him, even if an Israelite comes along and identifies it. For the owner will abandon hope of its recovery as soon as he loses the property, since he thinks that a heathen will find it. Yet even though it belongs to the finder, *if he wishes to follow* the good and upright path and do more than the strict letter of the law requires, he must return the lost property to an Israelite who identifies it.[65]

Curiously, Maimonides omits in his *Mishneh Torah* any mention of what constitutes *li-fenim mi-shurat ha-din* conduct in the money changer and porter cases. The omission leads Dr. Shilo to find in the Maimonidean view a further restrictive implication for the operational significance of the *li-fenim mi-shurat ha-din* moral principle: If acting *li-fenim mi-shurat ha-din* entails a monetary loss, even the *ḥassid* is not expected to waive his legal rights.[66]

Naḥmanides, however, regards the *li-fenim mi-shurat ha-din* imperative as being addressed to the ordinary man. Understanding the verse *You shall do what is right and good in the sight of the Lord* (Deuteronomy 6:18) to impart the admonishment to act *li-fenim mi-shurat ha-din*, Naḥmanides connects this verse with the previous verse, *You shall diligently keep the commandments of the Eternal your God, and His testimonies and His statutes, which He has commanded you*. After enjoining man to obey all God's commandments in his interpersonal relations, the Torah forewarns him to display accommodation and generosity toward his fellow-man even when the strict letter of the law does not require it, i.e., to act *li-fenim mi-shurat ha-din*.[67]

Adopting a viewpoint intermediate between Maimonides and Naḥmanides is R. Azaria Figo (Venice, 1579–1647). In his view, *li-*

fenim mi-shurat ha-din is an absolute behavioral requirement *(din)* for the *ḥassid*. Since the man of extraordinary piety usually waives his legal right in order to display generosity to his fellow-man, consistency of character demands such conduct of him in any situation that may arise. For the ordinary person, however, *li-fenim mi-shurat ha-din* is merely recommended conduct.[68]

Naḥmanides' view evidently represents mainstream Jewish thought as the *li-fenim mi-shurat ha-din* moral principle is routinely incorporated in a judicial proceeding. The nature of this integration will be discussed below.

Li-fenim Mi-shurat ha-Din and Judicial Coercion

Another dimension of the operational significance of the *li-fenim mi-shurat ha-din* concept concerns the question of whether Halakhah empowers the Jewish court to *force* an individual to give up his legal rights and act in accordance with this legal principle.

Espousing judicial coercion in the above matter, R. Mordecai b. Hillel (Germany, 1240–1298) validates the practice only if the individual who is asked to give up his legal rights is a man of wealth.[69] Following the above line, R. Joel Sirkes (Poland, 1561–1640) validates the practice even when the legal right involved is a damage claim against an employee, similar to the talmudic porter case.[70]

Another school of thought, led by R. Ḥananel b. Hushi'el (North Africa, 11th cent.) does not legitimize the use of judicial coercion to force a party to a lawsuit to act *li-fenim mi-shurat ha-din*. The judicial role, according to this school of thought, is confined to informing the party what *li-fenim mi-shurat ha-din* conduct consists of.[71]

Indicative of the widespread and profound impact the *li-fenim mi-shurat ha-din* concept has on the Jewish legal system is the following sampling of court cases:

1. In the twelfth century, R. Eliezer b. Nathan of Mainz (ca. 1090–1170) invoked the *li-fenim mi-shurat ha-din* principle to persuade a tenant to acquiesce to his landlord's request to temporarily move out so that alterations could be made in the house. Since the lessee was promised adequate housing in the interim and, in addition, the temporary move represented for him only an inconvenience but no loss, R. Eliezer b. Nathan urged the tenant to waive his legal right and accommodate the landlord's request.[72]

2. In a case similar to the talmudic porter case, R. David b. Moses (Russia, 1769–1836) urged an employer to waive his legal claim against his driver. The driver had been given money to purchase salt in the city of Pinsk, and the money was stolen from him before he arrived there. Comparing the circumstance to the talmudic porter

case, R. David b. Moses urged the employer to conduct himself *li-fenim mi-shurat ha-din* and waive his claim against the driver.[73]

3. Another area of labor relations where Jewish courts found appropriate application for the *li-fenim mi-shurat ha-din* principle is the issue of severance pay. Unless it is expressly stipulated in the labor contract, an employer bears no responsibility to pay his worker severance pay upon the termination of his labor relationship with him. Nevertheless, if, after determining both the circumstances surrounding the termination of the labor relationship and the relative financial position of the parties involved, the court assesses that *equity* demands that severance should be paid, the court, according to Rabbi Ben Zion Meir Ouziel (Israel, 1881–1953), should order the employer to pay the worker the appropriate amount.[74]

In contrast to Rabbi Ouziel's call for coercive judicial intervention in the severance-pay case, a Haifa rabbinic tribunal merely *urged* such conduct on a religious institution. After pointing out that the religious institution had no *legal* obligation to pay severance to the worker it let go, the court took note of both the long tenure of the employee and his impoverished state. Equity considerations, in the opinion of the court, recommended that the religious institution act with compassion and furnish the employee with severance.[75]

The Law of the Abutter

Basing themselves on the *li-fenim mi-shurat ha-din* behavioral imperative, the sages enacted the "law of the abutter" *(maẓranut)*.[76] What follows is a description of the essential details of this law:

With the aim of affording the abutter "first refusal," the sages prohibited an individual from buying property contiguous to someone else's property.[77] The interdict applies to immovable property, including land, real estate,[78] and even a seat in a synagogue.[79] Violation of the ordinance gives the abutter the legal right to displace the purchaser by paying the sale price to the vendor.[80] Since the purchaser should have yielded to the abutter, the former is regarded as having concluded the sale as the abutter's agent. Consequently, provision of the purchasing price to the vendor allows the abutter to automatically secure title to the property without performing any symbolic act *(kinyan)*.[81]

The abutter's displacement right is recognized, however, only if he initiates his protest as soon as the antecedent sale becomes public knowledge and the vendee begins making use of his purchase.[82] Delay in lodging a protest beyond this interval is taken as an implicit waiver of his right.[83]

The abutter's forfeiture of his displacement right also obtains when he refuses the seller's offer to allow him to match the price he negotiated for the sale of his contiguous property.[84] Nonetheless, in the event the nonabutting interested party did not actually consummate his purchase of the contiguous property, the abutter, according to R. Ḥayyim b. Israel Benveniste (Constantinople, 1603–1673), retains his right to insist that his equivalent bid be given preference.[85]

Once the nonabutter takes formal possession of the property, the mechanism called for to render the displacement right nugatory becomes less severe. No formal *kinyan* is required. Forfeiture of the displacement right obtains here when the behavior of the abutter makes it evident that he waives his right. Helping the nonabutter work the contiguous land or renting the land from him provide examples of such conduct.[86]

The Law of the Abutter and the Welfare of the Seller and Other Interested Buyers

Realizing that the law of the abutter may come into conflict with the best interests of both the vendor and nonabutting prospective buyers, the sages limited application of their ordinance to instances where it would not impose a loss on these parties.

Protection of the Seller's Rights

Halakhic concern for the interests of the seller is evidenced from the following considerations:

1. The abutter enjoys his right of first refusal only when he will *match* any offer other prospective buyers are prepared to make.

Illustrating nonequivalency is the abutter's offer to pay the purchasing price in currency that is not as negotiable in the marketplace as the currency a nonabutter offers to pay.[87]

Providing another case in point is the timing of the payments offered by the competing bidders. Should the abutter offer to match A's ready cash offer but request time to liquidate his assets in order to raise the necessary cash, his offer may be rejected by the seller as nonequivalent.[88] Delay in receiving payment constitutes a legitimate opportunity cost for the seller.[89] Nonetheless, in the event the abutter is a man of known wealth, a request by him to be given time to fetch the necessary cash from his home makes his offer equivalent to the ready cash offer and hence entitles him to first refusal.[90]

Another factor that may legitimately enter into the equivalency calculation is the creditworthiness of the bidding parties. In the event the contiguous property is being sold on credit, deference must be given to the seller's assessment that he regards the abutter as less creditworthy than other prospective buyers.[91]

2. Recognizing that the abutter's displacement right effectively lengthens the time necessary to conclude a sales transaction, the sages suspended the privilege when the motive behind the sale is the desire either to finance a pressing need or to take advantage of a fleeting investment opportunity.[92] Whether the abutter loses preference here even when he submits an equivalent offer at the same time as the other prospective buyer is a matter of dispute among decisors. While Maimonides and others suspend the abutter's privilege entirely in the case involving time constraint,[93] R. Solomon b. Isaac, on the interpretation of R. Israel of Krems (fl. mid-14th cent.), holds that the abutter's preferential status remains intact in the simultaneous-bid variant.[94]

In a related case, suppose the seller is confronted with an offer to buy up all his fields, which are scattered in various different locations. Such an offer is regarded as a rare business opportunity for the seller. Out of concern that the inevitable delay caused by the practical necessity[95] of first informing the abutter of the unusual offer might jeopardize the deal entirely,[96] the sages here suspended the abutter's displacement right. Indeed, preference for the abutter presumably does not arise as an issue unless he makes a *simultaneous* and identical offer to buy the same parcel of properties the other prospective buyer is bidding for.[97]

Protection of the Rights of Nonabutting Prospective Buyers

Recognizing that the law of the abutter may conflict with the economic interests of other prospective buyers, the sages either modified or suspended entirely the privilege of the abutter when equity demands that primacy be given to the interests of the nonabutting bidder.

1. Figuring prominently as an equity factor in the consideration of whether the abutter's privilege should be modified is the personal status of the other interested bidders. Women[98] and orphans[99] were regarded by the sages as being at a disadvantage in the real estate market. Since it was held to be unnatural for women and oprhans to engage in search activity in this market,[100] and thus it was difficult for them to acquire immovable property, the sages felt that it would be a matter of kindness not to recognize the abutter's displacement right in the event a woman or an orphan bought property contiguous with his property.[101] Should the abutter, however, submit a simultaneous and equivalent bid, preference, according to R. Asher b. Jeḥiel must be given to him.[102] Naḥmanides, however, suspends entirely the abutter's privilege when the competing buyer is a woman or an orphan.[103]

Similarly, in recognition of the difficulties women and orphans generally have in transacting business,[104] the sages, according to some authorities, disallowed the abutter from displacing anyone who purchased property from them.[105] Since the law of the abutter is entirely inoperative when the seller is a woman or an orphan, the sale of their property is greatly facilitated, as interested buyers would not hesitate to submit bids on account of concern for possible dealings with an abutter. R. Jacob b. Judah Weil (Germany, d. before 1456), however, holds that the abutter's displacement right remains intact in the above instance.[106] In any case, all authorities agree that if the woman or orphan is confronted by the abutter with a simultaneous and equivalent offer, the latter must be given preference.[107]

The abutter's displacement right is not recognized, according to some authorities, when the original purchaser was in financial straits and was also a fellow resident of the seller's town.[108] Nonrecognition of the abutter's displacement right here, according to R. Joshua ha-Kohen Falk (Poland, 1555–1614), is derived from the suspension of this right in the instance where the purchaser was a woman or an orphan.[109] Given this derivation, whether the abutter's simultaneous and equivalent bid gives him preference over the individual in financial straits would, in our view, be subject to the same dispute, cited above, in connection with women and orphans.

Other authorities, however, are of the view that the abutter's displacement right remains intact even when the original purchaser was both in financial straits as well as a fellow resident of the seller's town.[110]

A variant situation occurs when the property purchased was a house and the original buyer bought it not for investment purposes but as living quarters. Here, all disputants would deny the abutter a displacement right, provided that another house, even inferior to the one purchased, was not available to the poor man who bought the house adjoining the abutter's house.[111]

Another aspect of personal status which the sages take into account is the relationship of the nonabutter to the seller. Equity demands that the abutter's right be suspended entirely when the competing bidder owns a partnership interest in the immovable property up for sale. Here, the abutter must refrain from purchasing the property in order to give the partner the privilege of first refusal. Moreover, should the abutter ignore the procedure and make the purchase, the partner is entitled to displace him.[112]

The abutter's right is modified when a competing bidder enjoys a filial or business relationship with the seller. While submission of a simultaneous and equivalent bid requires the seller to give the abutter preference,[113] the latter's displacement right is not recognized in these instances.[114]

The above modification of the abutter's right applies also when the competing bidder happens to be the original owner of the parcel.[115] Attenuation of the abutter's right follows here from the sympathy Halakhah finds with the original owner's aim of recovering his inheritance plot.[116]

Halakhic concern for the interests of the nonabutting buyer also manifests itself in the compensation to which it entitles him when the displacement right is operative.

Displacing the original buyer by merely furnishing him with the purchasing price may not suffice when the sale to the nonabutter was concluded below fair market value. If the court concludes that the discount the seller tendered the nonabutter was due to a special relationship between them, the abutter may not displace the original buyer unless he pays him the fair market value of the property.[117]

In the event the contiguous property was sold to a nonabutter above market price, the abutter may not displace him unless he furnishes him with the purchasing price.[118] Should the purchasing price depart so widely from the fair market value that the transaction involves price fraud *(ona'ah)*, the abutter has the right to cancel the original sale,[119] provided the nonabutter does not want the original transaction to remain intact.[120] The abutter's right to cancel the original sale is, however, recognized only when the nonabutter concluded the sale unaware that it involved *ona'ah*. Should the nonabutter knowingly have entered into an *ona'ah* transaction, the abutter's displacement right is recognized only if he provides him with the purchasing price.[121]

Intended Use and the Law of the Abutter

Intended use also plays a role in deciding which competing bid the seller must give preference to. Promotion of population settlement is the criterion Halakhah adopts in deciding which of the competing bids should be given precedence. Application of this criterion results in giving one who intends to build a house or plant a tree preference over one intending to farm the land.[122] Accordingly, should a nonabutter express the intention of using the land for either tree-planting or building, his bid must be given preference over an identical bid by an abutter who wants to use the land for sowing purposes.[123] However, since trees have greater permanence than houses, R. Joshua ha-Kohen Falk denies the abutter preference if his intent is to build a house and another interested party wishes to use the land for tree-planting.[124] Disputing this view, R. David b. Samuel ha-Levi (Poland, 1586–1667) regards the abutter's right as remaining intact in the latter case. Since the abutter's house-building does minimally promote population growth, his privileged status remains intact despite the availability of competing tenders involving superior land use. Preference for the abutter is, however, no longer recognized when his intended use of the land does not even minimally promote population growth, while the land-use intent of competing bidders does promote this goal. This occurs when the abutter intends to use the land for sowing, while the competing bidders intend to use the land for either building or tree-planting.[125]

Suspension of the Law of the Abutter When the Buyer Is an Out-of-Town Resident

By increasing the transaction costs for the sale of immovable property, the law of the abutter could well have the effect of inhibiting commercial transactions in this market. This problem becomes particularly acute when the immovable property is located in one area and the owner finds a prospective buyer in a different town. Operation of the law of the abutter in this instance might make it almost impossible for the owner to effect the sale of the property. Lacking any firsthand information regarding the possible existence of an abutter, the prospective buyer might very well back off, despite assurances given to him by the owner. Realizing the acute inhibiting effect the law of the abutter would have on the ability of the owner to effect a sale in the above instance, the sages, according to R. Joseph Caro, suspended their ordinance here.

Concluding the sale outside the area in which the subject property is located, however, cannot be used as a device to evade the law of the abutter. When conspiracy between the seller and the nonabutter is evident, the Jewish court will punish the offenders by means of excommunication.[126] One authority, R. Ḥayyim b. Israel Benveniste, even confers the abutter with a displacement right in the latter instance.[127]

Kofin al Midat Sedom

Another dimension of the measure of generosity Jewish law demands of man in his interpersonal relations is the principle of *kofin al midat sedom*. This moral imperative calls for the Jewish court to *coerce* an individual not to act in the manner of the Sodomites. A is guilty of Sodomitic behavior when he refuses to allow B to infringe upon his right even though such infringement generates no loss for him and at the same time affords B the opportunity to secure a benefit or avoid a loss.

While the *kofin* principle is applicable to a wide variety of circumstances,[128] we will focus on how it alters property rights and contractural obligations. Illustrating the latter application is the following talmudic text in *Ketubbot* 103a:

> A certain man once leased his mill to another in [consideration of the latter's services in] grinding [his corn]. Eventually he [the former] became rich and bought another mill and an ass. Thereupon he said to the other, "Until now I have had my grinding done at your place, but now [that I have another mill in which to grind my corn], pay me rent." "I shall," the other replied, "only grind for you [but will pay no rent]." Rabina [in considering the case] intended to rule that it involved the very principle that was laid down in our Mishnah: The two husbands cannot plead, "We will maintain her jointly," but one must maintain her and the other allows her the cost of her maintenance. R. Awira, however, said to him: Are [the two cases] alike? There [the woman] has only one stomach, not two; but here [the lessee] might well tell the owner, "Grind [in your own mill] and sell; grind [in mine] and keep." This, however, has been said only in a case where [the lessee] has no [other orders for] grinding at his mill, but if he has [sufficient orders for] grinding at his mill, he may in such circumstances be compelled [not to act] in the manner of Sodom.

Rishonim infer from the above talmudic text that the possible loss the lessor may suffer as a result of the continuation of the old terms of the lease is irrelevant in deciding whether the lessee may be forced to accede to the lessor's request henceforth to make cash payment of the rent. The economic impact on the lessee is crucial in evaluating the merit of the lessor's request—that alone. Refusing to change the conditions of his lease to provide for a cash payment is legitimate only when the demand for his grinding services is not brisk enough to allow him to replace the grinding time he did for the lessor with other customer orders. When this is not the case, refusal to change to a cash payment amounts to Sodomitic behavior.[129]

Without the constraint imposed by the *kofin* principle, A's changed circumstances might afford B an opportunity to renegotiate his lease on more favorable terms. This occurs when A cannot sell or otherwise make use of the wheat he usually grinds in B's mill. Here, insistence on the old terms of the lease would generate a loss for A. Shrewd negotiation by B could allow him to reduce his rent in exchange for waiving his legal right to pay the rent in the form of a grinding service. What prevents this exploitation is the *kofin* principle. Since changing the rent payment from a grinding service to a cash transfer generates no loss for B, he must accommodate A, despite his ability to extract from him a consideration for agreeing to the change.

A case analogous to that of the "talmudic" miller came before the rabbinic court of R. David Ibn Zimra (Spain, 1480–1574): A sold land to B. The terms of the agreement called for B to pay half the purchasing price in cash and the balance in the form of providing A with tailoring services. Subsequently, A's financial position worsened and he was no longer in need of B's tailoring services. Given his changed circumstances, A demanded that B pay the balance due him in cash instead of in tailoring services. Noting that B had enough customers to fill his time without A's business, R. David b. Zimra invoked the *kofin* principle to force B to accede to A's request for a cash payment.[130] Here again, without the constraint the *kofin* principle imposes on B, he would be able to extract some consideration from A in exchange for A's not insisting that he pay the balance of the debt in the form of tailoring services. Though A would presumably pay some price to persuade B to give up his legal right, this potential gain is not regarded as a *legitimate* loss from the latter's perspective. Refusal to accede to the cash request when other customers would take up the slack of the loss of A's business, therefore, amounts to Sodomitic behavior.

The Lessee's Right to Make Improvements in His Rented Apartment

The *kofin* principle was again invoked by R. David Ibn Zimra to dismiss a landlord's objection to allowing his tenant to make improvements in a rented apartment. Since the improvements enhanced the market value of the apartment, the landlord's objection could only be described as Sodomitic.[131]

Intruding Upon the Air Space of a Neighbor's Property

While an individual may object to a neighbor making use of the air space of his property, such objection is regarded as Sodomitic when the intrusion generates no loss for him. Illustrating this case is A's petition to be allowed to extend a drainage pipe over B's land. If the intrusion involves no loss or inconvenience for B, the court will force B to accede to A's request.[132]

Limitations on the Operational Significance of the Kofin Principle

The operational significance of the *kofin* principle is limited from several standpoints. One limiting factor is the *liberality* the Jewish court adopts as to what constitutes *legitimate* loss for the party who is asked to waive his right, which, in turn, is used as a basis for rejecting the *kofin* petition. A second limiting factor is that Halakhah regards some rights as inalienable in the sense that even if infringement of the right would generate no loss to the possessor, he may not be forced to waive the right.

Elastic Definition of Loss

Evidencing the elastic attitude the Jewish court adopts regarding what constitutes a loss for the party who is asked to give up his right are several aspects of the laws protecting invasion of privacy.

Privacy-invasion law prohibits the owner of a house (A) from constructing a window in a wall located on his own property when the window would overlook a neighbor's (B's) courtyard. A's desire to allow light to enter his property is denied on the grounds that the overlooking window would invade B's privacy. Following R. Elai's opinion, talmudic codifiers deny A's request even when he offers to build the window at an elevation above his own height. The court's sympathy is with B's fear that A might on occasion place a stool at the foot of the wall and reach the overlooking window by standing on it. Taking this contingency into account characterizes A's window-building as an act of invasion of privacy, and his *kofin* petition is therefore rejected.[133]

Moreover, A's request for a window-construction permit is denied, according to R. Solomon b. Abraham Adret (Spain, ca. 1235–1310), even when the window would overlook a ruin owned by B. Insofar as private activities are not usually performed in a ruin, A's window-construction activity presents no immediate invasion of B's privacy. Nevertheless, credence is given to B's claim that he plans eventually to renovate the ruin. Should A be allowed to build or maintain his window, B will suffer immediately from A's ability to observe his domain. To spare B the nuisance of a possible future court battle, A will be immediately enjoined from building the window or required to board it up if he has already constructed it. Moreover, A's offer to draw up a document promising immediately to close up the window should B actually renovate the ruin may also be rejected by B. The court will sympathize with B's protest that the proposal would generate for him the inconvenience of having to *safeguard* the document. Given the predilection of most people to secure what is rightfully theirs with a minimum amount of litigation and nuisance, B's protest is not regarded as Sodomitic in character.[134]

Rights the Kofin Principle May Not Infringe Upon

The *kofin* principle does not invest an individual with a blanket license to infringe upon his neighbor's property right. Certain infringements are regarded as *unreasonable*, and resistance to such incursions, even when no loss is involved, does not amount to Sodomitic behavior.

One example of an unreasonable intrusion is a request to *settle* on a neighbor's land against his will. To be sure, settling on a neighbor's land without the latter's knowledge may at times allow the squatter to escape paying rent to the owner of the property. This occurs when the owner was not in the market to rent his land. Since the squatter causes the owner no loss, the owner's rent claim is denied.[135] Nevertheless, the owner is fully within his rights to object, in the first instance, to the squatter's desire to settle on his land,[136] and, for that matter, to evict him should he discover him there.[137]

Other aspects of the property right that the *kofin* principle may not make incursions into include the right to refuse a barter exchange[138] and the right to turn down an offer to buy the property.[139] A barter offer may be refused even if the exchange would admittedly leave the owner better or no worse off than before, while enhancing the welfare of the party requesting the deal.[140] Similarly, a property owner may legitimately refuse to sell his property to someone even if he admits to having no use for it.[141]

A further limitation of the incursions the *kofin* principle may make into the property right apparently proceeds from R. Jacob Tam's (France, ca. 1100–1171) interpretation of the following talmudic passage:

> A certain man bought a field adjacent to his father's estate. When they came to divide the latter's estate, he said: "Give me my share next to my own field." [The usual manner of dividing an estate is by drawing lots.] Rabbah said: "This is a case where a man can be compelled not to act after the manner of Sodom." R. Joseph strongly objected to this, on the grounds that the brothers can say to him: "We reckon this field as especially valuable like the property of the family of Marion." The law follows R. Joseph.[142]

In sharp contrast to other commentaries, R. Jacob Tam interprets R. Joseph as allowing the other brothers to run up the price of the field the adjoining brother seeks even when it is no more valuable to them than the other fields of the estate. Profiteering from the extra value the adjoining brother attaches to the field by allowing him to have it only at an inflated price is not regarded as Sodomitic.[143]

Strongly objecting to R. Jacob Tam's line, R. Asher b. Jeḥiel points out that every *kofin* application entails a request to secure some advantage which the petitioner presumably stands ready to pay some price for in the event the court refuses to order the defendant to allow him to enjoy it gratis. R. Tam's line, therefore, leads by logical extension to the rejection of the *kofin* principle entirely.[144]

R. Tam's position, in our view, rests on the proposition that forcing an individual to *renounce* an ownership claim, even if it is not definite in nature, lies beyond the ambit of the *kofin* principle. It follows from this that it is unreasonable for the adjoining brother to request that the other brothers exchange their possible title in the field he seeks in exchange for another estate parcel of equal quality and value.

R. Tam's disputants apparently do not delimit *kofin* to such an extent. They understand the rejection of the adjoining brother's *kofin* application to be grounded in the fact that the field he seeks is in some way more valuable than the other fields of the estate. Naḥmanides, for instance, interprets R. Joseph as allowing the other brothers to run up the price of the field the adjoining brother seeks only when it is *superior* in quality to the other fields of the estate.[145] Should all the fields of the estate be of equal quality, exploiting the extra value the adjoining brother attaches to the field by allowing him to have it only at an inflated price is regarded as Sodomitic.

R. Tam's disputants, in our view, could very well agree that A's request to B to exchange property with him amounts to an unreasonable encroachment upon the latter's rights. Consequently, B's refusal would not be regarded as Sodomitic even if he does not protest that the exchange would make him any worse off than before. What these disputants do regard as Sodomitic, however, is for B to refuse to renounce his inheritance title to a particular field in the estate in exchange for another field of the estate of equal quality and value.

Providing an alternative rationalization of the disputants' position is the proposition that the division of an estate by means of lot is an *expedient* rather than mandated by law.[146] This method is resorted to only when the division of the estate in some manner is not dictated by some legal principle, or, in the absence of the legal principle, when the brothers cannot voluntarily come to an agreement as to how they should divide up the estate. If division by lot is only an expedient, the *kofin* principle makes the adjoining brothers' plan for dividing the estate the *operative* method. R. Tam, however, would hold that the division of an estate by means of lot is a *mandated* method rather than merely an expedient. Consequently, running up the price of the field the adjoining brother seeks in exchange for giving up his possible lottery-conferred title to the field is not regarded as Sodomitic.

· 2

Advertising and Promotional Activities as Regulated in Jewish Law

Advertising plays a key role in the everyday functioning of the modern market economy. Its positive function consists of improving the information channels of the marketplace. Promotional activities make consumers more aware of alternatives open to them and allow firms who satisfy consumer wants to expand their sales and profits.

The objective of modern advertising clearly goes beyond an informational purpose. Sophisticated techniques are regularly employed to persuade and cajole people to buy products and services they would not otherwise buy. Likewise, favorable terms of credit allow consumers to effectively attain for themselves a much higher standard of living than would be possible if they were forced to live within their means.

Our task in this chapter will be to investigate the ethics of persuasion from the perspective of Jewish law. Modern advertising techniques will be analyzed in light of Jewish ethical principles. The moral imperatives developed in Chapter 1 will find ready application in the sphere of advertising.

One final issue of concern in this chapter will be the ethics of imposing a "dissuasion responsibility" on a salesperson when it becomes evident to him in the course of serving his customer that the latter's interests would best be served by the competition.

Bait and Switch

In its basic form, bait and switch involves the advertising of a popular article at a bargain price simply for the purpose of luring customers into the store. The deception becomes apparent when the bargain bait cannot be purchased, on one pretext or another, and salesmen, after disparaging the advertised product, attempt to convince customers to switch to higher-priced substitutes.

Since the vendor has no intention of selling the bait item, the advertisement is clearly an insincere offer and hence violates the "good faith" imperative. The *ona'at devarim* interdict is also violated here. Though the use of the bait and switch tactic may *eventuate* in the satisfaction of the customer, nothing removes the fact that the latter is filled with a sense of disappointment and annoyance *at the moment* he is advised the item is not available.

A variant of this tactic occurs when the vendor is in possession of the advertised item but only in limited supply. Suppose the offer for the attractive item is made for a specified period of time, and crude estimates of the demand for the product at the attractive price indicate that the supply of the advertised item will be exhausted considerably before the expiration date of the offer. Given the totally unrealistic duration of the offer, the advertisement remains insincere, and thus the advertiser violates both the "good faith" imperative and the *ona'at devarim* interdict.

Attaching a warning to the advertisement that supplies are limited and are available on a "first come first served" basis may, however, be sufficient to satisfy the "good faith" imperative and free the advertiser from the *ona'at devarim* interdict. In the final analysis, whether the above caveat does in fact make the advertisement morally acceptable depends, in our view, on the interpretation the majority of people attach to the advertisement. Consumer surveys could prove very helpful here.

The Weasel-Word Stratagem

Emulating the weasel's reputed habit of sucking the contents out of an egg while leaving the shell superficially intact, modern advertising, as documented by Carl Wrighter, often avoids making direct and forthright product claims. Ajax, for example, advertises that its product "cleans like a white tornado." By using this metaphor, Ajax avoids making a direct claim of superiority over competing brands and hence is not subject to possible challenges by rivals. Comparing a bottle of ammonia to a tornado is, of course, ludicrous. A tornado would not only lift dirt from a kitchen floor, but would uproot the entire house from its foundation as well. The metaphor, reinforced by animation, serves well to conjure up in the mind of the consumer an image of something much more glamorous than the odious job of scrubbing a floor. Weasel words, as Wrighter documents, often create false impressions. Two examples will be cited to illustrate this problem.

TWA offers two types of accommodations, first class and economy class. Calling its first-class accommodations Ambassador Service, TWA proceeds to copyright the name, and advertises that it is the *only* airline that offers Ambassador Service. By use of this ploy, TWA evades making any direct superiority claim over the first-class accommodations offered by competing airlines, but at the same time creates a definite impression of exclusivity.

Another example of the weasel-word stratagem is the preemptive claim. By being the first to direct the public's attention toward some little-known feature that its product shares in common with comparable products offered by rivals, a firm may secure an exclusivity image for its own product. Providing a case in point is Folger's pronouncement, made with passion and excitement, that its coffee is mountain grown. Since the public does not generally know that *all coffee* is mountain grown, Folger's preemptive claim creates a false impression of uniqueness, even though it makes no claim that competing brands are not mountain grown.[1]

We take note that Halakhah finds nothing intrinsically unethical about the weasel-word stratagem. Creative advertising does not necessarily deceive. If the association of the product with the advertising message injects an element of glamour or fantasy into an otherwise prosaic consumption experience, the message has effectively improved the *quality* of the product. Nonetheless, given its potential for deception, commercial use of the weasel-word stratagem would not be given legitimacy in the halakhic society, in our view, prior to its being pilot-tested. Scientifically designed, a pilot-test can ascertain what impressions the advertising message makes on the targeted group, as well as the inferences this group draws from it. Should these sets of expectations and impressions fail to conform to actuality, revision of the message would be in order.

Undeserved Good Will

Good will in the form of a reputation for fine customer service, low prices, or a high-quality product represents an important factor accounting for business success and expansion. Generating good will on the basis of deception and illusion violates Jewish business ethics. Such conduct is prohibited under the *genevat da'at* interdict. Several variants of the discount sale offer illustrate the generation of undeserved good will.

Advertising for discount sales often goes beyond merely informing the public that the customary selling price of a particular product has been reduced. Often, a strong impression is created that the lower price represents a *bargain opportunity,* available only for a limited time. Projecting a discount sale as a bargain opportunity generates not only a sense of appreciation from those who purchase the sale item, but, in addition, earns for the seller a favorable reputation from the general public.

A frequent motive behind a price discount is a desire on the part of the seller to increase his sales volume and profits. In a similar vein, a multiproduct firm may find it advantageous to discount one of its popular items, even below cost. Standing behind the price cut is an investment motive. Selling a popular item below cost generates good will for the firm. Capitalizing on this good will, the firm could induce customers to purchase along with the discounted item a whole line of complementary products. Good will is hence deftly parlayed into making the discounted item a "loss leader."

Notwithstanding the selfish motive behind the aforementioned discount sales, no moral issue is involved in characterizing the discounted price as a bargain opportunity for the consumer. This conclusion, in our view, is valid irrespective of the operational market structure. Within the framework of competitive conditions, the discounted price represents a bargain simply because the said article is available elsewhere only at a higher price. Should the discounted item be unavailable elsewhere, its bargain feature, nevertheless, remains intact. Given that the effective demand the seller faces for his product has not diminished, protecting his present profit-loss position in no way requires him to lower his price. Automatic market forces have not worked here to reduce the *objective* value of the subject product. Quite to the contrary, it is the *investment* motive of the seller that is *entirely* responsible for the discounted price of the article. With the price cut affording consumers the opportunity to purchase the article below its *objective market value,* one can characterize the discounted price as a true bargain opportunity.

Price discounts representing the seller's reaction to a sharp drop in demand for his product are, however, another matter. To illustrate, suppose a carpet dealer finds that particular lines of his broadlooms are not selling well. To stimulate sales, he advertises a big discount in the price of selected broadlooms, emphasizing the bargain opportunity the sale affords. What the discount amounts to here is nothing more than a downward adjustment of an overpriced item. While the discount generates sales volume that would not otherwise take place, no "bargain" element is present for those that purchase the item at the reduced price. Customers merely pay a "fair" price for what they purchase, acquiring *equivalent* value for the purchasing power they give up. Since the discount merely enables the firm to liquidate unwanted inventory and minimize its losses, it should call its promotion a *clearance* sale rather than a discount sale. Claiming that the discount represents a bargain generates for the seller an undeserved sense of appreciation on the part of the buyer.

Similarly, should stiff competition from the tile and linoleum industries prompt the carpet dealer to reduce his price, no element of bargain would be involved in the new lower price. Here, competitive conditions work to force down the market value of the carpet. Within the framework of the new market conditions, the buyer would be getting no bargain. Announcing the promotional effort as a clearance sale, instead of a discount sale, is appropriate here, too.

Another nuance of the discount sale which violates Jewish business ethics occurs when the firm projects the secondary motive behind the price reduction but conceals the primary motive. Disclosing the secondary purpose behind one's action, while concealing the primary purpose, as we discussed in Chapter 1, is a form of *genevat d'at*. To illustrate, Rachaman Automobile Company advertises that it is reducing the prevailing price of its entire line of cars, stressing the bargain opportunity the new price schedule represents. To this, Rachaman adds that its motive in running the sale is its deep concern for the crippling effect inflation has on society. Capitalizing on its position of prominence in the business community, Rachaman concludes its message with the hope that other business firms will follow its lead by reducing their prices. Widespread price reduction would lead, Rachaman argues, to increased consumer spending, which would benefit everyone. Notwithstanding Rachaman's firm belief in the beneficial effects of widespread price reduction, if, in fact, it was primarily adverse market conditions that motivated its discount, the advertising message is misleading.

Moreover, R. Aryeh Judah b. Akiba's remarks, discussed in Chapter 1, regarding the difficulty of assessing the *authenticity* of an *untested* feeling of altruism are, in our view, very relevant here. Does Rachaman's humanistic impulse independently account for the price reduction, or is the feeling of altruism entirely inspired by the happy prospect that the price discount will increase its profits?

Projecting a price reduction in a humanistic framework when the altruistic impulse is in fact either a derivative motive or an incidental consideration is not only a form of falseness, but generates for the firm a measure of good will beyond what it merits.

Disparagement of a Competitor's Product

Falsely maligning a competitor is a violation of the biblical interdicts against slander[2] and falsehood.[3]

Disparaging a competitor's product presents a moral issue in Jewish law even when no misrepresentation of fact is made and the motives of the disparager are sincere. One aspect of the disparagement issue is the halakhic parameters of warning the public regarding the unethical conduct of a competitor. We have dealt with this particular issue elsewhere.[4] Our concern here will be with three other aspects of the disparagement issue, namely, (1) the ethics of the comparative merit stratagem; (2) the exclusivity claim; and (3) the superiority claim.

The Comparative Merit Stratagem

We will discuss several aspects of the comparative merit technique. In one variant of this tactic the seller (A) demonstrates the superiority of his product to a prospective buyer (B) by drawing his attention to the *deficiencies* of rival models. Motivated by a desire to forestall B from engaging in comparison shopping, A, while careful not to impugn the integrity of his competitors, tries to persuade B that rival models are *inferior* in various ways. To illustrate, suppose A provides B with a demonstration of his vacuum cleaner. At the conclusion of the demonstration, A mentions that competitor C's *lower-priced* model operates very noisily. In addition, B is informed that D's *lower-priced* model is very cumbersome and difficult to maneuver. Since the rival models are cheaper than A's product, his effort to prevent B from comparison shopping by pointing the deficiencies present in these models cannot be legitimated on the grounds that this information enables B to avert financial loss. Moreover, insofar as B's favorable attitude toward A's product is secured by means of impressing him with the deficiencies of rival models, the stratagem, in our view, violates Jewish business ethics. While A has the legitimate right to point out to everyone the fine qualities of his product, *magnifying* the attractiveness of these qualities by pointing to the deficiencies of rival models amounts to elevating himself at the expense of his neighbor's degradation. Such conduct was severely condemned by the talmudic sages, as evidenced by R. Yose b. Ḥanina's (second half of the 3d cent.) dictum: "Anyone who elevates himself at the expense of his friend's degradation has no share in the world-to-come."[5]

Concretely illustrating the objectionable nature of such conduct is the following talmudic passage:

> R. Neḥunia b. ha-Kaneh was asked by his disciples: In virtue of what have you reached such a good old age? He replied: "Never in my life have I sought respect through the degradation of my fellow" . . . as illustrated by R. Huna, who once was carrying a spade on his shoulder when R. Hana b. Hanilai wanted to take it from him, but he said to him, "If you are accustomed to carry in your own town, take it, but if not, I do not want to be paid respect through your degradation."[6]

Why R. Huna's behavior is regarded as exhibiting extraordinary moral character is explained by R. Samuel Eliezer b. Judah ha-Levi Edels (Poland, 1555–1631). It stems from the fact that R. Huna did not merely refrain from requesting R. Hana to carry his spade for him but *rejected* the latter's offer to do so.[7] Refraining from making such a request is presumably a normal behavioral expectation and does not merit particular praise, since demanding honor at the expense of a fellow's degradation constitutes contemptible behavior. Akin to this, in our view, is the sales tactic of demonstrating the superiority of one's product by means of pointing up the defects of lower-priced competing models.

A variation of the preceding situation occurs when A demonstrates the superiority of his product by drawing attention to the defects of competing models priced at or above his product. Since this information can spare B an opportunity cost in the form of paying the same or a higher price for a product *inferior* to A's model, the conduct is apparently legitimized.

Exclusivity Claims

Another twist of the comparative merit stratagem is the exclusivity claim. Providing a case in point is A's advertising message that his vacuum cleaner is the only one in the marketplace featuring detachable parts. Since the absence of a detachable-part feature does not render a vacuum cleaner defective, A's exclusivity claim amounts to nothing more than pointing out an *advantage* his model has over competing models. A is not guilty of enhancing the attractiveness of his product by means of pointing up the defects of competing models, and thus his advertising message does not, in our view, violate Jewish business ethics.

Superiority Claims

Another variant of the comparative merit stratagem is the superiority claim. Superiority claims take the form of either limited or unrestricted assertions. The limited superiority claim often appears in connection with the multipurpose product. To illustrate, A advertises that his aspirin compound is more effective in relieving arthritic pain than competing brands. Insofar as aspirin is used to relieve an assortment of pains and aches, A's claim amounts to nothing more than an exclusivity claim. Since A does not enhance the attractiveness of his product by means of pointing out *defects* in competing brands, the tactic, in our view, does not violate Jewish business ethics.

An example of an unrestricted superiority claim is provided by A's general claim that his aspirin compound is the most effective nonprescription drug in relieving aches and pains. Since the superlative claim implicitly concedes adequacy to competing brands and certainly does not degrade them, the tactic, in our view, would be legitimated in Jewish law.

Supportive of the view that the general superiority claim does not violate Jewish ethics is the ruling of R. Ḥayyim Ḥezekiah Medini (Russia, 1832–1904) that voicing an opinion that A is a greater talmudic scholar than B does *not* amount to degrading B and is therefore a permissible statement.[8]

Puffery

Puffery, the practice of extolling the qualities of a product in an exaggerated manner, has proved to be an effective promotional device. Defenders of puffery maintain that exaggeration makes advertising more memorable. The more memorable advertising is, the more efficiently it can perform its informational role. Detractors of the practice, however, assert that exaggeration misleads and therefore makes the firm guilty of false claims.

In this section we will develop a guideline for the use of puffery as a promotional device from the standpoint of Jewish law. Puffery manifests itself in claims regarding either the aesthetic-sensual or the performance dimensions of a product. We will deal with each in turn.

An example of puffery in the aesthetic realm is provided by an artist's claim that his scenic portrait evokes a mood of serenity. Further illustrating puffery in the aesthetic realm is a furniture dealer's claim that his dining room set is elegant, decorous, and luxurious. A seller's description of his culinary products as palatable and savory represents an example of puffery in the sensuous realm.

Assessments regarding the aesthetic and sensuous impact a product will have on a customer fall into the realm of the subjective. In Jewish law, majority opinion does not establish fact or truth in a subjective matter relating to aesthetics. Examinations of the following talmudic text bears this point out:

> Our rabbis taught: How does one dance (what does one sing or recite) before the bride? Bet Shammai say: "The bride as she is." And Bet Hillel say: "Beautiful and charming bride!" But Bet Shammai said to Bet Hillel: "If she was lame or blind, does one say of her: 'Beautiful and charming bride'? Whereas the Torah said, *Keep thee far from a false matter.*" Said Bet Hillel to Bet Shammai: "According to your words, if one has made a bad purchase in the market, should one praise it in his eyes or deprecate it? Surely, one should praise it in his eyes." Therefore, the sages said: "Always should the disposition of man be pleasant with people."[9]

Talmudic decisors rule in accordance with Bet Hillel's view.[10] Why this school of thought does not regard an invariable bridal praise formula as a form of falseness, as Bet Shammai would have it, requires explanation. Rationalizing Bet Hillel's view, R. Judah Loew b. Bezalel (Worms, ca. 1525–1609) posits that while characterizing the bride as beautiful and charming may, at times, run counter to popular sentiment, the description presumably conforms well with the bridegroom's feelings in the matter. If he did not find his prospective bride beautiful and charming, he presumably would not have married her. Given that what constitutes beauty is a *judgmental* matter, pronouncing the bride beautiful and charming does not amount to a mischaracterization of reality, notwithstanding majority opinion to the contrary. Similarly, approving the buyer's glowing characterization of his "unseemly" purchase does not amount to falsehood, as a sales transaction creates a presumption of buyer satisfaction.[11]

Before any implications for the business practice of puffery can be drawn from Bet Hillel's bridal praise formula, further clarification of the latter case must be made.

Aside from the issue of falsehood raised by Bet Hillel's formula, calling for the wedding guests to regale the bridegroom with praise for his bride's beauty and charm, even when this sentiment runs counter to his own feelings, amounts to outright hypocrisy and insincerity. R. Judah Loew's analysis removes the falsehood issue, but the insincerity question appears to remain.

The insincerity question, in our view, is somewhat attenuated by consideration of the fact that the sages suspended the biblical injunction against lying when the purpose of the untruth is to bring about reconciliation. Classically illustrating this dispensation is the message Joseph's brothers sent him after Jacob's death: *Before his death, your father left this instruction: Thus shall you say to Joseph: "Forgive, I urge you, the offense and guilt of your brothers who treated you so harshly." So now, please forgive the crime of the servants of your father's God* (Genesis 50:16–17). Fearing that Joseph harbored ill feelings toward them for selling him into slavery, the brothers presented Joseph with a fabricated conciliatory plea from their father. Because their behavior was motivated by a desire for reconciliation, the use of a lie to further this end is found to be legitimate.[12]

Analogously, the behavioral requirement of absolute sincerity was apparently relaxed by the sages in connection with the biblical precept of gladdening the heart of a wedding couple. An essential feature of this precept apparently consists of complimenting the groom on his bride's beauty and charm. Note, however, the limited nature of the dispensation. Since the reconciliation motive does not apply here, complimenting the bridegroom by means of mischaracterizing reality is not permitted. What is relaxed here is only the behavioral requirement of absolute sincerity.

It follows from this interpretation of Bet Hillel's view that a wedding guest who does not feel that the bride is beautiful and charming is not permitted to relate the bridal praise formula to anyone but the bridegroom himself or to someone else in the bridegroom's presence. Similarly indicated is a restrictive interpretation of the "bad purchase" case. With A's true feeling toward the article very negative, approving B's purchase would appear proper only in direct response to B's solicitation for one's opinion or as a spontaneous reaction to B's glowing self-appraisal of the article he purchased.

We will now turn to the implications of the preceding discussion for the business practice of puffery. Of primary relevance is the finding that in a subjective matter relating to the realm of aesthetics, majority opinion does not establish fact to the extent that an individual's contrary opinion must be regarded as invalid. Accordingly, the seller would be entitled to advertise his or other people's judgments regarding either the aesthetic quality of his product or the satisfaction the product gave him or the endorser. Aesthetic judgments are, however, subject to the sincerity constraint. Moreover, such judgments may not be made in a manner that creates an impression that the judgment is shared by a larger group than the case may be.

Another ethical issue for the advertising practice of puffery is the admissibility of making aesthetic claims based on the product's popularity. Without conducting a survey to determine the reason(s) people are buying the product, the aesthetic claim remains unsubstantiated and therefore is misleading.

Puffery in the Performance Domain

In sharp contrast to puffery in the aesthetic domain, puffery of the product's performance effectively exaggerates its objective qualities. Hyperbole regarding the performance of the product amounts therefore to a false and misleading claim. Notwithstanding the deceptive potential of hyperbole in the performance realm, such statements do not mislead when they are not taken literally. Provided the public takes the element of puffery in the advertising message into account to such an extent as not to interpret the advertiser's claim as ascribing qualities to the product beyond its objective properties, the message would be free of any element of deception. Puffery here serves a useful purpose in the form of creating a memorable message, thereby improving the flow of information in the marketplace.

Jewish law's attitude toward nondeceptive puffery can, in our view, be derived from its treatment of vows of *incitement (nedrei zeiriezin)* made in a commercial setting. Suppose A and B are locked in a price negotiation. A asks $4 for his article. B counters with an offer of $2. Upon hearing B's bid, A proclaims, "If I accept anything less than $4, let bread be forbidden to me by force of a vow." B then counters, "If I offer anything more than $2, let bread be forbidden to me by force of a vow." Though each party has fortified his negotiating position by means of a vow, the vows are not regarded as the result of firm resolution. Since the vows lack legal force, the deal may be concluded at $3 and both parties may eat bread without prior resort to the absolution process.[13] The Tosafot (12th and 14th cent. French commentators) and others point out that common business practice makes the intention of the parties clear-cut. A is not indicating that he is intransigent in regard to his asking price, as the formulation indicates, but merely wants to convey his seriousness about not accepting B's original offer. B's intentions are similarly interpreted. Though unverbalized thoughts are usually of no account in Jewish law, A and B's unverbalized thoughts regarding their intentions are *universally* shared, i.e., anyone hearing the vow would interpret each party's intentions to consist of merely forewarning his opposite number to adopt a more flexible position. Since the unverbalized thoughts of each negotiating party are universally shared, it is legally regarded as if A and B *verbalized* an *addendum* to their explicit vows, explaining their true intentions.[14]

Though the vows of incitement are not legally binding, an individual is forbidden to utter such a vow. This lesson is exegetically derived from the verse *He shall not break (yaḥel) his word* (Numbers 30:3), i.e., he shall not make profane *(ḥullin)* his own words.[15]

Jewish law's treatment of vows of incitement provides, in our view, a criterion for the use of puffery as a promotional technique in the performance realm. If the puffery is not in the form of an oath or vow and does not generate deception, the advertising message would not violate Jewish business ethics. Certainty on the part of the advertiser that his hyperbolic claim does not have the effect of misleading the public does not appear, in our view, as sufficiently valid to safeguard against deception. Avoidance of violation of the *genevat da'at* law requires the seller, prior to the release of his advertising message, to confirm that his judgment of nondeception is shared by the general public. Conducting a survey to assess public reaction to the message would accomplish this.

Puffery as Treated in American Law: A Critique

American law recognizes the right of a seller to express an opinion regarding his product. This opinion, the law presumes, will naturally be favorable. Prospective buyers are therefore expected to understand that they are not entitled to rely literally upon the seller's assertions. Since an opinion makes no statement of fact, it cannot be characterized as misrepresentation. Finally, if the opinion is such that no reasonable person would believe it, no element of deception is involved.

The law recognizes most puffery as harmless and permits a firm to argue that a claim is puffery in defense against a charge of fraud or misrepresentation.

Commenting on the present state of affairs, Preston argues that the current legal approach to puffery is misguided. Statements of opinion or value often *imply* fact and thus should be considered as factual representation. To illustrate, a beer manufacturer's assertion that his product is "Milwaukee's finest" *implies* the fact that beer production/quality standards exist and that the advertised beer is superior to competitors' on the basis of these standards. Given that no such quality standards exist, the manufacturer's assertion is misleading and deceptive.

Instead of approaching the issue of puffery by making semantic distinctions between fact and opinion, advertising messages should be examined on the basis of their behavioral-psychological impact. Whether the claim is fact, opinion, or value, the legal test should be whether the message deceives, i.e., creates untrue expectations which influence purchasers.[16]

Following Preston's line, Oliver suggests that whenever consumers overrate a product relative to its actual merits as a result of puffery, the advertising message should be regarded as deceptive.

Recognition of exaggeration in an advertising message does not necessarily lead to the conclusion that the message does not have the capacity to deceive. To illustrate, if an advertiser states that detergent X gets clothes "cleaner than clean" or "whiter than white," this statement is likely to affect the consumer's expectation that X cleans in some superior sense. If the appropriate discount is not made, the puffery will influence the consumer to regard the cleaning power of X more favorably than would be the case had the advertiser simply said "clean" or "white."

The deception inherent in puffery is often reinforced by the consumer's inability to disprove the advertiser's exaggerated claim. A case in point occurs when disproof is beyond the physical capacity of the consumer. Illustrating this is the inability of the consumer to invalidate a manufacturer's claim that the "flutter and wow level" of his tape deck is under ".1% rms." Similarly, the consumer will be unable to disprove a claim when the product is such that he would not normally use all competing brands and measure differences in performance among them. Would the consumer be expected to buy three competing shock absorbers and interchange them on a weekly basis, for the purpose of testing manufacturer X's claim that his product gives the "most comfortable ride"?

In yet other cases, consumers may not recognize invalidation of the claim because of the phenomenon of cognitive dissonance.

The latter situation was illustrated in an early study by Kassarjian and Cohen investigating the effect of the Surgeon General's Report on smokers' attitudes and behavior. The findings showed that 36.5 percent of the surveyed smokers did not believe that the report had established a linkage between smoking and cancer. Moreover, the figure among heavy smokers was 41 percent, suggesting that the more committed one is to a product, the greater the dissonance and the less likely one is to admit the product's adverse effects.[17]

From the standpoint of Jewish law, advertising copy involving puffery may violate *genevat da'at* law. To avoid possible infringement of *genevat da'at* law, puffery, as we indicated earlier, requires pilot-testing before its commercial use can be legitimized. A scientifically designed pilot-test can ascertain the impressions the advertising message has on the target group, as well as the inferences this group draws from it. Should these sets of expectations and impressions fail to conform to actuality, revision of the copy would be in order. Hence Judaism's approach to the issue of puffery conforms with Preston's and Oliver's critiques of the current American legal approach to this issue.

The Testimonial Technique

A seller's comparative merit claim is often catapulted to a heightened level of credibility when it is accompanied by professional or expert endorsement. Expert opinion confers credibility and an aura of objectivity on an otherwise entirely subjective assertion.

Illustrating the testimonial technique is the Saam Drug Company's claim that a certain reputable, independent laboratory has determined that its aspirin tablet relieves arthritic pain more effectively than competing brands. Providing another example of the use of this technique is the Anavim Wine Company's announcement that a well-respected wine connoisseur has found its concord grape wine to be superior to competing brands.

Should the image of objectivity the testimonial message generates be misleading, *genevat da'at* law would be violated. This occurs when the professional or expert opinion cited is in fact biased.

What constitutes bias in Jewish law can, in our view, be derived from an examination of its judicial code of conduct.

Jewish law safeguards the integrity of the judicial decision-making process by means of both preventive measures and corrective action.

Preventive measures take the form of prohibiting the judge of a lawsuit from submitting to any influence that might taint his integrity and calling for him to disqualify himself on the basis of bias.

By force of the verse *You shall not distort justice* (Deuteronomy 16:19), the judge of a lawsuit is forbidden to accept a payment to acquit the guilty or to condemn the innocent. What constitutes a corrupting payment is considerably broadened by force of the verse *You shall take no gift* (Exodus 23:8). Exegetical interpretation of this verse prohibits the judge from accepting payment from one of the opposing litigants even with the instruction to acquit the innocent or to condemn the guilty.[18] Rava's (d. 352) rationalization of the latter point of stringency is very telling: "What is the reason for [the prohibition against taking] a gift? Because as soon as a man receives a gift from another he becomes so well disposed toward him that he becomes like his own person, and no man sees himself in the wrong. What [is the meaning of] *shoḥad? She-hu ḥad*—'he is one with you.' "[19]

Fully recognizing that bias may be created by means other than the acceptance of money, Jewish law prohibits the judge from submitting to even a bribe of words *(shoḥad devarim).*[20] Illustrating *shoḥad devarim* is the following talmudic incident: "Amemar was once engaged in the trial of an action, when a bird flew down upon his head and a man approached and removed it. 'What is your business here?' [Amemar asked him.] 'I have a lawsuit,' the other replied. 'I' came the reply, 'am disqualified from acting as your judge.' "[21]

The stringency of *shoḥad devarim* applies even to words of greeting. Accordingly, in the event A did not make it a practice to anticipate judge B's greeting with his own greeting, initiating this practice just prior to the time his lawsuit will come up in B's docket amounts to *shoḥad devarim.* Since B is regarded as being biased toward A on account of the latter's newfound friendliness toward him, B is disqualified from serving as judge in his lawsuit.[22]

A close friendship or enmity with one of the litigants similarly disqualifies an individual from serving as judge in his lawsuit.[23]

Judicial verdicts rendered under the influence of *shoḥad* are null and void.[24] Since the *shoḥad* payment is regarded as a forbidden receipt, the judge is legally bound to return the illicit fee. Though the Jewish court will not force the judge to return the *shoḥad* unless the claimant demands repayment,[25] he is, nevertheless, ethically bound to make restitution even in the absence of a petition by the claimant.[26]

The judicial code of conduct applies not only to the individual who adjudicates a formal litigation. Residents of a community, according to R. Moses Isserles (Poland, 1525 or 1530–1572), must cast their votes in a referendum in accordance with what they perceive the public's interest to be.[27] Noting this requirement, R. Moses Sofer (Hungary, 1762–1839) invalidated a communal election for the position of rabbi when it was discovered that some of the members of the community had accepted graft to cast their ballots for a particular candidate.[28] What follows, in our view, is the imposition of the judicial code of conduct on anyone who is called upon to make judgments in matters pertaining to the public interest and welfare.

Recognition that professional judgment is susceptible even to subconscious biases leads, in our view, to the necessity of regulating the use of the testimonial technique in advertising.

Bolstering his comparative merit claim by means of expert testimonial achieves heightened credibility for the seller. The heightened credibility the testimonial affords him may, however, be undeserved. This occurs when the expert opinion is in fact tainted, but is presented in a manner that effectively conceals the biasing influence. To illustrate, suppose Saam Drug Company contracts Emet Laboratories to conduct research to determine which of several pain relievers, including its own brand, most effectively combats arthritic pain. The arrangement calls for Saam to review the research every month and allows it the option of terminating the agreement within a week of each progress review. Another provision of the contract calls for Saam to pay Emet an escalating monthly fee for the lifetime of their contract. After eighteen months of research Emet concludes that among the competing brands tested, Saam tablets are the most effective in combating arthritic pain.

Given the arrangement outlined above, bias could very well be expected to enter Emet's judgment both in its selection of a research design and in its interpretation of data. Accordingly, the significance of its findings should be appropriately discounted. Reporting the findings without disclosing the nature of its arrangement with Emet catapults Saam's comparative merit claim to a level of credibility it does not deserve. Hence, by using the testimonial Saam violates the *genevat da'at* interdict. Emet's presumed awareness at the outset that disclosure of its arrangement with Saam would not accompany any eventual commercial use of its findings makes it guilty of complicity in Saam's crime. Receipt of its fees, nonetheless, does not constitute *shoḥad*, as Emet assumes here merely the role of Saam's employee, taking on no judicial role whatsoever.

Avoidance of *genevat da'at* infringement requires, in our view, pilot-testing of any testimonial message prior to its commercial use. The purpose of the pilot would be to ascertain the assumptions the public makes regarding the relationship between the sponsor and the endorser. Should the survey indicate public presumption of the absence of certain biasing factors that are in fact operative, the testimonial message would have to be either entirely discarded or modified accordingly.

Installment Plans Allowing the Buyer to Live Beyond His Means

Successful promotion frequently requires the seller not only to present his product in an attractive manner, but also to arrange favorable terms of payment for his customer. Both price discrimination on the basis of terms of payment and installment plans calling for a premium above the cash price are regulated in Jewish law. We have dealt with the details of these regulations elsewhere.[29] Our concern here will be with the ethics of installment plans which do not call for any premium above the cash price. Such transactions become a matter of halakhic concern when the credit terms effectively allow the buyer to live beyond his means.

Halakhic disfavor with living beyond one's means can be derived from an analysis of the sliding-scale sacrifice and Jewish charity law.

In the times of the Temple, the offering of sacrifices often formed a part of the expiation process for the transgressor seeking atonement. Sacrificial requirements in connection with certain classes of offenses allowed the penitent to offer a sliding-scale sacrifice. To illustrate the nature of the sliding-scale sacrifice, we will describe its application in connection with a particular qualifying offense, the false oath of testimony. This offense consists of A falsely swearing to B that he is not privy to information relevant to his case. The sacrificial aspect of A's atonement process requires him to offer a female sheep or goat. Should A's means not suffice, he may substitute two turtledoves or two young pigeons for the animal sacrifice. If his means do not suffice for birds, he offers a tenth of an ephah of fine flour.[30]

The means criterion, according to *Torat Kohanim,* translates into allowing the penitent to move down the sliding scale if bringing the more expensive sacrifice would put him into debt.[31]

Noting the means criterion, *Sefer ha-Ḥinnukh* advances the opinion that if the poor man offers the rich man's sacrifice he does not fulfill his obligation. This ruling is rationalized on the grounds that since the Almighty shows compassion to the poor man by allowing him to bring a sacrifice according to his means, it would not be proper for the poor man to reject the gesture by incurring an expense for his sacrifice beyond his means. Sound practical advice regarding living standards, continues *Sefer ha-Ḥinnukh,* should be derived from the sliding-scale sacrifice: An individual should not live beyond his means. Such conduct could lead the individual to unethical aggrandizement as a means of sustaining his habit of high living.[32]

Halakhic disfavor with living beyond one's means can also be inferred from the ordinance against donating charity in excess of 20 percent of one's income. The basis of the interdict is the fear that overgenerosity in giving charity could make the donor himself vulnerable to poverty.[33] The prescription of restraint in alms giving indicates that disfavor would certainly be directed against maintaining a standard of living beyond one's means.

Translating the halakhic disfavor of living beyond one's means into a precise formulation for contemporary society is somewhat elusive. The widespread prevalence of installment debt for home mortgages and consumer durables means that blanket adoption of *Torat Kohanim*'s debt-incurral criterion would result in denying masses of people the opportunity to attain the common standard of living in the society they live in. If a person incurs mortgage and consumer durables debts, but is able to meet the amortization and interest payments out of his anticipated income he should apparently not be viewed as living beyond his means. Incurring debt for the purpose of achieving a standard of living beyond the common standard is, however, another matter. Indeed, making the *Torat Kohanim* consistent with the above distinction requires us only to assume that penitents did not usually go into debt for the purpose of satisfying the sacrificial aspect of their atonement process. Given this assumption, the need to go into debt naturally becomes the criterion to determine eligibility to move down the sliding scale in the instance where the Torah prescribes an order of sacrifices relating to means. Understanding the *Torat Kohanim* in these terms results in interpreting the compassionate element of the sliding-scale prescription to consist of not requiring an individual to go into debt for an expenditure people usually do not go into debt for, even when the purpose is atonement. What follows is the halakhic disfavor of going into debt to acquire a style of living higher than the common standard.

It should be noted, however, that retaining use of liquid funds affords the asset holder a distinct advantage. This consideration will often make it more attractive to enter into a particular purchase on a credit rather than a cash basis. Therefore, whether a particular credit purchase affords the buyer the ability to live beyond his means depends, in the final analysis, on the degree of strain the purchase exerts on his present budget as well as how easily his anticipated future income will be able to meet the amortization and interest payments he obligates himself to pay. Since households differ in respect to income, wealth, sources of benefaction, and budget priorities, it is well-nigh impossible to *a priori* identify an installment purchase that allows the buyer to live beyond his means. While good business sense may dictate that the vendor check on the creditworthiness of his customer, inquiries beyond what is necessary for this purpose often infuriate and repel the customer. Since Halakhah has no *intrinsic* objection to installment purchases, the seller, as it appears to us, has no moral obligation to pry into the financial status of his customer in order to satisfy himself that the purchase will not allow him to live beyond his means.

Even though the seller has no investigative responsibility in respect to the financial status of his customer, offering a reluctant customer an installment plan as a means of inducing him to purchase an item he feels he cannot afford clearly violates Jewish business ethics. To illustrate, suppose crystal dealer A shows B an exquisite crystal chandelier. B reacts with excitement and admiration, but turns ashen when informed of its price. Eager to make a sale, A offers B the opportunity to pay out the purchase over a year in monthly installments. B remains reluctant, admitting that while the installment plan would make the purchase feasible for him, his budget, in consequence, would suffer considerable strain. Reminding B once again of the aesthetic qualities of the chandelier, A repeats his offer, expressing confidence that B will somehow make ends meet, the chandelier purchase notwithstanding. B is now persuaded and concludes the purchase. Since the purchase allows B to live beyond his means, A's *persuasion* clearly amounts to ill-suited advice and violates the *lifnei ivver* interdict.

Advertising That Incites Envy

In a materialistic culture where personal worth is often measured by invidious distinctions, maintaining an ostentatious lifestyle beyond the means of ordinary people secures status for the individual. Within this cultural milieu, successful advertising strategy for luxury items often dictates that the seller project an exclusivity image for his product. The more inaccessible the luxury article is thought to be, the greater the symbolic status attached to it.

Promotional messages designed to convey the idea that a certain luxury product is beyond the means of ordinary people present a moral dilemma in Jewish law.

Conduct having the effect of generating envy, as the following talmudic text indicates, is strictly prohibited in Jewish law:

> Our rabbis taught: . . . If one journeys from a place where they do not fast to a place where they do, he should fast with them. . . . If he forgot and ate and drank, let him not make it patent in public, nor may he indulge in delicacies, as it is written, *And Jacob said to his sons, "Why should you show yourself?"* [Genesis 42:1]. Jacob conveyed thereby to his sons, "When you are fully sated, do not show yourselves before Esau or before Ishmael, that they should not envy you."[34]

Differential living standards inevitably produce feelings of inadequacy, embarrassment, and envy among those of limited means.

With the aim of reducing the intensity of these ill feelings, the sages, in talmudic times, regulated the lifestyles of the wealthy in various ways. Mourning customs provide a case in point:

> Formerly, they were wont to convey [victuals] to the house of mourning, the rich in silver and gold baskets, and the poor in osier baskets of peeled willow twigs, and the poor felt shamed: they therefore instituted that all should convey [victuals] in osier baskets of peeled willow twigs out of deference to the poor.
>
> Formerly, they were wont to serve drinks in the house of mourning, the rich in white glass vessels, and the poor in colored glass, and the poor felt shamed: they instituted therefore that all should serve drinks in colored glasses out of deference to the poor.[35]

Out of concern that conspicuous consumption would ignite both internal discord and envy among neighboring non-Jews, autonomous Jewish communities in the Middle Ages regulated living standards. The medieval sumptuary laws typically imposed limitations on the type of dress residents could wear and restricted expenditures for weddings and other social festivities.[36]

Application of the aforementioned principles to commercial advertising disallows, in our view, use of the exclusivity stratagem for mass media promotion of luxury articles. While such messages are primarily directed to potential buyers, mass media advertising allows the message to reach huge audiences, including many who cannot possibly afford the product. For the latter group, the promotional message stirs up feelings of envy. The greater the intensity of the envy generated by the advertising message among nonbuyers, the more attractive the luxury product becomes to potential buyers, and thus, from the seller's standpoint, the generation of envy is, at the very least, a welcome consequence of the advertising message. Since Jewish law interdicts envy-generating conduct, such advertising messages violate Jewish business ethics.

Dissuading a Customer from Making a Purchase

Promotional and advertising campaigns not only enhance consumer awareness of market alternatives but, in addition, increase seller knowledge of what rivals are doing. Awareness of a rival's product line, pricing policy, and the amenities he offers customers creates the setting for a difficult moral dilemma. Suppose that Marfi, a salesperson for Alpha Carpets, in the process of servicing a customer, Rispah, becomes convinced that Rispah's interests would best be served by

Alpha's rival, Beta Carpets. Is Marfi morally obligated to dissuade Rispah from making his purchase at Alpha? Whether or not a dissuasion obligation devolves upon Marfi hinges, as it appears to us, on an analysis of the following three moral prescriptions: (1) the prohibition against price fraud *(ona'ah);* (2) the prohibition against offering ill-suited advice *(lifnei ivver);* and (3) the prohibition against standing by idly as a neighbor's blood is about to be shed *(lo ta'amod al dam rei'akha)*. We will take up, in turn, each of these prohibitions as they relate to the moral issue at hand.

Ona'ah

The law of *ona'ah* prohibits an individual from *knowingly* concluding a transaction at a price which is more favorable to himself than the competitive norm.[37] What is objectionable here is to prey on the opposing party's ignorance of market conditions in a commercial transaction.[38] A transaction involving *ona'ah* is regarded as a form of theft.[39] Depending on how widely the price of the subject transaction departs from the competitive norm, the injured party may have recourse to void or adjust the transaction. Provided the price discrepancy is assessed to be within the margin of error,[40] the plaintiff's right to void the transaction is recognized when the difference between the sale price and the competitive norm is more than one-sixth.[41] When the differential was exactly one-sixth, neither of the parties may subsequently void the transaction on account of the price discrepancy. The plaintiff is, however, entitled to full restitution of the *ona'ah* involved.[42] Finally, third-degree *ona'ah* occurs when the sale price differs from the market price by less than one-sixth. Here, the transaction not only remains binding, but, in addition, the complainant has no legal claim to the price differential.[43] In the latter instance, however, the plaintiff's claim would be denied only when the transaction involved a product which is nonstandardized in nature. Should the case involve a homogeneous product, the plaintiff's claim for the differential is honored.[44]

The aforementioned apparently indicates that Marfi has a clear-cut responsibility to dissuade Rispah from making the purchase when it is evident to him that the transaction at hand involves *ona'ah*.

While the *ona'ah* prohibition is of theoretical importance in assessing the appropriateness of the dissuasion responsibility in the case at hand, its operational significance, in the final analysis, hinges on the range of alternatives among the entire set of available opportunities that Halakhah regards as relevant in evaluating the merits of an *ona'ah* claim.

Pointing to a narrow range of consideration within the context of the modern differentiated-product market is R. Asher b. Jeḥiel's (Germany, 1250–1327) analysis of third-degree *ona'ah.* In the interest of brevity we will cite only that part of R. Asher's analysis that is germane to the present discussion. Noting the absence of any provision for legal redress in third-degree *ona'ah* cases, R. Asher speculates whether it might be permissible, in the first instance, to contract into third-degree *ona'ah.* Pivotal to the resolution of this question, in R. Asher's view, is the definition of market price. Is market price to be understood as a single value, or is it to be defined as the range of deviations of less than one-sixth from the price of the transaction? Adopting the latter view leads to the conclusion that third-degree *ona'ah* is not price fraud at all. Subscription to the former view leads, however, to the conclusion that knowledge of the market norm prohibits either party from contracting into a price agreement which is even slightly more favorable to himself than the norm. The absence of legal redress for third-degree *ona'ah* would then be explained by the presumption that when the degree of *ona'ah* involved is of such a relatively small amount, the plaintiff waives his claim to restitution. This presumption follows from our inability to fix the value of the article sold. While some experts would insist that *ona'ah* took place, others would just as vehemently deny it. Since the experts are divided as to whether *ona'ah* occurred, and, if it did, by how much we may safely presume that the victim of this possible price fraud waives his right to restitution.

Though offering no definitive resolution of the above dilemma, R. Asher urged the following guideline for third-degree *ona'ah* cases. Cognizant of the prevailing norm, an individual should not contract into a price agreement that is even slightly more favorable to himself than this value. Should an individual fall victim to third-degree *ona'ah,* on the other hand, he should accept his loss graciously and express no complaint.[45]

R. Asher's uncertainty as to why third-degree *ona'ah* is legally not subject to return is not shared by other Rishonim. Maimonides (Egypt, 1135–1204),[46] R. Jacob b. Asher (Germany, 1270–1343),[47] and R. Joseph Caro (Safed, 1488–1575)[48] understand the lack of provision for modification of the original transaction as stemming from a presumption that the plaintiff waives his claims against the offender when the degree of *ona'ah* involved is relatively small, i.e., third degree. What follows as a corollary, according to R. Asher's line of reasoning, is a prohibition against *knowingly* contracting into third-degree *ona'ah.* This latter action is explicitly prohibited by Naḥmanides (Spain, 1194–1270).[49]

Implicit in R. Asher's analysis of third-degree *ona'ah,* according to

R. Jeḥiel Michel Epstein (Belorussia, 1829–1908), is the proposition that the plaintiff's restitution claims are denied in this case only when the product market involved is *heterogeneous* in nature. R. Asher's explanation of why it is reasonable to assume that the plaintiff waives his claims against the offender in third-degree *ona'ah* cases forces this conclusion. The basis of this presumption, as will be recalled, is the division among experts as to whether or not *ona'ah* took place. Now, this disagreement among experts is only comprehensible when the product involved is standardized and homogeneous. Since the occurrence of *ona'ah* is not subject to dispute when the product market is homogeneous, the presumption that the plaintiff waives his claims for restitution is not defensible regardless of the inconsequential nature of the *ona'ah* involved.[50]

Another implication of R. Asher's analysis of third-degree *ona'ah,* in our view, is a narrow definition of what constitutes a product market. This narrowness follows from the fact that division among experts as to whether or not price fraud took place is only possible when the products being compared have offsetting advantages and disadvantages. Within this framework, when the difference in price is less than one-sixth, the plaintiff presumably waives his claim to the differential. If the difference in price is one-sixth or more, the trade-offs involved no longer justify the presumption of waiver. Differences among experts would, however, not be expected to emerge when the subject product contains all the features of competing products and displays, in addition, a distinctive characteristic as well. Differentiation here clearly separates the subject product from the competition and confers upon the seller an element of monopoly status. Monopoly status, in turn, vitiates the *ona'ah* claim.

From the above criterion for market separation, it follows that an *ona'ah* claim against a showroom furniture store on the grounds that an identical piece of furniture was available at a lower price in a catalogue furniture store is invalid. Since the showroom store offers differentiation in the form of product display, its product is traded in a market *separate* from the product in the catalogue store. The pricing policy of the latter establishment is therefore irrelevant in assessing the merits of an *ona'ah* claim against the showroom store.

One may well argue that within the context of the modern product world no two competing products are identical. Differentiation today has advanced considerably beyond the level of the physical properties of the product to include such factors as proximity to the consumer, convenience of hours, complementarities of consumption, product display, and service level. All market purchases involve some trade-off of offsetting advantages and disadvantages, and thus the law of *ona'ah* should have wide operational significance within the framework of the modern product market. Relating the argument for defining a product market in broad terms to the furniture market leads to the proposition that the showroom and catalogue stores should be lumped together in a single product market. While the showroom store offers differentiation in the form of product display, the catalogue store may offer the convenience of proximity to the consumer.

The above argument, in our view, is not entirely valid. Differentiation, as it appears to us, works to erode the distinctiveness of a competing brand only when a basis exists for presuming that consumers value the differentiation involved. Pointing clearly in this direction is the determining role R. Asher assigns to the agreement or disagreement of experts in adjudicating *ona'ah* cases. Clearly, cost differences among sellers play no role in judging the merits of an *ona'ah* claim. What does matter is the legitimacy of the presumption that consumers want to spend extra money for the differentiation involved. Following this line, proximity to the consumer would not be regarded as an offsetting advantage for the catalogue store in the furniture market. Since the furniture market is not a local, neighborhood market, proximity of the seller to the consumer cannot be said to generate a presumption that consumers are willing to spend extra money to acquire this advantage. In respect to the consumer nondurables market, proximity, within limits, expecially in the inclement-weather season, may be regarded by consumers as an advantage to which they attach a price significance. Scientific surveys could prove very helpful in determining which aspects of differentiation consumers are willing to pay extra money to acquire. Such information would naturally add a measure of refinement to the preceding analysis.

Ona'ah and Shadow Prices

Another factor working to limit the operational significance of the law of *ona'ah* in the consumer market is the multiproduct character of many of the firms serving this market. Within the framework of a multiproduct-firm market structure, a particular product may often sell below the price it can theoretically command in the marketplace. Reflecting an investment stratagem, the bargain price is designed either to attract customers to complementary products offered by the same seller or to generate good will for the purpose of increasing future sales. Since the discount represents a voluntary income transfer between the seller and the buyer, that price does not serve as a measure of the *objective market value* of the product. Using a discount price as the measure of the *market* opportunity cost the plaintiff incurred as a result of entering into the moot transaction is, in our view, inappropriate. The plaintiff's alternative *market* opportunity is more precisely measured by the price the competing outlet *could* have commanded at that time. In contradistinction to *market* price, economists call the latter price the "shadow" price of the article.

The preceding discussion of product-market identification and shadow prices indicates that the seller enjoys some latitude in deciding for himself that his "above-competitive" price does not violate *ona'ah* law.

Financial Ruination and the Ona'ah Interdict

Another factor in considering the appropriateness of a dissuasion responsibility in the case at hand is the adverse financial impact the disclosure might have on both the owner of Alpha Carpets and the job security of Marfi, its salesperson. Circumstances may be such that the disclosure would erode Alpha's competitive position and threaten Marfi's job security. Does a perception of financial ruination enter in any way as a mitigating factor in deciding the appropriateness of the disclosure obligation?

Relevant to the issue at hand is R. Mosheh Sofer's ruling regarding the dictum that an individual is not required to spend more than one-fifth of his income in order to fulfill a *mizvah.* R. Moses Isserles contends that the one-fifth rule does not apply in respect to a negative commandment. Avoidance of the infringement of a negative commandent requires an individual, if necessary, to go to any expense.[51] Disputing R. Isserles' view, R. Sofer extends the one-fifth rule to a negative commandment as well. To be sure, the leniency applies only if the negative commandment would be violated passively *(shev ve-al ta'aseh).* Avoidance of the violation of a negative commandment in an active manner requires an individual, if necessary, to go to any expense.[52]

Following R. Sofer's line, passive violation of the *ona'ah* interdict should be countenanced when avoidance of the prohibition is perceived by Marfi as threatening to his job security. Such an assessment apparently meets the one-fifth rule. The passivity condition is met when the violator plays no role in setting the *ona'ah* price and, in addition, does not actively persuade the customer to buy the product.

Lifnei Ivver and the Dissuasion Responsibility

Another consideration in assessing the appropriateness of the dissuasion obligation is that failure to do so may violate the *lifnei ivver* interdict. One aspect of this interdict is the prohibition against aiding someone in committing a sin. Maimonides regards "strengthening the hands of transgressors" as violating this aspect of the prohibition.[53] Extrapolating Maimonides' position, R. Judah Rosanes (Turkey, 1657–1727) theorizes that failure to voice objection also constitutes "strengthening the hands of transgressors." Evidencing this is Maimonides' ruling that a Jew may not permit a non-Jew to use a tree belonging to another Jew for the purpose of grafting a branch of one species to another.[54]

Following R. Rosanes' line, Rabbi Jacob Breisch (Israel, contemp.) posits that offering someone "passive" counsel which is ill-suited violates the *lifnei ivver* interdict. Accordingly, if A fails to provide B with timely information which would avert a financial loss for him, A has violated the *lifnei ivver* interdict.[55] Applying this principle to the case at hand apparently points to a dissuasion responsibility for Marfi when it is evident to him that Rispah's interests would best be served elsewhere. The dissuasion responsibility proceeding from the *lifnei ivver* interdict is, in our view, intact whether or not the law of *ona'ah* independently requires this responsibility. Irrespective of whether the seller would be in violation of the *ona'ah* law in the event of such a purchase, making the purchase may, in any case, be ill-advised. This distinction is illustrated by the proposition we advanced earlier regarding the appropriateness of referring to shadow prices rather than actual market prices in adjudicating the merits of *ona'ah* claims. Suppose that the shadow price of the alternative market opportunity is sufficiently above the market price so as entirely to vitiate the *ona'ah* claim. Despite the fact that the *ona'ah* claim has no validity in the above instance, making the purchase is, in any case, ill-advised in light of the availability of a cheaper alternative. Silence on the part of Marfi amounts to giving Rispah "passive" counsel to go ahead with the ill-advised purchase.

Given that the *lifnei ivver* interdict is violated here only in a passive manner, the impact the dissuasive responsibility would have on the livelihood prospects of Marfi must be taken into account. Marfi's perception that the dissuasion course threatens his job security relieves him, as the previous discussion indicated, of this responsibility.

Lo Ta'amod al Dam Rei'akha and the Dissuasion Responsibility

Finally, another relevant consideration in the moral dilemma at hand is that Marfi's silence may violate the biblical injunction of *Do not stand idly by the blood of your neighbor (lo ta'amod al dam rei'akha,* Leviticus 19:16). While the verse speaks of the prohibition of a bystander's remaining idle in a life-threatening situation, *Mekhilta* extends the interdict to the prohibition of witholding testimony in a monetary matter. Basing himself on *Mekhilta*, Rabbi Israel Meir ha-Kohen Kagan (Radun, 1838–1933) understands the monetary application of the *lo ta'amod* interdict in broad terms: A's failure to supply B with timely information that would avert a financial loss for B is a violation of the *lo ta'amod* interdict.[56] Applying the *lo ta'amod* interdict to the case at hand obligates Marfi to dissuade Rispah from making the purchase. The dissuasion obligation proceeding from the *lo ta'amod* interdict is operative, in our view, independent of any like responsibility that may proceed from the *ona'ah* injunction. Since it is evident to Marfi that the item in question is available elsewhere at a cheaper price, the purchase constitutes a loss for the customer, notwithstanding that the law of *ona'ah* may not have been violated.

Invoking the one-fifth rule here is apparently not valid. Passivity in the violation of the prohibition works to create a dispensation on the basis of financial ruination only when it is feasible to violate the prohibition in both the active and the passive form. Since the passive form represents a less severe form of the prohibition, legitimacy is given to the one-fifth rule. In sharp contrast, the *lo ta'amod* injunction is feasibly violated *only* in the passive form. With the essence of the prohibition consisting of inaction, legitimacy would not be given to invoking the one-fifth rule as a means of relieving Marfi of a dissuasion responsibility.

Release from the dissuasion responsibility in the above circumstances proceeds, in our view, from a different consideration. The applicability of this injunction in connection with the *mitzvah* of restoring lost property *(hashavat avedah)* proceeds from the understanding that the *lo ta'amod* interdict extends to the monetary realm. Both the positive commandment of *hashavat avedah* (Deuteronomy 22:1–3) and the negative commandment of *lo ta'amod* require the finder of lost property to take action to restore it to its owner. An individual is, however, not required to engage in the task of *hashavat avedah* when it would be at the expense of restoring his own property or losing time on his job. This exemption is exegetically derived from the verse *Save when there shall be no needy among you (efes ki lo yehiyeh bekha evyon,* Deuteronomy 15:4).[57] The word *efes* is interpreted to mean "end" or "prevent," with the meaning being: "Be careful not to engage in conduct that will result in poverty for you."[58]

From the preceding analysis, it follows that the obligation, should the opportunity arise, to take action to avert a loss for a fellow is by no means absolute. A's perception that his provision of timely information to B would be to his own detriment exempts him from the obligation.

Extension of the *efes* caveat to the *lifnei ivver* and *ona'ah* prohibitions is, in our view, entirely illegitimate. The potential violator's desire to avoid financial detriment neither vitiates nor mitigates the immorality of price fraud and proffering ill-suited advice. The *lo ta'amod* interdict, as it pertains to the monetary realm, on the other hand, amounts to nothing more than a moral imperative, should the opportunity arise, to avert financial loss for someone else. Conflict of interest between the parties involved is therefore a relevant consideration in determining whether the obligation is operative. Nonetheless, the passivity condition, as we discussed earlier, works to allow violation of these prohibitions, provided the one-fifth rule is met.

We should note that many authorities do not subscribe to R. Sofer's formulation of the one-fifth rule as it pertains to a negative commandment. Avoidance of the violation of a negative commandment, whether in the active or the passive form, according to this school of thought, requires an individual, if necessary, to expend all his resources.[59] Moreover, every instance of the dissuasion dilemma, in any case, is not necessarily either a job-threatening or a financially ruinous situation. Honest self-appraisal, as it appears to us, readily indicates this.

· 3

Supply-Side Economics: A Jewish Perspective

Introduction

Ronald Reagan's succession to the presidency of the United States in 1980 marked not only a dramatic shift to the right in political power, but a watershed in economic policy-making as well. Reagan's economic policy adopted many of the tenets of the supply-side school of economics.[1] It will be our purpose in this chapter to describe two of the prescriptions of this school of economics, namely, its advocacy of a reduction in taxes and deregulation of industry. These ideas will then be examined from the perspective of Jewish law.

Supply-Side Economics

One of the basic tenets of supply-side economics is that government tax policy can play an important role in promoting economic incentives in the marketplace. Specifically, work effort can dramatically be increased by reducing the tax liability associated with it. Similarly, a lower tax rate for investment income encourages increased investment activity. Increased investment, in turn, enhances society's capacity to produce goods and services, hence raising its standard of living.

Increasing the cost of an undesirable activity can also be done directly through taxation. Idleness, supply-siders claim, can be discouraged by linking unemployment compensation and welfare programs more imaginatively with work effort.

Another proposition of the supply-siders designed to increase the efficiency of the marketplace is their call for deregulation of industry. Supply-siders maintain that government regulation of the private marketplace has resulted in massive inefficiencies and increased costs; costs which far exceed any benefits which might be associated with such government interference. Thus, they are confident that as these regulations are relaxed, the business community will respond with an increase in supply.

Government regulation of the marketplace today is very extensive and is rooted in a variety of motivations. For the purpose of elucidating the supply-side position in respect to government regulation, we will draw upon the taxonomy Hailstones and Mastrianna have devised in categorizing government intervention in the marketplace.[2] Supply-siders have most stridently objected to government interference in the marketplace when its motivation is the prevention of excessive competition and the provision of better information to market participants. Much less vehemence is voiced in the areas of natural monopoly and market failure due to ill-defined property rights. Nonetheless, to the supply-sider, government regulation should only be carried to the point where the incremental costs equal the incremental benefits.

Preventing Excessive Competition

When an industry is characterized by a cost structure largely comprising variable rather than fixed cost, entry and exit into the industry by many small producers is relatively easy. This can produce wide swings in industry output and great instability in prices and profit in both the short and long run. These conditions create a maximum of uncertainty on the part of producers and consumers. The case for government regulation rests on the presence of excessive competition rather than excessive monopoly power and is justified to provide industrywide stability.

Supply-siders' advocacy of deregulation of the marketplace has scored its greatest success in those industries where government intervention is rooted in a desire to prevent excessive competition. Evidencing this success was the passage of the Airline Deregulation Act of 1978 and the Motor Carrier Act of 1980.

The most outstanding case of deregulation in the early 1980s has been that of the airlines.

Economic regulation of the airline industry dates back to 1938, with the creation of the Civil Aeronautics Board (CAB). The stated objectives of the CAB were to assure adequate, economical, and efficient air service at reasonable charges. To achieve these goals it acted to control entry and exit of domestic trunk lines to prevent excessive competition, and it supervised air fares to protect the public.

Under CAB regulations, airlines were prohibited from engaging in competitive pricing. Consequently, airlines were compelled to compete vigorously on the basis of customer service.

The most injurious form of service competition entailed flight scheduling in heavily trafficked markets. Individual airlines sought consumer identification by providing the largest number of daily flights between major cities so that customers would contact that airline first in making reservations to any destination. Many of these flights were duplicative, since the passengers they carried could have been accommodated easily by fewer flights. The resulting proliferation of flights created a chronic problem of excess capacity on these routes.

To compound the problem, airlines also competed heavily in other areas of costly nonprice competition. Over the years, airlines sought to attract passengers by providing greater comfort and more exotic foods and drinks than competitors. Such attempts to differentiate service also tended to increase the costs of providing passenger service.

The Airline Deregulation Act of 1978, which called for a gradual decrease in the control of routes and fares by CAB, has drastically changed that sector of the U.S. economy.

Deregulation has allowed airlines to utilize their aircraft more intensively. As anticipated, passenger comfort and costly service amenities have been curtailed. Market chaos has not resulted, but the scramble to reconstruct airline routes has created problems.

Route competition has intensified on many heavily traveled corridors, such as New York to California, where new entry has brought about price wars on discount fares. In lightly traveled markets, sharp declines in service have been recorded. However, commuter and regional airlines are expanding rapidly and are expected to pick up any slack.[3]

Regulation to Provide Better Information to Market Participants

Government intervenes in the marketplace for the purpose of protecting the consumer. An example of this form of social regulation is the Federal Trade Commission Act (1914). This act, as amended by the Wheeler-Lea Amendment of 1938, protects the consumer from false advertising claims and deceptive packaging. Similar protection is afforded the consumer in the drug market by the Pure Food and Drug Act.

The philosophy behind this regulation is the belief that consumers are unable to judge quality in advance of purchase. Because search costs for consumers are expensive, and the information gathered by individuals is difficult to disseminate, government intervention to improve the flow of information is appropriate.

On the factor-resource side, the same rationale has been applied to justify intervention in protecting laborers from unsafe working conditions in factories, mines, offices, and on construction sites.

The creation of government agencies for the purpose of protecting the consumer from fraud and misleading advertising is opposed by supply-siders. This position reflects a faith in the self-regulating nature of the marketplace. Fear of losing a customer to a competitor will restrain the seller from charging above the competitive norm, inhibit him from misrepresenting his product, and discourage him from adulterating it. Likewise, enterprises which fail to protect their labor force against accidents or industrial diseases or which work them unusually hard are penalized by the refusal of workers to work for them except at a higher wage than other employers pay.

The growing complexity of the products of the modern industrial economy has not dampened the faith of those believing in the self-regulating nature of the marketplace. While individuals may not be capable of judging the quality of complex products, specialists capable of making such assessments do exist. The success of these specialists, such as major retailers and other middlemen, hinges heavily upon the reputation for reliability they build up among their customers.

Product Safety

In the area of product safety, supply-siders are decidedly opposed to government regulation.

Given that safety is not a free good, the utility-maximizing consumer is well aware that the more safety he demands in the products and services he buys, the less other goods and services will be available to him. For this reason, the typical well-informed consumer would not be expected to demand the highest level of safety in the various goods and services he buys. Instead, the typical consumer is seen as constantly comparing the benefits of additional safety to the costs of that safety in terms of time, money, and effort. When the costs and benefits change, the level of safety the consumer desires also changes.

While government promulgation of safety standards has the effect of increasing the safety of the regulated products, it also increases their costs. Automobile safety legislation provides a case in point. Some estimates of the costs of automobile safety legislation have been made by Murray Weidenbaum and Robert DeFina of the Center for the Study of American Business at Washington University in St. Louis. The two economists reported that safety regulations enacted between 1968 and 1978 have added at least $450 to the price of a new car.

Higher prices, of course, lead to still other indirect effects. Other things being equal, as the price of a regulated product rises, fewer purchases will be made. Some consumers will turn to substitute products, which may be less safe than the regulated product. As a result, safety regulations can have the wholly unintended effect of reducing the overall level of safety.

In the face of higher prices for new cars, for example, potential buyers are encouraged to seek out alternatives. They may continue driving the cars they have; they may purchase used cars; or they may turn to less expensive forms of transportation, such as motorcycles, mopeds, or even bicycles. These are the kinds of indirect effects that are likely to decrease the level of safety. Working in the opposite direction to produce a higher overall level of transportation safety is the possibility of some shifting to public transportation.

Another indirect effect of safety regulation may be to induce consumers to exercise less caution in the use of the regulated products. The adverse effect of safer product design in product use was identified by Peltzman in his investigation of the effects of automobile safety legislation on traffic accidents and highway deaths. In particular, Peltzman found that a disproportionate share of accidents occurred in cars that had the new safety equipment as compared to those that did not have it. He also found that, after adjusting for other factors, the new safety standards had no overall effect on the highway death rate. In fact, the only major result of safety regulation was a change in the way people died. The death rate went down for the occupants of automobiles, but it went up, by an offsetting amount, for pedestrians, bicyclists, and motorcyclists.

Certification

As an alternative to government regulation in the area of product safety, supply-siders favor government certification. Through certification the government simply provides information to the consumer regarding the safety features and risks of products. Its aim is to prevent mistakes, not to coerce, and the ultimate choice is left to the consumers themselves.

The health hazard posed by cigarettes is an example of one problem handled through certification. Cigarettes are not outlawed, even though the surgeon general believes that smoking is hazardous to health. Instead, manufacturers are required to post warnings on cigarette packages and in cigarette advertisements. Consumers are, however, left free to smoke as many cigarettes as they want.[4]

Ill-Defined Property Rights

The workings of a market economy are predicated on recognizable private property rights, but where property rights are unassigned or indefinite, anyone can use the property without paying for it, so long as no one else is using it. As a result, social costs may differ from private costs, since users will not bear the full costs and are likely to overuse the property. Ill-defined property rights justify environmental regulation in the form of controlling air and water pollution.

Exemplifying the supply-siders' approach to environmental pollution is Ruff's *effluent fee scheme.* The plan calls for those who produce and consume goods which cause pollution to pay the costs involved. All that is needed to implement such a plan is a mechanism for estimating the pollution output of all polluters, together with a means of collecting fees. Under such a system, anyone could emit any amount of pollution as long as he pays the price which the government sets to approximate the marginal social cost of pollution. If pollution consists of many components, each with its own social cost, there would be different prices for each component. Prohibitive prices would be set for pollutants that endanger human life. Once the prices are set, polluters could adjust to them in any way they choose. Because they act in self-interest, they will reduce their pollution by every means possible, up to the point where further reduction would cost more than the price. Should the initial price prove to be too low to accomplish the desired amount of pollution abatement, the price could be increased to effect the desired reduction.[5]

Natural Monopoly

Natural monopoly occurs when one firm is capable of providing for the entire market at decreasing costs. Under these conditions the first firm to establish sufficient output to achieve very low production costs could drive out competing firms with higher costs, leaving a monopoly situation. The cost structure of the industry, therefore, serves as a barrier to entry; and the unregulated monopolist may be in a position to charge excessive prices, restrict output, and reap monopoly profits. Thus, the government awards monopoly franchises to such firms, protecting them from competition. In return for monopoly privileges, the government regulates services, prices, and profits. Cases of natural monopoly are few, with public utilities being the major example.

Recent research has suggested that even if a market is a natural monopoly, it may still not be a good candidate for regulation. This occurs when the subject market is contestable, i.e., entry and exit are relatively easy to achieve. When the market is contestable, potential competition will keep a monopoly from charging high prices. To illustrate, it may be efficient for only a single airline to provide passenger service between two specific cities. Yet this monopoly firm need not be regulated if other airlines have access to the same market (route). If the airline flying between these two cities charges a monopoly price, another airline can easily enter this route, and can do so very successfully by offering somewhat lower prices.[6]

Supply-Side Economics: A Halakhic Perspective

Underlying the supply-siders' preoccupation with designing a tax system that would work to maximize society's wealth is the premium they put on marketplace activity. Encouraging people to devote more of their time to activities that generate for themselves an economic reward represents to the supply-sider an unqualified social gain. It will be our purpose in this section to demonstrate that while Judaism regards the efficiency aspect of economic incentives as a positive good, designing an economic system to maximally encourage people to spend their time in the marketplace is not desirable.

Economic Incentives and Efficient Work Effort in the Rabbinic Literature

The talmudic insight into the paramount role economic incentives play in bringing forth efficient work effort is seen in connection with the rights of an assault victim to medical treatment: "If the offender says to him [the victim], 'I will bring you a physician who will heal you for nothing,' he might object, saying, 'A physician who heals for nothing is worth nothing' " (*Bava Kamma* 85a).

Commenting on this talmudic text, R. Solomon b. Isaac (France, 1040–1105) and others understand the case to refer to a situation where the physician is a relative of the offender. Presumably, the physician normally commands a fee for his medical services, but in this instance, as a favor to the offender, he is willing to render his services gratis.[7] Why the offer may be rejected by the victim is explained by R. Asher b. Jeḥiel (Germany, 1250–1327) on the grounds that anticipation of reward generates responsibility and diligence on the part of the party who obligates himself to render a service. A certain amount of potential diligence and responsibility will be lost when the service is rendered gratis.[8]

It should be noted that the adverse effect of noncompensation on work effort could very well be subliminal, as Jewish law presumes that a professional will do nothing consciously to ruin his reputation (*uman lo meira umnateih*).[9]

Further evidencing Judaism's recognition of the efficiency advantage inherent in economic incentives is R. Solomon b. Abraham Adret's (Spain, ca. 1235–1310) analysis of the appropriate method of filling the communal position of cantor. Rather than fill this position on a voluntary basis, R. Adret preferred the community to hire an individual specifically for this purpose. Defending his ruling, R. Adret points out that the former method suffers from the disadvantage of inevitably producing incessant disputes as to who should serve as cantor. Hiring an individual to serve as cantor avoids such disputes, as only the designated person may assume the role. Moreover, hired status pressures the employee to approach his cantorial duties more conscientiously than would be the case if he provided his services on a voluntary basis.[10]

Another example of Judaism's insight into the advantage of economic incentives is seen from the polemic that R. Eliezer b. Isaac of

Böhman (12th cent.) directed against a proposal to deny religious functionaries compensation for their services. Building his case for compensation, R. Eliezer points out that during the time of the *Mishkan* (Tabernacle) and the First and Second Temples, Kohanim and Levites were entitled to support in return for the Temple service they rendered. Compensation was called for despite the fact that competition to officiate in the Temple was fierce and intense. What follows is a background description of how the Temple service was organized and the nature of the rivalry among the Kohanim. For the purpose of establishing a rotation system, the Kohanim and Levites were divided into twenty-four guards, or *mishmarot*. Each week a different *mishmar* would officiate in the Temple on a rotating basis. *Mishmarot* were further subdivided into daily groupings, called *batei avot*. Generally, Kohanim and Levites were permitted to officiate only during the period their *beit av* served. Daily Temple service requirements were assigned to individual Kohanim on the basis of an allotment system. Originally, the first service of the day, i.e., the removal of the ashes from the altar, was not assigned by means of allotment, since those interested in performing this service would have to arise close to the crack of dawn, and vigorous competition was not expected. The sages provided, however, that if there was competition, the contending Kohanim would have to run a foot race up the thirty-two cubits of the ramp of the altar to determine who would officiate. Surprisingly, fierce competition did arise for the honor of removing the ashes. Indeed, the Talmud records an incident where the losing contestant of the foot race, venting his extreme frustration, fatally stabbed the winner. The occurrence of a subsequent incident where the foot race resulted in one of the contestants breaking his leg convinced the sages that the previous bloodshedding episode could not be dismissed as a mere quirk. Consequently, an allotment system was instituted for the assigning of the removal of ashes service as well.[11]

Given the intense rivalry to officiate in the Temple service, the call for compensation, argues R. Eliezer b. Isaac, can only be understood in terms of the debilitating long-term effect a system of voluntarism would produce. Without economic incentive, enthusiasm for the Temple service would eventually wane and possibly be subject to gross neglect.

While the destruction of the Sanctuary brought with it the disruption of the Temple service, Torah study and prayer, according to tradition, substitute for it. Maintaining the viability of the Torah and public prayer institutions requires the community to provide its religious functionaries with adequate compensation.

Providing sufficient economic incentives for religious functionaries proved to be an enormous burden for the poverty-stricken Jewish communities in the time of R. Isaac. The communal burden was lightened somewhat by the practice of making gifts to such functionaries at weddings and various other festivities. The joyous mood on such occasions helped to engender a spirit of generosity. Corresponding loosely to the prescribed method of supporting the Kohanim, this system of voluntary gifts, which provided a good part of the income of religious functionaries, enabled the community to avoid the burden of making relatively high payments to them at regular intervals.[12]

A similar, albeit less detailed rationale for compensating religious scholars is provided by R. Joseph Caro (Safed, 1488–1575). This decisor brings into play the significant link between productivity and compensation. For Torah scholarship to flourish, the Jewish community must be prepared to adequately compensate those who dedicate themselves to the holy work.[13]

Another dimension of Jewish law's recognition of the efficiency implication of economic incentives is its treatment of fees for medical services rendered on the Shabbat.

Normally, demanding or offering a fee for work rendered on the Shabbat is rabbinically prohibited *(sekhar shabbat)*.[14] Out of concern that the *sekhar shabbat* prohibition might cause a physician to hesitate in responding to a call for assistance on the Shabbat, the sages suspended the *sekhar shabbat* interdict in connection with medical fees.[15] On similar grounds the sages refrained from proclaiming that physicians taking *sekhar shabbat* would see no "sign of blessing" from the fee. Such a harsh pronouncement would surely deter physicians from demanding *sekhar shabbat*, but would at the same time remove the economic incentive for them to respond to a call for assistance on the Shabbat.[16]

While Judaism appreciates the efficiency aspect of economic incentives, it would decidedly disapprove of an economic incentive system designed to *maximally* encourage work effort. Analysis of the following tannaic dispute bears this out:

> Our rabbis taught: *that you may gather in your grain* [Deuteronomy 11:14]. What is to be learnt from these words? Since it says, *This book of the Law shall not depart out of your mouth* [Joshua 1:8], I might think that this injunction is to be taken literally. Therefore it says, *that you may gather in your grain*, which implies that you are to combine the study of them [the words of the Torah] with a worldly occupation. This is the view of R. Ishmael. R. Shimon b. Yoḥai says: Is that possible? If a man plows in the plowing season, and sows in

> the sowing season, and reaps in the reaping season, and winnows in the season of wind, what is to become of the Torah? No, but when Israel performs the will of the Omnipresent, their work is performed by others, as it says, *And strangers shall stand and feed your flocks* [Isaiah 61:5], and when Israel does not perform the will of the Omnipresent, their work is carried out by themselves, as it says, *that you may gather in your grain* [Deuteronomy 11:14]. Nor is this all, but the work of others also is done by them, as it says, *And you shall serve your enemy* [Deuteronomy 28:48].[17]

The apparent diametric opposition between the views of R. Shimon b. Yoḥai and R. Ishmael is somewhat narrowed by R. Edels' interpretation of this dispute. Pointing out that the phrase *that you may gather in your grain* is immediately preceded by the verse *And if you will carefully obey My commands which I give you today, to love the Lord your God and to serve Him with all your heart and with all your soul,* why then, asks R. Edels, does R. Shimon b. Yoḥai interpret verse 14 as referring to the circumstance where Israel does *not* perform the will of the Almighty? Noting that verse 13 curiously omits the phrase *and with all your wealth,* R. Edels, following the Tosafot's lead, posits that *you may gather in your grain* indeed refers to the circumstance where Israel does perform the will of the Almighty, albeit not with perfect righteousness. What follows is that R. Shimon b. Yoḥai's prescription for complete immersion in Torah study to the exclusion of worldly occupation is directed only to the perfectly righteous. Only this elite group has the right to rely on others to provide it with its material needs. This restrictive interpretation of R. Shimon b. Yoḥai's view is supported by Abaya's observation: "Many have followed the advice of R. Ishmael, and it has worked well; others have followed R. Shimon b. Yoḥai, and it has not been successful." With reliance on the support of others permitted only for the perfectly righteous, it is no wonder that out of the many that followed R. Shimon b. Yoḥai's lifestyle, few succeeded.[18]

Proceeding from R. Edels' analysis is the universally held principle that for the great majority of men pursuit of a livelihood is a positive duty.

Judaism apparently rejects disengagement from worldly occupation even as an ideal for the perfectly righteous. Strongly evidencing this rejection is the teaching of Rabban Gamaliel III (first half of the 3rd cent.), the son of R. Judah ha-Nasi: "It is seemly to combine the study of Torah with an occupation, for the wearying labor of both keep sin forgotten. All Torah study that does not have work accompanying it must in the end come to nothing and bring sin in its wake.[19]

R. Gamaliel's teaching is understood by the Polish decisor R. Joel Sirkes (1561–1650) to be directed at two distinct groups. Speaking in the first clause to people primarily immersed in occupational pursuits, R. Gamaliel warns that if they are to become God-fearing, Torah study must enter their lives. Addressing himself next to Torah scholars, R. Gamaliel cautions that preservation of their spiritual status requires them to combine an occupation with their Torah study.[20]

Another popular talmudic teaching which implicitly rejects the notion that complete disengagement from worldly occupation is an ideal is Ulla's dictum: "A man who lives from the labor [of his hands] is greater than the one who fears heaven."[21]

Further illustrating the importance Judaism attaches to gainful employment is the obligation it imposes on a father to prepare his son for a livelihood. This obligation, according to R. Meir,[22] may be satisfied by teaching the son either a trade or business skills.[23] Out of concern that business enterprises are prone to periodic slumps, R. Judah holds that the father cannot fulfill his obligation by teaching his son business management, for during slack periods, lacking capital or merchandise to transact with, the son may turn to crime.[24]

Apparently disputing both authorities is R. Nehorai's teaching:

> I abandon every trade in the world and teach my son Torah only, for man enjoys the reward thereof in this world while the principal remains to him for the world-to-come. But all other professions are not so; for when a man comes to sickness or old age or suffering and cannot engage in his craft, he must die of starvation, whereas the Torah is not so, for it guards him from all evil in his youth and gives him a future and hope in his old age.[25]

Reconciling R. Nehorai's view with R. Meir and R. Judah, R. Edels posits that R. Nehorai's intention was not to say that he entirely discarded teaching his son a trade, but merely that he refused to prepare him for a trade that would make a major claim on his time and energy. Instead, R. Nehorai concentrated on teaching his son Torah, with the faith that the merit of Torah study would allow his son to make ends meet from his meager source of livelihood.[26]

Another approach for reconciling R. Nehorai's dictum with the obligation of the father to prepare his son for a livelihood is advanced by R. Eliyahu b. Ḥayyim (Constantinople, ca. 1530–1610). Taking note that both of the opposing opinions are recorded by R. Asher b. Jeḥiel, R. Eliyahu posits that R. Nehorai's dictum relates only to the childhood years. Once the son reaches maturity and must begin thinking of earning a livelihood, his father is obligated to prepare him for this by teaching him a trade or business skill.[27]

The Subsidiary Role of Livelihood Activities

While Judaism takes a very positive attitude toward the pursuit of a livelihood, excessive preoccupation with the acquisition of wealth is looked upon very dimly. Judaism teaches that man must give primacy to the spiritual domain. Worldly pursuits are permitted only a minor and subsidiary claim on man's time and energy. Epitomizing Judaism's view of the role that pursuit of material needs should play in the total life experience is R. Judah b. Ila'i's pithy observation:

> See what a difference there is between the earlier and later generations. The earlier generations made the study of the Torah their main concern and their ordinary work subsidiary to it, and both prospered in their hands. The later generations made their ordinary work their main concern and their study of the Torah subsidiary, and neither prospered in their hands.[28]

Further clarification of the nature of the claim that livelihood activities may have on man's energies is provided by R. Judah Loew b. Bezalel (Worms, ca. 1525–1600). Material pursuits may claim man's energies only to the extent necessary to adequately support himself and his family. To avoid becoming a public charge, one should not regard any type of honest work as beneath him. In this vein Rav advised R. Kahana: "Flay carcasses in the marketplace and earn wages, and do not say, I am a priest and a great man, and it is beneath my dignity."[29]

Once subsistence needs have been met, however, King Solomon's admonishment, *Weary not yourself to become rich* (Proverbs 23:4), becomes applicable. At this point the spiritual domain must be given rein over man's energies and time.[30]

Economic Incentives and the Humane Impulse

Increasing the economic incentive to engage in work effort automatically increases the penalty for spending time on activity which produces no economic reward. Gearing society to maximally respond to economic incentives may therefore have the impact of shifting benevolent activity heavily in the direction of financial contribution and away from altruism in the form of personal involvement. Any significant reduction in benevolence of the personal-involvement variety has the effect, as we will argue in

Chapter 4, of blunting society's humane impulse. Since the fostering of a humane climate, as will be discussed in Chapter 4, represents one of the most important social welfare functions of the public sector of the halakhic society, increasing economic incentives to promote additional marketplace activity must be evaluated in light of its impact on this goal.

Economic Disincentives for Idleness and Halakhah

While Halakhah opposes government policies that have the effect of skewing society's energies away from Torah study and personal benevolence, it enthusiastically embraces methods of discouraging idleness by means of increasing the penalties it entails.

Indicative of the disdain Judaism has for idleness is its teaching that idleness brings on immorality.[31] Discouragement of idleness follows also from the halakhic disapproval of the "welfare mentality," as enunciated in Rav's advice to R. Kahana: "Flay carcasses in the marketplace and earn wages, and do not say, I am a priest and a great man, and it is beneath my dignity."[32]

Suggestive of halakhic approval of an unemployment compensation and welfare system designed with the aim of penalizing idleness among the employable members of society is one aspect of the halakhic definition of poverty. In talmudic times, an individual was not eligible to receive a stipend from the weekly disbursement of the public charity chest *(kuppah)* unless he did not have funds for fourteen meals. Having funds for fourteen meals makes an individual self-sufficient for at least a week and hence disqualifies him from becoming a public charge. Liberalization of the eligibility requirement to fifteen meals by dint of the religious duty to eat *three* meals on the Shabbat is rejected by the Talmud by invoking R. Akiva's dictum: "Treat your Shabbat like a weekday rather than be dependent on your fellow-beings."[33] Now, if the poverty standard of living implicit in the below-fourteen-meal criterion is not expanded to cover an additional food expenditure which is required as a religious duty,[34] then, *a fortiori*, the poverty standard is not expanded to include any amenities above bare subsistence.

What rejection of the third Shabbat meal in the eligibility requirement amounts to, in our view, is a definition of poverty in terms of bare subsistence. The discouragement of idleness inherent in this formulation can, of course, be expected to be significant.

Regulation of the Marketplace and Jewish Law

In this section we will develop the case that Judaism calls for government regulation of the marketplace in the form of protecting the consumer against defective and harmful products as well as against false and misleading advertising claims. Also indicated is government intervention to protect the laborer against unsafe working conditions. Finally, government regulation of environmental pollution is called for in the halakhic society.

Pointing to this conclusion is: (1) Judaism's conceptualization of the nature of the information channels of the marketplace; (2) the disclosure obligation it imposes on the seller; (3) the method Halakhah prescribes to assure that proper disclosure takes place; and (4) certain aspects of Jewish tort law. We will discuss each of these elements in turn.

The Nature of the Information Channels and Halakhah

Halakhah rejects the notion that the marketplace is permeated by any semblance of perfect knowledge. This assertion follows from an examination of the laws of *ona'ah* (price fraud).

The ethics of the price terms of transactions concluded within the framework of a competitive norm are governed in Jewish law by the laws of *ona'ah*. These regulations provide a taxonomy of grounds for invalidating or otherwise modifying transactions concluded at a price that diverges from the prevailing norm.

Individuals freely entering into market transactions are presumed, by Jewish law, to have an *approximate* notion of the value of the article involved. Hence, price agreements which diverge enormously from the prevailing norm are not regarded as having occurred as a result of ignorance of market conditions on the part of the participants. Divergent price agreements are, quite to the contrary, interpreted as representing a tacit understanding between buyer and seller to treat the price differential as a voluntary gift transfer.[35] Credence is given to a complainant's *ona'ah* claim only when the discrepancy between the sale price and the market price is more than one-sixth. Here, grounds exist for invalidating the original sale.[36]

Second-degree *ona'ah* occurs when the sale price differs from the market price by exactly one-sixth. Here, the transaction remains binding. Neither of the parties may subsequently void the transaction on account of the price discrimination. The plaintiff, however, is entitled to full restitution of the *ona'ah* involved.[37]

Finally, third-degree *ona'ah* occurs when the sale price differs from the market price by less than one-sixth. Here, the transaction not only remains binding, but in addition, the complainant has no legal claim to the price differential.[38]

We have demonstrated elsewhere that what stands at the basis of the *ona'ah* claim is the opportunity cost the plaintiff incurred at the moment he entered into the transaction. If the article of transfer was available at that time at a lower (higher) price, credence is given to the plaintiff's claim that he would either have insisted on an adjustment or walked away from the proposed deal, as the case may be. What follows is that the *ona'ah* claim is, in the final analysis, based on the imperfect knowledge of market conditions that Halakhah ascribes to market participants.[39]

Disclosure Obligations in Jewish Law

Jewish law requires the parties to a transaction to deal with each other in an open and forthright manner. Conveying a false impression *(genevat da'at)* by means of word or action is strictly prohibited.[40]

Proceeding from the *genevat da'at* interdict is a disclosure obligation for the seller. Proper disclosure requires the seller to divulge to his prospective buyer all defects in his product which are not visibly[41] evident.[42] The disclosure obligation extends even to a flaw whose presence does not depreciate the article sufficiently to allow the vendee an *ona'ah* claim.[43]

What constitutes a defect may depend upon the buyer's intended use of the product. The sale of a vicious ox illustrates the point. If the buyer intends to butcher the ox, its vicious nature would make no difference to him. If, on the other hand, the vendee intends to use the ox for plowing, its vicious character would render it unfit, as the ox would be regarded as a menace to society and the vendee would be prohibited from keeping it alive.[44] If the buyer discloses his intent to use the ox for plowing prior to the consummation of the transaction, he is entitled to cancel the sale on the basis of his discovery of the vicious character of the ox.[45] Seller awareness that the vendee is a farmer, according to R. Samuel b. Meir (Ramerupt, ca. 1080–1174), establishes a presumption that the latter's intent is to use the ox for plowing. Given this indirect awareness of the plowing-use intent, the vendee is entitled to cancel the sale on the basis of his discovery of the vicious nature of the ox.[46]

Discovery of a flaw not properly disclosed at the time of the sale may allow the buyer to void the original transaction. This occurs when the defect involved is objectionable to the extent that common practice would be to return the flawed article to the seller.[47]

The remedy available to the vendee when the product proves to be defective is confined to a recision right. The Jewish court will not, however, sustain the complainant's demand for a price adjustment on the basis of the defect he discovered. The latter's options consist of either demanding a refund or accepting the transaction as originally concluded.[48]

Forthright Disclosure

Disclosure of defects must be made in an open and forthright manner and not in a manner that deludes the vendee into discrediting the seller's declaration.[49]

Disclosure of the nonforthright variety, according to Maimonides (Egypt, 1135–1204), occurs when, for instance, a vendor (A) of an animal enumerates to his prospective buyer (B) a number of flaws in his beast, which, if present, would be readily apparent to him, e.g., lameness. Along with these defects, A admits to the presence of some specific *hidden* faults in his animal as well. Now, in the event that the readily apparent flaws were in actuality not present in the animal, subsequent discovery of the hidden flaw may allow B to void the original transaction. Credence is given to B's claim that he did not take seriously A's disclosure of the hidden flaw. Since the readily visible flaws mentioned by A were obviously nonexistent, B was presumably deluded into discrediting the existence of the real defect as well. B's claim of delusive disclosure is, however, not accepted when *one* of the readily visible flaws A mentioned was actually present in the animal. Here, B should have taken seriously A's disclosure of the hidden flaw.[50]

A variant of the latter case, according to R. Jacob b. Asher (Germany, 1270–1343) and R. Joseph Caro (Safed, 1488–1575), allows B to void the sale on the basis of the delusive disclosure. This occurs when A takes pains to *demonstratively point out only one* of the number of readily visible flaws he mentions. His failure to do likewise in regard to the other plainly visible flaws he mentions presumably leads B to discredit his disclosure of the hidden flaw. Subsequent discovery of the hidden defect may therefore allow B to void the original sale.[51]

The buyer's agreement to the vendor's demand not to void the sale on the basis of product defect does not nullify his recision right in the event he does subsequently find a defect in the article.

Why the recision right remains intact here is explained by Maimonides and others on the ground that acquiescence to a general disclaimer lacks specificity. For a waiver to be legally binding, the person making it must be aware of *specifically* what he is waiving. Now, since the seller here makes no mention either of specific defects that he is not responsible for nor of a specific depreciation in value that he is not responsible for, the vendee does not forfeit his recision right by accepting the disclaimer.[52]

Why the right to cancel the sale remains intact here is, however, explained by R. Joshua ha-Kohen Falk (Poland, 1555–1614) and others on the basis of the false impression such a disclaimer conveys to the vendee. The seller's insistence that the sale remain intact even if a flaw is discovered is interpreted by the buyer as conveying the message that the article at hand is such an extraordinary bargain that even if a defect is hypothetically present the article would still be a good buy. Since the buyer does not interpret the seller's disclaimer as an admission of the presence of any defects in the product, his acquiescence to it does not amount to an implicit waiver of his recision right.[53]

Vendee acquiescence not to void the sale on the basis of specific product defects does, however, nullify his right of cancellation in respect to the specific defects mentioned. The specificity requirement is met when the disclaimer clause either (1) details the defects the seller is not responsible for or (2) sets a limit to the depreciation in value from the sale price that the buyer must absorb on account of discovery of defects in the product.[54]

Seller Rights in the Defective Product Case

While the preceding discussion makes it clear that Jewish law rejects the doctrine of caveat emptor, a certain degree of mental alertness is expected of the buyer in a sales transaction. This expectation along with the various rights Jewish law confers on the vendor in product-defect cases, as discussed below, effectively qualify the disclosure obligation and limit the buyer's recision right.

1. The buyer's recision right—right of cancellation—is not recognized when the defect he bases his refund claim on is *visibly evident*. Since the defect is in plain view, the buyer was presumably aware of it at the time he entered into the transaction, and consequently he was agreeable to the terms of trade despite its presence. Buyer protest that the visibly evident flaw did not register in his mind at the time of the sale is greeted with incredulity.[55] Following this line, R. Eliezer of Toule (d. before 1234) denies the refund even on the strength of the buyer's sworn testimony that he did not notice the defect at the time he entered into the sale.[56]

It follows, in our view, from the denial of the recision right in cases where the defect is visibly evident, that forthright disclosure does not require the seller to point out to a would-be buyer the evident flaws in his article. Since the defects are plainly visible, the buyer is presumably aware of them at the time he enters into the sale. The vendor's failure to make mention of them or to point them out, therefore, does not amount to creating a false impression.

2. Another limitation on the buyer's recision right occurs in instances where the defect involved can be repaired or removed. The following real estate case recorded by R. Asher b. Jeḥiel illustrates this

point: A returns from an out-of-town inspection of a house B has put up for sale. Operating under the assumption that the house is in the same condition as he left it, A proceeds to purchase B's house. Before the sale went into effect, however, vandals entered the house, breaking the door and windows and smoking the walls. When A learns of this, he wants to void the sale on the basis of the vandalized condition of the house. B, however, demands that the sale remain intact, conceding only that A should be allowed a deduction from the original price to cover the expense of renovating the house. The Jewish court will here sustain the seller's position. Since the act of vandalism did not destroy the original identity of the article of transfer, it cannot be said that A actually acquired something essentially different than what he contracted for. The presence of a defect does not cause the transaction to be classified as one concluded in error, and rectification of the defect by the seller allows the sale to remain intact.[57]

Should the defect render the article something essentially different than what was contracted for, recognition would be given to the buyer's recision right. The following real estate case recorded by R. Moses Isserles (Poland, 1525 or 1530–1572) illustrates this point: A contracts to buy B's out-of-town house. Upon inspection he discovers that its walls are deteriorated. On the basis of this defect, A wants to void the transaction. B, however, insists that the sale remain intact, conceding only that A should be allowed a deduction from the purchase price to cover the expense of renovating the walls. The court here will sustain the buyer's position. Given the fact that a house with deteriorated walls loses its identity as a house, what A actually acquired is not what he contracted for. Since the defect here renders the original transaction as one concluded in error, recognition is given to the buyer's recision right, despite the seller's willingness to renovate the walls.[58]

3. Another limitation on the buyer's recision right occurs in the case of a standardized product. Here, the seller may insist on exchanging the defective product for a flawless model. If the market price of the standardized product went down in the interim, the buyer would, however, retain his recision right.[59]

The Seller's Testing Obligation

The seller's responsibility to his customer in the halakhic society clearly goes beyond forthright disclosure. Various halakhic norms point to various *testing* obligations for the seller before he can market his product.

Media advertising provides a case in point. Since media advertising reaches a very wide audience, the seller cannot rely upon his own conviction that his message is not misleading. Avoiding violation of the *genevat da'at* interdict, as we have argued in Chapter 2, requires that advertising messages be pilot-tested before being put into commercial use. Scientifically designed, a pilot-test can ascertain what impressions the advertising message makes on the targeted group, as well as the inferences this group draws from it. Should these sets of expectations fail to coincide with the actual properties of the product, revision of the message would be in order.

The seller's responsibility to test his product before he markets it to ensure that it is not defective or harmful proceeds, in our view, from the biblical prohibition against offering ill-suited advice *(lifnei ivver).*[60] Without premarketing testing, the seller's implicit claim that his product will serve the customer's need amounts to a possible violation of the *lifnei ivver* interdict. A case in point is the pharmaceutical manufacturer who fails to properly test his drugs for their effectiveness and possible side-effects before marketing them.

It should be noted that talmudic decisors differ as to whether the *mere offer* of ill-suited advice constitutes a violation of the *lifnei ivver* interdict. *Halakhot Gedolot* takes this view.[61] Maimonides, however, does not regard the interdict as being violated until the individual who received the ill-suited advice actually follows it.[62] What follows from our application of the *lifnei-ivver* interdict to the sale of a product without proper premarketing testing is that the mere offer for sale of an untested product, according to *Halakhot Gedolot,* constitutes a possible violation of *lifnei ivver.*

Marketing a product which is possibly harmful without prior testing may violate the interdicts cited in connection with the obligation the Torah imposes on the homeowner to construct a parapet around his roof: *When you build a new house, you shall make a parapet for your roof, so that you will not bring the guilt of bloodshed on your house if anyone should fall from it* (Deuteronomy 22:8).

Exegetical interpretation of this verse extends the positive duty *(aseh),*[63] *you shall make a parapet,* and the negative duty *(lo ta'aseh),*[64] *so that you will not bring the guilt of bloodshed,* to the requirement for the individual to properly *remove* from his property any object that may cause someone damage.[65] Now, argues Rabbi Jeroḥam Fishel Perla (Poland, 1846–1934), if the Torah forewarns us to clear our property of dangerous objects, then, *a fortiori,* it forbids us to *place* a possibly harmful object anywhere it may cause injury.[66] Following this line, another application of the parapet interdict would be the sale of untested drugs.

Just as the parapet interdict is violated by the *mere* placing of an object which is possibly dangerous,[67] the *mere offer* for sale of an untested drug constitutes a possible violation of this prohibition.

Similarly prohibited under the parapet interdict, in our view, is the dumping of noxious chemicals and wastes in lakes and streams. Since water pollution of this type has been linked to genetic diseases and cancer, such action constitutes the "placing" of a harmful object in the public domain.

Safe Working Conditions

By dint of the parapet interdict, Rabbi Ben Zion Meir Hai Ouziel (Israel, 1880–1953) obligates the employer both to provide his worker with safe working conditions and to make restitution to him in the event of injury in consequence of his neglect to do so. Nonetheless, since the parapet interdict merely adjures the removal from one's property of objects which might cause injury, monetary claims by the worker for injuries he suffers as a result of his employer's failure to provide him with safe working conditions are denied by the Jewish court.[68]

The Enforcement Mechanism for Judaism's Disclosure and Testing Obligations

The preceding discussion has demonstrated that Halakhah imposes on the seller an extensive disclosure obligation as well as a premarketing testing responsibility. Would Halakhah rely on a system of voluntary enforcement to ensure that these responsibilities are carried out? Indicative that Halakhah would insist on public-sector involvement here is its call[69] for the appointment of public inspectors to ensure the honesty of commercial weights and measures. Why voluntary self-enforcement is not relied upon to ensure the integrity of commercial weights and measures is explained by Rabbi Jeḥiel Michel Epstein (Belorussia, 1829–1908) as stemming from the unconscious, distorting impact the profit motive exerts on vendors. Rabbi Epstein uses this rationale to explain Maimonides' ruling[70] that in matters of Kashrut one may only patronize a vendor who is known to be reliable.[71] It follows that in the halakhic society, a voluntaristic system for enforcing proper disclosure and premarketing testing would be regarded as unreliable.

Certification and Regulation in Jewish Law

While the unconscious bias stemming from the profit motive necessitates government involvement in the area of product safety in the halakhic society, the form this intervention takes remains to be clarified. Certification and regulation present themselves as alternative approaches. Banning the product rather than just certifying the risks it imposes to users is clearly the indicated course when the premarketing testing determines that normal use of the product entails an imminent health risk to the typical consumer. Since Halakhah does not recognize the right of the individual to expose himself to an imminent health risk,[72] the public sector has no choice other than to ban the health-endangering product in the above instance.

Certification does, however, present itself as a viable alternative means of promoting product safety when the relevant health risk is assessed to be potential rather than imminent. This follows from R. Jacob Ettlinger's (Germany, 1798–1871) ruling that Halakhah only prohibits exposure to an imminent health risk, but not to a reasonable health risk which is assessed to be only potential. He derives this principle from an analysis of the Thanksgiving sacrifice *(korban todah)*. During the times of the Temple, this sacrifice was prescribed as an expression of gratitude when an individual was delivered from danger. Two qualifying circumstances consist of the safe return from a sea journey and the safe return from a trip across the desert. Since these safe returns are characterized as "deliverances from danger," sea voyages and desert trips were obviously regarded by the sages as fraught with danger. Given the prohibition of exposing oneself to danger, why, queries R. Ettlinger, didn't the sages prohibit these adventures in the first place? This dilemma leads R. Ettlinger to posit that Halakhah does not prohibit exposure to a reasonable risk when the danger is assessed to be only potential. Since most people who embark upon a sea journey or go on a desert trip return safely and, in addition, are not subject to immediate danger at the outset, the risk exposure is both reasonable and potential and hence is permissible.[73]

Validation of the certification approach as a means for the public sector to meet its responsibility to ensure product safety follows from R. Ettlinger's line in instances where the risk exposure involved is reasonable and the relevant danger is potential rather than immediate. While the distinction between immediate and potential danger cannot be precisely defined, the auto-safety area represents one clear-cut instance of a potential rather than an immediate risk.

Basing himself on R. Ettlinger's criterion, Rabbi Bleich posits that Halakhah does not prohibit cigarette smoking. Since the physiological changes caused by smoking are reversible, the risk involved should be characterized as potential rather than immediate. What follows is a halakhic approach which is in consonance with the current government certification approach to cigarette smoking.[74] Mounting recent scientific evidence in regard to the health dangers of smoking may, however, force this indulgence to be characterized as an "unreasonable" health-risk exposure and hence as halakhically prohibited.[75]

Another instance where a danger should be halakhically classified as potential rather than immediate occurs, as it appears to us, when a product exposes the consumer to an immediate danger only when it is used in an abnormal manner, but presents no danger when it is used in the conventional manner. Rotary lawn mowers provide a case in point. Using a lawn mower to cut hedges generates an immediate danger to the consumer, but in the halakhic society, it would be unwarranted to ban lawn mowers for this reason. Since cutting hedges with a lawn mower is clearly an abnormal use of the product, it can, at worst, be classified as only potentially dangerous. The certification approach, therefore, suffices here.

Elimination of Unnecessary Risks

Since exposure to potential danger is permissible only when the risk involved is a reasonable one, subjecting oneself to an unnecessary safety or health risk should be prohibited. An unnecessary risk is defined as a risk a well-informed individual would willingly spend money to eliminate. Given the average consumer's imperfect knowledge of the marketplace, the above line confers on the public sector the responsibility to promulgate design safety features for products when it assesses that the typical consumer, equipped with the necessary facts, would willingly spend money to secure those features. Auto safety provides a case in point. Since designing a car so that it can sustain a rear-end collision and requiring seat belts as a standard feature significantly reduce the probability of death or severe injury for the motorist, a presumption exists that the motorist would spend money to secure these features. Meeting its responsibility in the area of product safety requires the public sector, therefore, to mandate these provisions. Once the safety of product design reaches a certain level, we may no longer presume that the typical informed consumer would willingly expend more money to secure additional safety. Air bags provide a case in point. Installing this safety feature will add from $800 to $1,200 to the price of a car. Moreover, each time a bag is inflated the owner may have to pay twice that amount to have it replaced.[76] Given the present level of auto safety and the cost of achieving additional safety by means of installing air bags, mandating this safety feature cannot be said to eliminate an unnecessary risk. Since automobile use represents a potential rather than an immediate danger, mandating the elimination of a risk which cannot be characterized as unnecessary, e.g., the installation of air bags, would not fall within the purview of a product safety commission of the halakhic society.

Ill-Defined Property Rights and Jewish Law

Ill-defined property rights, as discussed earlier, justify environmental regulation in the form of controlling air and water pollution. Environmental pollution represents an example of a negative externality, i.e., an unintended negative side-effect of economic activity. Judaism's analogue to the negative-externality case is the law in circumstances where an individual conducts an activity on his own premises and this activity generates harm outside his premises. Involving many nuances, a negative externality is generally not subject to restraint unless two main criteria are met: (1) a direct link between the adverse effect and the action of the initiator must be established;[77] (2) the harm the plaintiff stands to sustain as a result of the defendant's activity must consist of actual or potential bodily harm or property damage.[78]

When an adverse side-effect is halakhically classified as a negative externality, the initiator, by force of a biblical interdict, must refrain from the activity generating it. R. Meir Abulafia (Spain, ca. 1170–1244) bases the interdict either on the verse *you shall not place an obstacle in front of the blind* (Leviticus 19:4) or on the verse *you shall love your neighbor as yourself* (Leviticus 19:18).[79] R. Asher b. Jeḥiel, however, bases the prohibition on the verse *Her ways are ways of pleasantness, and all her paths are peace* (Proverbs 3:17).[80]

In the absence of voluntary compliance, the courts will enjoin the activity by petition of the party that stands to be injured.[81]

Though the use of a restraining order does not preclude a *negotiated* change in the initial distribution of rights, the plaintiff would be within his rights to reject a scheme wherein he is compensated for damages actually sustained. Such a scheme amounts to licensing the defendant to inflict damage if he so chooses and only face penalties after the damage is already done. Jewish law clearly prohibits an individual from damaging his neighbor's property even if he promises to compensate the victim for losses sustained.[82] What follows is that unless the arrangement is voluntarily negotiated, the plaintiff may insist that the court impose a restraining order on an actionable negative externality.

The Reciprocal Nature of the Externality Problem

Economic theory has uncovered the truth that the externality problem is reciprocal in nature. Restraining the defendant gives primacy to the interests of the plaintiff. Nonintervention, however, favors the defendant's interests over the plaintiff's. When those adversely affected by the negative externality constitute an entire community, the reciprocal nature of the problem at hand assumes the proportions of a vexing social issue. Restraining a factory from polluting the atmosphere, for example, may force it to substitute more costly methods of production, placing it at a competitive disadvantage. Thus, the elimination of environmental pollution may take place at the cost of increased unemployment and a reduced standard of living.[83]

Given the reciprocal nature of the negative-externality problem, can a minority veto a majority-approved scheme that allows the industrial polluter to continue his enterprise and face only a schedule of fines for damage actually caused? From the perspective of the approving majority, the arrangement represents the most efficient means of allowing the community to maximize its economic interests: The enterprise, with its favorable impact on community employment, is allowed to continue, and at the same time its owners are made to pay, at least partially, for the damage it inflicts. Objecting to the arrangement on the ground that it effectively licenses the factory to inflict harm, the minority press for the relocation of the factory. What rights do the majority enjoy here?

Clarification of minority rights in a legislative matter requires an investigation of the halakhic view of both the parameters and the nature of the legislative process.

It should be noted at the outset that communal legislation enjoys no halakhic sanction when it comes into conflict with ritual prohibitions and permissions.[84] In matters of civil and criminal law, communal enactments are, however, generally recognized even if they come into conflict with a particular rule of Halakhah.[85]

Providing a basic source for the analysis of the halakhic view of the communal legislative process is the following *baraita* quoted in *Bava Batra* 8b: "The townspeople are also at liberty to fix weights and measures, prices and wages, and to inflict penalties for infringement of their rules."

Espousing the majority view, R. Isaac b. Jacob Alfasi (Algeria, 1013–1103) and others understand the communal legislative authority the *baraita* speaks of to become effective by means of a majority-decision rule.[86] Indicative that the coercive power of the majority over the minority is limited is the observation that all the actions the *baraita* speaks of are of a communitywide welfare basis. What may therefore be inferred is that in matters not pertaining to a communitywide interest, the majority may not pass legislation that favors one group at the expense of another. Clearly enunciating this principle is the fifteenth-century decisor R. Joseph Colon (Italy, ca. 1420–1480).[87]

In this vein R. Solomon b. Abraham Adret ruled invalid a communal edict calling for the taxation of a resident on the basis of his ownership of assets located in a different town. Majority decision, as R. Adret points out, cannot legitimize robbery. Since the edict effectively subjected a segment of the community to "double taxation," the provision amounted to outright robbery.[88]

Further limitation of the coercive power of the majority in legislative matters follows from R. Meir b. Baruch of Rothenburg's (ca. 1215–1293) comments on the *baraita* quoted earlier.

Taking the position that unanimous consent is required before legislative proposals become operative, R. Meir posits that the *baraita* implies that *verbal* consent alone suffices to make town ordinances effective law. Though verbal consent alone normally does not constitute a *kinyan*, and hence does not make a commitment legally binding, unanimously approved legislation becomes binding by means of verbal consent alone. By dint of the pleasure each member of the community derives from the knowledge that his fellows have consented to enter into a mutually advantageous agreement with him, he resolutely binds himself to the commitment.[89]

Notwithstanding the halakhic rejection of the unanimous-decision rule in favor of a majority-decision rule, R. Meir's interpretation of the *baraita* as describing proposed actions of mutual benefit has evoked much discussion. Such actions as fixing weights and measures, prices, and wages are of mixed effect, i.e., some of the townspeople will gain while others will lose. Why, then, did R. Meir characterize these actions as mutually advantageous?

Espousing majority rule, R. Moses b. Joseph Trani (Safed, 1500–1580) posits that R. Meir's characterization of the actions described in the *baraita* as mutually advantageous is essentially correct. Rather than imposing absolute gains and losses on the townspeople, the fixing of weights and measures, prices, and wages merely determines the *relative* gains of economic activity. Amounting to an implementation of the townspeople's concept of *equity* in the distribution of the relative gains of economic activity, these measures must be characterized as mutually advantageous.[90]

Characterization of the actions recorded in the *baraita* as mutually advantageous is also justified, according to R. Trani, on the grounds that the relative impact of these measures often changes over time.[91] To illustrate, economic growth and inflation may very well work to reverse an earlier prolabor characterization of a legislated wage structure as now favoring employers vis-à-vis workers.

The aforementioned has many implications for the design of an effluent-charge plan to effect pollution abatement. Given the underlying motive of maximizing wealth, such a plan would clearly qualify as a measure for communitywide welfare. Minority opposition to the plan would therefore not cause rejection of it in a Jewish court.

Making concessions to the industrial polluter in the name of advancing the goal of community wealth is, however, subject to a constraint. Communal legislation, by means of majority rule, can only renounce those rights which Halakhah regards as subject to waiver but may not contract out of the law of the Torah entirely.[92]

Proceeding from the above is the legitimacy of a majority-sponsored effluent-charge scheme which calls for the industrial polluter only to partially compensate society for damages actually inflicted. Since it is within the halakhic rights of an individual to waive his right to compensation due him, a majority decision to this effect requires everyone to renounce his rights to full compensation in accordance with the plan adopted.

Moreover, since an individual may expose himself to some degree of risk to his health and even to his life for the purpose of earning a livelihood,[93] a majority-approved effluent-charge scheme entailing some small degree of health- and life-threatening risk is fully valid.

Clearly contrary to Torah law, however, is an effluent-charge scheme which exposes the townspeople to extraordinary health- and life-threatening risk. Since the plan violates the biblical injunction of *Take you therefore good heed unto yourself* (Deuteronomy 4:15),[94] the legislation is, in our view, invalid, despite majority or even unanimous approval.

R. Trani's remarks, presented earlier, indicate another limitation on effluent-charge legislation. Careful attention must be given to ensure that the plan does not generate a discriminatory effect on certain segments of the community. Typically, residents located close to the industrial polluter will bear the brunt of any effluent-charge plan which entails property damage and health hazards for the townspeople. Provision for special compensation and relocation expenses for those we anticipate will suffer disproportionately from implementation of the effluent-charge plan represents a halakhic approach to this problem in line with the previous discussion.

Another important implication of the preceding discussion is that cost-benefit analysis is an invalid criterion for the halakhic society in determining whether a plant should be required to install pollution-abatement equipment. Though the cost-benefit criterion can be universally applied, it contains an inherent bias against the poor and the old. Because valuation of life is based on earnings potential, the lives and health of those who can expect little or no future earnings, like the unskilled, the handicapped, or the elderly, are valued at next to nothing. When benefits are measured in terms of anticipated health and longevity gains, the dollar value of the benefits proceeding from pollution abatement for a disadvantaged area would be calculated to be lower than the corresponding value in an affluent area. As a result, if a cost-benefit criterion is applied, plants located in disadvantaged areas would be more likely to continue to generate pollution than plants located in affluent areas. Amounting to a discriminatory license to injure people and damage property, such a scheme is halakhically invalid, even if approved by the majority.

It follows from the preceding analysis that the approach to pollution abatement in the halakhic society would stress cost-effectiveness rather than cost-benefit criteria. Specifically, goals in the form of pollution-abatement standards would be set, and these goals would then be pursued by means of the least-cost method. Any pollution-abatement plan in the halakhic society, as discussed above, would have certain special compensation provisions for the discriminatory impact it may impose on society.

Economic Regulation of the Marketplace and Halakhah

While the aforementioned indicates that there is a sharp division between Halakhah and supply-side economics in regard to government intervention to protect the consumer and worker, general convergence can be found in respect to the issue of economic regulation.

Convergence on the issue of economic regulation of the marketplace follows from the halakhic preference for a system of freedom of entry, as discussed in Chapter 6. Protectionist pleas by an established firm to enjoin a new entrant are given consideration only when the impact of competition would *ruin* the established firm. To be sure, another school of thought rejects the protectionist pleas of the established firm even in this instance.

Moreover, protecting an established firm against a seller of a substitute product finds no sympathy in the Jewish court even when the competitive presence of the substitute product threatens to *ruin* the established firm. Similarly, established firms are not afforded protection against substitute products embodying new technology. The Jewish court would not sympathize, for example, with a protectionist plea by the horse and buggy industry that it enjoin the entry of the automobile.

Natural Monopoly in Jewish Law

The concept of natural monopoly has explicit halakhic approval, according to the Hungarian decisor R. Mosheh Sofer (1762–1839), in the form of an ancient rabbinic edict prohibiting the publication of a religious work while copies of an earlier printing by another publisher were still available for sale. Within the spirit of this ancient ordinance, it became customary for prospective authors of religious works to secure from a rabbinic authority a formal ban on the publication of the same work by others for a specified period of time. The text of the ban was usually published in the preface of the work. Once conferred, the ban was effective not only in the jurisdiction of the issuing authority, but upon all of Israel as well.

Since the purpose of the edict was to promote the widest possible dissemination of Torah works, the ban, posits R. Sofer, does not extend beyond the sale of the earlier printing. Extension of the ban beyond this period would merely serve to create a commercial property right for the publisher of the previous printing, a windfall unintended by the ancient edict. Notwithstanding its lack of force, a ban extending beyond the sale of the previous printing remains operative within the jurisdiction of the issuing authority.

Promoting the social interest by means of conferring monopoly privilege apparently runs counter to Ezra's ancient ordinance. To afford Jewish women with easy access to beautification aids, Ezra (5th cent. B.C.E.) allowed itinerant cosmetics salesmen to peddle their wares from door to door, despite the competition this would create for local storekeepers. Encouraging free entry evidently represented for Ezra a more efficient means of promoting the social interest than protecting local tradesmen.

Defending the protectionist approach for the case at hand, R. Sofer posits that sufficient economic incentive would be lacking to motivate investors to undertake the publication of religious works without the expectation of monopoly status. Without this privilege entrepreneurs would direct their investments elsewhere. In sharp contrast, local stores, which carry, besides cosmetics, a whole line of other products, would not be likely to close down on account of the competition of cosmetics peddlers.[95]

Disputing R. Sofer's view, R. Mordecai Banet (Moravia, 1753–1829) argues, in effect, that the ancient decree described above could not have been promulgated. Drawing an analogy from Ezra's decree, R. Banet posits that promoting the widest dissemination of religious works calls for a free-entry rather than a protectionist approach.[96]

The dispute between R. Sofer and R. Banet, as it appears to us, is an empirical one. Rising standards of living and levels of education and religious observance may very well make competition feasible in a marketplace previously characterized as a natural monopoly. Moreover, identification of a natural-monopoly-product market may require the rabbinic authority, at times, to extend the ban on a new printing beyond the sale of the extant printing. This occurs when only multiple printings of the subject religious works are deemed sufficient to recoup for the publishers a reasonable return on their investment.[97] What constitutes a reasonable profit would, in turn, be determined by the opportunity cost of the publisher. Economic analysis is therefore of critical importance in determining whether, and under what conditions, it would be appropriate for the halakhic authority to impose the ban.

· 4
Social Welfare in Jewish Law

The responsibility society assumes for its poor and disadvantaged often reflects an underlying philosophy. It will be our task in this chapter to delineate Judaism's social welfare philosophy along with its implications for both individual and public sector responsibility.

Social Welfare Rooted in Self-Interest

Social welfare attitudes are often rooted in a self-interest doctrine, albeit in a disguised and even amorphous form. In its most noble form, altruism rooted in self-interest demands nothing less than an emotional identification with the deprived elements of society. Ideally, empathy for a victim of misery entails a feeling that our fellow man's suffering is *our* suffering and his pain is *our* pain.

Actualization of this form of social welfare philosophy at its highest level could very well result in a drive to assure our fellow-man that relief will be immediately available to him should the need arise. What this would involve is the establishment of altruistic institutions whose sole purpose would be to spring into immediate action as the need arises. The aim of these institutions would be nothing less than to restore the man of misery to a proper state of mental, physical, and financial health.

Empathetic identification with our fellow Jew represents, of course, one of the highest preachments of Judaism, taking the form of the commandment *you shall love your neighbor as yourself* (Leviticus 19:18). Demanding the quality of love in interpersonal relations is not the same thing as a call to respond to our fellow Jew's need based on what we vicariously imagine we would like done for us if we had the same need. To be sure, without empathetic attachment to our fellow Jew, we would never be *sensitized* to his needs, and even his most profound anguish would go unnoticed by us. But emotional solidarity with the man in need cannot serve as the *guide* of our reaction to that need. Social welfare policy touches many issues, including education, crime, interference in the labor market, family planning, public vs. private welfare, and the priority rating of needs. Our attitudes toward these and related issues is to some degree shaped by the secular culture in which we interact daily. This secular culture cannot, however, formulate for the Jew his social welfare philosophy and resultant policy prescriptions. Torah perspectives, rather than instinctive reactions, must provide for us the basis for constructing our social welfare attitudes and imperatives.

The insufficiency of the *love your neighbor* dictum as a social welfare policy is, in our view, clearly seen from the following tannaic dispute, recorded in the Jerusalem Talmud, *Nedarim* 9:4.

> R. Akiva said: "*Love your neighbor as yourself* [Leviticus 19:18] is a great principle of the Torah." Ben Azai said: "An even greater principle is expressed in the verse *This is the record of the descendants of Adam; when God created man, He made him in the likeness of God* [Genesis 5:1]."

Why Ben Azai regards the teaching that man is created in the image of God as superior to the *love your neighbor as yourself* dictum can, in our view, be explained on the strength of the former principle's self-sufficiency as a social welfare philosophy. If man is created in the image of God, then only God's Torah, the source of moral truth, can determine for us what constitutes duty and virtue in interpersonal relations. Since we cannot rely on our own instincts to tell us what duty and virtue are in interpersonal relations, the *love your neighbor as yourself* principle is not a self-sufficient social welfare philosophy.

The supreme model of moral conduct for us is, of course, God's own conduct toward man, as revealed to us in the Torah. It is for us to emulate this conduct. Ben Azai's dictum therefore alludes to Judaism's *imitatio Dei* principle, enunciated in *Sotah 14a*.

> Is it, then, possible to "walk after" the Divine Presence? Has not Scripture already said, *for the Lord thy God is a devouring fire* [Deuteronomy 4:24]? But it means, walk after the attributes of the Holy One. Even as He clothes the naked [clothing Adam and Eve with the garments of skins (Genesis 3:2)], so must you provide clothes for the naked. The Holy One visited the sick [appearing to Abraham after his circumcision (Genesis 18:1)]; so must you visit the sick. The Holy One consoled the bereaved [blessing Isaac after Abraham's death (Genesis 25:11)]; so must you console the bereaved. The Holy One buried the dead [interring Moses (Deuteronomy 34:6)]; so must you bury the dead.

What proceeds from the specific instances of Divine conduct the Talmud selects in demonstrating the *imitatio Dei* principle is the unreliability of our own instincts in telling us what constitutes duty and virtue in our interpersonal relations. Had the Torah not recorded that God conferred garments of skin on Adam and Eve after they had sinned by eating the fruit of the tree of knowledge (Genesis 4:21), would our instincts tell us that the obligation of kindness applies even when the recipient is underserving?[1] If the Torah had not recorded that the Almighty buried Moses, would our instincts tell us that our obligation to treat man with dignity applies even after his death? Since we cannot rely on our own instincts to tell us what virtue is in interpersonal relations, the *love your neighbor as yourself* principle is not a self-sufficient social welfare philosophy.

Virtue, in its highest form, Maimonides (Egypt, 1135–1204) teaches, is exemplified when conduct flows from an understanding that Divine truth requires it. If the same action is done out of sentiment or emotion, the conduct is not regarded as virtuous in the highest degree. The superiority of conduct which proceeds from a perception of truth is derived by Maimonides from an analysis of how Adam and Eve changed after they committed the sin of eating the fruit of the tree of knowledge. The lure of the tree of knowledge was presented by the serpent to Eve with the assertion *God well knows that on the day you eat from it your eyes will be opened and you will be the same as God, knowing both good and evil* (Genesis 3:5). After partaking of the forbidden fruit, Adam and Eve appear to acquire a dimension of existence they did not previously possess: *Then the eyes of both were opened, and they realized that they were naked* (Genesis 5:7). Is it possible that sin generated for Adam and Eve an *advantage* they did not previously possess? Maimonides answers in the negative. Sin can only have a degenerative effect on man. Evidencing Adam and Eve's superior nature before they sinned is the psalmist's declaration *yet you have made him only a little less than the angels* (Psalms 8:6). Before they sinned Adam and Eve related to God's commandments on an intellectual level in terms of *truth and falsehood.* After Adam and Eve ate the forbidden fruit, God's moral truth no longer exerted a compelling force on their moral conduct. Instead, human emotion biased moral choices. Moral conduct was now evaluated in terms of *good and evil.* An action would be deemed good if it offered the prospect of generating pleasure for the doer. Conversely, if the doer could anticipate pain from his conduct, the contemplated action would be deemed evil.[2]

While a magnificent edifice of altruism can be built on the cornerstone of a social welfare philosophy rooted in empathetic identification with human need and suffering, this philosophy may in some cases lead to a great weakening of the humane impulse.

Dramatically illustrating the inherent danger of a social welfare philosophy rooted in any form of self-interest is the following passage from the Mishnah (*Avot* 5:13): "There are four character types among people: One who says 'What is mine is mine and what is yours is yours' is an average character, and others say this is the characteristic of Sodom. . . ."

Now, the second view expressed in this passage is apparently astonishing. A Sodomitic nature is defined in the Talmud as denying one's fellow a benefit even though it is of no cost to oneself.[3] Sodom's fate of destruction was sealed, according to tradition, when its inhabitants executed a woman for violating their ordinance not to come to the aid of a poor person.[4] How then can the philosophy "what is mine is mine and what is yours is yours" be, in any way, equated with a Sodomitic character? What this view expresses, we submit, is that the above philosophy is capable of so weakening the practice of benefaction so as to make it disappear entirely. This occurs when A's simple act of charity to B is viewed by C as decidedly injurious to him.

As a means of illustrating that point, we will set forth a social welfare philosophy rooted in self-interest and demonstrate that through a series of stages this *very* philosophy could provide the rationale for an ordinance which makes the aiding of the poor a capital offense. Let us begin with the noble premise that by dint of our belief that man is created in the image of God, each individual has an unlimited potential to contribute to the economic well-being of society. To accomplish this, man needs merely the opportunity and proper motivation to develop the unique skills and talents the Creator endowed him with. Let us also suppose that self-realization in the economic sphere ranks high in society's priorities for achieving happiness.

Once self-realization in the economic sphere is taken to rank high among society's priorities, an identity is produced between the individual's material striving and society's material well-being. Within the framework of a market economy, anyone who offers a desirable product or service will command a reward for it. Income earned by A from providing his product or service for the marketplace will result in increased spending on his part. A's spending generates income for B, whose spending, in turn, generates income for C. This expansionary process, called the *multiplier effect,* will eventually peter out, as a certain amount of the increased income earned in each successive round is saved.

Realization of the multiplier process may lead many individuals to regard charity as a potentially very sound means of ensuring the viability of the economic environment. Optimal results proceed from the multiplier process when each member of society embodies a skill or offers a product for sale which other members of society regard as desirable to acquire. Hence, self-interest in the form of an ever-expanding standard of living requires society to tax a portion of its income for the purpose of providing an opportunity for its disadvantaged to become productive members of the economic system. Toward this end, tax monies would be used mainly to finance public employment, subsidize the education of the disadvantaged, and finance job-training programs.

With the passage of time, society may well become disillusioned with some and even all aspects of its public welfare policy. Regarding charity primarily as a form of "economic viability insurance" leads, naturally, to a concern that a climate of indolence and a state of dependency should not develop in society. This concern would immediately place the public employment element of the social welfare program under attack. If an individual could always rely on the public sector as an employer of last resort, would he have any incentive to exert himself to the utmost in cultivating his potential skills and talents?

Preventing the emergence of a climate of indolence was, indeed, one of the obssessive concerns of the ancient city of Sodom. This concern manifested itself in the city's system of economic organization and incentive rewards. The people of Sodom took turns pasturing the cattle of all the inhabitants of the city, instituting the rule that "whoever possesses one ox must watch everyone's animals one day. Someone who possesses no oxen must, however, guard everyone's animals for two days."[5]

Social welfare rooted in self-interest may inspire the emergence of measures designed to ensure that the benefits of the community's investment remain within its own environs and not spill over into other areas. Restrictive immigration laws and prohibitive tariffs represent familiar legislative means of preventing outsiders from reducing the local living standard and economic opportunities.

Concern for the spill-over effects of economic activity may well degenerate into an obsession and finally take the form of a sadistic contempt for foreigners. Sodom won its notoriety for the cruel and sadistic manner in which it treated strangers.[6]

Obsessively guarding its wealth against the intrusion of strangers, Sodom charged its judges with the responsibility to ensure that every wayfarer leave its midst penniless.[7] Sodom's laws permitted its citizens to rob and mistreat strangers with impunity.[8] Anyone who invited an outsider to a wedding was punished by having his clothes removed.[9] Evidencing the extent to which Sodom communicated to outsiders that they were not welcome, in our view, was its practice of pruning trees which grew on public property so that the birds should have no benefit from them.[10]

Concern for the prevention of the emergence of a climate of indolence leads logically to a call for the restructuring of public welfare and unemployment compensation so as to maximally discourage idleness. Increasing the disincentive for idleness is, indeed, one of the tenets of supply-side economics. Rather than concentrating its efforts on direct assistance, this school of thought insists that the long-term interests of the poor are best served when government allows the natural incentive system of the marketplace free rein. This will occur when the tax liability associated with work effort, savings, and investment is reduced and the welfare system is designed to maximally discourage idleness.

Supporting the economic argument against public social welfare would be the various elements who oppose this approach on grounds other than efficiency and welcome the opportunity to latch on to a respectable basis for attack. These groups include those who deny the basic premise of the economic potential of the disadvantaged elements of society, those who feel public subsidization of job training threatens their own job security, and those who feel that substantial abuse exists in public social welfare programs.

Once social welfare is no longer in the realm of the public sector, charity rooted in an insurance motive becomes vulnerable to disappearing entirely. What could bring this state of affairs about is the *free rider* phenomenon. This principle asserts that given the possibility of securing a benefit from the side-effect of someone else's economic activity, the opportunity would be taken with no thought of compensating the benefactor. If charity is indeed an "insurance premium" and no more, many people would rely upon others to make this expenditure with the anticipation of reaping the benefits of the spending gratis. In view of the widespread nature of the free rider motive, charity rooted in an insurance motive could very well become a sporadic activity.

The virtual disappearance of a charity rooted in self-interest would have the effect of catapulting instances of *selfless charity* to a prominence this phenomenon never received before. The drastic contrast in ideology between those who practice selfless acts of charity and the great majority of people, who regard such conduct as undermining the societal good of self-realization in the economic sphere, holds the prospect of producing friction and hostility between the two groups. Finding it unacceptable to view themselves as inferior to those who practice selfless charity, the majority could very well be cornered into branding certain forms of selfless charity as decidedly ruinous to the economic interests of society. What appears on the surface as an act of kindness may, in fact, unleash a harsh blow to society's interests. Aiding a family that becomes destitute on account of its failure to purchase health or life insurance provides a case in point. For the champion of the societal goal of self-realization in the economic sphere, the plight of the destitute family would be viewed as self-imposed and the consequence of blatantly exercising the free rider motive. The stricken family, it would be argued, must have reasoned that there was no need for them to purchase an economic good they had an obvious need for, i.e., health and life insurance, as the rest of society could be counted upon to come to their aid in the event of disaster. Coming to the assistance of the stricken family runs the grave risk of encouraging others to follow their example of not purchasing adequate insurance. Widespread emulation of this conduct could make the insurance business a failing enterprise. Private philanthropy would then, perforce, have to replace insurance as a means of dealing with the tragedy of the incapacitation or the death of a head of a household. The resultant diversion of resources from productive enterprise could only have the effect of dragging down society's standard of living.

For the compassionate, however, the above scenario pales into insignificance when compared to the tragedy of the stricken family. Instead of ascribing contemptible motives to the incapacitated or deceased, they would find various excuses and extenuating circumstances for the family's failure to purchase adequate insurance. In any case, they would hold that a man's mistake should not be allowed to make his family suffer eternally!!

What the "mine is mine and yours is yours" philosophy is capable of producing, therefore, is a situation in which A's simple act of charity to B is viewed by C as threatening to him.

To be sure, not all acts of selfless charity would evoke outrage by the adherents of the majority view. Nonetheless, a climate of callousness and insensitivity easily sets the stage for *toleration* of extreme expressions of opposition to public welfare activities. A new stage would be entered into when these extreme expressions are given the stamp of government approval. An economic crisis might prove to be the catalyst to bring about this state of affairs. Passive acquiescence to laws authorizing the state to sterilize individuals who are mentally unfit and even making certain forms of charity a capital offense now becomes distinctly possible.

Judaism's Social Welfare Program

We will now turn to a description of the basic elements of Judaism's social welfare program and how this program flows from its social welfare philosophy.

Judaism's charity obligation is expressed in terms of broad responsibility:

> *If your brother near you becomes poor and cannot support himself, you shall maintain him; he shall live with you, even when he is a resident alien* (Leviticus 25:35).

> *If one of your brethren is in need in any community of yours within your country which the Lord your God is giving you, you must not harden your heart nor close your hand against your needy brother. Instead, you shall open your hand to him and freely lend him enough to meet his needs* (Deuteronomy 15:7–8).

Exegetical interpretation of the phrase *you shall maintain him* (Leviticus 25:35) establishes that charity in its noblest form consists of aiding a faltering individual from falling into the throes of poverty. The position of such a person must be stabilized, with his dignity preserved, by either conferring a gift upon him, extending him a loan, entering a partnership with him, or creating a job for him.[11]

Preventing a faltering individual from falling into the throes of poverty is ranked by Maimonides as the first in his eight categories of charity-giving.[12] Why this form of benevolence is given first rank can, in our view, be explained on the basis that this conduct best exemplifies the *imitatio Dei* principle. One aspect of Divine grace, teaches R. Mosheh Ḥayyim Luzzato (Italy, 1701–1746), is that the Almighty bestows His bounty in a manner that allows man to *maximize* the potential enjoyment he can derive from it. Since man cannot feel a sense of pride unless he imagines that his achievements are due to his *own* efforts, the element of Divine grace in his successes is not made obvious to him. Despite the inherent danger of leading man to deny the true source of his bounty, God allows this delusion of human independence to persist for the purpose of maximizing for man the joy he derives from the Divine bounty.[13] Maimonides' first category of benevolence emulates the form of Divine grace described above. Given the charitable motive behind A's partnership or job offer to B, the transaction may very well entail an opportunity cost for A. This occurs when A, other things being equal, prefers to form the partnership or make the job offer to C, but out of consideration of B's straits makes the offer to B instead. A's shrewd concealment of his charitable motive will deceive B into believing that mutual interest is what prompted his offer. This conduct exemplifies *imitatio Dei* in the highest form.

Creating a false impression is normally prohibited under the *genevat da'at* interdict.[14] Employing deceptive conduct to delude a charity recipient into believing he was not the beneficiary of charity, however, actually enhances the good deed of the donor. That deceit can be employed in a meritorious manner represents, in our view, another application of the dictum stated by Yalta (R. Naḥman's wife):

> Yalta once said to R. Naḥman, "Observe, for everything that the Divine Law has forbidden us, it has permitted us an equivalent: it

has forbidden us blood but it has permitted us liver; it has forbidden us intercourse during menstruation but it has permitted us the blood of purification; it has forbidden us the fat of cattle but it has permitted us the fat of wild beasts; it has forbidden us swine's flesh but it has permitted us the brain of the *shibbuta;* it has forbidden us the *giruta* [a forbidden bird] but it has permitted us the tongue of fish; it has forbidden to us the married woman but it has permitted us the divorcee during the lifetime of her former husband; it has forbidden us the brother's wife but it has permitted us the levirate marriage; it has forbidden us the non-Jewess but it has permitted us the beautiful woman [taken in war]. I wish to eat flesh in milk [where is its equivalent?]." Thereupon R. Naḥman said to the butchers, "Give her roasted udders."[15]

Included in Maimonides' highest level of charity, as will be recalled, is the extension of a loan or gift to a needy individual. Concealing the charitable intent in these forms of altruism challenges the ingenuity of the donor to a greater extent than altruism in the form of a partnership or job offer. Unless a close friendship exists between A and B, B may very well take A's gift, not as a token of their friendship, but rather as a polite offer of assistance, with its accompanying humiliation. The challenge to A's ingenuity is perhaps even greater in the loan case.

Playing a central role in classifying acts of charity into the remaining seven categories is the extent to which the beneficence meets the needs of the recipient and at the same time preserves his dignity and self-esteem.

Ranking second is the chariable gift which manages to conceal both the identity of the benefactor from the recipient and the identity of the recipient from the benefactor. Closely related to this level of charity-giving, according to Maimonides, is making a contribution to a charity fund.

Falling into the third category is the charitable gift which manages to conceal the identity of the benefactor from the recipient, though the identity of the recipient is not unknown to the benefactor.

In the next lower category the recipient knows who the donor is, but the donor does not know who the recipient is.

Falling into the fifth category is the person who gives to a poor person before he asks.

In the sixth category is the one who gives appropriately to a poor man after he has been asked.

Ranking in the seventh category is one who gives less than is appropriate but in a pleasant and cheerful manner.

Finally, falling into the lowest category is the person who gives charity ungraciously.[16]

Dei Maḥsoro

The charity obligation in Jewish law consists of satisfying *fully* the needs of the poor *(dei maḥsoro)*.[17] Means permitting, even the purely psychological needs of the poor must be met. In this regard the Talmud relates that Hillel the Elder (1st. cent. B.C.E.–1st. cent. C.E.) provided a certain poor man with a horse on which to ride and a slave to run in front of him, because he had been accustomed to these luxuries while he was wealthy.

Satisfying *fully* the needs of the poor is by no means an absolute obligation. First, it is a collective rather than an individual obligation. Second, *dei maḥsoro* is subject to an overall limitation that Halakhah imposes on individual charity-giving. Finally, the priority schedule that Halakhah calls for in relation to its charity obligation may very well relegate the *dei maḥsoro* responsibility to only a theoretical significance. Let us discuss, in turn, each of the preceding caveats.

Dei Maḥsoro: A Collective Responsibility

Satisfying a supplicant's needs *fully* is, according to R. Moses Isserles (Poland, 1525–1572), mainly a collective rather than an individual responsibility. Confronted with a request for assistance, an individual is not himself required to shoulder the entire burden of financing the need. The entire community must share this responsibility. Nonetheless, in the event of refusal or absence of cooperation, the individual, means permitting, is required to shoulder *alone* the burden of financing the need.[18]

Rate Limitations

Talmudic decisors differ as to whether the 10 percent charity obligation the Torah imposes on agricultural produce applies to income as well.[19] Opinions in the matter range along the continuum from custom to rabbinical edict, to pentateuchal law.[20] In his survey of the responsa literature, Rabbi Ezra Basri concludes that majority opinion regards the 10 percent level as a definite obligation, albeit by dint of rabbinical decree.[21] In any case, devoting less than 10 percent of one's income to charity reflects an ungenerous nature.[22]

Out of fear that overgenerosity in giving charity could make the donor himself vulnerable to poverty, the sages enacted an interdict against donating more than 20 percent of one's income to charity.[23] This interdict has been variously interpreted. Some authorities understand it as a restriction on the proportion of income that an individual may devote to a charity fund in the absence of requests for assistance. Should an individual be confronted, however, with pleas for assistance, no maximum restriction on the amount of his aid is prescribed. Other authorities suspend the interdict only in relation to bequests and to situations where the aid would avert loss of human life.[24]

The base against which the 10 percent charity obligation applies is arrived at by deducting from gross receipts, business expenses,[25] business losses,[26] personal casualty losses, irrecoverable debts,[27] and income taxes[28] paid to various governments.[29]

Priorities in Charity-Giving

The priority issue in charity-giving is operative on two levels. Choices must be made among competing people as well as among competing requests.

In respect to competing people, relatives take precedence over other poor people,[30] with parents given the highest priority.[31] Using charity funds to support parents is, however, regarded as despicable when the children can maintain them otherwise.[32] Next in priority are children above the age at which one is halakhically[33] obligated to maintain them.[34] Other relatives come next. Brothers on the father's side precede those on the mother's side.[35] Among nonrelatives, one's neighbors take precedence over other supplicants.[36] The needy of the donor's town precede the poor of other towns.[37] Finally, among competing claims of poor from towns outside the locale of the donor, the poor of the Land of Israel take precedence.[38]

Within a given category there is also a priority list. A woman takes precedence over a man,[39] and a rabbinical scholar over one who is unlearned. For those at the same level of scholarship, the order is Kohen, Levite, and Israelite.[40]

Notwithstanding the above ordering of priorities, a pressing or more basic need, according to R. Pinḥas ha-Levi Horowitz (Germany, ca. 1731–1805), upsets this ordering and takes precedence. In respect to one's own poor relatives, however, their total needs take precedence over even the basic needs of other poor people.[41]

A somewhat different position in this matter is taken by R. Jeḥiel Michel Epstein (Belorussia, 1829–1908). The guidelines that Halakhah sets for mediating between competing charity claims are established, in his view, only for the purpose of determining the relative amounts each person gets, but do not work to exclude any supplicant entirely. If precedence was meant to imply exclusion, then any poor person who did not have a rich relative would likely be neglected entirely. Catering to the total needs of a relative while neglecting the basic needs of other poor people would, according to R. Epstein, be entirely inappropriate.[42]

A third view in this matter is advanced by Rabbi Mosheh Feinstein (New York, 1895–1986). He rejects the notion that relative need is a halakhically imposed criterion for the distribution of a private charity fund. Relative need is an equity benchmark and becomes operative only in deciding how to disburse public charity funds. Complete discretion is, however, given to an individual to disburse his own charity fund in any manner he sees fit. Notwithstanding its effect of excluding others, an individual may decide to disburse his entire amount of charity to a single qualified recipient.[43]

Eligibility for Public Assistance in Talmudic Times

Wealth and the liquidity of that wealth form the basic elements of the talmudic eligibility criterion for public assistance.

For the purpose of establishing eligibility standards for receiving the agricultural tithe, the Talmud classifies a household as poor if its net worth falls below 200 zuz. When net worth consisted of capital invested in business transactions, the sum was reduced to 50 zuz on the assumption that an active capital of such size would generate subsistence for a year.[44]

Liquidity also plays a role in determining a household's eligibility to receive charity. Claims for assistance on the basis of an inadequate cash flow are usually denied when net worth exceeds the poverty line. Under these conditions, the household is expected to liquidate its assets to increase its cash flow to an adequate level. Several exceptions to this general rule should, however, be noted. An individual is not expected to sell his apparel, home, or any essential household article to attain a liquidity level consistent with a subsistence standard of living. Nonetheless, if any of these essential items are made of gold or silver, blanket exclusion from the 200-zuz net-worth base no longer applies. If selling these items and replacing them with ordinary ones will bring the individual's net worth up to the 200-zuz level, he no longer qualifies for public assistance. Notwithstanding the above disqualification, to be eligible for private assistance, an individual is not made to sell either his apparel, house, or any essential household articles, regardless of their value.[45]

In addition, Jewish law recognizes the fact that the market value of farmland is subject to seasonal fluctuation.[46] Close to harvest-time, during the summer months, its value is relatively high. Immediately after the harvest, during the autumn, its market value is relatively low. Should the squeeze on a household's liquidity occur during the depressed autumn market, the household qualifies for public assistance until it can manage to sell its land for at least one-half of its harvest-time value.[47]

Should the household's liquidity squeeze compromise its bargaining position to such an extent that it cannot manage to sell its holdings at the prevailing market price, the household qualifies for public assistance until it can sell its holdings at the prevailing market price.[48]

However, when real estate values are generally depressed, a family, regardless of the size of the capital loss it would sustain by liquidating its real estate holdings, does not qualify for public assistance as long as its net worth remains above the poverty line.[49]

Another aspect of liquidity taken into account by the halakhic definition of poverty is the location of an individual's assets. For an asset to be included in net worth, it must be accessible to its owner. Hence, a traveler whose assets are situated in his place of permanent residence qualifies for public assistance when his funds run out. When he returns home he need not return any charity he received while on his travels.[50]

In the modern banking era, where electronic transfer of funds is commonplace, location, as it appears to us, would rarely render a cash asset inaccessible.

Eligibility for Public Assistance Today

While some authorities extend the 200-zuz criterion for accepting agricultural tithe to the eligibility requirement for accepting charity in general, R. Joseph of Corbeil (France, d. 1280) breaks new ground by rejecting this identification. The 200-zuz formula, in his view, applies only to former times when agricultural tithes were regularly available to the poor, as well as institutionalized public welfare in the form of the charity chest *(kuppah)* and the charity plate *(tamḥui)*. In the absence of these conditions, a person should be regarded as poor as long as the *income* of his capital does not generate subsistence for him.[51] R. Joseph's view is recorded approvingly by R. Joseph Caro (Safed, 1488–1575).[52]

Following this line, Rabbi Solomon Z. Auerbach (Israel, contemp.) posits that in contemporary society Halakhah would regard an unemployed person as poor if the income of his capital does not generate subsistence for him. (Presumably, any transfer payment he receives from the government counts toward this subsistence level.)

The employed individual is, however, not regarded as poor unless his earnings, including government subsidies, do not afford him a "reasonable" standard of living. What is reasonable will depend on many circumstances, in particular on the neighborhood in which he resides and the level of wealth to which he was formerly accustomed.[53]

Defining poverty for the unemployed in terms of *income* inadequacy creates an inequity in treatment between this class of poor and the working poor: A struggles to earn a livelihood through gainful employment, but does not manage to earn subsistence. B, on the other hand, does not work at all, but is capable of supporting himself by drawing on some part of his capital. Both individuals are treated alike and hence are eligible for the same level of assistance. This inequity can have no effect other than to create a work disincentive and foster a state of dependency on charity among the poor.

Closer examination of the reasoning behind R. Joseph of Corbeil's formulation indicates, in our view, the appropriateness of halakhically defining poverty for the unemployed in contemporary society in terms of *capital* inadequacy rather than income inadequacy. Application of the mishnaic 200-zuz criterion leads clearly to a capital-depletion approach. Departure from this approach is indicated only when societal conditions differ from the talmudic model under which the 200-zuz criterion is operative. Given the security blanket that surrounded the individual in talmudic times in the form of agricultural gifts and institutionalized public welfare, an individual could be reasonably expected to deplete his capital in the process of supporting himself, rather than draw upon charity funds. At worst, this individual would finish the year with his capital entirely depleted; but he would be able to rely upon the *regularized* charitable gifts the next year. In the absence of this security blanket, it borders on cruelty to expect an individual to literally run his net worth down to zero in the process of supporting himself. Without a "safety net" to rely upon, an unemployed individual is regarded as poor until his *capital generates enough income* to afford him subsistence. Given the commitment of the U.S. government to the social "safety net" concept, contemporary society is akin to that of the era in which the 200-zuz criterion was operative. We submit, therefore, that R. Joseph of Corbeil would define poverty for the unemployed in contemporary society in terms of *capital* rather than income inadequacy.

Further refinement of our criterion proceeds from an examination of the *dei maḥsoro* imperative. Talmudic explication of this imperative establishes that we are required to supply the poor man only with what he is *lacking,* but we are not obliged to make him rich.[54] It follows that providing luxuries to a poor man is only appropriate if he was once wealthy and was accustomed to them.[55] To ease the trauma of falling into the throes of poverty, we provide the poor man, means permitting, with the standard of living he was once accustomed to. As long as someone does not actually become poor, there is never an obligation to lavish any luxuries upon him, even if he enjoyed them when he was wealthier than his present state.

Translating this understanding of the *dei maḥsoro* principle to our capital-inadequacy criterion of poverty results in making an individual ineligible for assistance until his capital cannot provide him with subsistence for the year. Capital inadequacy, however, qualifies a household for assistance, means permitting, in a style it was previously accustomed to.

An examination of several aspects of the eligibility requirements Jewish law sets for receiving public assistance will show that the halakhic definition of poverty should be couched in terms of *bare subsistence,* in our view.

One aspect of the eligibility requirement, as will be recalled, is the exclusion of essential household articles and apparel from the 200-zuz net-worth base. Nonetheless, if any of these essential items are made of gold or silver, blanket exclusion from the 200-zuz net-worth base no longer applies. If selling these items and replacing them with ordinary ones will bring the individual's net worth up to the 200-zuz level, he no longer qualifies for public assistance. What emerges clearly from this point in law is that Halakhah admits no luxury items in its subsistence base.

Further evidence for our thesis that Halakhah defines poverty in terms of an inability to achieve bare subsistence is an aspect of the eligibility requirement it sets for receiving funds from the weekly disbursement of the public charity chest *(kuppah).* Having funds for fourteen meals, according to the Talmud, makes an individual self-sufficient for at least a week and hence disqualifies him from becoming a public charge. Liberalization of the eligibility requirement to fifteen meals by dint of the *religious* duty to eat *three* meals on the Shabbat is rejected by the Talmud by invoking R. Akiva's dictum: "Treat your Shabbat like a weekday rather than be dependent on your fellow-beings."[56]

Now if the poverty standard of living implicit in the fourteen-meal criterion is not expanded to cover an additional food expenditure which is required as a religious obligation,[57] then *a fortiori,* the poverty standard is not expanded to include any amenities above bare subsistence.

It should be noted that the fourteen-meal requirement only sets the benchmark for *eligibility* to draw from the *kuppah.* Once at the poverty line, however, an individual's allotment from the *kuppah* includes three meals for his Shabbat requirements.[58] This point of law can, in our view, be rationalized on the basis of the *dei maḥsoro* principle. Since eating three meals on the Shabbat is an aspect of the common standard of living, anyone who falls to a below-subsistence level is entitled to draw a public stipend large enough to allow him the amenity of eating three Shabbat meals.

Poor households consist of the unemployed and, in addition, those who work but who do not earn subsistence. Within the framework of Rabbi Auerbach's benchmark for poverty, the difference in treatment of the two classes of people is considerable. This sizable gap is the result of his definition of poverty for the unemployed in terms of *income* inadequacy to generate a "reasonable" standard of living for a year. Defining poverty for the unemployed, however, in terms of the inadequacy of the household's *capital* to support itself at a subsistence level for a year, considerably reduces the difference between the treatment of this class of poor and the working poor.

Defining the public social welfare role as heavily job oriented has the effect of reducing the inherent work disincentive generated by the more favorable treatment afforded the unemployed. This latter point will be developed below.

The Halakhic Definition of Subsistence

While the concept of subsistence defies precise definition contemporary social scientists have offered various approaches to defining poverty. It will be our task in this section to present these various criteria and relate them to the halakhic definition of subsistence.

One contemporary approach to defining poverty is the *amenity criterion*. It entails an assessment of what constitutes a decent level of consumption in such areas as caloric intake and the number of square feet of living space per person in a family. The availability of inside plumbing and running hot water provide examples of items included in the amenity index. A family is regarded as living in poverty if it has less than a certain level of such key amenities. This concept of poverty is optimistic because, under its terms, it is conceivable that poverty could be completely eliminated. By the amenity standards of the middle and late nineteenth century, poverty has today been almost eliminated in both Western Europe and North America, but not in the Third World countries where a great majority of the world's population lives.

Another approach to poverty is the *proportionality criterion*. This approach defines poverty in relative terms. Regardless of their absolute incomes, this school asserts, families located in the lowest tenth (or fifteenth or twentieth?) percentile of the national income distribution will feel psychologically alienated from society and believe they are victims of deprivation. Subscription to this criterion leads to the contention that there is no solution for the poverty problem short of something close to absolute equality of income and wealth.

Finally, poverty has been defined in *budgetary* terms. The first step in developing this criterion is to determine the cost of a set of standard food budgets providing nutritive diets for families of different sizes, ages, and environments. As applied in the United States, this food budget is multiplied by three, since surveys suggest that poor American workers spend about one-third of their income on food. When the basic food budgets are multiplied by three, the result is a series of *poverty lines,* or income levels below which poverty is said to exist. In the United States, the most publicized of these poverty lines is for an urban family of four including two small children. This poverty line was $9,300 in 1982–1983.

Among the criteria discussed, the budgetary approach, as it appears to us, best approximates the halakhic definition of subsistence. Halakhic distancing from both the amenity and proportionality approaches follows from the talmudic understanding that the *dei maḥsoro* imperative, as discussed above, does not obligate society to make the poor wealthy.

On the other hand, in the halakhic society, defining subsistence in terms of *physiological survival* alone is also not indicated. Evidence of this is the communal practice of conducting a special charity drive before the Passover season for the purpose of enabling the poor to purchase matzah for the holiday *(ma'ot ḥittin).*[59] Similarly, the community is obligated to finance the religious education of the children of indigent families.[60] Still another responsibility of the community is to help find the indigent a suitable mate and set up a household for the couple.[61]

The aforementioned extensions of physiological subsistence lead, in our view, to the generalization that Halakhah includes the wherewithal to fulfill definite religious obligations in its definition of subsistence. Consideration that Halakhah imposes certain definite obligations on the Jewish father in respect to his son opens up the possibility for further expansion of the subsistence index. These obligations include the duty to circumcise him,[62] redeem him (if he is a firstborn),[63] teach him Torah,[64] find him a mate,[65] and prepare him for a livelihood.[66] Others require the father to teach his son to swim, as well.[67]

Decisors understand the father's obligation to prepare his son for a livelihood to remain intact even after the son passes the age of majority.[68]

What the above obligation entails is a matter of tannaic dispute.

Satisfaction of this obligation is attained, according to R. Meir,[69] when the father teaches his son either a trade or business skills.[70] Out of concern that business enterprises are prone to periodic slumps, R. Judah holds that the father cannot fulfill his obligation by teaching his son business management, since during slack periods, lacking capital or merchandise to transact with, the son may turn to crime.[71] Decisors rule in accordance with R. Meir's more lenient view.[72]

Within the framework of contemporary society, fulfillment of the obligation to prepare his son for a livelihood will inevitably entail expenses for the father. Proceeding from the principle that the halakhic subsistence base includes the means to finance religious obligations is the requirement for society to defray the expense of preparing indigent children for a livelihood.

Another factor working to enhance the standard of living of the poor in the halakhic society is the tax exemption conferred upon this class of people.[73] Why tax-exemption status confers higher living standards on the poor, other things being equal, follows from the fact that Halakhah mandates certain functions on the public sector. Many of these functions can be characterized as pure public or collective goods. A *collective good* is a good whose benefits are indivisible, i.e., it is not feasible to exclude nonpayers from the consumption of the good. Mandated functions falling into the category of collective goods include security (defense) measures, public road repair, and a variety of communal projects of a religious character.[74] Since the poor are exempt from taxes, they effectively enjoy the benefits of the collective goods without bearing any responsibility to defray their cost. Similarly benefiting the poor would be any nonmandated expenditures the Jewish public sector adopts which cannot manage to exclude nonpayers entirely.

Eligibility for Private Assistance

An applicant is eligible for public assistance only if he fails to achieve a level of subsistence, but Halakhah adopts a more liberal criterion in respect to eligibility for private assistance, as shown by the blanket exclusion of essential household articles from the 200-zuz net-worth criterion the sages adopted in respect to eligibility for private assistance.[75] This liberalization of eligibility requirements, as will be recalled, is not allowed the public assistance supplicant. In the latter instance, if any of these essential items are made of gold and silver, blanket exclusion from the 200-zuz net-worth base does not apply. If selling these items and replacing them with ordinary ones will bring the individual's net worth up to the 200-zuz level, he no longer qualifies for public assistance.

The rationale behind this liberalization for the private charity supplicant is supplied, in our view, by the following caveat that *Geonim* attached to the *dei maḥsoro* imperative. This imperative, as discussed above, requires us to provide even luxuries to a poor person, if he was accustomed to them when he was wealthy. Commenting on this point, *Geonim* posit that this applies only *before* the indigent plight of the pauper is a matter of public knowledge. To *prevent* his indigent status from becoming public knowledge, we even create for him the facade that he continues to enjoy his previous status of affluence. Such treatment protects the pauper from the degradation that would inevitably accompany revelation of his indigent status. Once the pauper's indigent status becomes public knowledge, we are no longer obligated to maintain his affluent facade. At this stage, accordingly, *dei maḥsoro* no longer requires us to provide the pauper with luxuries, notwithstanding that he enjoyed the amenities when he was wealthy.[76]

The reason for the blanket exclusion of essential household articles from the 200-zuz net-worth base obtaining for the private charity supplicant proceeds from *Geonim*'s thesis. Since the sale of one's essential household articles amounts to a degradation,[77] and serves only to publicize the individual's desperate status, the sages excluded these items, regardless of their value, from the 200-zuz net-worth base for the private charity supplicant. Such deferential treatment serves to prevent exposure of the supplicant's needy status. Once this individual applies for public assistance, and his indigent status becomes a matter of public knowledge, he is no longer entitled to such deferential treatment. Accordingly, if selling his essential household items made out of gold and silver and replacing them with ordinary ones brings his net worth above 200 zuz, the supplicant is not eligible for public assistance.

Public Social Welfare

The Jewish community is required to establish and maintain charitable institutions to provide for the needs of the poor.[78] In talmudic times this obligation was carried out by means of weekly collections for the community charity box *(kuppah)* and daily collections for the community charity plate *(tamḥui)*.[79] In addition, a special charity drive was conducted before the Passover season for the purpose of allowing the poor to purchase matzah for the holiday *(ma'ot ḥittin)*.[80] Another dimension of the public subsidy to the poor consisted of a compulsory hospitality scheme, wherein the townspeople were forced to take turns providing lodging for guests.[81]

Townspeople were not required to participate in these levies unless residency requirements were met.[82]

Individual assessments in these collections were based on a proportional property tax.[83] If an individual refused to meet his assessment, the Jewish court was allowed to subject him to physical duress and/or to seize his property as a pledge, if necessary, to exact payment.[84]

Widespread poverty forced many Jewish communities in the rishonic period (mid-11th to mid-15th cent.) to abandon most of the above elements of public philanthropy in favor of private philanthropy.[85]

Jewish social welfare, posits R. Samson R. Hirsch (Germany, 1808–1888), historically consisted of both public and private components. Public social welfare never displaced private philanthropy even when the various communal levies were operative; thus we have the talmudic dictum (*Nedarim* 65b) that anyone who becomes needy does not immediately apply for public relief. Rather, his relatives and friends must first attend to his needs, and only then is the community required to make up the deficiency.[86]

An application of the above dictum is the ruling that public charity funds may not be used to support an indigent individual when the would-be public charge has a father of means. Instead, the father is forced to support his son. Coercion applies even when the father is not otherwise legally obligated to support his son, i.e., the son is not a minor.[87] Similarly, public charity funds may not be used to support an indigent individual who is known to have wealthy relatives in the local area. Since the wealthy relatives are expected to support their indigent kin out of their own resources, public funds may not be used for this purpose, even though the wealthy relatives made contributions to the public charity chest.[88]

Social welfare, consisting of both public and private components, is, of course, practiced in the State of Israel today as well as in Jewish communities in the Diaspora organized on the *Kehillah* model. Two issues present themselves. What form should the public component of social welfare take? In addition, what degree of importance should the public sector assume vis-à-vis the private sector in the social welfare program?

Shedding light on these issues is an analysis of why talmudic law empowers the Jewish community to impose various charity levies on its residents, even to the extent that the minority can coerce the majority to participate.[89] Why is Judaism not content with a system of voluntarism in respect to its charity obligation? Several approaches to this question suggest themselves. We will present each in turn and draw out their implications for Jewish public welfare policy.

1. *Creating a favorable economic environment.* One possible rationale

for the coercive element in Jewish charity law is suggested by the thesis, ascribed to Rabbi Ḥayyim Soloveichik (Russia, 1853–1918), that society as a collective, apart from its individual members, has a responsibility to relieve poverty. The purpose of the coercive levy is not to ensure that the individual members of the community *qua* individuals discharge their charity obligation, but rather is to allow the public sector to carry out its own distinctive social welfare responsibility. Bolstering the theory that the charity obligation consists of both an individual and a collective component, posits Rabbi Soloveichik, is the repetition of the charity obligation in the Torah. The charity obligation, as cited above, is set out once in Leviticus (25:35) and once in Deuteronomy (15:7, 8). The Leviticus passage, in R. Soloveichik's view, refers to society's collective responsibility to relieve poverty, while the Deuteronomy passage speaks of the individual's personal charity obligation. Noting that the reward, *for the Lord your God will bless you for this in all your works and in whatever you undertake,* is mentioned in connection with the Deuteronomy passage (Deuteronomy 15:10), Rabbi Soloveichik posits that coercion cannot be applied to the individual's personal charity obligation. This follows from the general talmudic principle that when a reward is mentioned in connection with a biblical positive precept, the Jewish court will not force compliance, but instead, will rely upon voluntarism. Since no reward is mentioned in connection with the Leviticus passage, coercion is applied to the individual to force him to finance society's collective charitable responsibility.[90]

Mention was made earlier of the obligation to prevent an individual from falling into the throes of poverty. Representing the highest level of charity giving, this obligation is derived by *Torat Kohanim* from the phrase *you shall maintain him* employed in the Leviticus passage. Understanding the Leviticus passage to refer to society's collective responsibility to relieve poverty adds a societal component to the poverty-prevention obligation.

Applying the obligation to prevent poverty to the public sector generates for it, in our view, a responsibility to pursue policies that would foster a favorable economic environment. Such policies would prevent the economy from falling into a recession. Public sector investment in the development of society's infrastructure, in the form of road, bridge, school, plant, mass transit, and hospital construction, represents one type of initiative which promotes this end. Investment in basic research is another area of vital concern for long-term economic growth. Reliance on the profit motive to bring forth an optimal level of investment in the above areas invariably results in an underallocation of resources.

Meeting its obligation to create a favorable economic environment requires the government, in our view, to build "automatic stabilizers" into the economic system, for the purpose of softening the impact of any sharp economic downturn in the private sector. An adequate unemployment compensation system and a progressive income tax serve this function. The operation of these automatic stabilizers guarantees that the federal budget will work to automatically increase the government deficit when the economy experiences a tailspin. Similarly, the automatic stabilizers work to reduce the federal deficit and hence retard the rate of government spending when the private sector is expanding at too rapid a pace. *Restoration* of a favorable economic environment in the face of a severe economic downturn requires discretionary expansionary monetary and fiscal policy initiatives to supplement the automatic stabilizers. Implementation of any measures currently regarded as necessary to promote a depression-free economy is also indicated. Mandatory insurance on bank deposits and margin requirements on the purchase of financial assets provide examples of these measures.

If the public sector limited its involvement in poverty relief out of concern that it would be at the expense of economic growth this world represent a clear-cut *abdication* of its charitable obligation. Nonetheless, once society has already devoted 10 percent or more of its income to a combination of poverty prevention and poverty relief measures, the possible conflict between these two objectives must be taken into account. To illustrate, suppose conventional economic wisdom insists that any further substantial increase in government spending, regardless of how it is financed, threatens the viability of the economy. If the spending were financed by increasing the tax burden, a work-disincentive signal would be generated to the marketplace. On the other hand, financing the increased spending by means of new money supply creation and/or borrowing would run the risk of both increasing inflation and causing a surge in interest rates. Within the context of this assessment, unless the federal government is willing to restructure its priorities, further poverty relief efforts must be shifted to the private sector. Deferring to voluntarism here follows from the public sector's responsibility to give poverty prevention primacy over poverty relief.

It should be noted that the coercive element in Jewish charity law does not in itself prove the thesis that society as a collective, apart from its individual members, has a responsibility to relieve poverty.

Addressing himself to the question of how judicial coercion can be justified in connection with the charity obligation when the Torah records a promise of reward alongside this imperative, R. Isaac of Dampierre (ca. 1120–1200) points out that the charity obligation consists of a negative interdict *(lo ta'aseh)* as well as a positive duty *(aseh)*. The negative interdict is worded, *you must not harden your heart nor close your hand against your needy brother* Deuteronomy 15:7). When a biblical duty is expressed in the form of both a positive duty and a negative interdict, judicial coercion to force a recalcitrant to meet his assessment is justified, notwithstanding the promise of reward mentioned in its connection.[91]

Rejection of the thesis that society as a collective, apart from its individual members, has a responsibility to relieve poverty, effectively makes the coercive element in Jewish charity law just another aspect of the individual's personal charity obligation. What follows is a number of rationalizations of the communal coercive element of Jewish charity law which operate under the assumption that the charity obligation in Jewish law consists only of the individual's personal obligation.

2. Halakhah's call for a communal charity levy may very well be rooted in a desire to elevate the quality of the individual's charity-giving. Left to his own devices, the private citizen may be confronted with precious few opportunities to give charity at the level of preventing someone from falling into poverty. The combination of risk aversion and limited resources may work to limit private loan initiatives to finance vocational and professional education as business ventures. Moreover, unless an individual owns his own business, he will not be in a position to disguise his charity by offering a needy person a job or partnership.

The communal charity levy accomplishes the pooling of some part of society's resources already destined for charity. This fund could then be used to extend interest-free loans to finance various job-oriented activities, such as vocational training, professional education, and job retraining. Repayment of these loans could be geared to the level of the beneficiaries' future earnings.

The creation of public jobs, especially when it is employed as a countercyclical measure, represents another manner in which the government can enhance the individual's charity obligation to prevent poverty. Job expansion in the public sector, at some point, however, comes into conflict with the goal of achieving noninflationary growth. Devising the optimal mix of policies that would promote economic growth with only moderate inflation represents one of the most formidable challenges the discipline of economics faces today.

The idea that the public sector's role in the charity levy is merely for the purpose of enabling the individual members of the community to discharge their personal charity obligations does not free the public sector of a responsibility to design its antipoverty program in a manner that would not be at the expense of creating a favorable economic environment. Since the prevention of poverty ranks for the individual as a higher priority than the relief of poverty, the public sector, *in its agency role,* must assure that the aggregate effect of its antipoverty programs is not to upset this hierarchy of priorities.

3. *Prevention of the free rider phenomenon.* Another rationale behind Judaism's call for a coercive charity levy is perhaps the concern that voluntarism may produce an underallocation of resources toward the reduction of poverty. People may abhor poverty as a social ill, but be quite content to rely on the efforts of others to bring about its elimination. To the extent that shirking of the charity obligation is a widespread phenomenon, the role of the public sector in the social welfare area perforce must expand.

4. *The responsibility to relieve poverty is proportional to wealth.* Another reason for the public sector's involvement in social welfare is that the obligation to relieve the plight of the poor is, according to R. Solomon b. Abraham Adret (Spain, ca. 1235–ca. 1310), not an equal per capita obligation but rather a responsibility proportional to wealth.[92] Without the imposition of a proportional-wealth tax, there would be no assurance that the community's pattern of antipoverty expenditures would be proportional to wealth. Kind-hearted individuals and individuals of high profile would, in all probability, bear a disproportionate burden of the relief expenditure within the framework of a system of voluntarism.

Alternative economic policy options often seem to be equally valid in the pursuit of a particular objective. To illustrate, suppose the economy finds itself suffering under a condition of runaway inflation. Suppose, further, that economists diagnose the inflationary spiral to be of the demand-pull variety. Alleviation of the condition calls for the government to implement policies that would choke off the excess spending. Two alternative, but not mutually exclusive, courses of action present themselves: (1) One approach would be to curtail the excess spending by pursuing a tight fiscal policy. What this entails is a combination of reductions in government spending and an increase in government taxation. Any significant reduction in the federal deficit reduces aggregate spending and hence eases inflationary pressures. (2) Another approach would be to introduce a tight monetary policy. This alternative involves money-supply contraction for the purpose of raising interest rates. Higher interest rates can be expected to curtail various types of spending, including residential construction, consumer installment debt, flotation of municipal bonds, and small business borrowing. Since the fostering of a favorable economic environment represents one aspect of society's *charity* obligation, the burden of creating this environment, following R. Adret's line, is not an equal per capita responsibility, but rather is proportional to wealth. It follows that government has a responsibility to explore alternative means of achieving a particular macroeconomic goal in terms of their impact on the wealth and income distribution of society. Preference must be given to those policies which offer the least prospect of increasing inequalities of wealth and income.

5. *Prevention of neglect of the unattended poor.* Following the line that an individual enjoys complete discretion in disbursing his own charity funds among qualified recipients, the public sector's involvement in social welfare is obviously necessary to assure that the unattended poor are not neglected entirely.

The Public Sector's Obligation to Uphold the Dignity of the Poor

To perform its social welfare function at the highest and most idealized level, the state must strive to uphold the dignity of the poor. Preserving and enhancing the self-image of the poor requires the state, in our view, to concentrate its social welfare efforts on job creation, rather than on relief programs. Relief programs would not be acceptable as the sole means of dealing with poverty except when the target group is deemed unemployable.

Rav's advice to R. Kahana is further proof of Judaism's disapproval for an assistance program for the employable which concentrates its efforts on relief, as opposed to job creation: "Flay carcases in the marketplace and earn wages, and do not say, I am a priest and a great man, and it is beneath my dignity."[93]

With the aim of increasing employment opportunities for the poor, government support of the following programs is suggested: (1) improving information channels in the labor market to better facilitate the matching of employers with job seekers; (2) monitoring the labor market and conducting research regarding future trends in respect to job opportunities; (3) running job-retraining programs; (4) relocating families from depressed to viable economic areas; (5) subsidizing employers who hire difficult-to-place workers, i.e., the handicapped and individuals having criminal records; (6) extending interest-free loans to poverty households for the purpose of pursuing higher education.

By using the proceeds of the charity levy to increase employment opportunities for the poor, the state is effectively elevating the character of the charity-giving of the taxpayers. It does this by removing the element of degradation of the poor that their charity-taking might otherwise involve.

The Public Sector and a Humane Environment

Another aspect of Judaism's social welfare ethos is the creation of a humane environment, reflecting the ideal of *love your neighbor as yourself* (Leviticus 19:18). The public sector can, as we will explain, play a vital role in promoting this ideal.

The meaning of the biblical imperative of *love thy neighbor as yourself* (Leviticus 19:18) has long been a cause of perplexity. How can love or, for that matter, any emotion be legislated? Various approaches have been offered.[94] Most relevant to our present concern is the approach advanced by Rabbi Eliyahu Eliezer Dessler (Great Britain, 1891–1954). Benefaction *itself,* in his view, generates for the benefactor a feeling of affection for the recipient of his good deed. To be sure, personal involvement in the welfare of the recipient is an essential ingredient in generating this feeling of affection.[95]

As a corollary to Rabbi Dessler's thesis, it follows that voluntarism in the form of personal involvement in the needs of the disadvantaged elements of society is essential in fostering a humane social environment.

Paradoxically, as the commitment to alleviate misery and deprivation intensifies in the form of the creation and growth of institutions specifically designed to deal with these problems, society's humane impulse may very well weaken. This occurs when professionals are hired to attend to every aspect of the operation of these institutions and the public's involvement does not extend beyond making financial contributions toward their maintenance. Within this framework, an encounter with another human being's suffering may very well produce a muted reaction. Personal involvement or intervention on any level, the passerby might argue, is not necessary, as the welfare institutions he himself created will surely spring into action to aid the victim.

Government can do much to encourage a humane spirit in society. It can, for instance, influence educational institutions to require students to spend a certain number of hours each week with the aged, shut-ins, and infirm. Moreover, by dint of their own personal example and recruitment efforts, government officials can help make voluntarism a status activity in society.

Investigative reporting, which is now so effectively employed to dredge up scandalous conduct, could serve society well by discovering, publicizing, and playing up exceptional acts of altruism.

Heroic and spectacular acts of altruism in the form of assisting people in peril often have an inspiring and elevating impact on society. Official encouragement of such acts of nobility can therefore contribute positively toward the development of an altruistic spirit in society.

Legal systems today, as Dr. Kirschenbaum points out, do not always encourage the Good Samaritan. Within the framework of the American legal system, for instance, the rescuer might be liable to tort action by the very person he saved.

Halakhah, in contrast, as Dr. Kirschenbaum points out, encourages the Good Samaritan. It does this by (1) conferring on the rescuer the right to sue the person rescued for all financial losses he incurs as a result of the rescue operation; (2) exempting the rescuer, while actively engaged in the rescue operation, from all legal, civil, religious, and ritual duties; and (3) providing the rescuer with immunity from liability for any tort committed in the course of the rescue operation.[96]

Legislating the above prerogatives for the Good Samaritan not only offers the prospect of increasing the frequency of rescue operations, but offers the promise of enhancing the spirit of altruism in society.

Another legal prerogative, one suggested by Dr. Kirschenbaum, which might reinforce both of the above effects is the provision for the dependents of a rescuer who is either killed or disabled in the course of his rescue efforts.[97]

To be sure, a law calling for a liberal *public reward* for the Good Samaritan could be expected to encourage rescue efforts. Such a provision, in our view, however, effectively commercializes an act of nobility. Once an act of nobility takes on a *quid pro quo* character it loses its potential of elevating the moral character of society.

To counteract the current trend which makes every human interaction a *quid pro quo* event, nothing less than a concerted campaign to foster selfless benefaction is necessary.

Obligations of the Recipient

The *dei maḥsoro* imperative, according to R. Ephraim Solomon b. Aaron of Lenczycza (d. 1619), becomes operative only after the supplicant has exhausted his efforts to generate subsistence for himself and his family by means of gainful employment. This limitation of *dei maḥsoro* may be derived from the biblical duty to come to the aid of a neighbor who requests assistance to help him unburden his animal which is faltering under the weight of the load it is carrying: *If you see the donkey of a man who hates you lying helpless under its load, you must refrain from deserting him; you must be sure to help him unburden the animal* (Exodus 23:5).

Exegetical interpretation of the phrase "to help *him*" *(immo)* understands the obligation of the passerby to consist of *assisting* the owner in the unloading operation. Demanding that the passerby unload the animal himself constitutes, however, an unreasonable request on the part of the owner, and consequently need not be heeded.[98] Under the assumption that the *immo* caveat applies to the charity obligation generally, R. Ephraim derives the principle that before a supplicant qualifies for public assistance, he must be willing to do his part, i.e., exhaust his efforts to secure gainful employment.[99]

The issue of whether the caveat is confined to the unloading case or applies generally to the charity obligation, points out Rabbi Aaron Lichtenstein (Israel, contemp.), was raised earlier by R. Menahem b. Solomon Meiri. No definitive conclusion was reached by Meiri in regard to this issue. Notwithstanding Meiri's uncertainty and rishonic silence on the matter, R. Ephraim's position apparently finds support in Maimonides' treatment of welfare fraud: "Whosoever is in no need of alms but deceives the public and does accept them, will not die of old age until he indeed becomes dependent upon other people. He is included among those of whom Scripture says, *Cursed is the man that trusteth in man* [Jeremiah 17:5]."[100] Now, if the deception Maimonides speaks of refers to outright fraud, i.e., becoming a public charge when one's net worth is above 200 zuz, why is the conduct described only as accursed behavior? More appropriately, such conduct should be characterized as constituting outright theft! Maimonides' failure to characterize the deceptive conduct as outright theft indicates that the deception he speaks of refers to the circumstance where the relief claimant is employable. Though he is technically qualified for relief on the basis of his below-200-zuz net-worth, his becoming a public charge before exhausting all possibilities of securing employment constitutes accursed behavior.

Since the job-search requirement for the would-be welfare applicant is derived from the *immo* caveat mentioned in connection with the unloading-assistance duty, one can argue for a liberal interpretation of this requirement. Relaxation of the requirement follows from the duty of the passerby to accede to the owner's request to unload the animal without his (the owner's) assistance when the latter is either a *zaken* or a sick person. *Zaken* usually refers to a talmudic scholar, but in the present context takes on the broader meaning of an individual of standing.[101] Since health reasons prevent the sick person from participating in the work of unloading, and such labor is beneath the dignity of the *zaken,* the passerby must shoulder the task of the unloading operation alone.[102]

Extension of the *zaken* and sick-person exemptions of the *immo* caveat to general charity law, in Rabbi Lichtenstein's view, calls for a liberalization of the job-search requirement for the public assistance applicant.[103] Exemption from the job-search requirement for the handicapped and the female head of a household falls, in our view, squarely in the spirit of this indicated relaxation.

Another candidate for relaxation of the job-search requirement is the applicant for public assistance who can secure employment, albeit not in his area of professional training. What the *zaken* exemption of the *immo* caveat points to, as it appears to us, is allowing an otherwise qualified public assistance applicant who is professionally trained to draw public relief for a limited time, even though he can, at that time, secure employment outside his area of training. This grace period temporarily spares the professionally trained individual the indignity and trauma of being forced to change careers and at the same time affords him the chance of getting rehired in his area of specialization.

Distributive Justice in Jewish Law

The various caveats of the *dei maḥsoro* imperative, as discussed above, make it clear that what Judaism calls for is responsibility to the poor, not income redistribution. It makes no judgment as to what constitutes equity in income distribution.

Moreover, a charity levy in excess of 20 percent of income may violate the rabbinical ordinance, referred to earlier in this chapter, against charity-giving at this level. Variously interpreted, as discussed above, this ordinance certainly implies that the government may not impose a higher than 20 percent charity tax on the rich for the *sole* purpose of effecting greater "equity" in the distribution of income.

While Judaism does not subscribe to the notion of income redistribution, many other factors work to enhance the economic well-being of the poor in the halakhic society.

One favorable circumstance for the poor in the Torah society, as we discussed earlier, is the inclusion in the subsistence base of amenities beyond physiological survival.

Another advantage enjoyed by the poor, as will be recalled, is their tax-exempt status. This privileged status enables the poor to effectively enjoy society's collective goods without any accompanying financial burden. Indirectly benefiting the poor is the exclusion from the tax base that Halakhah affords to income or property devoted to the needs of the poor.[104] Moreover, when an individual designates the income of a fund for charitable purposes, though retaining possession of the fund itself, his taxable income is reduced by the full amount of the fund.[105]

We noted earlier the obligation of the public sector in the Torah society to build automatic stabilizers into the economic system for the purpose of softening the impact of any sharp economic downturn in the private sector. Since the progressive income tax forms a critical part of the automatic stabilizer mechanism, macroeconomic stabilization policy requires a tax system which favors the lower-income brackets.

Another factor working to enhance the economic well-being of the poor in the Torah society is the restraint Halakhah imposes on both the price of necessities and medical fees. We will take up, in turn, each of these restraints.

Profit Regulation in the Necessity Sector

Out of concern for the subsistence needs of the masses,[106] the sages enacted a 20% profit-rate constraint for vendors dealing in commodities essential to human life *(ḥayyei nefesh)*.[107]

Providing the basis for the rabbinical ordinance against profiteering in essential foodstuffs, according to R. Joshua ha-Kohen Falk (Poland, 1680–1756), is the biblical injunction *and let your brother live with you* (Leviticus 25:36).[108] What the verse apparently intimates is that the seller of essential foodstuffs should sacrifice some part of the potential profits he could realize by means of voluntary exchange so as to lessen the deprivation effects the sale price would generate to the buyer.

Extension of the 20% profit-rate constraint both to necessities other than food and as a basis for rent control for subsistence housing appears to follow from R. Falk's comment.

The 20% profit-rate constraint is understood by Maimonides, on the interpretation of Rabbi Isser Zalman Meltzer (Israel, 1870–1953), to consist of the duty of the Jewish community to impose a price ceiling on essential foodstuffs. Rather than imposing a restraint on individual vendors, the 20% profit level merely serves as a guidepost in the design of the price ceiling in the essential foodstuffs sector.[109]

Medical Fees

Accepting compensation for the performance of a mitzvah is generally prohibited.[110] Since the rendering of medical services constitutes a mitzvah,[111] the legitimacy of accepting a fee for such services is a matter of concern in the rabbinic literature.[112] Naḥmanides' (Spain, 1194–1270) work *Torat-ha-Adam* is an early source which deals with this issue. Compensation for medical instruction or advice, in his view, is prohibited. Nevertheless, the physician is within his rights to demand a fee for his labor and for the time in which he could otherwise have been gainfully employed.[113]

Given the *mitzvah* character of medical services, the physician, according to R. Eliezer Fleckeles (Prague, 1754–1826), is obligated to treat an indigent patient without charge. Supporting this position is R. Moses Isserles' (Poland, 1525–1572) ruling that in the event that the father of a child requiring circumcision cannot afford the *mohel*'s fee, the latter must perform his service gratis. Inability to pay the fee makes such a case, according to R. Isserles, comparable to one in which the child requiring the circumcision has no father. In the latter instance, the members of the Jewish court themselves are required to perform the circumcision on the child. The role of the Jewish court here is merely to coerce any available person with the requisite skill to perform his duty. Similarly, since the physician is duty bound to attend to the patient at hand, he must do so without charge if the patient cannot afford the fee.[114]

Reference to the source of R. Isserles' ruling provides further clarification of the derivative indigent-patient case. The source of R. Isserles' ruling is a responsum written by R. Solomon b. Abraham Adret. In this responsum R. Adret rules that an indigent father bears no responsibility to seek out charity funds for the purpose of satisfying the *mohel*'s fee demands.[115] Analogously, points out Rabbi Eliezer Waldenberg (Israel, contemp.), the indigent patient bears no responsibility to solicit charity funds in order to meet the physician's fee demand. One important caveat is, however, pointed out by Rabbi Waldenberg. When more than one physician is available to attend to the patient, each physician can shift the responsibility to treat the patient to his colleague by claiming that someone else is available to provide the medical service. Analogously, when more than one *mohel* is available, the indigent father can be shunted in a similar manner. Two solutions are offered by Rabbi Waldenberg. One alternative would be for the community to make charity funds available for the purpose of covering the medical and circumcision costs of the indigent. Another alternative would be for the Jewish court to apportion the medical care and the circumcision needs of the needy in an equitable manner among the available practitioners.[116]

· 5

Issues Involving Inflation in Jewish Law

Introduction

Since 1960, the price level in the United States, as measured by the consumer price index (CPI), has increased more than threefold. Stated in other terms, the dollar today buys less than one-third as much as it did in 1960. While the CPI registered only a 3.8 percent rise in inflation for 1985, it recorded double-digit levels for years as recent as 1979 and 1980.

Inflation is decidedly injurious to anyone whose money income does not keep pace with the rising price level. Especially hard hit on this account are pensioners and other people who subsist on a fixed income.

Unanticipated inflation redistributes income from creditors to debtors as the latter group pay back dollars of less purchasing power than they received.

Still another impact of inflation is to create an unwillingness on the part of market participants to enter into long-term contractual agreements.

Inflation creates various issues for Jewish law. It will be our task in this chapter to explore these various issues.

Real vs. Nominal Interest Rates and the Ribbit Interdict

One area of Jewish law profoundly affected by the phenomenon of inflation is Judaism's prohibition against interest charges *(ribbit)*. Understanding the difference between the *real* and the *nominal* interest rate will clarify the subsequent discussion of *ribbit* law. The *real* rate of interest is the percentage increase in purchasing power that the borrower pays to the lender for the privilege of borrowing. It indicates the increased ability to purchase goods and services that the lender earns. In contrast, the *nominal* rate is the percentage by which the money the borrower pays back exceeds the money that he borrowed, making no adjustment for the fall in the purchasing power of this money that results from inflation. Does *ribbit* law merely prohibit the lender from realizing a *real* return on his loan, or is he interdicted from even earning a *nominal* return on his loan? Should the former view be taken, the practice of indexing the repayment of a loan to the consumer price index would be legitimated.

Many contemporary decisors prohibit the indexing of loans to the consumer price index.[1] Some authorities take a lenient view on this matter.[2] The following analysis is offered in support of the stringent view.

Bearing directly on the issue of real vs. nominal interest rates is an analysis of the following talmudic text in *Bava Kamma* 97b:

> Raba asked R. Hisda: What would be the law where a man lent his fellow something on [condition of being repaid with] a certain coin and that coin meanwhile was made heavier? He replied: The payment will have to be with the coins that have currency at that time." Said the other: Even if the new coin be of the size of a sieve? He replied: Yes. . . . But in such circumstances would not the products have become cheaper? R. Ashi therefore said: We have to look into the matter. If it was through the [increased weight of the] coin that prices [of products] dropped, we would have to deduct [from the payment accordingly], but if it was through the market supplies [increasing] that prices dropped, we would not have to deduct anything. Still, would the creditor not derive a benefit from the additional metal? [We must] therefore [act] like R. Papa and R. Huna the son of R. Joshua, who gave judgment in an action about coins, according to [the information of] an Arabian market commissioner that the debtor should pay for ten old coins [only] eight new ones.

Rishonic interpretation of the above talmudic text understands the case to refer to the circumstances where subsequent to the loan the government removed from circulation the coin that was lent. Not only did the old coin not circulate domestically, but it was not in use as a medium of exchange elsewhere, or if it was, the creditor did not enjoy ready access to merchants from the country where it did circulate. Prohibiting the old coin from being used as a medium of exchange, the government replaced it with a new one of greater metallic content. Given the obligation to make payment of a debt with a medium of exchange, the debtor must make payment with the new circulating medium.[3]

Since the new monetary unit embodies greater purchasing power than the defunct unit, the debtor, in order to avoid violating *ribbit* law, apparently must return *fewer coins* than he borrowed. A blanket downward adjustment on this basis is, however, rejected by the Talmud. Such an adjustment is not appropriate when the supply of commodities simultaneously increased in the relevant interval. Here, the debtor would be obligated to return the *same* number of coins he borrowed, notwithstanding the increased purchasing power embodied in the new coins. To be sure, a simultaneous increase in the supply of commodities does not automatically rule out favorable treatment for the debtor. Since a coin has intrinsic value, aside from its value as a medium of exchange, downwardly adjusting the debtor's payment obligation is in order when the increase in metal content of the new coin was at least 20 percent. Here, melting down the new coin and selling it for its metal content will surely fetch a higher price in the marketplace than the current value of the coin as a medium of exchange. No such advantage would presumably accrue to the coin holder when the increase in the metal content was less than 20 percent. Here, the cost of converting the coin into bullion as well as the loss of metal involved in the melting-down process combine to make the melting-down process unprofitable.[4]

This formulation sheds light on the halakhic treatment of the converse case involving currency debasement. Suppose the monetary unit A lent B was declared defunct by the government at the time repayment was due and was replaced with a monetary unit containing less metal than the old unit. Suppose further that the new monetary unit commands less real goods and services than the old unit. Does Halakhah require an upward adjustment in the debtor's payment obligation? Application of the above rules led decisors to call for such an adjustment only if the supply of commodities did not decrease in the interim. Under conditions of stable supply, such an adjustment would not be in order unless the metal content of the monetary unit decreased by 20 percent.[5]

R. Ashi's distinction requires an explanation. With inflation eroding the purchasing power of the monetary unit lent out, why is the debtor's obligation upwardly adjusted only when the exclusive cause of the inflation is an increase in the monetary unit but not when it is a decrease in the supply of commodities?

The distinction, in our view, can be rationalized on the assumption that given the stability of the community's consumption pattern, an increase in the monetary unit, other things being equal, will only cause the *absolute* price level to rise, while leaving the *relative* price structure intact. In contrast, when the supply of commodities is reduced, other things being equal, only the *relative* price structure will change, while the *absolute* price level will remain intact. What brings about the change in relative prices in the latter case is the competitive bidding for the commodities in short supply. More money is now spent on the commodities in short supply and less money is spent in other areas. This change in the community's spending pattern will change the relative price structure.

Why the absolute-relative price distinction should prove decisive in determining whether an upward adjustment in the debtor's obligation is in order requires explanation. Examination of the nature of the debtor's obligation to the creditor is critical here. Bearing directly on this issue is the following talmudic passage in *Bava Kamma* 97b:

> It was stated: If a man lends his fellow [something] on condition that it should be repaid in a certain coin, and that coin became obsolete. Rav said that the debtor would have to pay the creditor with the coin that had currency at that time, whereas Samuel said that the debtor could say to the creditor, "Go forth and spend it in Meshan." R. Nahman said that the ruling of Samuel might reasonably be applied where the creditor had occasion to go to Meshan, but if he had no occasion [to go there] it would surely not be so.

The Tosafot and others understand the dispute between Rav and Samuel to refer to the circumstance where A bought merchandise from B on credit or borrowed money from him, *with the stipulation that repayment should be made with the medium of exchange.* In the absence of this stipulation, all disputants agree that payment is made with the medium of exchange that existed at the time the loan was entered into, notwithstanding that the original monetary unit is now declared defunct and does not even circulate in a foreign country at the time payment is due.[6]

Extension of the nonstipulation case to the instance where the monetary unit consists of fiat money leads, apparently, to the startling conclusion that the debtor discharges his obligation with the original medium of exchange, notwithstanding that its defunct status renders it literally worthless. Rejecting this extension, R. Jeḥiel Michel Epstein (Belorussia, 1829–1908) and others posit that returning what was lent out is an appropriate course of action only when the original medium of exchange was metallic and hence had intrinsic value. Here, despite its becoming defunct, the monetary unit retains its intrinsic value. Consequently, discharging the debt with it can be viewed as a form of "payment." Discharging a debt with defunct fiat money, however, amounts to *no payment at all.* Hence, the debt must be discharged with the new monetary unit.[7]

Proceeding clearly from the above understanding of the dispute between Rav and Samuel is a rejection of the notion that the debtor's responsibility consists of an obligation to restore to the lender the purchasing power he gave up at the time of the loan. What the obligation consists of is merely to return what was lent out. In cases where there is *stipulation* that payment must be made with currency, Rav and Samuel are in dispute as to the debtor's obligation. Talmudic decisors follow Samuel's view.[8] Accordingly, payment is made with the original medium of exchange, even if it was declared defunct at the time of repayment, provided, of course, that it continues to circulate somewhere, e.g., in Meshan.

Since the debtor's obligation consists essentially of a duty to return what was lent out to him, discharging the debt with the original monetary unit satisfies the stipulation as long as it retains its identity as a medium of exchange at least *minimally.* "Minimal identity retention" obtains when the medium of exchange retains its purchasing power in respect to one or more of the *entire* set of commodities previously available, albeit now available only in a foreign country. Since the original medium of exchange still circulates in Meshan, it may be reasonably assumed that it retains its purchasing power in respect to at least one or more of the entire set of commodities previously available.

Rav, in our view, may very well also subscribe to the principle that minimum identity retention allows the original medium of exchange to be used to discharge a debt. Retaining its purchasing power in respect to one or more commodities available only in a foreign country does not, however, suffice. Minimum identity retention obtains only if the monetary unit retains its purchasing power in respect to one or more of the entire set of commodities available *domestically.* With the government declaring the original monetary unit defunct, payment must be made with the new monetary unit.

Proceeding clearly from the above is a rationale of why inflation induced by a commodity shortage, other things being equal, does not call for an upward payment adjustment for the debtor. Since the money supply is assumed to remain constant, the monetary unit can well be expected to retain its original exchange value in respect to one or more of the entire set of commodities available domestically. Since the medium of exchange retains its identity, Halakhah adopts a nominalistic approach to the obligation for repayment, despite the loss in real terms that this approach causes the lender.

In sharp contrast, when the inflation is caused by an increase in the money supply, other things being equal, the *absolute* price level will rise. With the medium of exchange losing its identity, a nominalistic approach is rejected in favor of a payment obligation that would effectively restore for the lender the purchasing power he gave up at the time of the loan.

When both commodity shortage and money-supply growth are simultaneously operational, the monetary unit could very well maintain its purchasing power in respect to one or more of the entire set of commodities, despite the rise in the absolute price level occasioned by the monetary growth. Should the medium of exchange maintain its identity despite the monetary growth, the nominalistic approach recommends itself.

In a modern economy, monetary expansion invariably has an impact on the relative price structure as well as the absolute price level. What brings this about is the workings of the fractional reserve system.

A fractional reserve system requires a bank to hold as idle cash only a fraction of a deposit it receives. To illustrate, a legal reserve requirement of 20 percent would require a bank to hold as idle cash only $200 of a $1,000 deposit received.

Within the framework of a fractional reserve rule, monetary expansion is accomplished when holders of cash assets decide to exchange these cash assets for demand deposits or bank credit. Creating a demand deposit for a cash asset holder does not in itself expand the money supply, as the increase in the money supply occasioned by the creation of the demand deposit is exactly counterbalanced by an equal reduction of the currency in circulation. While the initial deposit changes only the composition but not the size of the money supply, the stage is set for monetary expansion. Meeting the 20 percent reserve requirement allows bank A to lend out $800 of the $1,000 deposit. This process of monetary expansion continues as the loan is spent and its proceeds are redeposited in another bank. Successive rounds of expansion eventually come to a halt when the entire original cash deposit of $1,000 is held as idle cash by the banking system as a whole.

Monetary expansion also occurs in consequence of expansionary Federal Reserve credit policy. Financing a deficit by selling bonds to the Federal Reserve illustrates such an expansionary policy. Let us suppose, for instance, that for the purpose of financing a $20 billion deficit, the Treasury sells $20 billion of bonds to the Federal Reserve. The Federal Reserve pays for the bonds by increasing the Treasury's account with it by $20 billion. Given its newly created demand deposit, the Treasury can now write $20 billion of additional checks against its account at the Federal Reserve.

The foregoing description of commercial bank and Federal Reserve credit expansion indicates that monetary expansion profoundly affects the relative price structure. Farmers, consumers, and businessmen compete for the available credit. Each of these groups is by no means homogeneous. The spending pattern of the recipients of bank credit affects the relative price structure. Similarly affecting the relative price structure is the spending pattern of recipients of federal spending, financed by means of monetary expansion.

Inflation in a modern economy is rooted in causes other than an increase in the monetary unit and a reduction in the supply of commodities. Phenomena exerting an inflationary impact on the economy include: a general loosening of credit conditions; increased government deficits; a breakdown of the competitive structure of the economy; and an increase in the population. Besides exerting an upward pressure on the price level, these phenomena affect the relative price structure as well. The set of goods and services in a modern economy is indeed enormous, including commodity prices, consumer goods, fees for professional services, financial assets, and the country's foreign exchange rates. While inflation generally exerts an upward pressure on prices, some prices, such as bond prices and foreign exchange rates, actually decline. Since the medium of exchange in a modern inflationary economy can be expected to maintain its exchange value in respect to one or more of the entire set of available goods and services, the nominalistic approach recommends itself in the treatment of loan transactions.

Commodity Loans

Inflationary times often create an incentive for market participants to substitute barter transactions for cash transactions. Commodity loans calling for payment in kind instead of a cash payment guarantee for the lender that the same purchasing power he gave up in making the loan will be restored to him when repayment is made.

Out of fear that the market value of the commodity may increase at the time of repayment, the sages prohibited commodity loans in kind *(se'ah be'se'ah)*. Such a transaction violates the rabbinic extension of *ribbit* law, called *avak ribbit*.[9] The prohibited agreement places the creditor at a disadvantage: Should the commodity appreciate at the time of repayment, the debt may not be discharged by means of payment in kind. Instead, a cash payment is required, with the debtor's obligation set equal to the value the commodity had at the time the loan was entered into. Depreciation of the commodity, on the other hand, disallows a cash payment. Here, payment must be made in kind.

A commodity loan would be legitimate, however, when repayment is to be made in cash, based on the market value of the commodity at the time the loan was entered into. Since the commodity serves here merely as the medium of the loan, and the debtor's obligation is fixed in cash, the possible appreciation in the value of the commodity at the time of repayment is immaterial.[10]

Since the *se'ah be'se'ah* transaction is prohibited only because of the *avak ribbit* consideration, the sages suspended their interdict under certain conditions.

One qualifying circumstance occurs when the debtor is in possession of the commodity he borrows at the time the loan was entered into *(yesh lo).* To illustrate, suppose the loan consisted of a ton of wheat and the debtor had this amount of wheat in his possession at the time he entered into the loan. Given that correspondence, the amount of wheat the borrower has is regarded as if it were given immediately to the lender as payment at the time the loan was entered into. Any appreciation of the commodity subsequent to the loan is therefore regarded as having occurred while the commodity was in the domain of the lender.[11]

The *yesh lo* point of leniency in *se'ah be'se'ah* law extends even to the instance where the amount of the commodity in the debtor's possession at the time of the loan amounts to only a small portion of the commodity loan. Since the *se'ah be'se'ah* interdict is *only* prohibited because of *avak ribbit* law, the *yesh lo* loophole is valid even when its rationale is not entirely applicable.[12]

When a *se'ah be'se'ah* transaction is legitimized by means of the *yesh lo* mechanism, both parties must be aware that the debtor has some amount of the borrowed commodity at the time the transaction was entered into and that this circumstance is what halakhically validates their arrangement. Nevertheless, even if the parties to the agreement are ignorant of these facts, the debtor is not disallowed from returning the borrowed commodity, even if it appreciated in value.[13]

Thus, the *yesh lo* condition validates a transaction whose time frame is such that market conditions will cause a natural increase in the value of the commodity by the time of repayment. This condition, according to R. Shabbetai b. Meir ha-Kohen (Poland, 1621–1662), is valid even when the contract disallows early payment.[14]

Another circumstance that may suspend the *se'ah be'se'ah* interdict obtains when the commodity involved trades at a definite market price *(yaẓa ha-sha'ar).*[15] With repayment in kind possible at any time, the borrower is regarded as being capable of discharging his debt by making the requisite commodity purchase before it appreciates above its value at the time of the loan.[16] Maimonides (Egypt, 1135–1204) and others legitimize the above mechanism even when the borrower lacks the necessary cash to make the commodity purchase. Though lacking cash, the borrower is regarded as capable of securing the necessary commodity purchase by means of establishing a line of credit.[17]

The *yaẓa ha-sha'ar* mechanism is subject to several restrictions. Calling for the commodity loan to be repaid at a particular time is, according to Maimonides, prohibited. Such a stipulation indicates an expectation on the part of the lender of price appreciation at the specified date.[18] Disputing this position, R. Abraham b. David of

Posquières (1125–1198) and others legitimize the *yaẓa ha-sha'ar* mechanism even if the lender sets a date for repayment.[19]

A variation of the situation where the date of repayment is specified occurs when the *se'ah be'se'ah* transaction disallows early repayment. Since early repayment cannot be made, the borrower cannot be regarded as capable of making repayment before the commodity appreciates in value. The transaction is hence prohibited.[20]

Another restriction for the *yaẓa ha-sha'ar* mechanism, according to Maimonides, is that it is invalid when either the lender or the borrower is unaware that the loan commodity is traded at a definite price when he enters into the *se'ah be'se'ah* transaction.[21] Unawareness creates a presumption of intention to make repayment at such time that the commodity will appreciate in value.[22] Apparently equating the rationale of the *yaẓa ha-sha'ar* mechanism with the *yesh lo* method, R. Asher b. Jeḥiel (Germany, 1250–1327) legitimizes the former procedure even if one or both of the parties was unaware that the loan commodity was traded at a definite price.[23]

Taking a stringent view in this matter, R. David b. Samuel ha-Levi (Poland, 1586–1667) rules in accordance with Maimonides.[24]

Requiring parties to a *se'ah be'se'ah* arrangement legitimized by means of the *yaẓa ha-sha'ar* mechanism to be aware of the market price at the time they enter into their agreement, R. Shabbetai b. Meir ha-Kohen does not prohibit repayment in kind with an appreciated commodity in the absence of the awareness condition.[25]

Advancing a middle-ground view in this matter is R. Yonathan Eybeschuetz (Prague, 1695–1764). Requiring the awareness condition, he does not prohibit repayment in kind with the appreciated commodity in the absence of this condition unless the ignorant party was the lender.[26]

Still another restriction on the *se'ah be'se'ah* transaction is that it must be structured in a manner that would not be regarded as "near to profit and far from loss" from the standpoint of the lender. The following ruling of R. Isaac b. Sheshet Perfet (Spain, 1326–1408) provides a case in point: A sold several measures of wheat on credit to a Jewish community, calling for the option of demanding at the due date either a payment in kind or cash payment set equal to the value of the wheat at the time of the sale. Since such an arrangement hedges for the seller against the possibility of price depreciation of the commodity, the stipulation violates *avak ribbit* law. The *se'ah be'se'ah* arrangement is legitimized only when the lender is willing to absorb the risk of commodity depreciation. When he is unwilling to do so, the arrangement amounts to "near to profit and far from loss."[27]

Currency may also be subject to the *se'ah be'se'ah* interdict. This occurs when the currency involved is not the economy's main circulating medium of exchange. Providing a case in point is R. Yoḥanan's prohibition against a loan transaction calling for A to lend B a gold dinar and to be repaid in kind at a later date. In R. Yoḥanan's time, silver coins were the main circulating medium of exchange, and therefore a loan in kind consisting of a gold dinar must be treated in the same vein as a *se'ah be'se'ah* transaction.[28]

Currency loans taking on the legal character of commodity loans may nevertheless be arranged so as not to violate *avak ribbit* law. Use of the mechanisms described above accomplishes this end.[29]

Denominating Loans in a Foreign Currency

Denominating loans in a foreign currency, rather than in the domestic currency, is a frequently employed inflation hedge when the lender fears that the purchasing power of the domestic currency will fall over time more than the foreign currency. Since foreign currency is not the main medium of exchange of a country, it must legally be treated as a form of *perot* (commodity) and hence subject to the *se'ah be'se'ah* interdict. Nonetheless, given the accessibility of the foreign exchange in question, the *yesh lo* mechanism readily suggests itself as a means of structuring the foreign exchange loan so as to avoid *avak ribbit* violation.

Use of the *yaẓa ha-sha'ar* mechanism as a means of validating the foreign exchange loan is, however, another matter.

Rishonic clarification of the concept of *yaẓa ha-shar'ar* is found in connection with the futures contract: A's commitment to deliver a commodity to B over a period of time in exchange for the latter's prepayment of the order is normally prohibited. Out of fear that the market price of the commodity might advance over the delivery period, the commitment to deliver is viewed as a disguised interest premium in exchange for the prepayment. Legitimacy, however, is given to accepting prepayment for future delivery when the market price of the commodity was established *(yaẓa ha-sha'ar)* at the time the contract was entered into. With the commodity available at the stipulated price, A is regarded as capable of making *immediate* delivery to his client, before the commodity has a chance to appreciate in value. Subsequent delivery of the commodity at a point in time when it is traded at a higher price is therefore not regarded as a disguised interest premium.[30]

What constitutes *yaẓa ha-sha'ar* in the futures contract case is defined by R. Isaac b. Jacob Alfasi (Algeria, 1013–1103) as a price which has stability for two or three months.[31] Though making no mention of any specific time span, R. Ḥananel b. Hushi'el (North

Africa, 11th cent.) and R. Yom Tov Ishbili (Spain, ca. 1250–1330) also define *yaẓa ha-sha'ar* in terms of price stability.[32]

A wider band of price fluctuation for *yaẓa ha-sha'ar* proceeds from R. Moses Isserles' (Poland, 1525 or 1530–1572) validation of a futures contract entered into in a small town which based the delivery price on the market price of the commodity in that small town.[33] Why the above ruling implies a wider band of fluctuation for *yaẓa ha-sha'ar* is seen from R. Nissim b. Abraham Gerondi's (Barcelona, 1310–1375) comparison of price in a city versus a small-town market. Relative stability, according to R. Gerondi, is what differentiates the price of a commodity traded in a city market compared to the price of the same commodity traded in a small-town market. In a small town, posits R. Gerondi, supply will usually become more and more scarce relative to demand with the passage of time. With upward pressure always building up on the price of a commodity in a small town, the price cannot be expected to be stable for long. In sharp contrast, supply relative to demand remains stable for prolonged periods of time in the context of a huge city commodity market. Relative price stability for a commodity traded in a city market can therefore be expected.[34]

Technological advances in transportation and communications have considerably widened the marketplace today. Hardly any price, as a result, is free from the possibility of sudden change on account of the vicissitudes of aggregate supply-and-demand factors. Noting this phenomenon, Rabbi Basri posits that all prices today, with the exception of those under government control, are inherently unstable and should be regarded as not being well defined.[35]

What proceeds from the above is that *yaẓa ha-sha'ar* is not a validating mechanism unless the *stability* test is met. Foreign exchange rates today are no longer fixed by means of multilateral government agreements, but rather are free to fluctuate in response to market forces. To be sure, central banks occasionally intervene in the foreign exchange market for the purpose of shoring up their own currencies. These interventions are sporadic and, of course, not announced in advance. Given the *daily* volatility of foreign exchange rates, it is doubtful whether *yaẓa ha-sha'ar* is operative in this market.

Small Commodity Loans from a Neighbor

The *se'ah be'se'ah* prohibition may affect the common practice of borrowing a food item from a neighbor. Since the loan calls for the *replacement* of the borrowed item, e.g., a loaf of bread, rather than the return of its value, this practice should be prohibited unless the *yesh lo* or *yaẓa ha-sha'ar* mechanism is met. Indeed, R. Isaac b. Jacob Alfasi legitimized this practice only when the validating mechanisms are met.[36] Positing that neighbors are not particular with each other in respect to matters of insignificant value, R. Moses Isserles legitimizes neighbor commodity loans without the validating mechanisms.[37] Nonetheless, in certain areas, it is the custom not to lend a neighbor a loaf of bread before Passover with the stipulation that the loaf should be replaced after Passover. Since leaven is prohibited on Passover, the transaction amounts to a stipulation disallowing early payment.[38]

Reciprocal Labor Agreements

Inflation, especially when it is accompanied by recession, produces a marked substitution of barter transactions for market transactions. Barter allows a person, in some measure, to maintain his accustomed standard of living despite his loss in income and the higher price level he faces.

Reciprocal work agreements may violate *avak ribbit* law. This occurs when A commits himself to compensate B at some future date for services rendered by the latter by providing services that enjoy a higher market value[39] or require greater physical exertion than the work just done for him.[40] Since the arrangement confers on A the right to delay fulfilling his end of the agreement, the differential value of, or greater effort involved in, this reciprocal service amounts to compensating B for *tolerating the delay* in the payment due him *(agar natar)*. No infringement of *avak ribbit* law is involved when the time-delay element is absent from the agreement, however. Reciprocal labor agreements calling for simultaneous or consecutive performance of the respective services are therefore legitimate.[41]

Interpreting R. Joseph Caro's view, R. Mordecai Dov Twersky (Hornestopol, 1840–1903) understands the essence of the prohibition to consist of the stipulation between the two parties, rather than the actual reciprocation of a service of higher value or one entailing greater physical exertion than the service initially rendered. Hence, should A perform a service for B, and, at some future date, A agrees to allow B's higher-valued service (or service entailing greater physical exertion) to constitute compensation for his service, the arrangement does not violate *avak ribbit* law. Payment of a premium above what is due without prior stipulation at the outset of the transaction does not violate the biblical injunction against *ribbit (ribbit keẓuẓah)*. While the mere payment of a premium without prior stipulation violates the *avak ribbit* law when the transaction involved takes on the character of a loan, no prohibition is violated when the transaction represents payment for service or product rendered.

This leniency is not applicable, however, according to the opinion that regards payment of a premium without prior stipulation as a violation of *avak ribbit* law even when the transaction does not take on the character of a loan.[42]

R. Jacob b. Asher (Germany, 1270–1340), on the interpretation of R. Joshua ha-Kohen Falk (Lemberg, 1555–1614), advances a very stringent view in respect to the reciprocal labor agreement interdict.[43] Reciprocal labor agreements, in his view, may be prohibited even when the committed service is not assessed at the time of the stipulation to entail greater exertion or be of a higher value than the service initially rendered. This occurs when there is merely concern that the committed service may entail greater exertion at the time it will be rendered in reciprocation.[44]

R. Abraham b. David of Posquières understands the prohibited cases of reciprocal work agreements to fall under the rubric of the *se'ah be'se'ah* interdict, discussed above.[45]

The applicability of the interdict applies, therefore, even when the committed reciprocal service is not assessed, as a definite matter, to be of greater value than the service already performed.

On the other hand, the *se'ah be'se'ah* rationale for the prohibition on reciprocal work agreements results in a leniency as well. A and B can easily validate their reciprocal work agreement by assessing the market value of A's initial service and agreeing that, should B's service prove to be of a higher market value, A will make the necessary monetary adjustment.

Rabbi Jacob Blau posits, however, that R. Abraham b. David's rationale of the interdict on reciprocal work agreements represents a minority view and should therefore be rejected. The majority view, according to Rabbi Blau, regards the interdict on reciprocal labor agreements as separate from the *se'ah be'se'ah* prohibition. Given the distinctiveness of the former, concern that the committed service might entail *greater physical exertion*, as well as the concern that it might be more valuable than the service already rendered, forms the basis of the prohibition. Consequently, the assessment-adjustment procedure described above would not be valid when the labor services involved are different, even if they are assessed to be of equal value.[46]

The Charity Obligation and Inflation

Judaism's charity obligation consists of a duty to devote one-tenth of net income to the needs of the poor.[47] Falling within the income base against which the tithing obligation is calculated is the profit earned from the sale of an asset.[48] What is included in the base, according to

Rabbi Mosheh Feinstein (1895–1986), is the *real* profit rather than the *nominal* profit earned. To illustrate, suppose A purchased an asset for $1,000 and sold it two years later for $2,000. Suppose further that the rate of inflation in this interim period was 100 percent. Taking into account the 100 percent inflation rate, the nominal profit of 100 percent on the sale is reduced in *real* terms to zero. Consequently, the nominal profit earned here would not be subject to any tithing obligation. Rabbi Feinstein further posits that the difference in the purchasing power of the monetary unit in the relevant periods of time should take into account only changes in the prices of necessities. Changes in the prices of residential homes and luxuries, however, do not enter the index.[49]

Religious Functionaries and Inflation

Compensation for a religious functionary hired by the community to devote his time exclusively[50] to his communal responsibilities must be in accordance with his need.[51] Need takes into account both family size and the cost of living. This formula may very well allow the functionary to command a salary *above* what he could earn outside communal religious service. With need serving as the criterion for his compensation, his salary must be automatically increased when either his family size or the cost of living increases. Hence, such contracts are subject to automatic escalator clauses.[52]

Delinquency in the Payment of Wages and Inflation

Proceeding from the legal principle that wages are due at the end of the wage period is the prohibition against labor agreements calling for the worker to receive a premium in wages in the event the employer is delinquent in paying him on time. Since wages are due on the last day of the wage period, the premium offered in the event of delinquency amounts to an *avak ribbit* payment to the worker for tolerating the delay in receiving his wages.[53]

A mutually arrived at agreement between a worker and an employer calling for a premium wage in the event of delinquency in payment violates *avak ribbit* law, even if the agreement was not made at the outset of the labor contract. Accordingly, should the worker, upon demanding his pay at the end of the wage period, accept the employer's offer to pay him a premium wage at some later time, this agreement violates the *avak ribbit* law. Since an employer's delay in paying wages violates a specific biblical prohibition *(halanat sakhar)*,[54] the worker's acquiescence to the delay in payment amounts to an agreement on his part to treat the balance due him as a loan. The higher wage called for at the later date, therefore, amounts to a premium for tolerating *delay* in payment and consequently violates *avak ribbit* law.[55]

A variant of the above occurs when the employer is in default of the wages due to the worker, and the worker, in consequence, exerts a claim for the income he could have realized from the wages had he been paid on time. The legitimacy of the worker's claim here is disputed among talmudic decisors. While R. Eliezer of Toul (d. before 1234) and others validated the compensation claim,[56] R. Isaac b. Moses of Vienna (late 13th cent.) and others regarded the payment as constituting *avak ribbit*.[57]

Supporting R. Eliezer's view, R. Joel Sirkes (Poland, 1561–1640) offers the following rationale of why meeting the worker's compensation demand does not violate *avak ribbit* law: Since the wages are held in arrears against the worker's wishes, the worker cannot be said to have allowed the balance due him to take on the character of a loan for the duration of the delinquency period. With the loan aspect of the transaction absent, the extra payment the worker seeks can in no way be characterized as a premium for tolerating delay in the payment of his wages.[58]

Noting the indirect link between the worker's foregone earning and the action of the employer, R. Judah Rosanes (Turkey, 1657–1727) posits that while meeting the worker's compensation demand does not violate *avak ribbit* law, the employer is under no legal obligation to honor the demand. Responsibility for meeting the worker's extra compensation demand proceeds as a definite matter only when the employer invested at a profit the wages due the worker and the worker expressed an investment intent at the time he demanded his wages.[59]

In the context of the current inflationary spiral, holding wages in arrears constitutes not only a foregone earning for the worker but a definite loss in the form of reduced purchasing power. Noting this phenomenon, Rabbi Naḥum Rakover posits that legislating a penalty on the employer for delinquency in payment of wages is entirely appropriate.[60] In a similar vein, Rabbi Jacob Blau concludes from his survey of rabbinic literature that the majority view would not object to the employer appeasing the worker in some concrete way for having held his wages in arrears.[61]

Theft Liability and Price Changes

Another instance where price change is a matter of halakhic concern occurs in connection with a thief's obligation to return the stolen item. As long as the article remains intact and was not materially changed, the thief must return it, rather than make monetary compensation.[62] Should the article no longer be in the culprit's possession, i.e., it was stolen or lost, a monetary obligation is imposed on him. This payment is set equal to the value of the article at the time of the theft.

An exception to the above rule obtains when the thief damages or consumes the stolen item. Here, in the event the article appreciated above its value at the time of the theft, liability for the theft is set in accordance with the article's value at the time when the damage was committed.[63] Nevertheless, if the article depreciated in value in the interim, liability is set in accordance with the higher value prevailing at the time of the theft.[64] Imposing the higher penalty on the thief is justified on the ground that it would be morally reprehensible to allow him to gain when he compounds the theft with the commission of a tort.[65]

The criteria for theft liability apparently apply whether or not the change in the price of the subject article was accompanied by a general change in the price level in the same direction.

· 6
Efficiency as Treated in Jewish Law

Introduction

In this chapter we will, at the outset, define the concept of efficiency as discussed in the economic literature. We will then examine the extent to which Jewish law mandates the practice of efficiency as a *religious* duty. Another issue we will explore is the halakhic approach to technological advance as it affects the competitive marketplace. Specifically, what protection does Halakhah afford the firm that becomes noncompetitive as a result of its failure or inability to adopt the available technology?

Efficiency in Economic Theory

Production results from the coordination of land, labor, capital, and technology. Often, a given production goal can be achieved through alternative means. Efficiency requires that the *least-cost method* should be employed in the pursuit of a given objective. Concretely, this aspect of efficiency, called *allocational efficiency,* entails market search for the required inputs at the least-cost outlet. In addition, this aspect of efficiency calls for the substitution of a cheaper input for a more expensive one whenever feasible, without sacrificing the given objective.

Once input selection is completed, another dimension of efficiency, called *X-efficiency,* comes into play. X-efficiency requires the firm to combine, coordinate, and direct the inputs available to it in a manner that would maximize output.

Of particular importance in regard to the human input, X-efficiency entails the ability of the firm to motivate its personnel to perform at their maximum potential. Left to their own devices, human "inputs" can be expected to display considerable variation in their X-efficiency performance level. This variation follows from the fact that labor contracts are incomplete. It is exceedingly rare for all elements of performance to be spelled out in a labor contract. A good deal is left to custom, authority, and whatever motivational techniques are available to management as well as the individual worker's discretion and judgment.

The significant gaps in the specificity of contracts allow the individual worker some degree of latitude in deciding (a) the activities he will carry out; (b) the pace at which he will carry out these activities; (c) the quality of the activities; and (d) the time spent on the activities. Thus each individual chooses an activity–pace–quality–time (APQT) bundle. Since most individuals interact with others in their work, the nature of the interactions and the job interpretations set constraints on the APQT bundles each can choose. The formal system of financial payoffs, promotions, and potential dismissals determined by the contract is only part of the incentive system operative within the firm. Each person hired brings, in addition to his work potential, a set of desires, attitudes, and a sense of responsibility about the activities of others around him, and contributes to the creation of an atmosphere of approval or disapproval which determines, in part, the nature of the APQT bundles that are chosen. If individuals can choose, to some degree, the APQT bundles they like, they are unlikely to choose a set of bundles that will maximize the value of the output.[1]

Efficiency as Treated in Jewish Law

An analysis of the biblical prohibition against wasteful destruction *(bal tashḥit)* provides one basic strand in extrapolating Judaism's attitude toward both allocational and X-efficiency:

> *When you besiege a town for a long time in order to conquer it, you must not destroy its trees by putting an axe to them. You may eat their fruit, but you must not cut down the trees. Is a tree of the field a human being, that you should lay siege to it? Only trees which you know are not fruit trees may be destroyed and cut down, so that you may build bulwarks to reduce the town that makes war against you* (Deuteronomy 20:19–20).

While the biblical source of the *bal tashḥit* interdict makes mention only of the cutting down of fruit-bearing trees outside a besieged city, the Talmud understands the prohibition to extend to the destruction of anything beneficial to mankind regardless of location. Specific instances of violation of *bal tashḥit* law mentioned in the Talmud include breaking a utensil,[2] tearing a garment,[3] destroying an animal,[4] and causing a lamp to burn faster than its normal rate of fuel consumption.[5]

These extensions, according to majority view, take on the force of pentateuchal law.[6]

Bal tashḥit, in its most elemental form, involves an action carried out with no useful intent that results in the destruction of some material substance. Indeed, flagellation, according to Maimonides (Egypt, 1135–1204), is not incurred for the violation of this interdict unless the action can be characterized as *purposeless* destruction.[7]

Talmudic explication of the *bal tashḥit* prohibition clearly takes it beyond the level of purposeless destruction. Interpretation of this biblical passage establishes that the prohibition of cutting down a fruit tree to build a bulwark is *not absolute.* The Torah's intent is merely to give priority to a wild tree over a fruit tree in this regard. Moreover, if using the fruit tree for the bulwark will result in the creation of a higher value, this priority no longer holds.[8] This latter principle, which will be expanded upon below, is referred to as the *me'ulah bedamim* condition.

With the *bal tashḥit* law proscribing the transformation of a material substance into something else unless a higher value is obtained, negligent destruction of a material is *a fortiori* prohibited.

Studies of the modern business unit find that people and organizations normally work neither as hard nor as effectively as they potentially can. Leibenstein, the developer of the X-efficiency theory, rationalizes this conduct as follows: In situations where competitive pressure is light, many workers will trade the disutility of greater effort, of search, and of controlling the activities of other workers for the utility of feeling less pressure and of better interpersonal relations. But in situations where competitive pressures are high, and hence the costs of such trades are also high, they will exchange less of the disutility of effort for the utility of freedom from pressure, etc.[9]

What follows, however, from the above conceptualization of *bal tashḥit* law is a definite constraint on such trade-offs, regardless of the nature of the competitive market the firm finds itself in.

Because of the *bal tashḥit* interdict, it becomes the religious duty of a manufacturer to avoid unnecessary loss, wastage, and spoilage of materials he makes use of in his process. A clear-cut application of this principle is the requirement for a food manufacturer to monitor his production process so as to avoid unnecessary wastage and spoilage of the perishables he uses.

Within the context of the modern technological environment, raw materials wasted in an industrial process can often be reconstituted. Metal wasted in the process of cutting metal sheets into cylindrical tubes, for instance, can be sold as scrap metal and reshaped into metal sheets. Given the recycling phenomenon, inefficient use of the raw material in an industrial process cannot be said to amount to the negligent *destruction* of the raw material. Whether *bal tashḥit* law imposes X-efficiency requires further analysis of the *me'ulah bedamim* condition.

What circumstances the *me'ulah bedamim* case refers to is a matter of dispute among Rishonim. R. Menaḥem b. Solomon Meiri (Perpignan, ca. 1249–1306) and others understand the circumstance to refer to the instance where the bulwark can be effectively constructed from either the fruit tree or the wild tree, but the wild tree is more valuable in an alternative use than the value of the fruit tree in its natural state. Halakhah here mandates use of the fruit tree for the construction of the bulwark.[10] Interpreting the condition in this fashion transforms the *bal tashḥit* interdict into an efficiency mandate. Construction of the bulwark must be accomplished by means of the least-cost method. Since the wild tree is more valuable than the fruit tree, minimizing the cost of constructing the bulwark requires use of the fruit tree for this purpose.

Given that the biblical source of the *bal tashḥit* interdict deals with a specific case, i.e., the cutting down of a fruit tree for the purpose of building a bulwark, Meiri's understanding of the *me'ulah bedamim* condition as consisting of a least-cost caveat amounts to nothing more than imposing this constraint on the transformation of a fruit tree into a bulwark. By extension, *any* material substance may not be transformed into something else unless the transformation represents the least-cost method of achieving the given objective.

Imposing the least-cost condition to aspects of X-efficiency other than material transformation and to any aspect of allocational efficiency does not, however, follow from Meiri's position. Hence, Meiri's conceptualization of *bal tashḥit* does not directly produce a general halakhic mandate for efficiency.

Another school of thought, led by R. Yehonatan of Lunel (ca. 1150–1215) and others, understands the *me'ulah bedamim* condition to deal with a case where the *fruit-bearing tree* has greater value as a bulwark than as a fruit tree. Here, Halakhah prescribes no order of preference. To build the bulwark, either the fruit or wild tree may be cut down.[11] Now, if *bal tashḥit* law prohibits transforming a material substance having a present use into something else unless the transformation represents the least-cost method of achieving the given objective, why does Halakhah take an indifferent stance here? The alternative uses of the fruit and wild trees should enter as a prime consideration in deciding which tree should be used for the bulwark. Under the assumption that both trees provide equally effective building material for the bulwark and only the fruit tree has an alternative use, efficiency clearly demands use of the wild tree for the bulwark. This prescription allows society to maximize its output with its given resources. The bulwark will be produced from the wild tree and the fruit tree will continue to provide fruit. Constructing the bulwark from the fruit tree results, however, in a smaller output for society. While the bulwark will be constructed, society will be permanently deprived of the services of the fruit tree.

What follows from this interpretation of the *me'ulah bedamim* case is a delimitation of the scope of the *bal tashḥit* interdict. *Bal tashḥit* law merely prohibits the production of a material substance unless the outcome creates a superior value. Provided a superior value is achieved, it matters not whether the transformation represents the least-cost method of achieving the given objective. Since providing building material for the bulwark represents a higher value for both the wild tree and the fruit tree, either tree may be used to construct the bulwark.

Before relating this dispute to the issue of to what extent Halakhah imposes efficiency on the manufacturer, one point must be clarified. Insofar as the biblical source of the *bal tashḥit* prohibition speaks of the prohibition of cutting down a fruit tree, does this apply only to a material substance that, like a fruit tree, has a definite current use as well as a current market value? Or is only current market value, and not current use, crucial in making the interdict operative? The extension of the prohibition to the casting away of money would argue for the latter.[12] Now, money has no specific current use but only a value in the form of generalized purchasing power and yet the *bal tashḥit* interdict applies to it.

Applying the *bal tashḥit* law to any material substance having a current market value generates profound consequences for the manufacturer. The manufacturer may not transform the raw materials he purchases into an intermediate or final product unless the value he expects to create exceeds the value of the raw material. Given the profit motive, this criterion cannot be expected to restrain a single-product manufacturer more than good business practice would in any case dictate. Nonetheless, when applied to manufacturing activity rooted in a long-term investment motive, this condition amounts to a halakhic constraint on the amount of risk a manufacturer may voluntarily assume. To illustrate, suppose a toy manufacturer estimates that the revenue he can expect to earn from the initial run of space shuttle tinker toys will not likely allow him to recover even his raw material cost. Nonetheless, once the fad catches on, he feels he can earn a handsome profit on the venture, more than making up the initial loss. Since the manufacturer does not even anticipate recovery of his raw material cost on the initial run of his product, the activity would be interdicted under the *bal tashḥit* prohibition.

Prohibiting a manufacturer from transforming a material substance into something else unless the value he expects to create exceeds the value of the materials used up makes the "loss leader" pricing stratagem employed by a multiproduct firm questionable. What is involved here is the pricing below cost of a key item which has complementary products manufactured by the same firm. This is done to increase demand for the entire line by outlets which do not carry competing brands. A cosmetics manufacturer, for instance, might offer to sell his face makeup below cost in order to stimulate an increased demand for the rest of his line of cosmetics. Selling below the raw material cost need not, of course, violate *bal tashḥit* law, as for instance when misjudgment of market conditions or a sudden change in them *forces* this pricing stratagem on the manufacturer. But does Halakhah perhaps prohibit this stratagem when it proceeds by *design* from the very outset of the production process? R. Asher b. Jeḥiel's ruling that the *me'ulah bedamim* case includes the circumstances where the *site* of the tree is needed by the tree-cutter,[13] for example, to build a house,[14] sheds light on this matter. Commenting on R. Asher's dictum, R. Jacob Emden (Germany, 1697–1776) understands it to be limited to the instance where the tree-cutter will use the site to create a greater value than the natural value of the fruit tree.[15] Understanding the *me'ulah bedamim* case in these terms implies that cutting down a fruit tree may be legitimized even when the tree itself is not used to create a higher value. Contributing to the creation of a higher value suffices to allow the cutting down of the fruit tree. Analogously, if selling a product below its raw material cost increases the profits of the multiproduct manufacturer, this practice should be legitimized. It should be noted, however, that R. Asher's dictum is not universally held by talmudic decisors.[16] Rejection of R. Asher's dictum imposes the stringency that a fruit tree may not be cut down unless the fruit tree itself will be used to create a product of higher value. Generalizing this condition to all extensions of *bal tashḥit* law results in a prohibition of the transforming any material substance into anything but a product of higher value than the original one. What follows is a constraint on the "loss leader" strategem of the multiproduct firm. To stimulate increased demand for his entire line, the manufacturer may not plan to produce one (or more) of his products with the intent to sell it (them) at or below the raw material cost. Selling the product at or below the raw material cost violates the *bal tashḥit* interdict.

Rejection of R. Asher's dictum does not, in our view, automatically call for the imposition of the constraint on the "loss leader" pricing stratagem of the manufacturer. Since the product targeted for pricing below the cost of the raw materials of which it is composed *can objectively* command a market price above this level, the transformation should be regarded as creating a superior value. While the product may sell below the cost of its raw material component, its "shadow" or real price is above that level. Selling the product below its raw material component amounts to nothing more than a *voluntary* income transfer from the manufacturer to the consumer of part of the superior value created.

Let us now relate the dispute among the Rishonim regarding the *me'ulah bedamim* condition to the efficiency requirement Halakhah imposes on the manufacturer. Following R. Yehonatan's line of reasoning, we must disallow the manufacturer from converting raw materials into an intermediate or final product unless the value created exceeds the value of the raw materials. Provided this condition is met, *bal tashḥit* law is not violated despite the occurrence of any amount of material waste which can be recycled. Industrial processes involving negligent material waste which cannot be recycled do, however, infringe the *bal tashḥit* interdict, as the *me'ulah bedamim* condition is violated.

The efficiency standards described above apply with equal force to the view of Meiri and those who follow his line of reasoning. In addition, this view imposes a measure of X-efficiency on the manufacturer. The X-efficiency constraint comes into play when the process becomes so wasteful that substitute inputs would enable the manufacturer to achieve his objectives at a lower cost. Notwithstanding that the process transforms the inputs into a higher value, *bal tashḥit* law is violated, as the transformation does not represent the least-cost method of achieving the given objective.

Supporting Meiri's conceptualization of the *bal tashḥit* interdict, in our view, is the following talmudic discussion at *Kiddushin* 32a:

> R. Huna tore up silk in the presence of his son Rabbah, saying: "I will go and see whether he flies into a temper or not." But perhaps he [Rabbah] would get angry, and then he [R. Huna] would violate *you shall not place an obstacle in front of the blind* [Leviticus 19:14]? [Rabbah might act disrespectfully to his father, and violate the Fifth Commandment.] He renounced his honor for him. But he [R. Huna] violated *you must not destroy its trees by putting an axe to them* [Deuteronomy 20:19]. He did it in the seam [as it could be easily resewn, there was no real damage]. Then perhaps that was why he displayed no temper? He did it when he was [already] in a temper [when he could not have noticed this, and yet he did not affront his father].

Now, R. Huna's purpose in tearing the silk garment in the presence of his son was to ascertain the degree of self-control he would maintain under provoking circumstances. Presumably, the importance of ascertaining this information exceeded for R. Huna the value of the garment. Now, if *bal tashḥit* law merely prohibits the transformation of a material substance into something else unless the transformation creates a higher value, why did R. Huna find it necessary to wait until his son was already in a fit of temper and then tear the garment only at the seam? One interpretation of R. Huna's conduct yields Meiri's least-cost caveat. Since R. Huna's objective could be achieved without *destroying* the garment, its destruction is prohibited, notwithstanding the higher value achieved thereby. R. Huna therefore waited until he could give the appearance of destroying the garment without doing so.

Another talmudic passage that appears to follow Meiri's approach to the *bal tashḥit* prohibition is recorded at *Shabbat* 129a.

> R. Ḥiyya b. Abin said in Samuel's name: If one lets blood and catches a chill, a fire is made for him even on the Tammuz [summer] solstice. A teak chair was broken for Samuel; a table [made] of juniper wood was broken up for R. Judah. A footstool was broken up for Rabbah, whereupon Abaye said to Rabbah: But you are infringing *you must not destroy. . . . you must not destroy* in respect to my own body is more important to me.

What proceeds from the above talmudic passage is the legitimacy of using furniture for fuel to avert[17] or relieve[18] physical danger and suffering. The Rishonim interpret the above passage as limiting its application to the instance where conventional fuel is not available.[19] Now, since the purpose of the fire was either to prevent or relieve a chill resulting from the bloodletting, the burning of the furniture generates a definite benefit. Undoubtedly, this health-preservation value exceeded the furniture value of the articles. Why then does *bal tashḥit* law prohibit the use of the furniture as fuel when conventional sources are available? What follows is Meiri's least-cost caveat. *Notwithstanding* the anticipated outcome of creating a higher value, the *bal tashḥit* law is violated unless the transformation represents the least-cost method of achieving the given objective. Accordingly, in the case at hand, should conventional fuel be available, furniture may not be used as fuel, despite the higher value achieved thereby.

In the light of the difficulties the above two talmudic passages present for R. Yehonatan's position, a reformulation of the position of this school of thought, as it appears to us, is in order: By the operation of the *bal tashḥit* law, a material substance having a current market value may not be transformed into something else unless the outcome is a higher value. Higher value obtains either when the outcome represents higher *market value* or when the transformation is undertaken by the producer to satisfy a personal need which is subjectively more important to him than the original value. That need is, however, not regarded as superior to the original use unless the transformation represents the least-cost method of achieving the given objective. Attaching the above caveat to the personal consumption–subjective value case follows, in our view, from several considerations. Most basically, if the least-cost condition was not imposed, the *me'ulah bedamim* condition would be almost completely emasculated. Moreover, the *me'ulah bedamim* case, according to R. Yehonatan, refers to the permissibility of constructing a bulwark from a fruit tree when the former value is higher. The biblical source of the *bal tashḥit* interdict, hence, speaks specifically of the case where the fruit tree is *objectively* more valuable as a bulwark than in its natural use. All applications of the *me'ulah bedamim* principle must therefore be, at the least, akin to the transformation of something of present use to another use of greater objective value. While denying entirely the admissibility of subjective value arising out of the needs of personal consumption is obviously rejected by the Talmud, as shown by the R. Huna incident cited above, imposing the least-cost condition establishes an affinity between the personal-consumption case and the biblical *me'ulah bedamim* case. The least-cost condition makes the transformation *objectively* necessary in order to achieve the desired personal-consumption outcome. Since the producer regards this outcome as more valuable than the original value of the material substance, the transformation can be characterized as an elevation of purpose, rather than as a destructive act.

It follows from the preceding analysis that R. Huna's character-testing objective did not confer blanket permissibility on him to rend the silk garment in his son's presence. Since promoting his objective cannot be said *objectively* to elevate the silk garment to a value higher than its present value, his use of it to test Rabbah's degree of filial respect does not legitimize tearing the garment unless it cannot be achieved by other means. Since R. Huna could have achieved his objective by waiting until his son was in an emotional state before rending the garment in the seam, causing the garment irreparable damage to promote his objective was not legitimized. Moreover, what emerges from the talmudic bloodletting cases is that the least-cost caveat is invoked even when personal need consists of the avoidance of physical pain or injury. Avoidance of possible suffering *(bal tashḥit degufa)* does not automatically legitimize the transformation of a material substance into an inferior value. It is only when averting the suffering unavoidably requires the inferior transformation that it becomes permitted.

Subsidizing Farm Income by Destroying Crops

Meiri's *me'ulah bedamim* criterion has important implications for the modern agricultural setting. For the purpose of stabilizing the price of agricultural products, governments have often adopted the policy of purchasing surplus from the farmers and then destroying it. This tactic effectively reduces supply relative to demand and hence raises price.

In the United States, farmers have formed into marketing co-ops. The operation of the orange growers' marketing co-op is typical. The co-op sets quotas for its members. Each member agrees not to market any surplus above its quota. Heavy penalties are imposed on violators. Surplus is either sold as animal fodder or is destroyed outright.

Meiri's *me'ulah bedamim* criterion puts to question any scheme, public or private, designed to subsidize farm income by means of destroying surplus crops. Moreover, programs allowing farmers to store grains in government storage bins, without requiring their release before the grains suffer physical deterioration, may similarly violate the *bal tashḥit* law. Such programs would be regarded as legitimate only if the approach represented the least-cost method of achieving the goal of subsidizing the farmer.

Mention was made earlier that members of the orange growers' marketing co-op comply with their quotas by selling surplus for animal fodder. Economic analysis is once again essential in assessing the halakhic permissibility of this practice. Using foodstuffs fit for human consumption as animal fodder is prohibited under the rubric of the *bizzuy okhelim* (degrading of food) interdict.[20] Spurning use of a Divine bounty designed for human consumption and consigning it to an animal's use reflects an ingratitude to the Creator.[21] Nonetheless, the interdict is suspended when a benefit is derived from the degraded use of the foodstuff. Illustrating the suspension of the interdict is the permissibility of drenching bread in wine and applying it as an eye salve.[22] The interdict is, however, not suspended when the sought-after benefit can be achieved by means other than degrading foodstuffs. Illustrating this distinction is the following case: Making use of a beverage to wash one's hands is only permitted if water is not available. If water is available, using the beverage for this purpose constitutes *bizzuy okhelim*.[23] In light of the above, using oranges as animal fodder to raise the price of oranges is justified only if the goal cannot be achieved more efficiently by other means.

Notwithstanding the above discussion, Meiri's point of leniency in *bizzuy okhelim* law should be noted. Consigning food fit for human consumption to animals is, in his view, prohibited only when the foodstuff was specifically prepared for a meal. Consigning the food to an animal after it was in a *state of readiness* for human consumption constitutes *bizzuy okhelim*. There is no objection to using food fit only for human consumption as animal fodder, however.[24] Therefore, oranges may be sold as animal fodder without any qualification.

Allocational Efficiency and Jewish Law

We will now turn to the halakhic perspective on the issue of allocational efficiency. Shedding light on this issue is a responsum by the Hungarian decisor R. Mosheh Sofer (1762–1839). In it he analyzes the biblical source of the *bal tashḥit* interdict and finds an apparent superfluity in the phrase *only trees which you know are not fruit trees may be destroyed and cut down.* Given the generally accepted view that in respect to biblical law, stringency must be followed even when the contemplated conduct will not as a certainty violate the law, it appears quite obvious that when we are in doubt as to whether the subject tree is a fruit tree or not, it may not be cut down. Adopting Maimonides' lenient position in the biblical case of doubt does not lessen this difficulty. Maimonides sanctions leniency in a case of doubt only when a prior status of prohibition was not established *(lo itḥazek issura).* This is not the case at hand, as Maimonides interprets the phrase *only trees which you know* to refer to a fruit tree that, because of aging, is no longer sufficiently productive to warrant halakhic characterization as a fruit tree.[25] Now, since the old fruit tree was at one time prohibited from being cut down, it does not become free of its prohibited status until it is determined as a matter of certainty that it is no longer halakhically called a fruit tree. Why then is it necessary for the Torah to stress *only trees which you know?*

Surveying all the various interpretations of the biblical source of the *bal tashḥit* interdict, R. Sofer asserts that only R. Solomon b. Isaac's (Rashi) understanding of the phrase *only trees which you know* removes the difficulty. In R. Solomon b. Isaac's view, *know* means proximity of distance rather than certainty of knowledge. What we are taught is that if the fruit tree is more *accessible* than the wild tree, the fruit tree may be used to construct the bulwark against the enemy.[26]

This difficulty leads R. Sofer to broaden the applicability of the *bal tashḥit* prohibition. Prior to the introduction of the phrase *only trees which you know, bal tashḥit* amounts to nothing more than a prohibition against *purposeless* destruction. If only *purposeless* destruction is prohibited, the *me'ulah bedamim* constraint must be given the widest possible latitude. Concretely, the cutting down of a fruit tree would be legitimized by a mere assessment that the value achieved is higher than the value of the fruit tree in its natural use. Though the estimation may be inaccurate, the *me'ulah bedamim* constraint is not violated, since only purposeless destruction is prohibited. Introduction of the phrase *only trees which you know,* however, legitimizes the cutting down of a fruit tree only where there is *certitude,* rather than mere *assessment,* that the value sought is greater than the value of the fruit tree in its natural use.

It will be recalled that Rashi interprets the clause *only trees which you know* to refer to proximity of distance. If this clause is not superfluous, R. Sofer's broadened conceptualization of the *bal tashḥit* law apparently does not follow. Nonetheless, R. Sofer proposes his thesis even according to Rashi's understanding of the *bal tashḥit* biblical passage. This follows from the fact that the Talmud records the testimony of R. Hanina that his son Shikhat died prematurely only because he cut down a date tree before it was dead.[27] Since situations involving possible danger to human life are always treated more stringently than cases involving possible violation of the law, the certitude condition, argues R. Sofer, follows even according to Rashi's interpretation of the *bal tashḥit* interdict.[28]

It appears to us that another understanding of Rashi's position is possible. Since there is nothing intrinsic in the source of the *bal tashḥit* interdict that indicates this condition, it should apply only to the cutting down of a fruit tree where the extraneous consideration of danger to life for the violator is operative.

It should be noted that R. Sofer advances yet another point of stringency in respect to the biblical source of the prohibition. Cutting down a fruit tree to achieve a higher value is legitimized only when it is not possible to uproot the tree and plant it elsewhere. When the tree can be transplanted elsewhere, it may not be transformed into something else, despite the fact that the transformation achieves a higher value than the value of the tree in its natural use.[29]

Let us now relate the certitude condition to the previous discussion regarding the nature of the *bal tashḥit* interdict. If the *bal tashḥit* interdict entails a least-cost caveat, then the certitude condition imposes a market-search requirement. Transforming a material substance having a current value into something else is legitimized only if we are certain that the production represents the least-cost method of achieving the particular objective. Since certainty obtains only after appropriate market search regarding both the input prices of competing outlets and the availability of substitutes, the certitude condition implies an allocational-efficiency responsibility.

However, the certitude condition requires a narrower market-search responsibility when *bal tashḥit* is formulated as nothing more than a prohibition against transforming a material substance into something else unless a higher value is created. Alternative means of achieving the given objective need not be considered. Provided the transformation results in the creation of a higher value, the action is legitimized. Clearly violating the certitude condition, however, is the transformation of a material substance into something else on the *speculation* that the new value will prove superior to the original value.

Efficiency Obligations Halakhah Imposes on a Businessman in a Competitive Environment

It was theorized earlier that in Rashi's view nothing intrinsic in *bal tashḥit* law indicates the imposition of the certitude condition beyond the fruit tree case. Nonetheless, Rashi may very well be in agreement that Halakhah imposes a certain degree of market-search responsibility on the *businessman* in the pursuit of his livelihood. Within a dynamic, competitive environment, gross neglect on the part of a firm to either price out its input requirements or keep abreast of new technologies and developments in the field could quickly result in its ruination. Halakhah offers no protection to a firm that becomes noncompetitive on account of inefficiency that it is capable of correcting. This is evidenced from the following talmudic discussion at *Bava Batra* 21b:

> R. Huna [d. 296] said: If a resident of an alley sets up a handmill and another resident of the alley wants to set up one next to him, the first has a right to stop him, because he can say to him, "You are interfering with my livelihood.". . .
>
> Said Ravina [d. 422] to Rava [d. 352]: May we say that R. Huna adopts the same principle as R. Judah? For we have learnt: R. Judah says that a shopkeeper should not give presents of parched corn and nuts to children, because he thus entices them to come back to him. The sages, however, allow this!—You may even say that he is in agreement with the rabbis also. For the ground on which the rabbis allowed the shopkeeper to do this was because he can say to his rival: "Just as I make presents of nuts, so you can make presents of almonds"; but in this case they would agree that the first man can say to the other: "You are interfering with my livelihood."

Given the permissibility of business promotional activities in Jewish law, in accordance with the sages' view,[30] the import of the Talmud's question, "May we say that R. Huna adopts the same principle as R. Judah?" is that R. Huna's protectionist philosophy is rooted in R. Judah's minority view and should therefore be rejected. What follows is that the distinction the Talmud draws in its rejoinder between ability to counter a rival's initiative and inability to do so, is critical in rationalizing R. Huna's protectionist philosophy. To qualify for protection against a competitive tactic, a complainant must demonstrate to the court's satisfaction that it is not within his means to counter the tactic.

Within this framework, the court would deny a complainant umbrella price protection whenever it assessed that it was within his means to reduce costs by improving the efficiency of his operation. To illustrate, suppose A and B are rival leather bag manufacturers. A sells at a profit, but his price falls below B's per-unit cost. Examination of their respective enterprises reveals, however, that A's operation is much more efficient than B's. While B tolerates slack on the production line, A does not. Similarly, B's cutting technique wastes relatively more leather than the technique A employs. Since it is within B's means to modify his operation and reduce costs, he is not entitled to umbrella price protection.

Given that correctable inefficiency halakhically invalidates a firm's petition for protection, grossly neglecting its managerial function amounts to conduct that carries with it a self-imposed poverty potential. Such conduct, according to Rashi,[31] is prohibited on the basis of the biblical verse *Save when there shall be no needy among you* (*efes ki lo yehiyeh bekha evyon*, Deuteronomy 15:4). The word *efes* is interpreted to mean "end" or "prevent," with the meaning being: "Be careful not to engage in conduct that will result in poverty for you."

By dint of this verse, salvaging one's own property takes precedence over restoring the property of one's *rebbe* (religious teacher) or father.[32] Standing at the basis of this prescribed procedure is the presumption that neglecting to restore one's own property in favor of salvaging someone else's property constitutes conduct that carries with it the potential of causing poverty for oneself.[33]

It follows that the *efes* imperative imposes some degree of responsibility to be efficient on the firm.

Technological Innovation: A Halakhic Perspective

Economic progress brings in its wake new and more efficient methods of production. Integrating these technologies into its operations often entails a large investment for the firm. Economies of scale provide a case in point. A large-scale enterprise often has inherent cost advantages over a competitor operating on a smaller scale. These advantages may include the ability to substitute capital for labor, making use of division of labor, taking advantage of bulk discounts, and reducing risk by diversifying its product line. Given these advantages, the profit-seeking larger firm can easily undersell a smaller rival and drive it out of business. Similarly, the use of new technology may allow the larger firm to price its product above cost, yet sell below the per-unit cost of a rival.

In both instances, the smaller firm is unable to become competitive by means of short-term adjustments. It is not within the resources of the small firm to achieve the improvements in efficiency inherent in large-scale operations. Similarly, it may not be profitable for a firm to introduce new technology into its operations until its presently employed plant and equipment depreciate entirely. Given that the firm is operating efficiently within its financial means, does Halakhah afford it protection against advancing technology?

Shedding light on this issue is Jewish law's attitude toward freedom of entry in the marketplace. In this regard, R. Huna's protectionist view was cited earlier. In opposition to his view, the Talmud at *Bava Batra* 21b records R. Huna b. Joshua's position:

> R. Huna b. Joshua said: "It is quite clear to me that the resident of one town can prevent the resident of another town [from establishing a competing outlet in his town]—not, however, if he pays taxes to that town—and that the resident of an alley cannot prevent another resident of the same alley [from establishing a competing outlet in his alley]." R. Huna b. Joshua then raised the question: "Can the resident of one alley prevent the resident of another [from competing with him]?" This question remains unresolved.
>
> Talmudic decisors rule in accordance with R. Huna b. Joshua's view.

What follows from this advocacy of freedom of entry is that an established firm is entitled to protection against intrusion into its territory only when the potential entrant is an out-of-town tradesman who does not pay taxes in the complainant's town. Given the moot entry status of a resident of a different alley, the Jewish court would not enjoin him from entering the complainant's alley.[34] (Rabbinic courts in Israel today have understood the modern "neighborhood" to correspond to the talmudic "alley.")[35]

While R. Huna's protectionist philosophy is apparently rejected, several rulings by the Rishonim indicate that his view is not entirely discarded.[36] This leads the Hungarian decisor R. Mosheh Sofer to reconcile the dispute between R. Huna and R. Huna b. Joshua: R. Huna's protectionist philosophy is restricted to instances where the effect of the new entry would ruin, not merely reduce, the livelihood of the established firm. The free entry advocacy of R. Huna b. Joshua, on the other hand, is confined to instances where the new entry would merely reduce the profit margin of the entrenched competitor and not deprive him of his livelihood entirely.[37]

Rabbi Mosheh Feinstein (New York, 1895–1986), one of the leading contemporary decisors, concurs with R. Sofer's requirement that the interloper deprive the established firm of its livelihood.[38]

Thus umbrella price protection is indicated only when the new technology threatens the established firm with ruination. Moreover, in the event that the threatened firm can avoid ruination by improving its efficiency within its financial constraints, protection would be denied by the Jewish court.

The more superior the new technique is, the more likely it is that it will result in the ruination of an established firm, and so the operation of the above guideline has the consequence of inhibiting the rapid integration of a superior new technology. This criterion, then, amounts to an expression of the attitude that new technology should be introduced into society in a gradual manner. While this approach sacrifices potential economic growth, it avoids the severe dislocation and social trauma often concomitant with rapid economic change. Jewish law appears, therefore, to place a premium on the development of new technology in the form of modifying and perfecting current practices, rather than devoting creative energy to the discovery of techniques radically departing from current practices.

The economic disincentive to develop vastly superior new technology inherent in the above criterion is somewhat attenuated in consideration of Dr. Warhaftig's contention that the guideline does not call for umbrella price protection when the competitors involved are located in different towns.[39]

Illustrating this principle is the "tavern case" dealt with by the decisor R. Ḥayyim Sofer (1821–1886). A and B owned taverns situated in adjacent towns. The price difference between the competitors was insignificant, and each was able to capture his local market. Now C opened a tavern in a nearby third town. Realizing that the local market was not large enough to allow him to earn a livelihood from his enterprise, C tried to expand his market by significantly undercutting A and B. Attracted by C's low prices, many customers switched their patronage from A and B to C. Protesting that their livelihood was threatened by C's pricing policy, A and B petitioned R. Sofer to require C to increase his prices to a level that would allow them to recapture their original local customers. Noting that C charged the same low prices to both his local and nonlocal patrons alike, and that ordering C to raise his prices would make it impossible for him to attract a sufficient clientele to support his livelihood, R. Sofer refused to order umbrella price protection.[40]

A variant of the above case came to the court of the Lemberg decisor R. Isaac Aaron Ettinger (1827–1891): A and B owned taverns situated in adjacent towns. Both A and B paid license fees to their respective local noblemen. While A's fee was nominal, B's fee was very high. Since the other cost conditions were similar, the license fee differential allowed A to sell his whiskey profitably at a price B could not match. B's petition for umbrella price protection was rejected by R. Isaac Aaron Ettinger. What entitles a complainant to umbrella price protection is the inevitable loss of customers to his lower-priced rivals. Inevitable loss of customers on account of price difference can only be said to occur when the competitors involved are situated in the same local area. Geographic separation, however, frees a competitor of an umbrella price obligation even according to R. Huna's protectionist view.[41]

Noting that R. Huna's protectionist stance refers to the right of a firm to exclude a rival from locating in its closed alley, a contemporary decisor, Rabbi Mordecai Jacob Breisch, posits that R. Huna would not entitle a firm to enjoin a rival from locating outside its closed alley, despite its deprivation-generating effects.[42]

In our view, the critical factor making this exception to the umbrella price rule operational is market separation of the rivals, rather than mere geographic separation on the basis of political jurisdiction.

Relating this criterion to the modern urban product market, the extent of umbrella protection afforded an individual competitor would depend on the nature of the market he serves. Standing at one end of the continuum is the firm serving its local neighborhood exclusively. Here, only rivals located inside the neighborhood are subject to the deprivation requirement. Competitors located outside the neighborhood, however, need not restrain their competitive conduct so as to ensure the viability of firms located inside the neighborhood. Clearly falling into this category are retail grocery, drug, and dry-cleaning stores. Should their market extend beyond the neighborhood area, umbrella protection would be extended up to the boundary of the relevant market. Firms dealing in wholesale trade and consumer durables provide examples of product markets extending beyond the immediate neighborhood of the firm's location.

Since a firm is not entitled to umbrella protection from firms outside its product market, a sequence of events can be imagined wherein the umbrella obligation is dropped entirely. Suppose A operates a small-scale grocery store in his local neighborhood. Now, B makes known his intent to open a supermarket in the same area. While the competitive presence of B per se would not reduce the livelihood of A below his opportunity-cost earnings, underpricing him would drive him out of business. The Jewish court would, accordingly, allow B to locate in the neighborhood but would impose an umbrella protection constraint on him. At this point in time C establishes a supermarket outside the neighborhood. Economies of scale allow C to operate his enterprise profitably and yet significantly undersell A and B. Attracted by C's low prices, many customers desert A and B in favor of C. While B is capable of avoiding ruination by matching C's prices, small-scale competitor A cannot meet the challenge and faces bankruptcy. Since A faces ruination regardless of what B will do, the Jewish court, in our view, would, at this point, remove the umbrella protection obligation from B.

Analysis of the one area of agreement between R. Huna and R. Huna b. Joshua indicates another avenue for the entry of new technology. On all accounts, a local tradesman may block the entry of a nontaxpaying, nonresident competitor. Nonetheless, should the out-of-town vendor offer for sale merchandise unobtainable locally, the community may not obstruct his entry. Heterogeneity of product, in R. Joseph Caro's view, is what is crucial in generating free trading rights. Hence, should the out-of-town merchant offer to sell a product available locally, but superior or inferior in quality, the outsider's freedom of entry is vouchsafed.[43] Loss of local profits due to the substitution effect apparently provides no grounds for excluding the nonlocal merchants.

Applying R. Caro's criterion as a guideline for the introduction of new technology results in a narrow band of protection for firms whose viability is threatened by new technology. Protection against the incursion of new technology proceeds as a definite matter only when the product embodying the new technology is identical with the product offered by established firms which make use of the old technology. The use of new technology to introduce a product that is not available in the marketplace is in stark contrast. Protectionist pleas by the horse and buggy industry, for example, to enjoin the entry of the automobile would not find sympathy in the Jewish court.

It should be noted that another school of thought regards the dispute between R. Huna and R. Huna b. Joshua as irreconcilable and rules, in accordance with R. Huna b. Joshua, to allow free entry.[44]

Noting the controversy surrounding the deprivation rule, the highest rabbinic tribunal in Israel has expressed the view that it would not enjoin a religious teacher from enrolling children from the neighborhood of a competitor. Similarly, in a case involving an alleged breach of contract between a newspaper and a publisher of Talmud, the court refused to enjoin the newspaper from entering into a distributorship agreement with a competing publisher of Talmud, notwithstanding the deprivation the arrangement would generate to the first publisher.[45]

Thus, the free entry position would allow unimpeded entry of new technology in the halakhic society.

Efficiency Obligations Halakhah Imposes on the Worker

The *bal tashḥit* law addresses not only the resource owner. Clear evidence for this is the biblical source of the prohibition which deals with the cutting down of the fruit tree of a besieged enemy. Making the above observation, R. Shneur Zalman of Lyady (1745–1813) extends the prohibition to ownerless property as well.[46] R. Ezekiel b. Judah ha-Levi Landau (Prague, 1713–1793), however, posits that the prohibition is operative only when the destruction will result in a loss for someone. Accordingly, hunting down an animal in a forest does not violate the *bal tashḥit* law. Since the forest animal generates no benefit to man while it is alive, hunting it down cannot be said to cause someone a loss.[47]

With the *bal tashḥit* law, at the very least, operative whenever destruction of a material substance will result in a loss for someone, the interdict clearly pertains to a hired worker. While the employee falls under the ambit of the *bal tashḥit* law, the market-search requirements discussed above may not fully pertain to all types of employees. Two types of employees can be identified. At one extreme stands the managerial type. He is given an objective with wide discretionary authority to carry it out. Because of the latitude inherent in his job title, this type of employee should, in our view, be bound by the same market-search requirements as his employer would be.

At the other extreme stands the nondiscretionary worker. This worker is simply given a set of instructions or orders and is expected to carry them out to the letter. Notwithstanding his nondiscretionary status, the *bal tashḥit* law prohibits the worker from accepting employment that might entail his violating of this interdict. To illustrate, if the worker is offered a job consisting of cutting down a fruit tree, he must refuse the job unless he is satisfied that the *me'ulah bedamim* condition will not be violated. We theorized earlier, as will be recalled, that the *me'ulah bedamim* condition is minimally satisfied when the production creates a higher value than the value of the raw materials used up. Since the *me'ulah bedamim* condition does not require that the production process result in profit, being employed by a profit-oriented firm should create a presumption for the worker that the *me'ulah bedamim* condition is not being infringed. This presumption is, however, upset when the production worker is employed by a non-profit-oriented firm. This circumstance obligates the worker, in our view, to ascertain for himself prior to accepting employment that the *me'ulah bedamim* condition will not be infringed.

Another variant occurs when the employer's particular need calls for the material substance to be transformed into something outside its ordinary use. Here, prior to accepting the job, the worker must ascertain both that the employer *subjectively* values the outcome more than the market value of the raw materials used up and, in addition, that the transformation represents the least-cost method of achieving the objective.

Labor Productivity and Halakhah

Another aspect of the efficiency requirement that Halakhah imposes on the worker is the prohibition of idling on the employer's time.[48] The extent to which Halakhah is concerned with this duty is indicated by the prohibition it imposes on the worker not to stand up for a rabbinic scholar while engaged in his work.[49] In a related matter, the Talmud records that Abba Ḥilkiah refused to return a greeting to a delegation of rabbinic scholars who approached him while he was engaged in his work as a day-laborer. Being employed as a day-laborer, Abba Ḥilkiah felt it was unethical on his part to interrupt his work to return a greeting to the delegation.[50]

With the objective of minimizing time lost from work, the Talmud prescribed for the day-laborer *(po'el)* an abbreviated version of the grace after meals formula as well as a shortened version of the *Amidah* prayer.[51] Eventually employers generally began to voluntarily allow their day-laborers to recite the *standard* texts prescribed for these religious duties. The consequence of this liberalization of attitude was that the right to recite the standard formulae for these religious duties became an *implicit* condition of employment for the day-laborer.[52] Once the practice of the worker's reciting the standard formulae became established, an explicit stipulation on the part of the employer to disallow it, according to R. Jeḥiel Michel Epstein, was no longer recognized.[53]

One can only surmise why there was no similar liberalization of employer attitudes that would have allowed day-laborers to stand up for rabbinic scholars. One possible explanation, in our view, involves the element of *predictability*. Since both the grace after meals and the *Amidah* prayer must be recited at predictable times, the employer can allot time for them in a manner that will not disrupt the worker's routine or concentration level. Because of this element of predictability, we may assume, employers eventually became willing to allot sufficent time for the recitation of the standardized formulae in fulfillment of these religious duties. In sharp contrast, the appearance of the rabbinic scholar on the work scene is a random event, not within the control of the employer. Conferring the worker with the privilege of standing up for a rabbinic scholar, therefore, runs the risk of disrupting his routine and concentration. A liberal attitude toward allowing workers to stand up for rabbinic scholars, therefore, did not develop.

A worker who idles on his employer's time forfeits the wages he would have earned for this time period.[54]

The prohibition of idling on the employer's time, according to R. Isaac b. Moses of Vienna (late 12th cent.–mid-13th cent.), applies only to the day-laborer *(po'el)* and not to the piece-worker *(kabbelan)*. What legally distinguishes the day-laborer from the piece-worker in Jewish law is that the former is either hired for a specified period of time or is required to work at fixed hours. The piece-worker, in contrast, is hired to perform a specific task, with no provision made regarding fixed hours. Since the piece-worker is paid for the completed job, rather than by the hour, breaking off the job whenever he so desires should be his prerogative.[55]

The above discussion has, in our view, much relevance for the contemporary American work scene. Casual observation suggests that it is common practices for desk-job employees briefly to telephone their spouses during lulls in their work routine. Unless they are explicitly prohibited from doing so, this conduct should be viewed as an implicit right. Long-distance calls and prolonged or frequent local calls provide examples of abuses of this implicit privilege and cannot be sanctioned or rationalized on the knowledge that co-workers are guilty of the practice.

Accepting "outside calls," other than those of an emergency nature, is, however, a questionable practice. Since the call may very well disrupt the employee's routine or concentration level, the employer may implicitly object to the practice. In the final analysis, the permissibility of this practice rests, in our view, on a study of the industry involved regarding both employer and supervisory personnel attitudes toward the conduct.

Another aspect of the efficiency requirement that Halakhah imposes on the worker is his obligation to exert himself on behalf of his employer with his *utmost* energy.[56]

Proceeding from the requirement of *energetic* exertion is the prohibition of the worker working at night while under contract during the day.[57] Similarly, a worker may not refuse to use his wages to provide himself with minimum nourishment, even if the money saved is used toward the support of his family.[58] Similarly, a schoolteacher may not stay up late at night or rise very early.[59] In all these instances, the conduct reduces the worker's productivity while performing his contracted work and is therefore prohibited.[60]

Conduct engaged in outside the working schedule which adversely affects the worker's productivity during working hours is prohibited, according to R. Jeḥiel Michel Epstein, only for the *po'el,* but not for the *kabbelan.* Since the *kabbelan* is paid for the completed job, rather than by the hour, conduct engaged in by him outside his work schedule which adversely affects his productivity during his working hours should present no moral issue.[61]

Dr. Warhaftig posits that the prohibition against outside night work applies only when the workday extends from sunrise to sunset. Here, outside night work makes it well-nigh impossible for the worker to recharge himself overnight and discharge his duties with vigor the following day. Nowadays, when the workday typically extends only eight hours, outside night work cannot be said to exert a debilitating effect on the performance of the worker in his daytime job.[62]

Blanket liberalization of the outside-work interdict on account of the shortened workweek, in our view, does not follow. What is crucial in determining the appropriateness of relaxing the interdict is not the amount of leisure time available to the worker today compared to previous times, but the *impact* the extra work exerts on the efficiency level of the worker in his regular job. Should the extra work reduce the worker's productivity in his regular job, the outside work should be disallowed.

If it is the common practice of members of a particular profession to accept extra work outside their regular routine, according to R. Gershom Me'Or ha-Golah (France, ca. 960–1040), the practice is thereby legitimized. What stands behind this dispensation, in our view, is that widespread practice creates an unverbalized, common set of expectations between the employer and the worker at contract time. Since outside work is a commonly accepted practice, no mention of this issue at contract time signals that it is tolerated by the employer.[63]

A variant of the preceding situation occurs when no widespread practice of accepting outside work in the subject profession can be identified, but the adverse impact of taking on the extra work does not reduce the worker's productivity below the performance level of co-workers in identical jobs. Following the above line suggests a set of conditions that point to a permissibility ruling in the latter case. Central in creating a presumption that the employer expects no more of the new worker than the performance level of established workers engaged in identical tasks is the condition that the new worker enjoys no higher compensation than his counterparts. Being hired under conditions of stable or rising demand for the product or service and under factory-utilization circumstances that do not generate expectations of diminishing returns provide examples of factors that tend to reinforce the validity of presuming that the *prevailing productivity norm* forms the employer's expectation level for the new worker. Given the presence of these presumption-validating conditions, a worker who takes on extra work that does not reduce his performance level below the prevailing productivity norm does not violate his contract with the employer. However, use of the prevailing productivity norm as the expectation level for the new worker may not be justified when all or some of the above conditions fail to obtain. For the worker, taking on extra work when the presumption-validating conditions fail to obtain constitutes a breach of contract with his employer.

Limits on the Employer's Right to Impose Productivity Standards

While the worker is prohibited from idling on the employer's time, the latter's right to assign him work for no reason other than to keep him busy during working hours is limited. An analysis of the *Torat Kohanim*'s interpretation of the prohibition in Leviticus 25:43 against working a Jewish slave rigorously *(lo tivdeh bo be-perekh)* tends to support this limitation: "You are not to tell him to warm a cup which is not wanted at all, or say to him, 'Cool this cup,' and you do not require it, or, 'Go on hoeing under this tree until I come.' "

The *lo tivdeh bo be-perekh* interdict is understood by *Torat Kohanim* to apply only to a Jewish slave but not to a hired worker.[64] Notwithstanding this legal permissibility, pious conduct, posits *Sefer ha-Ḥinukh,* requires an individual to refrain from injecting a *perekh* element in his interpersonal relations.[65]

Consideration of the various possible motives the employer may have for assigning his worker a useless task leads, in our view, to the conclusion that such conduct may at times violate halakhic norms, in addition to failing to meet expectations in the realm of extraordinary piety.

Useless work categorizes into three distinct cases. The variant posing the least serious halakhic objection occurs when the assignment is intrinsically useless but is, nevertheless, rooted in a profit motive on the part of the employer. By eliminating observed instances of idleness on the work scene, the employer hopes to foster a highly pressurized work environment, which, in turn, will result in high performance standards. Given *Torat Kohanim*'s formulation of the *perekh* interdict as consisting of intrinsically useless work, the master's possible productivity motive in no way changes the *perekh* characterization of his assignment. Since the Torah does not prohibit the employer from assigning a *perekh* task to his worker, such conduct, provided it is rooted in a profit motive, does not violate the strict letter of Halakhah.

Another variant of useless work occurs when the assignment reflects a begrudging attitude on the part of the employer. Meanness drives the employer to deny his employee a respite from his routine even when he has no work to give him. Since the respite generates no loss to the employer and at the same time affords the worker a welcome break in his routine, filling the gap in the worker's time by assigning him a useless task amounts to Sodomitic behavior on the part of the employer. To be sure, it would be difficult for the worker to obtain a judicial remedy, for the employer could easily defend himself by claiming either that the assignment was, in fact, useful and needed, or alternatively, that it was rooted in a profit motive.

A third variant occurs when the motive behind the useless assignment is the employer's desire to demoralize the worker by impressing upon him the power and leverage he has over him by dint of his employee status. Assigning the worker a menial task makes the power motive behind the useless work obvious. Given the employer's demoralizing intent, such conduct clearly violates the prohibition of *ona'at devarim*. Moreover, since the benefit the employer derives from the useless work consists of a forbidden pleasure, i.e., enjoying the feeling of power by demeaning an underling, the behavior is Sodomitic as well.

· 7
Speculation as Treated in Jewish Law

Modern financial markets offer opportunities for speculation in a variety of sophisticated instruments. Speculative activity presents two major areas of concern for Jewish law. First, some of the available investment vehicles may violate aspects of *ribbit* and contract law. The second issue relates to the legitimacy of speculation as a profession.

Investment Vehicles and Jewish Law

In this section we will explore investment in corporate bonds and certain forms of preferred stock in light of *ribbit* law. We will then turn to an examination of a very common feature of investment vehicles today, the margin agreement, in light of both *ribbit* and Jewish contract law. Finally, we will turn to a discussion of the techinque of selling short a financial security in light of an aspect of *ribbit* law, called the *se'ah be'se'ah* interdict.

Corporate Bonds

Inter-Jewish loan transactions are prohibited from calling for an interest premium.[1] Invoking a variety of legal principles, many authorities suspend the *ribbit* interdict when the majority-interest ownership of either the lending or the borrowing entity is non-Jewish.[2]

Independent of the nature of the majority interest, some authorities suspend the *ribbit* interdict when the *borrower* is a corporation. Standing at the basis of this point of leniency is the limited-liability feature of the corporate entity. Since the corporate bondholder enjoys only a lien on the business assets of the corporation but no lien on the personal assets of the shareowners, the shareowners do not assume the halakhic status of debtors.[3] This point of leniency is, however, sharply disputed by many other authorities. Holding a personal lien on the debtor *(shi'abud ha-guf),* according to the latter school of thought, is not critical in creating the halakhic status of debtor.[4]

Preferred Stock

Preferred stock is a type of security issued by a corporation. It has claims or rights ahead of common stock, but after all bonds. Typically, the holder of preferred stock enjoys no right to elect the directors of the corporation.

The nonvoting feature of the preferred-stock certificate effectively confers an *iska* relationship between this security holder and the common-stock shareowners of the corporation. *Iska* is a special type of business partnership which Halakhah regulates. The distinctive feature of *iska* is that the financier plays no operational or managerial role in the business enterprise.[5]

One of the regulations *iska* is subject to is an obligation on the part of the silent partner to provide the active partner with compensation for the term of the *iska* for his labor services.[6] This fee, called *sekhar tirḥa,* must be set at the very outset of the agreement. Provided it is set at the very outset, the *sekhar tirḥa* requirement may be satisfied with a nominal fee.[7]

The *sekhar tirḥa* requirement follows from an examination of the legal status of the *iska.* Given that responsibility for accidental loss is what differentiates the legal status of the debtor from that of the bailee, Halakhah confers a loan-deposit status on the *iska* arrangement. The portion of the capital transfer that the active partner assumes responsibility for takes on the character of a debt, while the remaining portion takes on the character of a deposit. Now, since the agreement calls for the active partner to invest the funds for the benefit of both himself and his financier, performing his managerial function gratis amounts to a disguised interest premium as a precondition for receiving the loan.[8]

What follows from the above rationale of the *sekhar tirḥa* requirement is its inapplicability to preferred stock. Unlike the talmudic *iska,* which calls for prorating in the event of loss, no sharing of losses is called for in the preferred-stock case. Instead, the preferred shareholder enjoys a *limited* claim against the common shareholder in the form of a prior claim to the assets of the corporation in the event of liquidation. Since the preferred shareholder's original investment assumes *entirely* the character of a loan, the *sekhar tirḥa* requirement should be dispensed with.

Another regulation the talmudic *iska* is subject to is the symmetrical profit-loss constraint. An *iska* agreement calling for the financier to reap more than 50 percent of the profits and absorb less than 50 percent of the losses is prohibited. A nonsymmetrical division of profits and losses favoring the financier is "near to profit and far from loss" and hence violates *avak ribbit* law (i.e., *ribbit* prohibitions proscribed by dint of rabbinic enactment, as opposed to pentateuchal law).[9]

Analysis of the typical provisions of the preferred-stock certificate indicates a possible violation of the "near to profit and far from loss" prohibition.

In respect to earnings potential, the preferred shareholder apparently enjoys an advantage over the common shareowner because of his lower exposure to risk. Many provisions in a preferred-stock certificate are designed to reduce risk to the purchaser in relation to the risk carried by the holder of common stock. Preferred stock usually has priority with regard to earnings and assets. Two provisions designed to prevent the undermining of these preferred-stock priorities are often found. The first states that, without the consent of the holders of the preferred stock, there can be no subsequent sale of securities having a prior or equal claim on earnings. The second provision seeks to hold earnings in the firm. It requires a minimum level of retained earnings before common-stock dividends are permitted to be distributed. In order to assure the availability of liquid assets that may be converted into cash for the payment of dividends, the maintenance of a minimum current ratio of assets to liabilities may also be required.

Another advantage of preferred stock is its cumulative dividend provision. The cumulative feature requires that all preferred dividends must be paid before common dividends may be paid.

In respect to losses, the preferred shareholder enjoys an advantage in the form of a prior claim on the assets of the corporation in the event of liquidation.

The advantages described above, it should be noted, work to characterize a capital transfer as "near to profit and far from loss" only from the vantage point of the risk-averter. For the risk-seeker, however, trading off low risk exposure in the event of loss and a chance to earn a fixed dividend for the prospect of earnings considerably above the fixed dividend represent a welcome opportunity. Whether preferred stock violates the "near to profit and far from loss" prohibition depends therefore upon one's attitude toward risk. Since preferred stock is not *intrinsically* "near to profit and far from loss," it cannot be compared to an asymmetrical profit-loss arrangement and therefore does not violate *avak ribbit* law.

One variety of preferred stock, called a nonvoting, participating preferred stock, may, however, present a problem for *avak ribbit* law. This security calls for the stated preferred dividend to be paid first. Revenues permitting, income is then allocated to common-stock dividends *up* to an amount equal to the preferred dividend. Any remaining income is then shared *equally* between the common and the preferred shareowners. When the risk-protection feature combines with the participation provision described above, the preferred-stock certificate effectively creates a relationship between this security holder and the common shareholder that is "near to profit and far from loss" from the standpoint of the latter.

The preceding discussion demonstrates that investment in certain securities issued by a business enterprise whose majority-ownership interest is Jewish violates the *avak ribbit* law. These include debt instruments and nonvoting, participating preferred stock.

While the form of these investment vehicles violates the *ribbit* law, the terms they call for can be achieved within the framework of Jewish law by means of the *hetter iska* mechanism. What follows is a general description of this mechanism and its application to the investment instruments discussed above.

Hetter Iska

The *hetter iska* mechanism essentially makes it possible for a capital transfer to take on the form of the talmudic *iska*. To this basic structure the *hetter iska* document adds various clauses to insure the financier's capital against loss and to increase the probability he will earn a return on his investment.

To insure his principal, the financier (A) may attach conditions to the *iska* and stipulate that if they are not met, responsibility for losses devolves entirely on the managing partner (B). Specifications of the types of investments B may enter into with the *iska* and the security measures he must adopt for the *iska* income are examples of conditions A might want to attach to the *iska*. Since fulfillment of the conditions is feasible, and B may avert full responsibility for losses by adhering to them, the arrangement is not regarded, from A's standpoint, as "near to profit and far from loss."[10] Thus, the setting of conditions that are either impossible to fulfill or are not usually undertaken by business people is not permitted. Such stipulations on the part of A constitute a subterfuge to collect *ribbit* and are therefore forbidden.[11] On similar grounds, Rabbi Abraham Y. Karelitz (Israel, 1878–1953) forbids the financier to stipulate conditions that do not in any way relate to the *iska* arrangement. A violation of the *avak ribbit* interdict on this account, for example, would be a stipulation forbidding B to eat grapes for the entire term of the *iska* agreement and calling for his assumption of full responsibility for losses should he violate this condition.[12]

Stipulations of the permissible variety, it should be noted, do not impede the managing partner's flexibility to depart from the conditions. Since his intention is to seize upon opportunities for greater profit, his departure from the stipulation is not morally objectionable as long as he faces the consequences of failure.[13]

Another clause that may be inserted into the *iska* agreement for the purpose of securing A's principal is the stipulation that B's claim for loss will be accepted only if it is corroborated by the testimony of designated witnesses (C and D).[14] Disqualifying the testimony of all witnesses except C and D is permissible, according to R. David b. Samuel ha-Levi (Poland, 1586–1667), as long as the designated individuals are known to be at least slightly conversant with the *iska* affair.[15]

To increase the chances of earning a profit on the capital transfer, A may stipulate that B's claim regarding the amount of profits from the *iska* will be accepted only by means of his solemn oath *(shevuah ḥamurah)*. Insofar as B can always maintain accurate records of the *iska* transactions and take the solemn oath in regard to the profits realized, the solemn oath element of the agreement does not characterize it, from the standpoint of A, as "near to profit and far from loss."[16]

Further to increase his chances of earning a profit, A may stipulate that payment of an agreed-to sum, referred to as *sekhar hitpashrut*, would relieve B of both his solemn oath obligation and any further monetary obligation should A's share in the profits exceed this sum. Similarly, the *iska* agreement may call for A to receive a fixed sum as his share in the profits, with the proviso that B may reduce this payment by any amount by taking a solemn oath that A's share in the profit did not amount to this sum.[17] To increase the probability that A will actually realize the *sekhar hitpashrut*, the *iska* agreement may call for the attachment of all B's business profits to the *iska* venture.[18] This clause effectively precludes B from opting for the solemn oath unless A's prorated share in the profits of *all* B's ventures earned during the *iska* term fell short of the *sekhar hitpashrut* sum.

What makes the *hetter iska* arrangement attractive from the standpoint of the financier is the likelihood that profits will not be verified by means of the solemn oath and losses will not be validated by means of designated witnesses. Likely rejection of the oath follows from the assumption that a Jew will typically spurn an oath even when he is asked to confirm a matter he knows to be true. Likely nonfulfillment of the designated-witness clause follows from the fact that these witnesses are not the actual managers of the *iska* and therefore will probably not have the precise knowledge to testify with certainty about a loss. Nonfulfillment of the profit-loss reporting clauses triggers the restoration-of-principal and *sekhar hitpashrut* requirements.

The mechanism outlined above finds ready application to any debt instrument. Instead of structuring the bond instrument as a loan, *hetter iska* would characterize the investment as a capital transfer that A confers on the corporation for *iska* purposes. Next, a symmetrical profit-loss arrangement would be called for along with a specified *sekhar tirḥa* for the corporation. The document would call for the reporting of profits and losses only by means of the solemn-oath and designated-witness methods, respectively. Nonfulfillment of the designated-witness clause triggers an obligation on the part of the corporation to restore to A his original capital transfer. Nonfulfillment of the solemn-oath clause triggers the *sekhar hitpashrut* payment. The *sekhar hitpashrut* would be set equal to the desired interest rate.

The same procedure recommends itself for the nonvoting, participating preferred-stock certificate, with the simplification that the *sekhar tirḥa* clause, as discussed above, may be dispensed with.

Application of this mechanism to the investment vehicles discussed above presents several difficulties however. Validating profits by means of a solemn oath and verifying losses by means of designated witnesses amounts to an impossibility within the framework of the modern business organization. What is recorded as profits and losses in the firm's financial report often reflects the transactions conducted by numerous people. Some transactions may escape recording altogether. As the firm grows in size and in complexity of organizational structure, the proportion of its transactions of which any single individual has first-hand knowledge diminishes markedly. In the final analysis, the accuracy of the various items that go into the profit-loss statement reflects the honesty and efficiency of those who directly and indirectly furnished the data. As a result, it would be inappropriate to enforce the solemn-oath clause in the *hetter iska* agreement. Given the *first-hand testimony* intent of this clause, administering the oath to a representative of the firm amounts to causing him to make a false oath. Now, if the investor cannot demand the solemn oath, the *sekhar hitpashrut* clause will not be triggered.

The same line of reasoning renders the designated-witness clause nugatory. Nonfulfillment of the designated-witness clause triggers a requirement on the part of the active partner to restore the principal only when verification of losses through this means is at least slightly possible. Should verification of losses by means of designated witnesses be *entirely impossible,* nonfulfillment of this condition does not automatically generate the obligation to restore the principal.[19]

The aforementioned points to a need to replace the solemn-oath and designated-witness clauses with another procedure for reporting profits and losses. Ideally, to be both valid and practical the procedure would have to be both feasible to fulfill and sufficiently onerous as to generate an expectation that the business firm will opt to reject it and thereby trigger the *sekhar hitpashrut* payment and/or the restoration-of-principal requirement. With the above objective in mind, the investor could stipulate that he will accept the profit-loss statement only by means of the *accounting* methods he specifies. Since standard accounting practice tolerates considerable diversity with respect to such matters as inventory valuation, the treatment of depreciation, and the amount of reserves set aside for bad debts, it may be possible for the investor to come up with procedures more favorable to him than the procedures the firm customarily employs. Refusal on the part of the firm to report the profit-loss in the specified manner triggers the *sekhar hitpashrut* payment and/or the restoration-of-principal requirement.

Another approach to the above dilemma would be for the investor to stipulate that the financial statement of the firm will be accepted as the reporting method for profits and losses only if verified by an independent audit. Given the feasibility of carrying out this condition, the *sekhar hitpashrut* and restoration-of-principal clauses do not make the agreement "near to profit and far from loss."

The latter approach is, however, of no practical value in the event the corporation is publicly held. Since the public corporation is, in any case, required by law to independently certify its financial statement, the investor's insistence that profits be verified by means of an audit is entirely consistent with routine corporate practice. With the investor's insistence on an audit an entirely superfluous request, the *sekhar hitpashrut* clause will not be triggered.

Margin Agreements

Securities are often purchased on margin rather than on a cash basis. A margin purchase entails the partial payment of the value of a stock, with the outstanding balance extended as a loan by the brokerage house. To illustrate, Goldenglick purchases 1,000 shares of Oaf Corporation stock at $10 a share. Tehome, the brokerage house that arranges the transaction, allows Goldenglick to make the purchase at 50 percent margin. The agreement calls for Goldenglick to pay only $5,000 as a down payment, with the remaining $5,000 of the purchasing price extended to him as a loan. Goldenglick is charged 15 percent per annum interest on this loan. For the purpose of securing the loan as well as collecting the interest due, Goldenglick is required to maintain a margin acount with Tehome. In accordance with New York Stock Exchange rules, Goldenglick signs a hypothecation agreement, pledging the 1,000 Oaf shares as collateral for the loan. Should the loan become undercollaterized because of a decline in the price of Oaf stock, Goldenglick agrees to add the necessary funds to the margin account to meet the required balance. If he fails to answer the margin call, Tehome is allowed to sell the hypothecated shares in order to recover the balance of the loan and interest due them.

One questionable aspect of this transaction from the point of view of Jewish law is the interest premium it calls for. Loan transactions among Jews may not involve an interest premium. Accordingly, if the majority ownership of Tehome is Jewish, Goldenglick's agreement to pay interest on his margin purchase violates Judaism's *ribbit* law.[20]

The *hetter iska* arrangement described above immediately suggests itself as a means of overcoming the *ribbit* problem in the margin agreement. Adopting the conventional *hetter iska* arrangement for the margin agreement presents several difficulties, however. One difficulty relates to the designated-witness clause. Nonfulfillment of the designated-witness method of reporting losses triggers an obligation on the part of the active partner to restore the principal only when the failure of the *iska* is not self-evident. With the *iska* here consisting of the margin stock purchase, its performance is a matter of public record. Tehome cannot therefore claim nonfulfillment of the designated-witness clause as a means of securing restoration of the principal should the stock decline in value. The problem in regard to the solemn-oath clause is similar. Since the performance of the *iska* is a matter of public knowledge, calling for profit to be reported by means of a solemn oath amounts to Tehome's insisting that Goldenglick take an oath in regard to matters it already has knowledge of. Forcing an individual to take an oath attesting to facts already known to the party demanding the oath is forbidden by many authorities as an oath taken "in vain."[21] Now, if the solemn oath cannot be imposed, then the *sekhar hitpashrut* in lieu of the oath cannot be demanded.

Inclusion of a clause in the *hetter iska* document calling for the attachment of all Goldenglick's business profits to the *iska* venture recommends itself as a means of validating the designated-witness clause. With the profits of all Goldenglick's ventures attached to the margin stock purchase at hand, a plea of self-evident loss would be admissible only if it were common knowledge that all Goldenglick's business dealings during the *iska* term had failed. With the performance of the *iska* a matter of public record, the attachment clause does not, however, validate the solemn-oath clause.

Incorporating Rabbi Meir Arak's substitution clause[22] in the *hetter iska* document provides, in our view, an approach to validating the solemn-oath clause for the margin stock purchase. Mechanically, the *hetter iska* agreement would call for Goldenglick to substitute another business asset for the capital sum extended him. What this accomplishes is to make the substitute asset the *iska* capital instead of the margin stock purchase. To ensure its desired return, Tehome could stipulate that Goldenglick's report regarding the instrument he selected for the *iska* along with its performance would be accepted only by means of his solemn oath. Goldenglick would, however, be given the option of freeing himself of the solemn-oath obligation by the payment of the *sekhar hitpashrut* sum.

The adequacy of the above solution hinges upon the predictability that Goldenglick will not opt for the solemn oath and in consequence the *sekhar hitpashrut* clause will be invoked. Confidence in the outcome is in turn predicated on the presumption that Goldenglick abjures oaths and will avoid swearing even when he knows that his testimony is not perjurious. Oath aversion, as Rabbi Shiloh Raphael has pointed out, should, however, not be taken for granted today.[23] Given this element of uncertainty, Tehome may very well fear that Goldenglick would invest the substitute capital in some very secure, yet relatively low yielding instrument and opt to affirm this by means of the solemn oath. This scenario will, of course, result in Tehome's not realizing its desired return.

The foregoing approach may be salvaged, in our view, by introducing the following variation in design: Instead of conferring Goldenglick with complete flexibility in his choice of an investment instrument for the *iska,* the agreement could *specify* the instrument. Payment of an agreed-upon sum *(sekhar hitpashrut),* however, frees Goldenglick from the restricted-investment clause. With the aim of increasing the likelihood that Goldenglick will opt to pay the fee to achieve investment flexibility, Tehome could purposely select an instrument it feels would be unattractive from Goldenglick's standpoint. If Goldenglick's investment needs, for example, place a premium on liquidity and safety, the vehicle Tehome would impose on him would be characteristically high-risk and nonliquid. The instrument Tehome selects for Goldenglick's *iska* would, however, have to be on its *recommended list.* Without this constraint, Tehome's selection amounts to no more than a subterfuge to circumvent the *ribbit* law.

In order to structure the *hetter iska* document for the margin stock purchase in the nonconventional manner described above, Tehome is required to relinquish some of the control it might otherwise want to exert over the designated-substitute *iska* investment. Tehome, for instance, may not insist that the designated-substitute *iska* investment be acquired through its auspices. *Iska,* as will be recalled, takes on a part-loan, part-deposit character. The brokerage fee Tehome earns by executing the *iska* investment amounts, therefore, to an inducement Goldenglick must pay to receive his loan. Moreover, execution of the commission-generating *iska* transaction through Goldenglick's own initiative amounts to an *avak ribbit* violation unless Goldenglick customarily used Tehome's brokerage service in the past, before the *iska* was entered into.[24]

A variation of the substitution-clause approach suggests itself for solving the *ribbit* problem inherent in the margin stock purchase case. Instead of designating the substitute *iska* investment, Tehome could allow the substitute instrument to be open-ended. To ensure its desired return, Tehome could play on Goldenglick's strong preference for independent decision-making. Toward this end, Tehome would require Goldenglick to declare his selection and reserve for itself the right to determine when the investment should be liquidated. Payment of an agreed-upon sum would, however, vest decision-making authority regarding the *iska* entirely in the hands of Goldenglick. Without undertaking to monitor the investment closely, the above reserve clause would not only be unpalatable from Goldenglick's standpoint but might amount to a subterfuge to evade the *ribbit* law. Tehome's assumption of a monitoring responsibility in respect to the *iska,* as it appears to us, effectively removes its silent-partner status in the *iska* venture. With Tehome regarded as an *active* partner in the *iska* venture, the *sekhar hitpashrut* clause is entirely legitimized. Since the reserve clause effectively transforms the *iska* agreement into a nonregulated form of business partnership, the symmetrical profit-loss division clause and the *sekhar tirḥa* requirement, discussed earlier, can be dispensed with.

Asmakhta

Another issue the margin stock purchase presents for Jewish law is the maintenance-of-margin clause. For an obligation to become legally binding in Jewish law, two critical tests must be met. First, the commitment must be made with deliberate and perfect intent *(gemirat da'at)*. Second, the commitment must generate reliance *(semikhat da'at)* on the part of the party it was made to.[25] Both these related conditions may be absent in a transaction which projects the finalization of an obligation into the future, becoming operative only upon the fulfillment of a specific condition. A transaction containing these elements is referred to in the talmudic literature as *asmakhta*. With the obligation becoming operative only when a condition is fulfilled, the person obligating himself may very well rely on the probability that the condition will not be fulfilled, and thus that he will not become obligated. Because the presumption of perfect intent is lacking, the presumption that the commitment generated reliance is equally lacking.

A transaction characterized as *asmakhta* does not confer title.[26] With the *asmakhta* transaction regarded as invalid *ab initio,* a transfer made subsequent to the fulfillment of the condition is characteristically involuntary and hence a form of robbery.[27]

The affinity of the maintenance-of-margin agreement to the *asmakhta* transaction is readily apparent. Fully expecting the price of the security to move in the desired direction, the customer undertakes to add funds to his margin account should an adverse price movement necessitate it. In the final analysis, the halakhic validity of the maintenance-of-margin agreement hinges on whether it satisfies the various criteria Rishonim have proposed as to what constitutes an *asmakhta* undertaking.

One widely held view, espoused by R. Solomon b. Isaac (Troyes, 1040–1105) and others, takes the position that *asmakhta* obtains only when the obligating condition is within the power of the individual making the stipulation *(toleh be-da'at atsmo)*. When the obligating condition is, however, not within the power of the individual making the stipulation *(toleh be-da'at aḥerim)*, the commitment is fully valid.[28]

An illustration of *asmakhta* is the case discussed in the Mishnah at *Bava Batra* 10:15. A pays part of his debt to his creditor (B) and deposits the note of indebtedness with a third party (C), instructing him to surrender the note to B if he does not pay the balance by a certain date. Nonfulfillment of the condition does not, according to R. Judah, obligate A to pay the *full* debt to B. A's undertaking to pay the full debt after he had already paid an installment is presumed to lack perfect intent. It was merely an expression of good faith to demonstrate his sincere hope of paying the balance on time.

Another instance of *asmakhta* discussed in the Talmud is the following: Renting a field as a tenant farmer, A agrees to pay a percentage of the crop as rent and obligates himself to pay 1,000 zuz (i.e., a huge penalty) should he be guilty of allowing the land to lie fallow. Since it is both A's intent and within his power to cultivate the field, he presumably does not anticipate that the penalty clause will become operative. A's undertaking to pay the huge penalty in the event of neglect on his part is therefore not regarded as having been made unreservedly. Consequently, in the event of neglect, A is liable only for the loss the landlord sustains, estimated on the field's potential productivity.[29]

Why games of chance are not regarded as *asmakhta* is explained by R. Solomon b. Isaac (Rashi) on the basis of his *toleh be-da'at atsmo* criterion. Since the outcome of the game does not depend on the skill of either player, each participant unreservedly makes up his mind to confer ownership of his contribution to the pot on his opponent should he lose.[30]

Following this line of reasoning, R. Isaac b. Sheshet Perfet (Spain, 1326–1408) legitimized a cargo insurance contract. Since the safe arrival of the cargo at its destination is not an event subject to the insurer's control, the latter, by dint of the premium he receives from the policy holder, unreservedly undertakes to make good on any loss which might occur.[31]

Toleh be-da'at atsmo is taken very broadly by the disciples of the Rashba (early 14th cent.). Partial control over the obligating condition suffices, according to this school of thought, to confer an *asmakhta* designation on a conditional commitment. This is shown by the following ruling: A gives B money to buy wine for him at a certain relatively low price. B stipulates that should he fail to make the purchase at the stipulated price, he will make good A's loss. Since wine is available for sale, B's stipulation must be regarded as partly within his control. Nonetheless, the stipulation is not entirely within B's power, as his success obviously depends upon the willingness of others to sell him the wine at the stipulated price. Given the availability of wine for sale, the disciples of the Rashba regard B's undertaking to make good on A's loss as an *asmakhta*.[32] Disputing the above ruling, Naḥmanides (Spain, 1194–1270) and others regard the above conditional commitment as an *asmakhta* only if B formulates his commitment in terms of his own actions, but not if it is formulated in terms of the seller. Accordingly, if B stipulates, "I will make good on A's loss if the sellers do not sell me the wine at a particular price," the conditional commitment would not take on the character of *asmakhta*.[33]

Disputing Rashi's criterion, R. Jacob Tam (Ramerupt, ca. 1100–1171) regards the salient feature of *asmakhta* to consist of the circumstance where it is evident that both parties desire the completion of the underlying agreement and the conditional commitment is given merely as an assurance of good faith. These elements are clearly present in the debtor-assurance case, discussed above. Both parties desire that the balance should be paid on time. As a matter of good faith, however, the debor (B) instructs a third party (C) to return the note of indebtedness to the creditor (A), should he (B) fail to pay the balance on time. In constrast, a mutually desired outcome in a game of chance is impossible, as one player will win at the expense of the other. The undertaking each player makes in the event he loses the game is therefore not merely an assurance of good faith but part and parcel of each player's primary intention: Each player desires to win the stakes and unreservedly commits himself to the agreed-upon liability should he lose the game.[34]

R. Solomon b. Abraham Adret (Spain, ca. 1235–ca. 1310) advances still another criterion as to what constitutes *asmakhta*. Formulating an undertaking in terms of a penalty, in R. Adret's view, is what makes a conditional commitment an instance of *asmakhta*. The cases of the debtor and the tenant farmer discussed earlier both entail a conditional penalty and for this reason take on an *asmakhta* character. A conditional agreement calling for consequences for the principals should specific conditions obtain is, however, not regarded as *asmakhta*.[35]

The broadest conceptualization of *asmakhta* is that of Maimonides (Egypt, 1135–1204). Any conditional obligation, including a game of chance,[36] is in his view an *asmakhta*. For an undertaking to be free of an *asmakhta* designation, it must incorporate the phrase "from now" *(me-akhshav)*. The operation of this distinction is illustrated by the following case: A conditionally confers ownership of his house on B, stipulating to B, "if I do not return to this location by such and such date, my house is yours from now." Without the use of the phrase "from now," B's undertaking is regarded as *asmakhta*, as the commitment is conditional. Use of the phrase "from now," however, counteracts *asmakhta*. If A did not unreservedly commit himself to confer title to his house on B in the event he fails to return by the date he stipulated, he would not have conferred the conditional ownership from the time of the stipulation.[37]

Another means of counteracting *asmakhta*, according to Maimonides, is for A to reinforce his conditional commitment by performing a symbolic act (i.e., *kinyan sudar*) in the presence of a Jewish court *(kanu b'vet din)*. In addition to the symbolic act, A must entrust to this court the rights he has in the property he wishes to transfer conditionally to B. What the latter accomplishes is to make the court rather than A the principal who confers title on B in the event the obligating condition is triggered.[38]

Maintenance of Margin and Asmakhta

Let us now set the conventional maintenance-of-margin agreement against the various criteria of *asmakhta* described above. The element working to free the margin purchaser's undertaking from an *asmakhta* character is the triggering of the obligation by an adverse price move, an event completely outside the control of the customer. *Toleh be-da'at aḥerim*, as will be recalled, frees a transaction from an *asmakhta* designation according to Rashi and those who follow his reasoning.

Another favorable feature of the maintenance-of-margin agreement is that it amounts to nothing more than an assurance on the part of the customer that the collateral he provided the brokerage house should not fall below the capital sum extended him. Since the customer's conditional obligation does not take on a penalty character, the stipulation does not fall in the ambit of R. Adret's *asmakhta* criterion.

The maintenance-of-margin agreement does, however, apparently meet both R. Tam's and Maimonides' *asmakhta* criteria.

Unlike a game of chance, where one player's gain is predicated on the other player's loss, a successful margin stock purchase does not inevitably entail a loss for the other party to the agreement, i.e., the brokerage house: If the price of the stock rises, the customer's gain consists of an unrealized capital gain as well as a right to withdraw some portion of the margin deposit he originally posted. Since the brokerage house may not legally, in any case, make use of the funds in a customer's margin account, the latter's withdrawal privilege resulting from the price advance of the margin stock purchase cannot be viewed as a loss or disadvantage from the standpoint of the brokerage house. Should the stock decline, the customer would be obligated to add funds to the margin account, but again no consequences are generated for the brokerage house. Given that perfect resolve to undertake an obligation in the event of nonfulfillment of a condition is evident only if nonfulfillment of that condition entails a *loss* to the other principal of the agreement, the maintenance-of-margin agreement may halakhically amount to no more than a good faith assurance on the part of the customer. Fully expecting the stock price to advance, with no consequence generated for the brokerage house, the customer obligates himself to add funds to the margin account should his expectations fail to materialize.

Selling Short and Asmakhta

Affinity to a game of chance does apply to some short-sale cases. Selling short entails the selling of a security that the seller does not own. An investor would employ this technique if he anticipated a decline in the price of the security. To effect a short sale for a customer, a brokerage house would arrange a stock loan for him.

One source of a stock loan is the account of the brokerage house itself. Here, an upward price movement signals an unrealized gain for the brokerage house and an obligation on the part of the customer to add funds to his margin account. A downward price movement, on the other hand, generates an unrealized loss for the brokerage house and an unrealized gain for the customer. With one principal gaining at the expense of the other, the maintenance-of-margin agreement for this type of short sale does not fall into the ambit of R. Tam's *asmakhta* criterion.

Most frequently, the source of the stock loan in a short sale is the margin account of another customer of the brokerage house. This type of short sale differs markedly from a game of chance. In a game of chance, one player's gain is always at the other's expense. In contrast, the short seller's gain in this type of short sale is never the loss of the brokerage house, but rather of a third party, who is not party to the maintenance-of-margin agreement between the brokerage house and the short seller. Perhaps R. Tam frees an undertaking of an *asmakhta* character only when A's gain is *directly* predicated on the loss of another party to the agreement (B). Should A's gain entail only an inevitable loss to a third party (C), A's undertaking amounts only to an expression of good will and hence must be characterized as *asmakhta*. Moreover, since the most frequent source of a stock loan is the margin account of another customer of the brokerage house, it may not be unreasonable to assert that the typical short-seller presumes that the source of the stock loan is not the brokerage house that arranges the short sale for him. Following this assumption, any short sale, regardless of the source of the stock loan, should be regarded as merely an undertaking in good faith and, hence, takes on, according to R. Tam, an *asmakhta* character.

Remedy for Asmakhta

While Maimonides' *asmakhta* criterion clearly calls for the maintenance-of-margin agreement to be halakhically invalid, a ready remedy is available. This remedy is the inclusion of a "from now" clause in the maintenance-of-margin agreement. This approach suffers, however, from several practical difficulties. To confer the brokerage house with title "from now" to all the monies the customer might be called upon to add to the margin account requires advance knowledge as to what this maximum sum would be. Advance calculation of this maximum sum is well-nigh impossible, as it depends on the price variation of the stock, the term of the investment, and the interest rate the brokerage house desires to charge over this term. While the maximum price variation is known in advance in instances of margin purchases, the latter two elements are variables not subject even to approximate advance calculation. Closer approximation of the desired figure is, however, achieved by setting a time interval for the investment, beyond which it must be liquidated. All that is needed now to arrive at a precise figure for this sum is a mutual agreement between the customer and the brokerage house regarding the maximum return the latter will demand for the capital sum it extends the customer over the term of the investment. Since the maximum variation of the stock price in the short sale cannot be determined in advance, what is needed is an additional clause in the form of a maximum termination price for the investment.

The maintenance-of-margin agreement, as will be recalled, fell squarely into R. Tam's *asmakhta* criterion. Counteracting the *asmakhta* character of this agreement by means of the "from now" clause would, however, not be valid according to R. Tam. Maimonides' contention that "from now" alone counteracts *asmakhta* is disputed by R. Tam and those who follow his reasoning. *Asmakhta,* according to this school of thought, is counteracted when the undertaking is validated by means of *kinyan sudar* in an authoritative Jewish court *(bet din ḥashuv).*[39] If the undertaking was not validated by means of *sudar* in an authoritative Jewish court, inclusion of a "from now" clause would generally[40] not counteract *asmakhta.*[41]

While the *asmakhta* character of the maintenance-of-margin agreement can be validated, according to R. Tam, by means of *kinyan sudar* in an authoritative Jewish court, involvement of the Jewish court in this transaction may prove both impractical and unattractive from the standpoint of the brokerage house.

Application of the approach the "Spanish scholars" used to counteract *asmakhta* suggests, in our view, a *generally* acceptable method of halakhically freeing the maintenance-of-margin agreement from an *asmakhta* designation. The basic elements of this approach are: first, the maximum liability to which the customer may be subject over the term of the investment is calculated; the customer then unconditionally obligates himself to pay this amount to the brokerage house immediately. In a separate document, the brokerage house waives its right to collect any amount of the debt up to the entire debt *in certain agreed-upon eventualities.* This waiver is made "from now" and is validated by means of *sudar.* The eventualities, of course, relate to the price movement of the stock. If the eventualities, i.e., the specified price movements, do not occur, the customer's debt obligation is not cancelled and the brokerage house collects the debt in accordance with its specified schedule of payments.[42]

Selling Short and the Ribbit Interdict

Selling short entails the selling of a security that the seller does not own. An investor would employ this technique if he anticipated a decline in the price of the security. To illustrate, suppose Goldenglick anticipated a sharp decline in the price of Amalgamated Lighting Systems stock (ALS), but did not own shares in this company. Selling ALS stock short provides Goldenglick with a mechanism for capitalizing on his intuition. Mechanically, a brokerage house (Tehome) will arrange a stock loan of the desired number of ALS shares (e.g., 1,000 shares) for Goldenglick. Initially, Goldenglick will be required to deposit as security with Tehome the value of the 1,000 ALS shares. Serving as the measure of this value is the price of the shares at the time the short sale was executed. It is the practice in short selling for the loan to be secured at all times by approximately 100 percent of the market value of the stock. Accordingly, if ALS moves up by even a few points, Goldenglick will be required to deposit more cash with Tehome. Should ALS stock decline in price, however, Tehome will be required to credit Goldenglick's account accordingly. Anticipating a decline in the price of ALS stock, Goldenglick plans to buy in the 1,000 shares at a price that would leave him with a profit above the security value of his account at Tehome.

New York Stock Exchange rules allow either party to a stock loan to terminate the transaction by notice. Upon notice, the stock must be returned to the lender within five business days.

Given the stock-loan character of the short-sale transaction, this investment vehicle may conflict with an aspect of the *ribbit* law, called the *se'ah be'se'ah* interdict.

Out of fear that the market value of the commodity may increase at the time of repayment, the sages prohibited commodity loans in kind *(se'ah be'se'ah)*. Such a transaction violates one of the rabbinic extensions of the *ribbit* law, called *avak ribbit*.[43] The prohibited agreement places the creditor at a disadvantage: Should the commodity appreciate at the time of repayment, the debt may not be discharged by means of payment in kind. Instead, a cash payment is required, with the debtor's obligation set equal to the value the commodity had at the time the loan was entered into. Depreciation of the commodity, on the other hand, disallows a cash payment. Here, payment must be made in kind.[44]

Investigation of the sources of the stock loan in the short sale of a security surprisingly multiplies the number of instances in which this transaction might violate the *se'ah be'se'ah* interdict.

One source of the stock loan might be the brokerage house (Tehome). If the majority-interest ownership in Tehome is Jewish, the stock loan violates the *se'ah be'se'ah* interdict.

In most cases the source of the stock loan would be the margin account of another customer of Tehome. To illustrate, Silberglick purchases 1,000 shares of ASL stock through Tehome on margin. A margin purchase entails the partial payment of the value of the stock, with the outstanding balance extended as a loan by the brokerage house. Prior to opening a margin account, NYSE rules require the customer to sign a hypothecation agreement, pledging any stock purchased as collateral for the loan. The stock is left with the broker in street name, and the broker is authorized to sell the shares should the loan become undercollaterized. Customers who sign margin agreements often sign loan-consent forms, authorizing the brokerage house to lend their hypothecated securities to other customers. Notwithstanding the consent form, NYSE rules do not allow a brokerage house to borrow securities from a margin account unless the margin customer's debit balance (amount owed the brokerage house) equals or exceeds the value of the security.

Given the likelihood that a margin account will be the source of the security loan, the *se'ah be'se'ah* issue is not only a concern for the short seller but of concern to the margin stock *purchaser* as well.

Since the *se'ah be'se'ah* transaction is prohibited only because of the *avak ribbit* law, the sages suspended their interdict under certain conditions. Examination of these conditions points to a possible means of freeing the short sale of the *se'ah be'se'ah* problem.

Yaẓa ha-Sha'ar

One circumstance that may suspend the *se'ah be'se'ah* interdict applies when the commodity involved trades at a definite market price *(yaẓa ha-sha'ar)*. With repayment in kind possible at any time, the borrower is regarded as being capable of discharging his debt by making the requisite commodity purchase before it appreciates above its value at the time of the loan.[45]

Legitimacy is given to this mechanism even when the borrower lacks the necessary cash to make the commodity purchase. Though lacking cash the borrower is regarded as capable of securing the necessary commodity purchase by establishing a line of credit.[46]

Yaẓa ha-sha'ar validates a *se'ah be'se'ah* transaction, according to Maimonides, only if both parties are aware that the loan commodity is traded at a definite price when they enter into their *se'ah be'se'ah* transaction.[47] Unawareness creates a presumption of intention to make repayment at such time that the commodity will appreciate in value.[48]

While R. Asher b. Jeḥiel (Germany, ca. 1250–1327) does not mention the awareness condition, and apparently does not require it at all,[49] the condition finds general acceptance among talmudic decisors. Adopting the most stringent position, R. David b. Samuel ha-Levi (Poland, 1586–1667), for instance, prohibits repayment in kind for the appreciated commodity in the absence of awareness.[50] Departing from the above line, R. Yonathan Eybeschuetz (Prague, 1695–1764) prohibits repayment in kind only when the "ignorant" party was the lender.[51] R. Shabbetai b. Meir ha-Kohen (Poland, 1621–1662) takes a lenient view. Awareness, in his view, is required in the first instance to validate the *yaẓa ha-sha'ar* mechanism. Its complete absence does not, however, prohibit repayment in kind with the appreciated commodity.[52]

Since securities are actively traded in the financial markets, the *yaẓa ha-sha'ar* mechanism apparently provides a ready means of freeing the short sale from the *se'ah be'se'ah* problems. The interpretation of *yaẓa ha-sha'ar* by the Rishonim, however, casts doubt on the applicability of this approach to the problem at hand.

Clarification by the Rishonim of the concept of *yaẓa ha-sha'ar* is found in connection with the futures contract: A's commitment to deliver a commodity to B over a period of time in exchange for the latter's prepayment of the order is normally prohibited. Out of the fear that the market price of the commodity might advance over the delivery period, the commitment to deliver is viewed as a disguised interest premium in exchange for the prepayment. Accepting prepayment for future delivery when the market price of the commodity was established *(yaẓa ha-sha'ar)* at the time the contract was entered into is permitted. With the commodity available at the stipulated price, A is regarded as capable of making *immediate* delivery to his client, before the commodity has a chance to appreciate in value. Subsequent delivery of the commodity at a time when it is traded at a higher price is therefore not regarded as a disguised interest premium.[53]

What constitutes *yaẓa ha-sha'ar* in the futures contract case is defined by R. Isaac b. Jacob Alfasi (Algeria, 1013–1103) as a price which has stability for two or three months.[54] R. Ḥananel b. Hushi'el (North Africa, 11th cent.) and R. Yom Tov Ishbili (Spain, ca. 1250–1330) also define *yaẓa ha-sha'ar* in terms of price stability, though without mention of a specific time.[55]

A wider range of price fluctuation for the applicability of the *yaẓa ha-sha'ar* condition may be derived from R. Moses Isserles' validation of a futures contract entered into in a small town which based the delivery price on the market price of the commodity in that small town.[56] Why the above ruling implies a wider band of fluctuation for yaẓa ha-sha'ar is seen from R. Nissim b. Abraham Gerondi's (Barcelona, 1310–1375) comparison of the behavior of price in a city versus a small-town market. Relative stability, according to R. Gerondi, is what differentiates the price of a commodity traded in a city market from the price of the same commodity traded in a small-town market. In a small town supply will usually become more and more scarce relative to demand with the passage of time. With upward pressure always building on the price of a commodity in a small town, the price cannot be expected to be stable for long. In sharp contrast, supply relative to demand remains stable for prolonged periods of time in a huge city commodity market. Relative price stability for a commodity traded in a city market can therefore be expected.[57]

Thus, *yaẓa ha-sha'ar* is not a validating mechanism unless the *stability* test is met. Given the *daily* volatility of the prices of financial instruments, it is doubtful whether *yaẓa ha-sha'ar* is operative in any of the financial markets today.

Technological advances in transportation and communication have considerably widened the marketplace. Hardly any price, as a result, is free from the possibility of sudden change on account of the vicissitudes of aggregate supply-and-demand factors. Noting this phenomenon, Rabbi Basri posits that all prices today, with the exception of those under government control, are inherently unstable and should be regarded as not being well defined.[58]

Yesh Lo

While the *yaẓa ha-sha'ar* mechanism may not work to free the short sale from the *se'ah be'se'ah* prohibition, another approach suggests itself. A commodity loan in kind when the debtor is in possession *(yesh lo)* of the commodity he borrows at the time the loan was entered into is permitted. To illustrate, suppose the loan consisted of a ton of wheat and the debtor had this amount of wheat in his possession at the time he took the loan. In such a case, the amount of wheat the borrower has is regarded as if it were given immediately to the lender as payment at the time the loan was entered into. Any appreciation of the commodity subsequent to the loan is therefore regarded as having occurred while the commodity was in the domain of the lender.[59]

The *yesh lo* leniency in *se'ah be'se'ah* law extends even to the case where the quantity of the commodity in the debtor's possession at the time of the loan amounts to only a small portion of the commodity loan. Since the *se'ah be'se'ah* interdict is prohibited only because of the *avak ribbit* law, the *yesh lo* loophole is valid even when its rationale is not entirely applicable.[60]

When a *se'ah be'se'ah* transaction is legitimized by means of the *yesh lo* mechanism, both parties must be aware that the debtor has some amount of the loan commodity at the time the transaction was entered into and that this circumstance is what halakhically validates their agreement. The awareness condition is, however, not indispensable. Its absence allows the debtor to return the loan commodity, even if it appreciated in value.[61]

The *yesh lo* caveat yields a ready halakhic mechanism to legitimize one type of short sale, called "selling against the box." In this short sale, the seller is in actual possession of the security he is selling short. Hedging provides the motivation for such a transaction. To illustrate, Goldenglick purchases 1,000 shares of ASL stock at $50 a share. The stock subsequently climbs to $70 a share. At this point Goldenglick fears a decline in price. Not certain of his judgment, however, he prefers to hedge rather than make an outright sale. He therefore hedges by short selling 1,000 shares of ASL stock. If the stock falls, his gain on the short side exactly offsets the loss on his long stock, disregarding taxes and commissions. If the stock goes up, his gain on his long stock offsets his loss on the short sale. This strategy allows Goldenglick to lock in on the $20 price increase of his ASL stock.

With the investor in possession of the stock he borrows in selling against the box, all that is needed to validate the transaction halakhically is the awareness condition. This condition, as discussed above, is, however, not indispensable.

For the short sale not against the box, avoidance of violation of the *se'ah be se'ah* prohibition requires the investor to acquire at least one share of the stock he intends to sell short before he executes the short sale. In addition, the awareness condition is, of course, required.

Speculative Activity as Treated in Jewish Law

Throughout the ages, various elements of society have looked askance at speculative activity. Attacks against speculation have centered around two concerns. One concern is the impact speculative trading has on the consumers of the product involved. In addition, it has been objected that speculation is a sterile activity akin to gambling, and has no socially redeeming value. What attitude does Judaism take toward speculation with respect to the above points of concern?

The Prohibition Against Hoarding

Judaism's concern for the adverse impact of speculation has taken the form of a prohibition against hoarding essential commodities. The prohibition was operative in Eretz Israel as well as in any local community where the majority of the inhabitants were Jewish. Specifically, the interdict disallows market purchases of essential commodities in excess of normal consumption needs.[62] Hoarders of essential commodities are regarded by the Talmud in the same contemptuous light as those who lend money on interest.[63] Producers, though, may normally withhold any part of their crop from market sale. Nevertheless, during a period of famine, producers too are subject to a quota in regard to the amount of produce they may store. The quota allows the producer to store no more than one year's supply of foodstuffs for himself and his family.[64]

Judaism's diatribe against hoarders of essential commodities apparently runs diametrically counter to the favorable regard modern economic theory has for the speculator in the agricultural sector. Grain is harvested in the autumn but must be made to last all year if privation is to be avoided. This desirable state of affairs is brought about through the action of speculators. Driven by the profit motive, speculators purchase some of the autumn crop while it is cheap, withhold it in storage, and sell it later when the price has risen. While this action increases the autumn grain price, at the same time it increases the supply of grain in the spring and lowers its price. Hence, speculation in agricultural products performs the socially desirable service of equalizing consumption over the entire year. Brisk competition among speculators works to reduce the return for their services to the minimum cost necessary to bring forth their efforts.

Recognition of the revolutionary changes in agricultural production and distribution since talmudic times (end of 5th cent.) leads, however, to a ready reconciliation of talmudic law with economic theory.

In talmudic times agricultural production served a predominantly local market.[65] Producers themselves were apparently capable of handling the function of supplying the market for the entire year.[66] Evidence of this is the fact that the talmudic sages found no social value in the warehousing and wholesale functions per se. Middlemen dealing in essential commodities in Eretz Israel were, accordingly, prohibited from earning a markup unless they worked to *process* the products they purchased.[67] To be sure, the social value of the retailer was recognized by the talmudic sages, and thus the retailer was permitted to include an allowance for his toil and effort in his selling-cost markup. The retailer's total markup could not, however, exceed 20%.[68]

In sharp contrast, agricultural production today is mainly for the regional, national, or international market. Warehousing and distribution are clearly differentiated from production. Without middlemen performing the former two functions, the economic viability of the agricultural sector could not be assured.

Efficient distribution of stockpiles intended for the national and international markets is greatly facilitated by the existence of an organized commodity exchange. By fostering liquidity, active trading in these markets encourages people to undertake such fuctions as warehousing and distribution. Moreover, wide participation in commodity trading reduces the price volatility that would otherwise occur on account of market thinness.

What the aforementioned indicates, in our view, is that the talmudic interdict against hoarding of essential commodities does not apply to trading in the modern organized commodity exchanges.

Speculative purchases of essential commodities in present-day local markets may, however, violate the talmudic interdict against hoarding. Since the stockpile is intended for the local market, the speculative purchase cannot be said to directly or indirectly enhance the efficiency of its distribution to its intended customers. In fact, this speculative purchase generates the talmudic concern for shortages and their accompanying deprivation effect on consumers. To be sure, the integration of the local market with the wider markets makes bottlenecks short-lived; nonetheless, the short-term effect could be quite disconcerting.

Speculation and Gambling

Those who disapprove of speculation, as noted above, have often equated this activity with gambling. Let us now turn to a consideration of both the Halakhah's view of gambling and whether the assimilation of gambling with speculation has any validity from a halakhic standpoint.

Judaism regards gambling as an immoral pursuit.[69] The intensity of the halakhic condemnation of this vice is shown by the fact that professional gamblers are disqualified from serving either as judges[70] or as witnesses.[71] This disqualification obtains, however, only when the individual has no profession other than gambling.[72]

The basis for the Halakhah's objection to gambling is that this activity does not contribute to the welfare of society.[73] However, the concern for social welfare can break the nexus between gambling and at least certain forms of speculative activity.

Gambling certainly makes no contribution to the social welfare. It involves no more than a sterile transfer of money or goods. Creating no output, gambling nevertheless absorbs time and resources. Gains from this activity represent nothing more than a reward for assuming an artificial risk.

Unlike gambling, many forms of speculative activity have socially useful purposes.

The Social Usefulness of the Stock and Bond Markets

One of the most common forms of speculative activity today is trading in stocks and bonds on the New York and American Stock Exchanges. These exchanges promote vital economic functions. What follows is a description of these functions and the role the speculator plays in enhancing these functions.

Business units raise capital for the purpose of financing plant, equipment, tools, and inventory by issuing securities in the primary, or over-the-counter, market. Stock exchanges provide a secondary market for these securities. Sales in the primary market are facilitated by a dependable secondary market in which any holder of a security can *resell* his stock or bond at a fair price. Moreover, the auction nature of the securities markets provides an efficient method for allocating funds among competing sectors in a free economy. Since widespread and informed participation in the stock exchanges enhances the markets' capital-formation and capital-rationing functions, speculative activity in these markets contributes to their efficient working.

The Social Usefulness of the Futures Markets

Another popular form of speculation is trading in the futures market. A futures contract entails a commitment to deliver or receive a certain quantity of a commodity, such as wheat or cotton, at some stated time in the future.

The futures markets provide a mechanism for the transfer of risks associated with economic activity. To illustrate, Cornglick, a grain-elevator operator, purchases 5,000 bushels of wheat from local farmers at $3.00 a bushel in November and would like to sell the wheat in June at $3.10 a bushel. The anticipated $0.10 profit per bushel represents for Cornglick a fair return on his warehousing service. Fearful that the price of wheat may decline in June, Cornglick wants to hedge against this eventuality. He is prepared to forgo some part of his return so that he can transfer the risk of a downward price movement to someone else. Toward this end, Cornglick enters into a futures contract with a speculator (Mehlglick). Cornglick commits himself to deliver 5,000 bushels of wheat in June at $3.09 a bushel. Regardless of what the price of wheat may be in June, Cornglick has locked in a $0.09 return per bushel for his warehousing service. Mehlglick absorbs the entire risk of price fluctuation. Since Mehlglick is not in the warehouse business, he will sell the wheat Cornglick delivers to him in June at the spot price of wheat at that time. Should the spot price at that time be higher than $3.09, Mehlglick will have profited from his speculation. A lower spot price at that time will, however, translate into a loss for him.

What the aforementioned has demonstrated is that the futures market provides a mechanism where individuals engaged in legitimate economic activities have an opportunity to transfer unwanted risks to others.

Risk transfer, as Telser has pointed out, can be accomplished without an organized futures market. Merchants wanting to avoid the price risk of holding inventories need only enter into forward contracts calling for deferred delivery of their stocks. Forward contracts of the same maturity are, however, not perfect substitutes for each other, as the identity of the parties involved is essential in judging the safety and reliability of the agreement. By creating a highly liquid trade instrument, the organized futures market significantly enhances the risk-transfer function, otherwise accomplished by means of the forward contract.

Liquidity is promoted by the organized futures market by both the nature of its rules and the operation of its clearing house.

An organized futures market confines trades to those who are its members. This limitation has definite advantages. Each member has a proprietary interest in the survival of the exchange and in the value of his membership. He wants the other members to be reliable. Members who trust each other can trade more quickly at a lower cost. Members may also trade as agents of nonmembers. Since they are liable to the exchange for trades they carry out for nonmembers, exchange members will only accept accounts for those in whom they have confidence. All these considerations work to increase the volume of the exchange's transactions, promoting liquidity.

The clearing house of the exchange also works to promote liquidity. A member who buys futures contracts obtains liabilities of the clearing house that are offset by the sale of the futures contracts that constitute the assets of the clearing house. In terms of the quantities of futures contracts bought and sold, the assets and liabilities of the clearing house are always equal. Thus, the clearing house is to its members as a bank is to its depositors and debtors. Since the clearing house of the exchange backs each futures contract, liquidity is promoted.

Telser asserts that the futures contract acquires the same advantages over the forward contract as trade conducted with the aid of money has over barter. Because a futures contract has some of the attributes of money, it becomes suitable as a temporary abode of purchasing power. It is this aspect of a futures contract that is relevant to hedging. An inventory holder can sell futures in a liquid market so that he can choose the best time for making final sales of his inventory with little effect on the current futures price. Similarly, one who has made commitments to sell the commodity can buy futures contracts as a temporary substitute for the purchases of the actual commodities and also have little effect on the price.[74]

Demonstrating the social utility of the futures market does not, however, automatically confer redeeming value to all the participants in this market. We need only point out that while every hedger must find himself a speculator in order to make a futures contract, the converse is not true. All that it takes for a futures contract to be entered into is the meeting in the marketplace of two individuals who entertain contrary opinions regarding the future direction of the market. Does a futures contract between two speculators entail any social value? Telser's analysis of the liquidity function of the futures market gives an affirmative reply to this question. By promoting liquidity, and limiting price volatility which is rooted in market thinness, speculator participation in the futures market actually enhances the risk-transfer function of this market. With the expected volatility inherent in market thinness working to increase the unwillingness to absorb the hedger's risk, speculator participation in the futures market, other things equal, reduces the cost of risk transfer.

A more sympathetic view of the social value of speculation in the futures market emerges from Working's research on the economics of the futures market. Risk transfer, Working contends, is not the only function of the futures market. Most commercial hedging, his research indicates, is a form of arbitrage. The grain merchant's spot purchase of wheat and simultaneous short sale of an equivalent contract on the futures market is not usually based on a fear that the absolute price of wheat will decline, but rather on an expectation of a favorable change in the relation between spot and future prices. Believing that the spot price is low relative to the futures price, and anticipating an advance in the spot premium, the grain merchant buys spot wheat and sells short the futures contract.

Working's analysis leads him to conclude that the basic function of the futures market has been to promote an economically desirable adjustment of commodity stocks, reducing price fluctuation. By merely supplying simultaneous quotations applying to various subsequent dates, futures trading makes the holder of stocks sharply aware of any losses that must be expected from carrying unnecessary stocks in times of relative shortage of supplies, and provides good prospects for returns for storage over periods when there is a surplus to be carried. For Working, the social function of speculation is the improvement in the accuracy with which market prices reflect informed opinion.[75]

Stock Index Futures and Options

In recent years a proliferation of new investment vehicles have been introduced into the futures market. The social value of these new instruments, purportedly, has been to provide new and better means of hedging for individuals engaged in legitimate economic activity. New financial instruments in the futures market may, however, have the effect of both duplicating hedging instruments and diverting resources away from capital formation. A brief description of stock index futures and option contracts on this index will serve to focus on these issues.

Stock index futures, introduced in February 1982, are futures contracts based on broad stock market indexes. The Standard and Poor 500 Stock Futures Index, for example, is based on the value of five hundred representative stocks listed in the New York, American, and regional stock exchanges. To calculate the value of a stock index futures contract, the value of the stock index at the time of purchase or sale is multiplied by $500. Stock index futures are traded on a quarterly delivery-month cycle of March, June, September, and December.

Stock index futures represent an agreement to buy or sell the market value of stocks included in a specific market index. Unlike traditional futures contracts, which are based on an underlying specific product, stock index futures represent only a *hypothetical* portfolio of stocks. Because no underlying product or financial security is involved, stock index futures do not entail the physical delivery of securities. Instead, when the stock index futures contract is entered into, an initial margin must be deposited. Net gains or losses resulting from any change in the market value of the contract are calculated daily and credited to, or debited against, the account.

Stock index futures offer traders and investors, for the first time, an effective means of separating specific stock risk from general market risk. Specific stock risk relates to factors that affect a particular company and industry, while broad market risk involves considerations that have an impact on the whole market. Index futures offer traders new opportunities to profit from volatility by correctly determining market trends.

Most importantly, stock index futures contracts represent an innovative *hedging* tool for portfolio managers. Managers concerned that their stock portfolios will drop in value because of an anticipated market decline can hedge against this eventuality by selling stock index futures contracts. This short hedge helps protect against losses without liquidating stock positions, as any overall decline in the market will produce an offsetting gain on their short futures position. Conversely, portfolio managers who expect a market rally, but have not yet identified their stock selections, can buy stock index futures contracts. If the market does rally, the gains on the long futures position help offset the increased costs of purchasing the stocks at the higher prices.

A major attraction of futures trading is leverage. Buyers and sellers of futures contracts are required to make only a nominal margin deposit—in effect, a security deposit—to assure that adequate funds will be available to cover any day-to-day losses on their futures position. A profit on a futures transaction can thus provide a substantial percentage return on capital placed at risk. Leverage carries with it, however, equal potential for losses greater than the original margin posted.

Options

The option contract was developed as a means of limiting potential losses for participants in the futures market. Options take the form of either a call or a put. The buyer of a call option obtains the right—but with no obligation—to purchase a stock index futures contract at a specified price at any time during the life of the option. In contrast, the buyer of a put option obtains the right to sell a stock index futures contract at a specified price at any time during the life of the option. Expiration dates of options coincide with the last day of trading in the underlying futures contract. Unlike futures participants, whose potential losses are unlimited, the maximum loss the options buyer can incur is the price paid for the option.

Given the limited-risk feature described above, the options market is more attractive to the speculator than the stock index futures market. The significance of options futures for the owner or manager of a portfolio of stocks may, however, not extend beyond the availability of yet another hedging tool. If the options market primarily serves speculators, having only a marginal significance for those who want to transfer economic risk, the social value of this market is immediately put into question. By drawing resources away from the stock index futures market, the option futures thin out the former market and makes it work less efficiently. An additional drain on resources can be expected to occur by the arbitrage activity that usually springs up when a new financial instrument related to an existing market is introduced. Finally, resources devoted to speculation in option futures are at the expense of real capital formation.

Conclusion

The preceding discussion points to the need for financial innovation to be regulated in the halakhic society. Before a new financial futures instrument could be introduced, it would have to meet a social value test. The essence of social value for a financial futures instrument is, as discussed above, the risk-transfer function. If the new financial instrument promises only to serve as an attractive tool for speculators, its introduction would be denied. Trading in financial instruments which primarily serve speculators may fall afoul of Halakhah's disapprobation of gambling.

Glossary of Economic and Legal Terms

AGGREGATE SPENDING. Total spending for consumption, investment, and government goods and services. It increases as the national income increases.

ALLOCATIONAL EFFICIENCY. The optimal search for and selection of the inputs which would best promote the production objectives of the firm.

ARBITRAGE. The act of buying a currency or other commodity in one market and simultaneously selling it in another market at a higher price. Arbitrage is an important force in eliminating the price discrepancy, thereby making markets function more efficiently.

ASSET. A physical property or intangible right that has economic value.

AUTOMATIC STABILIZERS. Government spending, taxation, and transfer programs which automatically (i.e., without legislative action) act to increase aggregate spending during economic downturns and decrease aggregate spending during periods of prosperity.

BASIS (COMMODITY). The difference between the spot price and the futures price.

BOND. A corporation's promise to pay the holder a fixed sum of money at the specified maturity date and some other fixed amount of interest every year up to the date of maturity.

CAPITAL FORMATION. The creation of physical productive facilities, such as buildings, tools, equipment, and roads.

CAVEAT EMPTOR. Latin for "Let the buyer beware."

CENTRAL BANK. A government-established agency (in the United States, the Federal Reserve System) responsible for control over the nation's money supply and credit conditions, and for the supervision of commercial banks.

CLEARANCE SALE. A retail sale of merchandise at reduced prices to clear out seasonal stocks, overstocked, or slow moving items.

CLEARING HOUSE. An organization that guarantees fulfillment of futures contracts or options contracts.

COMMON STOCK. Represents proportional ownership of an incorporated enterprise. Common stockholders are the residual claimants for earnings and assets after all holders of debt and preferred stocks have received their contractual payments.

CONSUMER PRICE INDEX (CPI). A measure of inflation based on a market basket of goods and services purchased by urban households.

CUMULATIVE PREFERRED STOCK. Shares requiring that before common stock dividends may be paid, preferred dividends must be paid not only for the dividend period in question but also for all previous periods in which no preferred dividends were paid.

DEMAND–PULL INFLATION. A rise in prices believed to occur because consumers and investors with rising incomes increase their wants and compete for a relatively limited supply of available goods.

DIMINISHING RETURNS. An economic principle which states that if equal amounts of one variable input are added, while all other inputs are kept fixed, total product may increase, but after some point the additions to total product will begin to decrease.

DIVISION OF LABOR. The separating of an overall task into separate tasks so that each worker involved performs only a small part of the overall task. Division of labor usually results in increased efficiency.

ECONOMIES OF SCALE. The reduction in unit cost as a producer makes larger quantities of a product. Such reduction results from a decreasing marginal cost due to increasing specialization, use of capital equipment, and the benefit of quantity purchasing.

EFFICIENCY. Achieving maximum output value from a given set of inputs, or achieving the desired output with minimum cost of inputs.

EFFLUENT FEE. A charge levied on firms or consumers based on their rate of discharge of pollutants.

ESCALATOR CLAUSE. Clauses in long-term contracts that provide for automatic adjustment for general price increases (inflation).

FIAT MONEY. Money decreed as such by the government. It has little value as a commodity, but it maintains its value as a medium of exchange because people believe the issuer will back it and limit its issuance.

FISCAL POLICY. Government's efforts to use its spending, taxing, and debt-issuing authority to smooth out the business cycle and maintain full employment without inflation. It can occur through variations in the spending and tax rate of the government for the purpose of affecting the level of economic activity, employment, and price level.

FOREIGN EXCHANGE RATE. The rate, or price, at which one country's currency is exchanged for the currency of another country.

FORWARD CONTRACT. Risk-shifting technique by which farmers sell specified quantities of product or livestock at the current price for future delivery.

FRACTIONAL RESERVE RULE. A regulation in modern banking systems whereby a commercial bank is legally required to keep a specified fraction of its deposits in the form of deposits with the central bank (or in vault cash).

FREE RIDER. Anyone who receives benefits from a good or service without having to pay for them.

FUTURES CONTRACT. Instrument which requires the delivery of a specified quantity of a specified commodity at a specified future date.

HEDGING. Buying one security and selling another in such a way as to produce a riskless portfolio.

HYPOTHECATION AGREEMENT. The pledging of securities as collateral for a loan by delivering the securities without giving up title to them.

INCOME REDISTRIBUTION. Change in the aggregate amount of income which is enjoyed by each of several identified blocs of income recipients.

INFRASTRUCTURE. The foundation underlying a nation's economy. It includes transportation and communication systems, power facilities, and other public services.

INPUT. Anything that goes into the production of goods and services. Inputs consist of land, labor, capital, and entrepreneurial ability.

LIABILITY. Debt owed by an individual or organization.

LIQUIDITY. Ease with which an investment can be converted into cash for approximately its original cost plus its expected accrued interest.

LOSS LEADERS. Retail goods priced at less than cost so as to attract customers who will then buy other, regularly priced merchandise.

MACROECONOMICS. Analysis dealing with the behavior of the economy as a whole in respect to output, income, prices, and unemployment.

MARGIN ACCOUNT. Customer's brokerage "credit" account which allows the broker to borrow money from a financial institution on behalf of the customer. Investor deposits money or securities to meet the margin requirement.

MARGIN REQUIREMENT. Percentage of the purchase price of stocks, bonds, or commodities that a customer must pay when there is borrowing for the purchase.

MONETARY POLICY. The policy of the central bank in exercising its control over money, interest rates, and credit conditions.

MONEY SUPPLY. The "narrowly defined" money supply (M1) consists of coins, paper currency, plus all demand or checking deposits.

MULTIPLIER. The number of times by which the change in total income exceeds the size of the expenditure change that brought it about.

NATURAL MONOPOLY. A firm or industry whose average cost per unit of production falls sharply over the entire range of its output. Thus, a single firm, a monopoly, can supply the industry output more efficiently than can multiple firms.

NEGATIVE EXTERNALITY. An adverse side-effect of economic activity. Economic theory assumes that the perpetrator will not take the detriment into account unless society's property rights require him to do so.

NET WORTH. The excess of assets over liabilities.

NOMINAL INTEREST RATE. The percentage by which the money the borrower pays back exceeds the money that he borrowed, making no adjustment for any fall in the purchasing power of this money that results from inflation.

NOMINAL PROFIT RATE. The profit rate unadjusted for inflation.

OPPORTUNITY COST. The dollar amount that would be derived from the employment of a resource in its best alternative use.

OPTIONS. A privilege sold by one party to another which offers the buyer the right to buy (call) or sell (put) a security at an agreed-upon price during a specified period or on a specified date.

OUTPUT. The goods and services which a firm produces.

PARTICIPATING PREFERRED STOCK. Preferred stock that may pay an extra dividend increment if the issuing firm is especially profitable.

PREFERRED STOCK. Shares whose indicated dividends and liquidation values must be paid before common shareowners receive any dividends or liquidation payments.

PRIMARY FINANCIAL MARKET. Market involving the creation and issuance of new securities, mortgages, and other claims to wealth. It is the market for initial sales of securities.

PROGRESSIVE TAX. A tax whose rate rises as income increases. Thus those with high incomes pay a greater percentage of their incomes as tax than do those with lower incomes.

PURE PUBLIC GOOD. Commodity or service whose benefits are not depleted by an additional user and for which it is generally difficult or impossible to exclude people from its benefits, even if they are unwilling to pay for it.

REAL ASSETS. Assets which include direct ownership of land, buildings, machinery, inventory, and precious metals.

REAL INTEREST RATE. The percentage increase in purchasing power that the borrower pays to the lender for the privilege of borrowing. It indicates the increased ability to purchase goods and services that the lender earns.

REAL PROFIT RATE. The profit rate adjusted for inflation.

REAL RETURN. A return adjusted for changes in the price level. If the nominal rate of return were 11 percent, a 3 percent inflation rate would reduce the real return to 8 percent.

RECISION RIGHT. The legal right to cancel an agreement.

SECONDARY FINANCIAL MARKET. Market involving the transfer of existing securities from old investors to new investors. It is the market for already issued securities.

SELLING SHORT. The act of selling a security that is not owned. Securities belonging to someone else are borrowed and sold. When the short-seller covers, equivalent securities are bought back and restored to the original owner.

SHADOW PRICE. Price imputed to a good, service, or resource that is not priced by the marketplace or that is incorrectly priced by the market.

SHORT SALE AGAINST THE BOX. The short-selling of stock which is owned; usually employed as a tax device for extending the date of realizing a gain.

SPOT PRICE. The price of a commodity quoted for immediate sale and delivery in a commodity exchange.

STREET NAME. Securities held in customer accounts at brokerage houses, but registered in the firm's name.

SUPPLY-SIDE ECONOMICS. A view emphasizing policy measures to affect aggregate supply or potential output.

THIN MARKET. A market in which volume is low and transactions relatively infrequent.

UMBRELLA PRICING. A pricing policy of a firm entailing the setting of price sufficiently high so as to ensure the viability of less efficient rivals.

UNREALIZED GAIN (LOSS). The appreciation (depreciation) of the market value of an asset which the owner has not, however, realized in the form of an actual sale.

X–EFFICIENCY. The optimal arrangement, combination, and coordination of the inputs available to the firm for the purpose of best promoting its production objective.

Glossary of Hebrew and Aramaic Terms

ASMAKHTA. An agreement which either lacks the presumption of firm resolve on the part of the obligator or fails to generate a presumption of reliance on the part of the party to whom the commitment was made.

AVAK RIBBIT. Lit. "the dust of interest." Violations of Jewish law's prohibition against interest by virtue of rabbinical, as opposed to pentateuchal, decree.

BAL TASHḤIT. The prohibition against the wasteful destruction of a material substance.

BARAITA. A teaching or a tradition of the Tannaim that was excluded from the Mishnah and incorporated in a later collection compiled by R. Hiyya and R. Oshaiah.

BIZZUY OKHELIM. The prohibition against degrading foodstuffs.

DEI MAḤSORO. Lit. "sufficient for his need." Judaism's charity obligation, consisting of the duty, means permitting, to provide for the entire needs of the poor, both physical and psychological.

GAON, GEONIM. Formal title of the heads of the academies of Sura and Pumbedita in Babylonia from the end of the sixth to the end of the eleventh century.

GEMIRAT DA'AT. A firm resolve to conclude an arrangement at hand.

GENEVAT DA'AT. Conduct designed to deceive or create a false impression.

HALAKHAH. Jewish law.

HETTER ISKA. An elaborate form of the *iska* business partnership wherein conditions are attached with the design of protecting the financier from absorbing a loss on his principal and increasing the probability that he will realize a profit as well. These clauses are structured in such a manner that *ribbit* law is not violated.

ISKA. A form of business partnership consisting of an active partner and a financier who is a silent partner. In the absence of stipulation, half the capital transfer takes on the legal character of a loan, while the remaining half takes on the character of a pledge. The *iska* arrangement may violate *ribbit* law and is therefore subject to regulation.

KABBELAN. A pieceworker hired to perform a specific task, with no provisions regarding fixed hours.

KEHILLAH. Autonomous Jewish community.

KINYAN. Acquisition of legal rights by means of the performance of a symbolic act.

KINYAN SUDAR. A legal form of acquisition of objects or confirmation of agreements, executed by the handing of a scarf (or any other article) by one of the contracting parties (or one of the witnesses to the agreement) to the other contracting party as a symbol that the object itself has been transferred or the obligation assumed.

KOHEN, KOHANIM. The principal functionaries in the divine services. Their special task was to engage in rituals which they conducted mainly in the Temple. The priests' post is authorized by hereditary right, and they constitute a distinct class separate from the rest of the people.

KUPPAH. Communal charity box.

LEVITES. Descendants of the tribe of Levi, consecrated by Moses to assist the Kohanim in the service in the Tabernacle and later in the Temple.

MAẒRANUT. Abutter. The right of preemption available to the owner of land over the abutting land of his neighbor, when the latter is sold.

ME'ULAH BEDAMIM. Lit. "enhancement of value." A leniency in *bal tashḥit* law which permits the destruction of a material substance when the action results in the creation of a higher value.

MISHKHAN. The tabernacle, i.e., the portable sanctuary constructed by the children of Israel in the wilderness at the command of God.

MISHNAH. Compiled and codified by R. Judah ha-Nasi in 200 C.E., it contains the essence of the Oral law as it had been handed down from the time of the Bible.

ONA'AH. Price fraud involving selling above or below the competitive norm.

ONA'AT DEVARIM. Conduct causing needless mental anguish to others.

PEREKH. Crushing labor or labor which is useless from the standpoint of the employer's need.

PO'EL. Day-laborer hired for a specific period of time and required to work at fixed hours.

RISHON, RISHONIM. Designation of scholars who were active in the period from the eleventh to the middle of the fifteenth century.

SEKHAR HITPASHRUT. Agreed-to sum of money.

SEKHAR TIRḤAH. Remuneration for toil and effort.

SEMIKHAT DA'AT. Mental reliance. Without the presumption of mental reliance on the part of the principals to an agreement, the transaction lacks legal validity in Jewish law.

SHEVUAH ḤAMURAH. A severe oath, i.e., an oath imposed on an individual by dint of pentateuchal, as opposed to rabbinic, law. In cases requiring the pentateuchal oath, the deponent holds the Scroll of the Torah in his hand and swears by God. Before administering the oath, the court warns the deponent of the gravity of the oath and the inescapability of divine punishment for any false oath. In cases involving the oath administered by dint of rabbinic law, the former feature is absent and the latter is not required.

SODOMITIC. Exhibiting the character trait of a citizen of Sodom, i.e., denying a neighbor a benefit or privilege which involves no cost to oneself.

TABERNACLE. *See* MISHKAN.

TALMUD. The record of the discussions of scholars on the laws and teachings of the Mishnah. It consists of two parts, the Babylonian and the Palestinian Talmuds. The former was codified in ca. 500 C.E. and the latter in ca. 400 C.E.

TAMḤUI. Community charity plate.

TANNA, TANNAIC. Designation of scholars active in the period from the beginning of the common era up to 220 C.E. The period of the Tannaim spans six generations of scholars from Gamliel the Elder and his contemporaries to Judah ha-Nasi (the redactor of the Mishnah).

Notes

NOTES TO CHAPTER 1

1. Adam Smith, *An Inquiry into the Nature and Causes of the Wealth of Nations* (New York: Modern Library, 1937) p. 14.
2. Ibid., pp. 717–734.
3. *Berakhot* 61a.
4. *Sifre Deuteronomy* 33; *Shabbat* 105b; *Midrash Rabbah Genesis* 22:6; R. Eliyahu Eliezer Dessler, *Mikhtav M'Eliyahu*, vol. 1 (B'nei Berak: L. Carmel and N. S. Dessler, 1964), pp. 32–51.
5. *Berakhot* 5a.
6. *Midrash Rabbah Genesis* 9:7.
7. *Tanḥuma, Vayeḥi.*
8. Abaye, *Bava Meẓia* 49a; Maimonides (Egypt, 1135–1204), *Yad, De'ot* 2:6.
9. R. Solomon b. Isaac (France, 1040–1105), *Rashi* commentary at Leviticus 19:14. The Torah makes use of the phrase *And you shall fear your God* in connection with the following moral imperatives: (1) the prohibition against offering ill-suited advice (Leviticus 19:14); (2) the duty to bestow honor to a talmudic scholar (Leviticus 19:32); (3) the injunction against causing someone needless mental anguish (Leviticus 25:17); (4) the interdict against charging interest (Leviticus 25:36); and (5) the prohibition against working an Israelite slave oppressively (Leviticus 25:43).
10. *Torat Kohanim*, Leviticus 19:14; *Yad, Roẓeaḥ* 12:14.
11. Mishnah, *Bava Meẓia* 4:10; R. Isaac b. Jacob Alfasi (Algeria, 1012–1103), *Rif, Bava Meẓia* 58b; *Yad, Genevah* 14:12; R. Asher b. Jeḥiel (Germany, 1250–1327), *Rosh, Bava Meẓia* 4:22; R. Jacob b. Asher (Germany, 1270–1343); *Tur, Ḥoshen Mishpat* 228:1; R. Joseph Caro (Safed, 1488–1575), *Shulḥan Arukh, Ḥoshen Mishpat* 228.1; R. Jeḥiel Michel Epstein (Belorussia, 1829–1908), *Arukh ha-Shulḥan, Ḥoshen Mishpat* 228:1.
12. R. Menaḥem b. Solomon Meiri, *Beit ha-Beḥirah, Bava Meẓia* 59a. Pricing an article with no intention to buy it is prohibited, according to R. Samuel b. Meir (France, ca. 1080–1174), *Rashbam, Pesaḥim* 114b, on account of the possible financial loss this behavior might cause the vendor. While the vendor is preoccupied with the insincere inquiry, serious customers may turn elsewhere.
13. *See* commentary of R. Solomon b. Isaac (France, 1040–1105), *Rashi*, Leviticus 25:17.
14. Genesis 31:6; *Midrash Rabbah Genesis* 70:20; *Bava Meẓia* 93b; *Midrash Tanḥuma, Parshat Va-yetse; Midrash ha-Gadol Genesis* 30:42; *Yad, S'khirut* 13:7.
15. Genesis 31:39; *Bava Meẓia* 93b; R. Naphtali Ẓevi Judah Berlin (Russia, 1817–1893), *Ha'Amek Davar*, Genesis 31:39.

16. R. Samson Raphael Hirsch commentary at Genesis 30:27.
17. Genesis 30:32–33 and commentaries ad loc.
18. *Genesis Rabbah* 75:5.
19. R. Joseph Kimḥi, quoted by R. David Kimḥi (Narbonne, 1160–1236), *Radak*, Genesis 31:7.
20. Genesis 30:1. Naḥmanides (commentary at Genesis 30:37) finds no element of dishonesty in Jacob's use of the striped rods. Given that the contract called for offspring of a certain color to belong to Jacob, the latter had every right to promote his own interest by seeking to ensure such births. Given Laban's ignorance regarding the ramification of the use of the striped rods, it is even possible, avers Naḥmanides, that Jacob negotiated with Laban the legitimacy of their use at the outset of the agreement. For other defenses of Jacob's use of the striped rods, see *Radak* and R. Eliyahu Mizraḥi (Turkey, 1440–1525), *Mizraḥi,* ad loc.
21. Samuel, *Ḥullin* 94a; *Rif* ad loc.; *Yad, Genevah* 18:3; *Rosh, Ḥullin* 7:18; *Tur,* op. cit. 228:6; *Sh. Ar.,* op. cit. 228:6; *Ar. haSh.,* op. cit. 228:3.
22. Mishnah, *Bava Meẓia* 4:12; *Rif* ad loc., *Yad, Mekhirah* 18:2; *Rosh, Bava Meẓia* 4:24; *Tur,* op. cit. 228:9; *Sh. Ar.,* op. cit. 228:9; *Ar. haSh.,* op. cit. 228:5.

R. Jeḥiel Michel Epstein *(Ar. haSh,* op. cit. 227:1) regards a sale accomplished by means of misrepresentation as violating the *ona'ah* (price fraud) interdict. Earlier decisors do not, however, explicitly make this point.

23. R. Yom Tov Ishbili, *Ritva, Ḥullin* 94a.
24. R. Jonah b. Abraham Gerondi, *Sha'arei Teshuvah, sha'ar* 3, *ot* 184.
25. *Ar. haSh.,* op. cit. 228:3.
26. Samuel, *Ḥullin* 94a; *Rif* ad loc.; *Yad,* op. cit. 18:3; *Rosh, Ḥullin* 7:18; *Tur,* op. cit. 228:6; *Sh. Ar.,* op. cit. 228:6; *Ar. haSh.,* op. cit. 228:3.
27. Generating undeserved good will in the gift case is permitted according to R. Asher b. Jeḥiel *(Rosh,* loc. cit.) and Tosafot, *Ḥullin* 94b, on the interpretation of R. Joel Sirkes *(Baḥ, Tur,* loc. cit.). Members of the school of thought prohibiting such action include R. Jacob Tam (quoted in *Rosh, Ḥullin* 7:18); R. Solomon b. Abraham Adret *(Rashba, Ḥullin* 94a); R. Isaac b. Jacob Alfasi, Maimonides, and R. Moses of Coucy on the interpretation of R. Solomon b. Jeḥiel Luria *(see Yam shel Shelomo, Ḥullin, siman* 19).
28. Rabbi Joseph David Epstein, *Miẓvat ha-Shalom* (New York: Torat ha-Adam, 1969) p. 243.
29. R. Samuel Eliezer b. Judah ha-Levi Edels, *Maharsha, Yevamot* 65b.
30. Jerusalem Talmud, *Makkot* 2:6, *Shevi'it* 10:32.
31. R. Yom Tov Ishbili, *Ritva, Makkot* 12b.
32. See *Pesaḥim* 13a, *Yoma* 38a, *Mishnah Shekalim* 3:2, *Ta'anit* 11b.
33. *Pesaḥim* 13a; *Yad, Mattenot Aniyyim* 9:11; *Tur, Yoreh De'ah* 257:2; *Sh. Ar., Yoreh De'ah* 257:2; *Ar. haSh., Yoreh De'ah* 257:10.
34. *Sefer Zohar,* quoted in R. Jacob Culi (Constantinople, 1685–1732), *MeAm Lo'ez,* Kaplan trans, (New York: Maznaim Publishing Co., 1977), pp. 373–374.
35. Cf. R. Solomon b. Isaac (Troyes, 1040–1105), *Rashi,* Genesis 25:34; *Da'at Zekenim Mi'Ba'Alei HaTosafot* (France, 13th cent.), Genesis 25:34; R. Ḥayyim Ibn Attar (Jerusalem, 1696–1743), *Or haḤayyim,* Genesis 25:34.
36. Naḥmanides, *Ramban,* Genesis 25:34.
37. R. Abraham Ibn Ezra, *Ibn Ezra,* Genesis 25:34.
38. *Ramban,* loc. cit.
39. R. Solomon b. Isaac, *Rashi,* Genesis 25:34.
40. R. Ephraim Solomon b. Aaron of Lenczycza, *Keli Yakar,* Genesis 25:32.

41. R. Judah b. Samuel He-Ḥasid of Regensburg, quoted in *Da'at Zekenim Mi'Ba'Alei HaTosafot*, Genesis 25:34.

42. *Tanna Kamma, Mishnah, Bava Mezia* 4:7; R. Hai b. Sherira of Pumbedita (939–1038), quoted in *Rif, Bava Meẓia* 4:7 and in *Rosh, Bava Meẓia* 4:21; *Yad, Mekhirah* 13:13; *Tur, Ḥoshen Mishpat* 227:15; *Sh. Ar., Ḥoshen Mishpat* 227:15.

43. *Bava Meẓia* 10a; *Rif, Bava Meẓia* 77b; *Yad, Sekhirut* 9:4; *Rosh, Bava Meẓia* 6:6; Tur, op. cit. 332:2; *Sh. Ar.*, op. cit. 333:3; *Ar. haSh.*, op. cit. 333:6. For a discussion of the nature of this right, *see* Aaron Levine, *Free Enterprise and Jewish Law: Aspects of Jewish Business Ethics* (New York: KTAV Publishing House and Yeshiva University Press, 1980), pp. 44–49.

44. *Bava Meẓia* 75b; Rif ad loc.; *Yad*, op. cit. 9:4; *Tur*, op. cit. 333:3; *Sh. Ar.*, op. cit. 333:5–7; *Ar. haSh.*, op. cit. 333:18–22.

45. *Yad*, loc. cit.; *Ar. haSh.*, op. cit. 333:19.

46. *Rosh, Ḥullin* 7:18; *Tur*, op. cit. 228:7; *Sh. Ar.*, op. cit. 228:6; *Ar. haSh.*, op. cit. 228:3.

47. *Tosafot, Ḥullin* 94b.

48. R. Aryeh Judah b. Akiba, *Lev Aryeh, Ḥullin* 94a.

49. Rabbi Mosheh Mordecai Epstein, *Levush Mordecai* 24.

50. Rabbi Eliezer Meir Preil, *ha-Me'Or* 1:26–27.

51. Rabbi Mosheh Feinstein (New York, 1895–1986), *Iggerot Mosheh, Yoreh De'ah* 2:61.

52. *Bava Kamma* 100a.

53. *Bava Meẓia* 30b.

54. Tosafot, *Bava Meẓia* 24b.

55. R. Pappa, *Bava Kamma* 99b; *Rif* ad loc.; Maimonides (Egypt, 1135–1204), *Yad, S'khirut* 10:5; *Rosh, Bava Kamma* 9:16; *Tur*, op. cit. 306:10; *Sh. Ar.*, op. cit. 306:6; *Ar. haSh.*, op. cit. 306:13. Some of the above authorities (R. Isaac Alfasi, Maimonides, and R. Joseph Caro) hold that the nonexpert money changer is not liable for his erroneous free advice unless it is evident to the court that the inquirer relied upon his judgment. R. Asher b. Jeḥiel, however, holds the nonexpert liable even if the above condition is not met. R. Moses Isserles (Poland, 1525 or 1530–1572, *Rema, Sh. Ar.*, loc. cit.) rules in accordance with R. Asher b. Jeḥiel.

56. *Rif*, loc. cit.; *Yad*, loc. cit.; *Rosh*, loc. cit.; *Tur*, loc. cit.; *Sh. Ar.*, loc. cit.; *Ar. haSh.*, loc. cit.

57. *Ar. haSh.*, loc. cit. *Garme* is a term in the Talmud used to describe tortious damage caused indirectly by the tortfeasor's person. For a discussion of the various damages that fall under the rubric of *garme*, see *Encyclopedia Talmudit*, vol. 6, pp. 461–497.

58. Tosafot, *Bava Meẓia* 24b.

59. R. Solomon b. Isaac *(Rashi, Bava Meẓia* 24b), however, understands Samuel's father to have *found* the donkeys more than twelve months after their owner reported them lost. By the strict letter of the law, Samuel's father was not obligated to return the donkeys, as constructive abandonment on the part of the owner could safely be presumed after such a prolonged period of loss. Acting *li-fenim mi-shurat ha-din*, Samuel's father restored the donkeys to their owner.

60. Tosafot, *Bava Meẓia* 24b.

61. Most commentaries (*Rashi, Bava Meẓia* 83a, Tosafot, *Bava Meẓia* 24b, and *Tur, Ḥoshen Mishpat* 304:1 on interpretation of *Beit Yosef* ad loc.) interpret the incident to refer to the circumstances where the barrels were broken

through the negligence of the porters. R. Samuel Eliezer b. Judah ha-Levi Edels (Poland, 1555–1631), however, understands Rabbah b. Bar Ḥannan to have instructed the porters to transport the barrels over an incline. The porters could therefore not be held responsible for the subsequent breakage. Rav wryly indicated this to Rabbah b. Bar Ḥannan by quoting to him the verse *That you shall walk in the way of good men*. A play on the word *way* was meant. Since Rabbah b. Bar Ḥannan instructed the porters to transport the barrels over an incline instead of a *good way* (i.e., a smooth and even road), the porters cannot be held responsible for the breakage.

62. Tosafot, Bava Meẓia 24b.

63. *Rashi, Bava Meẓia* 83a; *Tur,* loc. cit.; R. Joel Sirkes (Poland, 1561–1640), *Baḥ, Tur,* op. cit. 304, 1; R. Menaḥem Mendel Krochmal (Moravia, 1600–1661), *Responsa Ẓemaḥ Ẓedak* 89; R. Mosheh Teitelbaum (Hungary, 1759–1841), *Responsa Heshiv Mosheh, Yoreh De'ah* 48.

64. *Yad, De'ot* 1:5.

65. *Yad, Gezelah ve'Avedah* 11:7.

66. Dr. Shmuel Shilo, "On One Aspect of Law and Morals in Jewish Law: *Li-fenim Mi-shurat Ha-din," Israel Law Review* 13, no. 3 (1978): 371–374.

67. Naḥmanides, commentary at Deuteronomy 6:18. See also his commentary at Leviticus 19:2.

68. R. Azario Figo, *Bina Le'Itim,* no. 12.

69. R. Mordecai b. Hillel, *Mordecai, Bava Meẓia* 2:257.

70. R. Joel Sirkes, *Baḥ, Tur,* op. cit. 12, n. 4.

71. R. Ḥananel b. Hushi'el, *Bava Meẓia* 24b; *Rosh, Bava Meẓia* 2:7; R. Yom Tov Ishbili (Spain, 1270–1342), *Bava Meẓia* 24b; R. Joseph Caro, *Beit Yosef, Tur,* op. cit. 12:6; R. Shabbetai b. Meir haKohen, *Sh. Ar. Ḥoshen Mishpat 259, n. 3; Ar. haSh.,* op. cit. 304:11.

72. R. Eliezer b. Nathan of Mainz, quoted in *Responsa* R. Meir of Rothenburg, no. 687.

73. R. David b. Moses, *Galya Masekhet, Ḥoshen Mishpat* 13.

74. Rabbi Ben Zion Ouziel, quoted in R. Mosheh Findeling, *Ḥukat Avodah,* p. 133.

75. *Piskei Din Rabanniyim,* vol. 3, p. 95.

76. *Nehardai Bava Meẓia* 108a; *Responsa* R. Abraham b. Maimonides (Egypt, 1186–1237), *Sefer Kinyan,* no. 63, Shulsinger ed.; *Rosh, Bava Meẓia* 9:24.

77. *Rashi, Bava Meẓia* 108a; R. Joshua ha-Kohen Falk, *Sma, Sh. Ar.,* op. cit. 175, n. 7, 63, 67; *Ar. haSh.,* op. cit. 175:1.

78. *Tur,* op. cit. 175:83; *Sh. Ar.,* op. cit. 175:53; *Ar. haSh.,* op. cit. 175:59.

79. R. Abraham b. David of Posquières (ca. 1125–1198) quoted in *Tur,* op. cit. 175:85; *Sh. Ar.,* loc. cit.; *Ar. haSh.,* op. cit. 175:60.

80. Nehardai, *Bava Meẓia* 108a; *Yad, Shekhenim* 12:5; *Tur,* op. cit. 175:6; *Sh. Ar.,* op. cit. 175:6; *Ar. haSh.,* op. cit. 175:2.

81. *Yad,* op. cit. 13:7; *Tur,* op. cit. 175:7; *Sh. Ar.,* op. cit. 175:6; *Ar. haSh.,* op. cit. 175:1.

82. R. Asher b. Jeḥiel, quoted in *Tur,* op. cit. 175:50–52; *Sh. Ar.,* op. cit. 175:32; R. Akiva Eger (Halberstadt, 1761–1837), *Sh. Ar.,* op. cit. 175, s.v. *Shakh, ot* 26; *Ar. haSh.,* op. cit. 175:21.

83. R. Joshua ha-Kohen Falk, *Sma, Sh. Ar.,* op. cit. 175, n. 57.

84. R. Meir Abulafia (Spain, ca. 1170–1244), quoted in *Tur,* op. cit. 175:47; R. Israel of Krems (fl. mid-14th cent.), *Haggahot Asheri, Rosh, Bava Meẓia* 9:22; *Sh. Ar.,* op. cit. 175:31; *Ar. haSh.,* op. cit. 175:20.

85. R. Ḥayyim b. Israel Benveniste, *Kenneset ha-Gedolah, Ḥoshen Mishpat* 175, notes on *Beit Yosef* 37.

86. *Yad*, op. cit. 14:2, quoted in *Tur*, op. cit. 175:48; *Sh. Ar.*, op. cit. 175:30; *Ar. haSh.*, op. cit. 175:18.

87. *Bava Meẓia* 108b; *Rif* ad loc.; *Yad*, op. cit. 14:1; *Rosh*, op. cit. 9:32; *Tur*, op. cit. 175:37; *Sh. Ar.*, op. cit. 175:23; *Ar. haSh.*, op. cit. 175:12.

88. *Bava Meẓia* 108b; *Rif* ad loc.; *Yad*, loc. cit.; *Rosh*, op. cit. 9:33; *Tur*, op. cit. 175:41; *Sh. Ar.*, op. cit. 175:25; *Ar. haSh.*, op. cit. 175:11.

89. *Sma*, *Sh. Ar.*, op. cit. 175, n. 37.

90. *Bava Meẓia* 108b, *Rif* ad loc.; *Yad*, loc. cit; *Rosh*, loc. cit.; *Tur*, loc. cit.; *Sh. Ar.*, loc. cit.; *Ar. haSh.*, loc. cit. R. Meir Abulafia (quoted in *Tur*, op. cit. 175:42, and *Sh. Ar.*, loc. cit.) expresses a minority opinion here. Provided the abutter did not approach the seller with his proposal after having already known the details of the competing offer, his offer to go and fetch the necessary cash must be regarded as equivalent to the nonabutter's ready cash offer even if the former is not known to be a man of wealth. With the abutter unaware of the details of the competing offer prior to his approach to the seller, his offer to go and bring the necessary cash should not be regarded as a dilatory tactic. Approaching the seller with such an offer after having already been aware of the details of the competing offer does, however, create a suspicion of a stalling tactic. Such a suspicion is removed only when the abutter is known to be a man of wealth. Hence, only when the abutter is a wealthy man can his offer be regarded as equivalent to the ready cash offer of the nonabutter.

91. *Sh. Ar.*, op. cit. 175:8; Rabbi Binyamin Rabinowitz-Teumim, *Ḥukat Mishpat* (Jerusalem: Harry Fischel Foundation, 1957), p. 229. For a variant view, see *Rosh*, op. cit. 9:24.

92. *Bava Meẓia* 108b; *Rif* ad loc.; *Yad*, op. cit. 12:9; *Rosh*, op. cit. 9:29; *Tur*, op. cit. 175:63; *Sh. Ar.*, op. cit. 175:43; *Ar. haSh.*, op. cit. 175:25.

93. *Yad*, loc. cit.; R. Ḥananel b. Hushi'el and Talmedei ha-Rashba on the interpretation of R. Israel of Krems (*Haggahot Asheri, Rosh, Bava Meẓia* 9:29).

94. *Haggahot Asheri*, loc. cit.

95. *Sma*, *Sh. Ar.*, op. cit. 175, n. 63.

96. *Rosh*, op. cit. 9:27.

97. *Bava Meẓia* 108b; *Rif* ad loc.; *Yad*, op. cit. 12:6; *Rosh*, loc. cit.; *Tur*, op. cit. 175:54; *Sh. Ar.*, op. cit. 175:36; *Ar. haSh.*, op. cit. 175:22.

98. Preferential treatment is extended to divorced and widowed women. A married woman, however, is conferred the privilege only when we are reasonably certain that she is transacting in behalf of herself rather than acting in behalf of her husband. See R. Joseph Ḥabib (early 15th cent.), *Nimmukei Yosef, Bava Meẓia* 108b; R. Solomon b. Abraham Adret (ca. 1235–1310), quoted in *Beit Yosef, Tur*, op. cit. 175:69 and in *Rema, Sh. Ar.*, op. cit. 175:47.

99. An orphan can qualify for privileged status only if he is also a minor. See R. Vidal Yom Tov of Tolosa (fl. 41th cent.), *Maggid Mishneh, Yad*, op. cit., 12:13.

100. *Yad*, op. cit. 12:13–14; *Rosh*, op. cit. 9:30; *Tur*, op. cit. 175:69; *Ar. haSh.*, op. cit. 175:29.

101. *Bava Meẓia* 108b; *Rif* ad loc.; *Yad*, loc. cit.; *Rosh*, loc. cit.; *Tur*, loc. cit.; *Sh. Ar.*, op. cit. 175:47; *Ar. haSh.*, loc. cit.

102. R. Asher b. Jeḥiel, quoted in R. Bezalel Ashkenazi (Egypt, 1520–1591), ed., *Shittah Mekubbeẓet, Bava Meẓia* 108b.

103. *Naḥmanides, Milḥamot, Rif, Bava Meẓia* 108b.
104. *Sma, Sh. Ar.*, op. cit. 175, n. 87.
105. Authorities quoted in *Rema, Sh. Ar.*, op. cit. 175:47.
106. R. Jacob b. Judah Weil, *Responsa Maharyu* 99, quoted in *Sma*, loc. cit.
107. R. Eliezer b. Ḥayyim, quoted in *Kenesset ha-Gedolah* 175, comments on *Beit Yosef*, n. 92.
108. *Some authorities*, quoted in *Rema, Sh. Ar.*, op. cit. 175:49.
109. *Sma, Sh. Ar.*, op. cit. 175, n. 89.
110. *Some authorities*, quoted in *Rema*, loc. cit.
111. See *Sma, Sh. Ar.*, loc. cit.
112. *Rosh*, op. cit. 9:30; quoted in *Tur*, op. cit. 175:5; *Rema, Sh. Ar.*, op. cit. 175:5; *Ar. haSh.*, op. cit. 175:32.
113. *Tur*, op. cit. 175:56; *Sma, Sh. Ar.*, op. cit. 175, n. 88; *Ar. haSh.*, op. cit. 175:33.
114. *Responsa Baḥ* 13; *Ar. haSh.* op. cit. 175:23; *Bava Meẓia* 108b; *Rif* ad loc.; *Yad*, op. cit. 12:5; *Rosh*, op. cit. 9:31; *Sh. Ar.*, op. cit. 175:49; *Ar. haSh.*, op. cit. 175:33.
115. *Bava Meẓia* 108b; *Rif* ad loc.; *Yad*, op. cit. 12:6; *Rosh*, op. cit. 9:27; *Tur*, op. cit. 175:55–56; *Sh. Ar.*, op. cit. 175:37 and *Rema*, loc. cit.; *Ar. haSh.*, 175:23.
116. *Ar. haSh.*, op. cit. 175:23.
117. *Bava Meẓia* 108a; *Rif* ad loc.; *Yad*, op. cit. 14:4; *Rosh*, op. cit. 9:24; *Tur*, op. cit. 175:13; *Sh. Ar.*, op. cit. 175:7; *Ar. haSh.*, op. cit. 175:3.
118. *Bava Meẓia* 108a; *Rif* ad loc.; *Yad*, op. cit. 14:4; *Rosh*, op. cit. 9:25; *Tur*, op. cit. 175:14; *Sh. Ar.*, op. cit. 175:9; *Ar. haSh.*, op. cit. 175:4.
119. *Sma, Sh. Ar.*, op. cit. 175, n. 14: R. Jacob Moses Lorberbaum (Lisa, 1760–1832), *Netivot ha-Mishpat, Sh. Ar.*, op. cit. 175, n. 8.
120. *Ḥukat Mishpat*, p. 229.
121. R. Israel Isser b. Ze'ev Wolf (Russia, d. 1829), *Sha'ar Mishpat, Sh. Ar.*, op. cit. 175:9.
122. See R. David b. Samuel ha-Levi, *Turei Zahav, Sh. Ar.*, op. cit. 175:26; *Sma, Sh. Ar.*, op. cit. 175, n. 44.
123. *Bava Meẓia* 108b; *Rif* ad loc.; *Yad*, op. cit. 14:1; *Rosh*, op. cit. 4:33; *Tur*, op. cit. 174:43; *Sh. Ar.*, op. cit. 175:26; *Ar. haSh.*, op. cit. 175:55.
124. *Sma*, loc. cit.
125. *Turei Zahav*, loc. cit.
126. R. Joseph Caro, *Beit Yosef; Tur*, op. cit. 175:48.
127. R. Ḥayyim b. Israel Benveniste, *Kenesset ha-Gedolah, Ḥoshen Mishpat* 175, comments on *Tur*, n. 55.
128. For an excellent survey and analysis of the *kofin* principle in the talmudic and responsa literature, see Dr. Shmuel Shilo, "*Kofin al Midat Sedom:* Jewish Law's Concept of Abuse of Rights," *Israel Law Review* 15, no. 1 (1980): 49–78.
129. *Rosh, Ketubbot* 12:5; Maimonides and R. Joseph Caro, on the interpretation of R. Joshua ha-Kohen Falk (*Sma, Sh. Ar.*, op. cit. 318, n. 2). *Tosafot* (*Ketubbot* 103a) expresses an opposing view. R. David b. Samuel ha-Levi (*Turei Zahav, Sh. Ar.*, op. cit. 318:1), however, reconciles both views.
130. R. David Ibn Zimra, *Responsa Radbaz*, vol. 2, no. 1002.
131. Ibid., vol. 1, no. 146.
132. *Rosh, Bava Batra* 3:72; *Tur*, op. cit. 153:13; *Rema, Sh. Ar.*, op. cit. 153:8.
133. R. Elai, *Bava Batra* 59a; *Rif* ad loc.; *Yad, Shekhenim* 7:4; *Rosh, Bava Batra* 3:73; *Sh. Ar.*, op. cit. 154:6; *Ar. haSh.*, op. cit. 154:12.

134. R. Solomon b. Abraham Adret, *Responsa Rashba* 1:1,143.
135. R. Kahana, reporting in the name of R. Yoḥanan, *Bava Kamma* 20b; *Rif* ad loc.; *Yad, Gezelah* 3:9; *Rosh, Bava Kamma* 2:6; *Tur,* op. cit. 363:6; *Sh. Ar.*, op. cit. 363:6; *Ar. haSh.*, op. cit. 363:6.
136. *Tosafot, Bava Kamma,* 20b; R. Israel of Krems, *Haggahot Asheri, Rosh, Bava Kamma* 2:6; *Rema, Sh. Ar.*, op. cit. 363:6; *Ar. haSh.*, op. cit. 363:16.
137. *Sma, Sh. Ar.*, op. cit. 363, n. 14.
138. R. Shmuel de Medina (Turkey, 1506–1589), *Responsa Maharashdam,* no. 409; R. Aaron Sasson (Turkey, ca. 1553–1626), *Responsa Torat Emet,* no. 129.
139. R. Shalom Mordecai Schwadron (Galicia, 1835–1911), *Responsa Maharsam* 5:5.
140. *Responsa Maharashdam,* no. 409; *Responsa Torat Emet,* no. 129.
141. *Responsa Maharasham* 5:5.
142. *Bava Batra* 12b.
143. R. Jacob Tam, *Tosafot Bava Batra* 12b.
144. *Responsa Rosh* 97:2, quoted in *Beit Yosef, Tur,* op. cit. 174:2.
145. Naḥmanides, *Ramban, Bava Batra* 12b. For other interpretations of the talmudic text, see *Rashi* ad loc. and R. Abraham b. David (Posquières, 1120–1198), *Rabad* in *Shittah M'kubbezet Bava Batra* 12b.
146. For a development of this theory, see Rabbi Mosheh Feinstein, *Dibberot Mosheh, Bava Batra,* vol. 1, pp. 84–92.

NOTES TO CHAPTER 2

1. Carl P. Wrighter, *I Can Sell You Anything* (New York: Ballantine Books, 1972), pp. 23–72.
2. R. Eliezer derives the warning against slander from Leviticus 19:16. R. Nathan derives the admonishment from Deuteronomy 23:11 (see *Ketubbot* 46a).
3. Leviticus 19:11.
4. Aaron Levine, *Free Enterprise and Jewish Law* (New York: KTAV Publishing House and Yeshiva University Press, 1980), pp. 128–130. See also Rabbi Alfred S. Cohen, "Privacy: A Jewish Perspective," *Journal of Halacha and Contemporary Society* 1, no. 1 (Spring 1981): 73–77.
5. Jerusalem Talmud, *Ḥagigah* 11:1.
6. *Megillah* 28a.
7. R. Samuel Eliezer b. Judah ha-Levi Edels, *Maharsha, Megillah* 28a.
8. R. Ḥayyim Ḥezekiah Medini, *Sedei Ḥemed* IV, K'lal 86.
9. *Ketubbot* 17a.
10. R. Jacob b. Asher (Germany, 1270–1343), *Tur, Even ha-Ezer* 65:1; R. Joseph Caro (Safed, 1488–1575) *Shulḥan Arukh, Even ha-Ezer* 65:1; R. Jeḥiel Miçhel Epstein (Belorussia, 1829–1908), *Even ha-Ezer* 65:1.
11. R. Judah Lowe b. Bezalel, *Maharal, Ketubbot* 17a.
12. *Yevamot* 65b.
13. *Nedarim* 21a; R. Isaac b. Jacob Alfasi (Algeria, 1012–1103) ed. loc.; Maimonides (Egypt, 1135–1204), *Yad, Nedarim* 4:3; R. Asher b. Jeḥiel (Germany, 1250–1327), *Rosh, Nedarim* 4:1; *Tur, Yoreh De'ah* 232:1; *Sh. Ar., Yoreh De'ah* 232:2.

Given the negotiating intent of both buyer and seller, some authorities take the view that the respective vows are not legally binding even in regard to the original positions which prompted the vows. Hence, the buyer would not be prohibited by force of his vow from finally agreeing to conclude the transaction at the initial $4.00 asking price of the seller. Similarly, the seller's vow would not prohibit him from concluding the transaction at the initial $2.00 bid of the buyer. Other authorities regard the vows as legally not binding only in respect to some compromise sum. By force of these vows, each party, however, would be prohibited from concluding the transaction at the initial price of his opposite number. (See R. Nissim b. Abraham Gerondi, *Ran, Nedarim* 21a, and R. Moses Isserles, *Rema, Sh. Ar., Yoreh De'ah* 22:2.) R. Joel Sirkes (*Baḥ, Tur,* loc. cit.) points out that common practice is in accordance with the lenient view.

14. Tosafot, *Nedarim* 21a; R. Yom Tov Ishbili (Spain, 1270–1342), *Ritva Nedarim* 21a.

15. Tosefta, *Nedarim* 4:4; *Yad,* op. cit. 4:4; *Tur,* op. cit. 232:20; *Sh. Ar.,* op. cit. 232:13.

16. Ivan L. Preston, "Logic and Illogic in the Advertising Process," *Journalism Quarterly* 44 (Summer 1967): 231–239; idem, "A Comment on Defining Misleading Advertising and 'Deception in Advertising,' " *Journal of Marketing* 40 (July 1976): 54–60; idem, "The FTC's Handling of Puffery 'and other Selling Claims Made by Implication,' " *Journal of Business Research* 5 (June 1977): 155–81.

17. Richard L. Oliver, "An Interpretation of the Attitudinal and Behavioral Effects of Puffery," *Journal of Consumer Affairs* 13 no. 1 (March 1979): 8–27.

18. *Ketubbot* 105a; *Yad, Sanhedrin* 23:1, *Tur; Ḥoshen Mishpat* 9:1; *Sh. Ar., Ḥoshen Mishpat* 9:1; *Ar. haSh., Ḥoshen Mishpat* 9:1.

19. *Ketubbot* 105b.

20. *Ketubbot* 105b; *Yad,* op. cit. 23:3; *Tur,* op. cit. 9:4; Sh. Ar., op. cit. 9:1; *Ar. haSh.,* op. cit. 9:1.

21. *Ketubbot* 105b.

22. R. Joshua ha-Kohen Falk (Poland, 1555–1614), *Sma, Sh. Ar.,* op. cit. 9, n. 4; *Ar. haSh.,* loc. cit.

23. *Sanhedrin* 29a; *Rif* ad loc.; *Yad,* op. cit. 23:6; *Rosh, Sanhedrin* 3:23; *Tur,* op. cit. 7:8, 10; *Sh. Ar.,* op. cit. 7:7; *Ar. haSh.,* op. cit. 7:9–10.

Judicial disqualification proceeds as a definite matter, according to majority opinion, only when the judge is either a *close* friend or a presumed enemy of one of the litigants. Here, the judge must, as a matter of strict law, remove himself from the case. Should he preside over the case, his verdict would be rendered null and void. An association of a more superficial nature with one of the litigants requires the judge only as a matter of propriety to remove himself from the case. Should he preside over the case, his verdict would here not be rendered void. Maimonides, according to interpretation of R. Joel Sirkes (*Baḥ, Tur,* op. cit. 7:11) equates the superficial and close relationship cases. In both instances, the judge must remove himself from the case only as a matter of propriety, as opposed to strict law. In both instances, presiding over the case does not render the verdict null and void, despite the impropriety committed.

24. *Baḥ, Tur,* op. cit. 9, n. 9.

25. *Yad,* op. cit. 23:1; *Tur,* op. cit. 9:2; *Sh. Ar.,* op. cit. 9:1; *Ar. haSh.,* op. cit. 9:1.

26. *Ar. haSh.,* loc. cit.

27. *Rema, Sh. Ar. Ḥoshen Mishpat* 163:1.
28. R. Moses Sofer, *Responsa Ḥatam Sofer, Ḥoshen Mishpat* 160.
29. Levine, *Free Enterprise and Jewish Law*, pp. 95–97, 110–112.
30. Leviticus 5:1–13; *Keritot* 10b; *Yad, Shegagot* 10:1–4.
31. *Torat Kohanim* 5:7.
32. *Sefer ha-Ḥinnukh* 123. The authorship of this work is unknown. Some authorities attribute it to R. Aaron ha-Levi of Barcelona (1235–1300). According to R. Joseph b. Moses Babad (Poland, 1800–1874), the position that the poor man who offers the rich man's sacrifice is not fulfilling his obligation is contradicted by Mishnah *Nega'im* 14:12. *See Minḥat Ḥinnukh* ad loc.
33. *Ketubbot* 50a; *Rif* ad loc.; *Yad, Arakhin* 8:13; *Rema, Sh. Ar., Yoreh De'ah* 249:1; *Ar. haSh., Yoreh De'ah* 249:1.
34. *Ta'anit* 10b; *Rif* ad loc.; *Yad, Ta'anit* 1:15; *Rosh Ta'anit* 1:7; *Tur, Oraḥ Ḥayyim* 574:1; *Sh. Ar., Oraḥ Ḥayyim* 574:2–3; *Ar. haSh., Oraḥ Ḥayyim* 574:2–3.
35. *Mo'ed Katan* 27a; *Rif* ad loc.; *Yad, Avel* 13:7; *Tur, Yoreh De'ah* 378:12; *Ar. haSh., Yoreh De'ah* 378:7.
36. Rabbi Bezalel Landau, "Takanot Neged ha-Motarot," *Niv ha-Medrishah*, 1971, pp. 213–226.
37. *Baraita, Bava Meẓia* 51a; *Rif* ad loc.; *Yad, Mekhirah* 12:1; *Rosh, Bava Meẓia* 4:17; *Tur, Ḥoshen Mishpat* 227:1; *Sh. Ar., Ḥoshen Mishpat* 227:1; *Ar. haSh., Ḥoshen Mishpat* 227:1.
38. For the development of this thesis, see Levine, *Free Enterprise and Jewish Law*, pp. 105–109.
39. *Bava Meẓia* 61a; *Tur, Ḥoshen Mishpat* 227:1; R. Joshua ha-Kohen Falk (Poland, 1555–1614), *Sma, Sh. Ar., Ḥoshen Mishpat* 227, n. 1.
40. *Bava Batra* 78a and *Rashi* ad loc.; *Rif* ad loc.; *Yad*, op. cit. 27:5; *Rosh, Bava Batra* 5:7; *Tur*, op. cit. 220:5; *Sh. Ar.*, op. cit. 220:8; *Ar. haSh.*, op. cit. 220:7.
41. *Bava Meẓia* 50b; *Rif* ad loc.; *Yad*, op. cit. 12:4; *Rosh, Bava Meẓia* 4:15; *Tur*, op. cit. 227:6; *Sh. Ar.*, op. cit. 227:4; *Ar. haSh.*, op. cit. 227:3.
42. *Bava Meẓia* 50b; *Rif* ad loc.; *Yad*, op. cit. 12:2; *Rosh*, op. cit. 4:15; *Tur*, op. cit., 227:3; *Sh. Ar.*, op. cit. 227:2; *Ar. haSh.*, loc. cit.
43. *Bava Meẓia* 50b; *Rif* ad loc.; *Yad*, op. cit. 12:3; *Tur*, op. cit. 227:4; *Sh. Ar.*, loc. cit.; *Ar. haSh.*, loc. cit.
44. *Ar. haSh.*, op. cit. 227:7.
45. *Rosh*, op. cit. 4:20.
46. *Yad*, op. cit. 13:3.
47. *Tur*, op. cit. 227:4.
48. *Sh. Ar.*, op. cit. 227:2.
49. *Naḥmanides*, commentary at Leviticus 25:14.
50. *Ar. haSh.*, op. cit. 227:27.
51. R. Moses Isserles, *Rema, Sh. Ar. Oraḥ Ḥayyim* 656:1. *See* also *Sedai Ḥemed*, vol. 9, pp. 7, 64.
52. R. Mosheh Sofer, Responsa *Ḥatam Sofer Ḥoshen Mishpat* 177 and his gloss at *Sh. Ar., Oraḥ Ḥayyim* 656:1. For an extended discussion of the one-fifth rule as it applies to the disclosure of professional confidences, see Rabbi Alfred S. Cohen, "Privacy: A Jewish Perspective," *Journal of Halakha and Contemporary Society* 1, no. 1 (Spring 1981): 82–82. For an opposing view in respect to this issue, see Rabbi Mosheh HaLevi Spero, "Halakhic Definitions of Confidentiality in the Psychotherapeutic Encounter: Theory and Practice," *Tradition* 20, no. 4 (Winter 1982): 313–314, fn. 73.
53. *Yad, Roẓeaḥ* 12:4.

54. R. Judah Rosanes, *Mishneh le-Melekh, Kelayim* 1:6. For an opposing view, see R. Joshua ha-Kohen Falk (Poland, 1555–1614), *Derishah, Yoreh De'ah* 297.

55. Rabbi Jacob Breisch, *Ḥelkat Ya'akov* 3:136.

56. Rabbi Israel Meir ha-Kohen Kagan, *Ḥafeẓ Ḥayyim, Be'er Mayim Ḥayyim, Hilkhot Issurei Rekhilut* 9:1.

57. Mishnah, *Bava Meẓia* 2:13; *Rif, Bava Meẓia* 33a; *Yad, Gezalah* 12:1; *Rosh, Bava Meẓia* 11:30; *Tur*, op. cit. 264:1; *Sh. Ar.*, op. cit. 264:1; *Ar. haSh.*, op. cit. 264:1.

58. R. Judah, *Bava Meẓia* 33a and *Rashi* ad loc.; *Ar. haSh.*, loc. cit.

59. R. Ḥayyim Ḥezekiah Medini, *Sedei Ḥemed*, vol. 9, pp. 7–11, 64–65.

NOTES TO CHAPTER 3

1. For a presentation and critique of supply-side economics, see Thomas R. Swartz, Frank J. Bonello, and Andrew F. Kozak, *The Supply Side: Debating Current Economic Policies* (Guilford, Conn.: Duskhin Publishing Group, 1983).

2. Thomas J. Hailstones and Frank V. Mastrianna, *Contemporary Economic Problems and Issues*, 6th ed. (Cincinnati: South-Western Publishing Co., 1982), pp. 120–122.

3. Ibid., pp. 131–133.

4. John C. Goodman and Edwin G. Dolan, *Economics of Public Policy: The Micro View*, 3d ed. (St. Paul: West Publishing Company, 1985), pp. 39–57.

5. Larry E. Ruff, "The Economic Common Sense of Pollution," *Public Interest*, no. 19 (Spring 1970): 69–85.

6. William J. Baumol, John C. Panzar, and Robert D. Willig, *Contestable Markets and the Theory of Industry Structure* (San Diego: Harcourt Brace Jovanovich, 1982).

7. R. Solomon b. Isaac, *Rashi, Bava Kamma* 85a; R. Asher b. Jeḥiel (Germany, ca. 1250–1327), *Rosh, Bava Kamma* 8:1.

8. *Rosh*, loc. cit.

9. *Rashi, Menaḥot* 43a.

10. R. Solomon b. Abraham Adret, *Responsa Rashba* 1:450, quoted by R. Joseph Caro (Safed, 1488–1575), *Beit Yosef, Tur, Oraḥ Ḥayyim* 53.

11. *Yoma* 22a, 23a.

12. R. Eliezer b. Isaac, quoted by R. Isaac b. Moses of Vienna (ca. 1180–ca. 1250), *Responsa Or Za'rua*, vol. 1, no. 113.

13. R. Joseph Caro, *Kesef Mishneh, Yad, Talmud Torah* 3:10.

14. *Tosefta Shabbat* 18:16; Maimonides (Egypt, 1135–1204), *Yad*, Shabbat 6:25; R. Jacob b. Asher (Germany, 1270–1340), *Tur, Oraḥ Ḥayyim* 306:5; R. Joseph Caro, *Shulḥan Arukh, Oraḥ Ḥayyim* 306:4; R. Jeḥiel Michel Epstein (Belorussia, 1829–1908), *Arukh haShulḥan, Oraḥ Ḥayyim* 306:9.

15. R. Ḥayyim Isaac Algazi (Smyrna, late 18th cent.), *Derekh Ez ha-Ḥayyim*, responsum no. 2; R. Ḥayyim Modai (Turkey, 1700–1784), *Ḥayyim L'olam*, p. 130; Rabbi Yehoshu'a Yesha'yah Neuwirth (contemp.), *Shmirat Shabbat ki-Hilkhata*, p. 164, n. 135.

16. *Ḥayyim L'olam*, loc. cit.

17. Berakhot 36b.

18. R. Samuel Eliezer b. Judah ha-Levi Edels (Poland, 1555–1631), *Maharsha, Berakhot* 35b.

19. *Avot* 11:2.
20. R. Joel Sirkes, *Baḥ Tur, Oraḥ Ḥayyim* 154.
21. *Berakhot* 8a.
22. The teaching is recorded in the Mishnah anonymously. R. Yoḥanan (*Sandedrin* 86a), however, identifies R. Meir as the author of an anonymous mishnaic teaching.
23. *Baraita, Kiddushin* 29a.
24. *Baraita, Kiddushin* 29a, *Kiddushin* 30b, and *Rashi* ad loc.
25. R. Nehorai, *Mishnah Kiddushin* 4:14.
26. *Maharsha, Kiddushin* 82a.
27. R. Eliyahu b. Ḥayyim, *Imrei Shefer* 52.
28. R. Judah Ila'i, *Berakhot* 35b.
29. *Pesaḥim* 113a.
30. R. Judah Loew b. Bezalel, *N'tivot Olam*, vol. 2; *N'tiv h'Osher*, chaps. 1–2.
31. R. Shimon, *Mishnah Ketubbot* 5:5.
32. *Pesaḥim* 113a.
33. Shabbat 118a; *Yad, Mattenot Aniyyim* 9:13; *Tur, Yoreh De'ah*, 253:1; *Sh. Ar., Yoreh De'ah*, op. cit. 253:1; *Ar. haSh., Yoreh De'ah* 253:1.
34. *Shabbat* 117b; R. Isaac b. Jacob Alfasi (Algeria, 1013–1103), *Rif* ad loc.; *Yad, Shabbat* 30:9; *Rosh, Shabbat* 16:15; *Tur, Oraḥ Ḥayyim* 291:1; *Sh. Ar., Oraḥ Ḥayyim* 291:1; *Ar haSh., Oraḥ Ḥayyim* 291:1–2.
35. *Bava Batra* 78a and *Rashi* ad loc.; *Rif* ad loc.; *Yad, Mekhirah* 27:5; *Rosh, Bava Batra 5:7; Tur, Ḥoshen Mishpat* 220:5; *Sh. Ar., Ḥoshen Mishpat* 220:8; *Ar. haSh., Ḥoshen Mishpat* 220:7.
36. *Bava Meẓia* 50b; *Rif ad loc.; Yad*, op. cit. 12:4; *Rosh*, op. cit. 4:15; *Tur*, op. cit. 227:6; *Sh. Ar.*, op. cit. 227:4; *Ar. haSh.*, op. cit. 227:3.
37. *Bava Meẓia* 50b; *Rif* ad loc.; *Yad*, op. cit. 12:2; *Rosh*, op. cit. 4:15; *Tur*, op. cit. 227:3; *Sh. Ar.*, op. cit. 227:2; *Ar. haSh.*, loc. cit.
38. *Bava Meẓia* 50b; *Rif* ad loc.; *Yad*, op. cit. 12:3; *Tur*, op. cit. 227:4; *Sh. Ar.*, loc. cit.; *Ar. haSh.*, loc. cit.
39. See Aaron Levine, *Free Enterprise and Jewish Law* (New York: KTAV Publishing House and Yeshiva University Press, 1980), pp. 105–109.
40. *Yad*, op. cit. 18:1; *Tur*, op. cit. 228:5; *Sh. Ar.*, op. cit. 228:6; *Ar. haSh.*, op. cit. 228:3.
41. Rabbi Binyamin Rabinowitz-Teomim, *Ḥukat Mishpat* (Jerusalem: Harry Fishel Foundation, 1957), p. 90.
42. *Yad*, op. cit.; *Tur*, op. cit.; *Sh. Ar.*, op. cit.; *Ar. haSh.*, op. cit.
43. See R. Joshua ha-Kohen Falk (Poland, 1555–1614) *Sma, Sh. Ar.*, op. cit. 228, n. 7; *Ar. haSh.*, op. cit. 228:3.
44. *Sma, Sh. Ar.*, op. cit. 232, n. 57.
45. *Bava Batra* 92a; *Rif* ad loc.; *Yad*, op. cit., 16:5; *Rosh, Bava Batra* 6:1; *Tur*, op. cit. 232:21; *Sh. Ar.*, op. cit. 232:23; *Ar. haSh.*, op. cit. 232:36.
46. R. Samuel b. Meir, *Rashbam*, Bava Batra 92a.
47. *Yad*, op. cit. 15:5, quoted in *Tur*, op. cit. 232:6; *Sh. Ar.*, op. cit. 232:6; *Ar. haSh.*, op. cit. 232:7.
48. *Yad*, op. cit. 15:4; *Tur*, loc. cit.; *Sh. Ar.*, op. cit. 232:4; *Ar. haSh.*, op. cit. 232:6.
49. See *Sma, Sh. Ar.*, op. cit. 228, n. 7; *Ar. haSh.*, op. cit. 228:3.
50. *Yad*, op. cit. 15:7–9.
51. *Tur*, op. cit. 232:8; *Sh. Ar.*, op. cit. 232:8, both on interpretation of R. Jeḥiel Michel Epstein (*Ar. haSh.*, op. cit. 232:13.
52. *Yad*, op. cit. 15:6; *Sh. Ar.*, op. cit. 232:7.

53. *Sma, Sh. Ar.*, op. cit. 232, n. 15; *Ar. haSh.*, op. cit. 232:11.
54. *Yad*, loc. cit.; *Tur*, op. cit. 232:7; *Sh. Ar.*, op. cit. 232:6; *Ar. haSh.*, loc. cit.
55. *Kiddushin* 11a; *Yad*, op. cit. 15:12; *Tur*, op. cit. 232:10; R. Joseph Caro, *Kesef Mishneh, Yad, Zekhiyyah* 1:1; *Ar. haSh.*, op. cit. 232:16; *Ḥukat Mishpat*, op. cit., p. 90.
56. R. Eliezer of Toule (d. before 1234), quoted in R. Ḥayyim b. Israel Benveniste (Smyrna, 1603–1673), *Kenesset ha-Gedolah, Ḥoshen Mishpat* 232 comments on *Tur*, n. 21.
57. R. Asher b. Jeḥiel, *Responsa Rosh K'lal* 96:6, quoted in *Tur*, op. cit. 232:5; *Sh. Ar.*, op. cit. 232:5; R. Moses Isserles (Poland, 1525–1572), *Rema, Sh. Ar.* ad loc.; *Ar. haSh.*, op. cit. 232:10.
58. *Rema*, loc. cit.; R. Jacob Lorberbaum (Poland, ca. 1760–1832), *N'tivot haMishpat, Sh. Ar.*, op. cit. 232, n. 7; *Ar. haSh.*, loc. cit.
59. Rabbi Ezra Basri, *Dinei Mamonot*, vol. 2 (Jerusalem: Sukkat David, 1976), p. 205.
60. *Torat Kohanim*, Leviticus 19:14; *Yad*, Roẓeaḥ 12:14.
61. *Halakhot Gedolot* on interpretation of R. Jeruḥam Fishel Perla, commentary on *Sefer ha Miẓvot* of *R. Saadiah Gaon, minyan ha-Lavin* 54. The authorship of this work is disputed, but it is generally dated to the geonic period. See *Encyclopaedia Judaica*, vol. 7, col. 1169.
62. Yad, loc. cit., on interpretation of R. Jeruḥam Fishel Perla, loc. cit.
63. *Sifre*, Deuteronomy 22:8.
64. Ibid.
65. Ibid.
66. Rabbi Jeruḥam Fishel Perla, loc. cit.
67. Maimonides, *Sefer haMiẓvot lavin* 298 on interpretation of R. Judah Fishel Perla, loc. cit.
68. Rabbi Zion Ouziel, *Mishpetei Uzzie'l*, vol. 3, *Ḥoshen Mishpat* 43.
69. Rami b. Ḥamma, reporting in the name of R. Yiẓḥak, *Bava Batra* 89a; *Rif* ad loc.; *Yad, Genevah* 8:20; *Rosh*, Bava Batra 5:22; *Tur*, op. cit. 231:2; *Sh. Ar.*, op. cit. 231:2; *Ar. haSh.*, op. cit. 232:3.
70. *Yad, Maakhalot Asurot* 11:25.
71. *Ar. haSh., Yoreh De'ah* 119:2.
72. Deuteronomy 4:15; *Shabbat* 32a; *Rif* ad loc.; *Yad, Roẓe'aḥ* 12:4–7; *Rosh, Shabbat* 2:21; *Sh. Ar., Oraḥ Ḥayyim* 170:16; *Rema, Sh. Ar., Yoreh De'ah* 116:5; *Ar. haSh., Yoreh De'ah* 116.
73. R. Jacob Ettlinger, *Binyan Ẓion* 137.
74. Rabbi J. David Bleich, *Tradition* 16, no. 4 (Summer 1977): 121–123; idem, *Tradition*, 17, no. 3 (Summer 1978): 140–142.
75. Dr. F. Rosner, "Cigarette Smoking and Jewish Law," *Journal of Halacha and Contemporary Society* 4 (Fall 1982): 33–45.
76. *Economics of Public Policy*, p. 43.
77. Ruling of R. Judah in the name of Samuel, *Bava Batra* 25b; *Rif* ad loc.; *Yad, Shekhenim* 10:5; *Rosh*, op. cit. 2:25; *Tur*, op. cit. 155:44–46; *Sh. Ar.*, op. cit. 155:32; *Ar. haSh., Ḥoshen Mishpat* 155:1.
78. R. Solomon b. Abraham Adret, quoted in *Shittah M'kubbeẓet, Bava Batra* 22a; *Tosafot, Bava Batra* 22a; Rabbi Aaron Kotler (1892–1962), *Mishnat Rabbi Aharon*, vol. 1, p. 68; Rabbi Yeḥezkel Abramsky (1886–1976), *Ḥazon Yeḥezkel, Tosefta Bava Batra* 1:5. For a treatment of the negative externality issue in Jewish law, see Levine, *Free Enterprise and Jewish Law*, pp. 58–77.
79. R. Meir Abulafia (Spain, 1170–1244), *Ramah, Bava Batra* 11:107.
80. R. Asher b. Jeḥiel, *Responsa Rosh, k'lal* 108, par. 10. A variant minority view in this matter is held by R. Moses b. Joseph Trani (Safed, 1500–1580). He

regards the prohibition as only *rabbinical* in origin, since biblical law merely requires the defendant to *compensate* his victim for damage he is responsible for, but would not enjoin a harmful act with the objective of preventing damage from occurring (*Kiryat Sefer, Shekhenim* 9). *See* also R. Jacob Tam (Ramerupt, 1100–1171), *Sefer ha-Yashar, siman* 522.

81. *Bava Batra* 25b, 26a.

82. *Yad, Nizkei Mamon* 5:1; Naḥmanides, *Ramban, Bava Batra, dinei d'garme;* Rabbi Jacob Kanievsky (Israel, contemp.), *K'hilot Yaakov, Bava Batra, siman* 1.

83. For the seminal treatment of the reciprocal nature of the externality problem, see Ronald H. Coase, "The Problem of Social Cost," *Journal of Law and Economics,* October 1960, pp. 1–45.

84. *Responsa Rashba,* vol. 3:411; R. Simeon b. Ẓemaḥ Duran (Algeria, 1361–1444), *Tashbeẓ* 2:132 and 239.

85. R. Gershom b. Judah (Germany, ca. 960–1028), Responsa R. Gershom *Me'or ha-Golah,* ed. Eidelberg, no. 67; R. Joseph b. Samuel Bonfils (France, 11th cent.) quoted in Responsa *Maharam of Rothenburg* 423; *Responsa Rashba,* vol. 4, no. 311; R. Asher b. Jeḥiel, *Responsa Rosh* 101:1; R. Ẓemaḥ b. Solomon Duran (North Africa, 15th cent.), *Responsa Yakhin u-Vo'az,* pt. 2, no. 20.

86. R. Isaac b. Jacob Alfasi (Algeria, 1013–1103), *Responsa Rif,* ed. Leiter no. 13; R. Joseph b. Samuel Bonfils, quoted by R. Meir b. Baruch of Rothenburg (1215–1293), *Responsa Maharam* 423; R. Ḥayyim (Eliezer) b. Isaac (Germany, 13th cent.), Responsa *Ḥayyim Or Zaru'a,* no. 222; R. Eliezer b. Joel ha-Levi (Bonn, 1140–1225), quoted by R. Mordecai b. Hillel (Germany, 1240?–1298), *Mordecai, Bava Batra* 1:482; Naḥmanides (Spain, 1194–1270), *Responsa Rashba* (attributed to *Ramban*) 280; R. Solomon b. Abraham Adret (Spain, ca. 1235–ca. 1310), *Responsa Rashba,* vol. 2, no. 279; vol. 5, nos. 126, 270, 242.

87. R. Joseph Colon, *Responsa Maharik, shoresh* 14. See, however, R. Ḥayyim Halberstamm (Zanz, 1793–1876), *Divrei Ḥayyim* 2:60.

88. *Responsa Rashba,* vol. 1:788; see also *Responsa Rashba,* vol. 1:399.

89. R. Meir b. Baruch, *Responsa Maharam* (Prague ed.) 941.

90. R. Moses b. Joseph Trani, *Responsa Mabit* 1:237.

91. *Responsa Mabit* 1:307.

92. See *Responsa Rashba* 1:787, 4:185; R. Moses Isserles (Poland, 1525 or 1530–1572), *Responsa Rema* 73.

93. See R. Ezekiel b. Judah ha-Levi Landau (Prague, 1713–1793), *Noda bi-Yhudah, Mahadura Tinyana Yoreh De'ah* 10; Rabbi Mosheh Feinstein (1895–1986), *Iggerot Mosheh, Ḥoshen Mishpat* 104.

94. See *Berakhot* 32b; *Noda bi-Yhudah,* loc. cit.

95. R. Moses Sofer, *Responsa Ḥatam Sofer, Ḥoshen Mishpat,* nos. 41, 57, 79.

96. R. Mordecai Banet (Moravia, 1753–1829), *Perashat Mordecai,* no. 8.

97. See Rabbi J. David Bleich, *Contemporary Halakhic Problems,* vol. 2 (New York: KTAV Publishing House and Yeshiva University Press, 1983), pp. 126–127.

NOTES TO CHAPTER 4

1. In his kabbalist work *Tomer Deborah,* the sixteenth-century mystic R. Moses Cordovero (Safed, 1522–1510) posits that *imitatio Dei* conduct requires an individual not to withhold his goodness even from someone who insulted him and has not yet sought forgiveness. He derives this principle by means of the following reasoning: Since man cannot exist for a single moment

without the grace of God, it follows that even in the *very* moment man sins against God, the life-sustaining power within him is not denied. Despite the fact that man uses the Divine power within him to sin, God, in his infinite mercy, does not arrest this power. Instead, God bears the insult and continues to empower man to move his limbs. Applying the Divine attribute to the realm of interpersonal conduct requires an injured party to not deny goodness to his offender, even while the offense has in no way been rectified. R. Moses' principle can, as it appears to us, be derived from God's conduct of providing Adam and Eve with clothing after they had sinned.

For a discussion and analyses of several aspects of the *imitatio Dei* principle which we have not discussed in the text, see Rabbi Dr. Norman Lamm, "Notes on the Concept of Imitatio Dei," in Leo Landman, ed., *Rabbi Joseph H. Lookstein Memorial Library* (New York: KTAV Publishing House, 1980), pp. 217–229.

2. Maimonides (Egypt, 1135–1204), *Moreh Nevukhim* 2:1. For an elaboration of Maimonides' view, see Rabbi Yehudah L. Kagan, *Halikhut Yehudah,* vol. 1, pp. 268–277.

3. Cf. *Ketubbot* 103a, *Bava Batra* 12b.

4. *Midrash Tanḥuma, Vayyera* 19.

5. *Sanhedrin* 109a.

6. Ibid.

7. *Pirke d'R. Eliezer* 25.

8. *Bereshit Rabbah* 50:10.

9. *Sanhedrin* 109a.

10. *Pirke d'R. Eliezer* 25.

11. *Torat Kohanim B'har;* Maimonides, *Yad, Mattenot Aniyyim* 10:7; R. Jacob b. Asher (Toledo, 1270?–1340), *Tur, Yoreh De'ah* 249:7; R. Joseph Caro (Safed, 1488–1575), *Shulḥan Arukh, Yoreh De'ah* 249:6; R. Jeḥiel Michel Epstein (Belorussia, 1829–1908), *Arukh ha-Shulḥan* 249:15.

12. *Yad,* loc. cit.

13. R. Mosheh Ḥayyim Luzzato, *Da'at Tevunot, siman* 18. For an elaboration of this concept, see R. Shelomo Harkavi, *M'Imrei Shelomo,* pp. 3, 16.

14. Samuel, *Ḥullin* 94a; R. Isaac b. Jacob Alfasi (Algeria, 1013–1103) ad loc.; *Yad, Mekhirah* 18:1–4; R. Asher b. Jeḥiel (Germany, 1250–1327), *Rosh, Ḥullin* 7:18; *Tur, Ḥoshen Mishpat* 228:5–9; *Sh. Ar., Ḥoshen Mishpat* 228:6–9; *Ar. haSh., Ḥoshen Mishpat* 228:3–5.

15. *Ḥullin,* 109b.

16. *Yad, Mattenot Aniyyim* 10:8–14.

17. Deuteronomy 15:8; *Ketubbot* 67b; *Rif* ad loc.; *Yad,* op. cit. 7:3; *Rosh, Ketubbot* 6:8; *Tur, Yoreh De*'ah 250:1; *Sh. Ar., Yoreh De'ah* 250:1; *Ar. haSh., Yoreh De'ah* 250:1–3.

18. R. Moses Isserles (Poland, 1525–1572), *Sh. Ar. Yoreh De'ah* 250:1; see Ar. haSh., op. cit. 250:4–5.

19. Deuteronomy 14:22.

20. See Cyril Domb, ed., *Maaser Kesafim* (New York: Association of Orthodox Jewish Scientists, 1980), pp. 26–29.

21. Rabbi Ezra Basri, *Dinei Mamonot,* vol. 1 (Jerusalem: Rubin Mass, 1974), p. 403.

22. *Yad,* op. cit. 7:5; *Tur,* op. cit. 249:1; *Sh. Ar.,* op. cit. 249:1; *Ar. haSh.,* op. cit. 249:1.

23. *Ketubbot* 50a; *Rif* ad loc.; *Yad, Arakhin* 8:3; *Rosh, Ketubbot* 4:15; *Tur,* loc. cit.; *Sh.Ar.,* loc. cit.; *Rema,* op. cit.; *Ar. haSh.,* loc. cit.

24. See *Dinei Mamonot*, vol. 1, p. 405.

25. R. Ya'ir Ḥayyim Bachrach (Worms, 1638–1701), *Responsa Ḥavot Ya'ir* 224; Domb, *Maaser Kesafim*, pp. 59–60.

26. Domb, *Maaser Kesafim*, pp. 74–79.

27. Ibid., p. 81.

28. Authorities dispute whether indirect taxes, such as sales taxes, are deductible; see Domb, *Maaser Kesafim*, pp. 79–81.

29. Rabbi Moses Feinstein (New York, 1895–1986), *Iggerot Mosheh, Yoreh De'ah* 143.

30. *Tanna De-Bei Eliyahu* 27; *Yad, Mattenot Aniyyim* 7:13; *Tur*, op. cit. 251:4; *Rema*, op. cit. 251:3; *Ar. haSh.*, op. cit. 251:3.

31. *Tanna De-Bei Eliyahu*, loc. cit.; *Tur*, loc. cit.; *Rema*, loc. cit.; *Ar. haSh.*, loc. cit.

32. *Rema*, op. cit. 240:5; *Ar. haSh.* 251:8.

33. R. Shabbetai b. Meir ha-Kohen (Poland, 1621–1663), *Siftei Kohen, Sh. Ar., Yoreh De'ah* 151, n. 4, understands the child-support obligation to end at age six. Theorizing that the child-support obligation ends at the age children customarily go to work. Rabbi Mosheh Feinstein posits that R. Shabbetai's six-year-old benchmark is considerably expanded today. In circles where it is customary for children not to go to work until they marry, the child-support obligation would extend until the child actually gets married. See *Iggerot Mosheh, Yoreh De'ah* 143.

34. *Tanna De-Bei Eliyahu*, loc. cit.; *Tur*, loc. cit.; *Rema*, loc. cit.; *Ar haSh.*, loc. cit.

35. *Sifre*, Deuteronomy 15:7.

36. *Tanna De-Bei Eliyahu*, loc. cit.; *Rema*, loc. cit.; *Ar. haSh.*, op. cit. 251:1.

37. *Sifre*, Deuteronomy 15:7; *Yad*, op. cit. 7:13; *Tur*, op. cit.; Rema, loc. cit.; *Ar. haSh.*, loc. cit.

38. *Sifre*, Deuteronomy 15:7; *Sh. Ar.*, op. cit. 251:3; *Ar. haSh.*, loc. cit.

39. *Ketubbot* 67a; *Rif* ad loc; *Yad*, op. cit. 8: 15–16; *Rosh, Ketubbot* 6:7; *Tur*, op. cit. 251:8; *Sh.Ar.*, op. cit. 251:8; *Ar. HaSh.*, op. cit. 251:10. Faced with the competing claims of food and clothing made by a man and a woman, respectively, the man's food request, however, takes precedence, as relieving hunger is more pressing than relieving the indignity of tattered clothing (*Ar. haSh.*, loc. cit.).

40. *Yad.*, op. cit. 8:17–18; *Tur*, op. cit. 251:9; *Sh. Ar.* 251:9; *Ar. haSh.* 251:11. See, however, *Siftei Kohen, Sh. Ar.*, op. cit. 251, n. 16.

41. R. Pinḥas ha-Levi Horowitz, quoted in R. Moses Sofer (Hungary, 1762–1839), *Ḥatam Sofer, Yoreh De'ah* 231.

42. *Ar. haSh.*, op. cit. 251:4.

43. *Iggerot Mosheh, Yoreh De'ah* 144.

44. Mishnah, *Pe'ah* 8:8–9 and commentary of R. Ovadiah Yarei Bertinoro (Italy, c. 1445–1505) ad loc.

45. Mishnah, *Pe'ah* 8:8; Yad, op. cit. 9:14; Tur, op. cit. 253:4–5; *Sh. Ar.*, op. cit. 253:1; *Ar. haSh.*, op. cit. 253:5.

46. Tosafot, *Bava Kamma* 7a; *Rif* ad loc.; *Tur*, op. cit. 253:8–9, quoted in *Rema*, op. cit. 253:3. For a different view, see *Yad*, op. cit. 9:16, and *Sh. Ar.*, op. cit. 253:3.

47. *Bava Kamma* 7a; *Yad*, op. cit. 9:17; *Tur*, op. cit. 253:8; *Sh. Ar.*, op. cit. 253:3; *Ar. haSh.*, op. cit. 253:8.

48. R. Joseph Caro, *Kesef Mishneh, Yad*, op. cit. 9:17; *Tur*, loc. cit.; *Ar. haSh.*, loc. cit.

49. Mishnah, *Pe'ah* 5:4; *Yad,* op. cit. 9:15; *Tur,* op. cit. 253:9; *Sh. Ar.,* op. cit. 253:4.

50. R. Isaac of Vienna (ca. 1180–ca. 1250) and Rabbeinu Efraim (North Africa, late 11th–early 12th cent.), quoted in *Beit Yosef, Tur,* op. cit. 253.

51. R. Joseph of Corbeil, quoted in *Tur,* op. cit. 253:2 and in *Sh. Ar.,* op. cit. 253:2; *Ar. haSh.,* op. cit., 253:2.

52. *Beit Yosef, Tur,* op. cit. 253.

53. Rabbi S. Z. Auerbach, quoted in Domb, *Maaser Kesafim,* p. 126.

54. Ketubbot 67b; *Rif* ad loc.; *Yad* op. cit. 7:3; *Rosh, Ketubbot* 6:8.

55. *Yad,* loc. cit.; *Tur,* op. cit. 250:1; *Sh. Ar.,* op. cit. 250:1; *Ar. haSh.,* op. cit. 250:1–2.

56. *Shabbat* 118a; *Yad,* op. cit. 9:13; *Tur,* op. cit. 253:1; *Sh. Ar.,* op. cit. 253:1; *Ar. haSh.,* op. cit. 253:1.

57. *Shabbat* 117b; *Rif* ad loc.; *Yad, Shabbat* 30:9; *Rosh, Shabbat* 16:5; *Tur, Oraḥ Ḥayyim* 291:1; *Sh. Ar., Oraḥ Ḥayyim* 291:1; *Ar haSh., Oraḥ Ḥayyim* 291:1–2.

58. Tosafot, *Shabbat* 118a; R. David b. Samuel ha-Levi (Poland, 1586–1667) *Turei Zahav, Sh. Ar., Yoreh De'ah* 253, n. 2; *Ar. haSh., Yoreh De'ah* 253:1.

59. T. J., *Bava Batra* 1:4; R. Mordecai b. Hillel ha-Kohen (Germany, ca. 1240–1298), *Mordecai, Bava Batra* 1:477; R. Isaac b. Moses of Vienna (ca. 1180–ca. 1250), *Or Zaru'a, Hilkhot Pesaḥim, ot* 255.

60. *Ar. haSh.,* op. cit. 245:9, 27.

61. *Tur,* op. cit. 250:1; *Sh. Ar.,* op. cit. 250:1; *Ar. HaSh.,* op. cit. 250:3.

62. *Kiddushin* 29a; *Rif* ad loc.; *Yad, Me'ilah* 3:1; *Rosh, Kiddushin* 1:40; *Tur,* op. cit. 260:1; *Sh. Ar.,* op. cit. 260:1; *Ar. haSh.,* op. cit. 260:4.

63. *Kiddushin* 29a; *Rif* ad loc.; *Yad, Bikkurim* 11:1; *Rosh, Kiddushin* 1:40; *Tur,* op. cit. 305:1; *Sh. Ar.,* op. cit. 305:1; *Ar. haSh.,* op. cit. 305:1–2.

64. *Kiddushin* 29a; *Rif* ad loc.; *Yad, Talmud Torah* 1:1; *Tur,* op. cit. 245; *Sh. Ar.,* op. cit. 245; *Ar. haSh.,* op. cit. 245:1–13.

65. *Kiddushin* 29a; *Rif* ad loc.; *Yad, Issurei Bi'ah* 21:25; *Rosh, Kiddushin* 1:40; *Tur, Even Ha-Ezer* 1.

66. Kiddushin 29a; *Rif* ad loc.; *Rosh, Kiddushin* 1:40; R. Abraham Abele b. Ḥayyim ha-Levi Gombiner (Poland, ca. 1637–1683), *Magen Avraham, Oraḥ Ḥayyim* 156, n. 2.

67. *Kiddushin* 29a; *Rif* ad loc.; *Rosh, Kiddushin* 1:40.

68. Rabbi Binyamin Adler, *Halakhot ve-Halikhot Bar-Miẓvah* (Jerusalem: Or ha-Torah, 1978), p. 192. R. Eliyahu b. Ḥayyim (Constantinople, ca. 1530–ca. 1610) understands the father's obligation to prepare his son for a livelihood to be operative only when the son is beyond the age of majority (*Imrei Shefer* 52).

69. The teaching is recorded in the Mishnah anonymously. R. Yoḥanan (*Sanhedrin* 86a), however, identifies R. Meir as the author of an anonymous mishnaic teaching.

70. *Baraita, Kiddushin* 29a.

71. *Baraita, Kiddushin* 29a; *Kiddushin* 30b and *Rashi* ad loc.

72. R. Nethanel b. Naphtali Ẓevi Weil (Germany, 1687–1769), *Korban Netanel, Rosh, Kiddushin* 1:40, n. 90; *Magen Avraham,* op. cit.

73. Responsa Rosh 6:4, 12.

74. For a discussion of the pure public good case as it pertains to the Jewish public sector, see Aaron Levine, *Free Enterprise and Jewish Law* (New York: KTAV Publishing House and Yeshiva University Press, 1980), pp. 131–160.

75. Mishnah, *Pe'ah* 8:8; *Yad, Mattenot Aniyyium* 9:14; *Tur, Yoreh De'ah* 253:4–5; *Sh. Ar., Yoreh De'ah* 253:1; *Ar. haSh., Yoreh De'ah* 253:5.

76. *Geonim* quoted in *Shittah M'kubbeẓet Ketubbot* 67b.
77. See *Responsa Rosh* 102.
78. *Rema, Sh. Ar., Ḥoshen Mishpat* 163:1; *Ar. haSh., Ḥoshen Mishpat* 163:1.
79. *Baraita, Bava Batra* 8a; *Rif* ad loc.; Yad, op. cit., 9:1–3; *Rosh, Bava Batra* 1:27; *Tur*, op. cit. 256:1–2; *Sh. Ar.*, op. cit. 256:1; *Ar. haSh.*, op. cit. 256:1–2.
80. T.J., *Bava Batra* 1:4; R. Mordecai b. Hillel ha-Kohen (Germany, 1240–1298), *Bava Batra* 1:477; R. Isaac b. Moses of Vienna, *Or Zaru'a, Hilkhot Pesaḥim, ot* 255.
81. *Rema*, op. cit. 163:1; *Ar. haSh.* op. cit. 163:1.
82. The residency requirement is not the same for each of the various charity levies. Twelve months is required for inclusion in the *ma'ot ḥittin* drive (*Or Zaru'a*, quoted in *Rema, Sh. Ar., Oraḥ Ḥayyim* 429:1). Nine months are required for inclusion in the burial fund, and six months for the clothing levy (*Bava Batra* 8a). The residency requirement for inclusion in the daily charity collection and the weekly food collection is a matter of dispute. R. Isaac b. Jacob Alfasi (*Rif, Bava Batra* 8a) and Maimonides (*Yad*, op. cit., 9:12) require thirty days for the former and three months for the latter. Reversing these requirements, R. Asher b. Jeḥiel (*Rosh, Bava Batra* 1:27) and R. Jacob b. Asher (*Tur*, op. cit. 256:5) prescribe thirty days for inclusion in the weekly food collection and three months for inclusion in the daily charity collections.
83. R. Solomon b. Abraham Adret (Spain, ca. 1235–ca. 1310), *Responsa Rashba*, vol. 3:381.
84. *Yad*, op. cit. 7:10; Tur, op. cit. 248:1–2; *Sh. Ar.*, op. cit. 248:1–2; *Ar. haSh.*, op. cit. 248:4–5. For a minority view regarding the nature of the coercion the recalcitrant may be subject to, see the opinions quoted in *Tosafot, Bava Batra* 8b.
85. *Ar. haSh.*, op. cit. 250:12.
86. R. Samson R. Hirsch, *The Pentateuch, Translation and Commentary*, vol. 5 (Gateshead: Judaica Press, 1982), p. 272.
87. *Responsa Rashba*, vol. 3:292, quoted in *Sh. Ar.*, op. cit. 251:4.
88. R. Eliezer b. Samuel of Metz, *Nedarim* 65a, quoted in *Sh. Ar.*, op. cit. 257:8.
89. *Rema, Sh. Ar., Ḥoshen Mishpat* 163:1; *Ar. haSh., Ḥoshen Mishpat* 163:1.
90. Rabbi Ḥayyim Soloveichik, quoted in the name of Rabbi Joseph B. Soloveichik by Rabbi Daniel Lander, "be-Inyan Dei Maḥsoro," in *Kavod ha-Rav* (New York: Student Organization of Yeshiva Rabbi Isaac Elchanan Theological Seminary, 1984), pp. 202–206.
91. R. Isaac of Dampierre, *Tosafot, Bava Batra* 8b.
92. *Responsa Rashba* vol. 3:380, quoted in *Beit Yosef, Tur*, op. cit. 250:5; *Rema*, op. cit. 250:5.
93. *Pesaḥim* 113a.
94. Cf. commentary of R. Solomon b. Meir (France, 12th cent.) and Naḥmanides (Spain, 1194–1270) at Leviticus 19:18.
95. Rabbi Eliyahu Eliezer Dessler (Great Britain, 1891–1954), *Mikhtav MeEliyahu*, 5th ed. (Bnei Berak: A. Kaplan, A. Halperin, 1964), pp. 32–52.
96. Dr. Aaron Kirshenbaum, "The Good Samaritan in Jewish Law," *Diné Israel* 7 (1976): 7–85.
97. Ibid., pp. 84–85.
98. Mishnah, *Bava Meẓia* 2:10; *Rif* ad loc.; *Yad, Roẓeaḥ* 8:8; *Rosh, Bava Meẓia* 2:28; *Tur*, op. cit. 272:4; *Sh. Ar.*, op. cit. 272:7; *Ar. haSh.*, op. cit. 272:7.
99. R. Ephraim Solomon b. Aaron of Lenczycza, *Keli Yakar*, commentary at Exodus 23:5.

100. *Yad, Mattenot Aniyyim* 10:19.

101. *Baḥ, Tur, Ḥoshen Mishpat* 272-8; *Ar. haSh.*, op. cit. 272:9.

102. Mishnah, *Bava Meẓia* 2:10; *Rif* ad loc.; *Yad*, op. cit., 13:8; *Rosh*, op. cit. 2:28; *Tur*, op. cit. 272:8; *Sh. Ar.*, op. cit. 272:3; *Ar. haSh.*, op. cit. 272:7.

103. Rabbi Aaron Lichtenstein, "Sa'od Tis'od Immo-Hishtatfut ha-Mekabbel bi-Gmilot Ḥasadim," in *A. Spiegelman Memorial Volume* (Israel: Moreshet, 1979), pp. 81–93.

104. R. Nissim b. Reuben Gerondi (Spain, 1488–1575), *Responsa Ran*, no. 2.

105. R. Ḥayyim Palaggi (Salonica, 1788–1869), *Massa Ḥayyim, Missim ve-Aroniyyot Maarekhet Alef.*

106. R. Joshua b. Alexander ha-Kohen Falk (Poland, 1555–1614), *Sma, Sh. Ar., Ḥoshen Mishpat* 231, n. 43.

107. *Bava Batra* 90a; *Rif* ad loc.; *Yad, Mekhirah* 14:1; *Rosh, Bava Batra* 5:2; *Tur, Ḥoshen* Mishpat 231:27; *Sh. Ar., Ḥoshen Mishpat* 231:20; *Ar. haSh., Ḥoshen Mishpat* 231:20.

108. *Sma*, op. cit.

109. Rabbi Isser Zalman Meltzer, *Even ha-Ezel, Yad, Mekhirah* 14:9. For an economic analysis of the price ceiling Halakhah imposes in the necessity sector. see Levine, *Free Enterprise and Jewish Law*, pp. 93–95.

110. R. Solomon b. Isaac, *Rashi, Kiddushin* 58b; Naḥmanides, *Torat ha-Adam, sha'ar hasakanah b'hashavat gufo.*

111. Maimonides (commentary at *Mishnah Nedarim* 4:4) regards the obligation to provide medical treatment as an aspect of the duty to restore lost property *(hashavat avedah)*. Included in the Torah's command *and you shall return it to him* (Deuteronomy 22:4) is the duty, should the opportunity arise, to restore an individual *to himself* by effecting a cure for him. Given the health- and life-maintenance nature of medical treatment, Naḥmanides (commentary at Leviticus 28:36) places the obligation to heal under the rubric of the biblical command *and let your brother live with you* (Leviticus 25:36). Finally, R. Yeshayah of Trani I ha-Zaken (ca. 1180–1260, *Tosafot Rid, Berakhot* 60a) and R. Asher b. Jeḥiel (*Tosafot ha-Rosh, Berakhot* 60a) regard the duty to heal as obligatory by dint of the verse *do not stand idly by the blood of your neighbor* (Leviticus 19:16). Since the physician is equipped with the expertise to restore his fellow's health, failing to act when the opportunity arises amounts to a violation of the above negative command.

112. In respect to the question of whether medical treatment as such constitutes a *mitzvah*, independent of its results, see Rabbi Dr. Norman Lamm, "Is It a Mitzvah to Administer Medical Therapy," *Journal of Halacha and Contemporary Society* (Fall 1984): 5–14.

113. For a survey of the rabbinic literature on the permissibility of medical fees, see Rabbi J. David Bleich, *Contemporary Halakhic Problems*, vol. 2, (New York: KTAV Publishing House, Yeshiva University Press, 1983), pp. 68–74.

114. R. Eliezer Fleckeles, *Teshuvat me-Ahavah*, 3:408.

115. R. Solomon b. Abraham Adret, *Responsa Rashba* 1:472.

116. Rabbi Eliezer Waldenberg, *Ramat Raḥel*, no. 24 sec. 3

NOTES TO CHAPTER 5

1. Rabbi Isaac Jacob Weiss (Jerusalem, 1902–), *Responsa Minḥat Yiẓḥak* VI:161; Rabbi Isaac Glickman, "BeDin Hetter Iska le-Halvaot Ẓemudot le-

Madad Yoker ha-Miḥyah o le-Matbe'a Zar," *Noam* 16 (1972): 153–160; Rabbi Jacob Blau, *B'rit Yehudah* (Jerusalem: R. Blau, 1976), pp. 354–335.

2. Cf. Rabbi Shear-Yashuv Cohen, "Piḥut ve Tisuf Matbe'a," in *Torah she-be-Al Peh*, vol. 19, 1977.

3. R. Samuel b. Isaac Sardi (Spain, ca. 1185–1255), *Sefer Ha-Terumot, sha'ar* 46, *ḥelek* 8, *ot* 2; R. Asher b. Jeḥiel (Germany, 1250–1327), *Rosh, Bava Kamma* 9:12; R. Solomon b. Abraham Adret (Spain, ca. 1235–1310), *Rashba, Bava Kamma* 97b.

4. *Rosh*, loc. cit. R. Abraham b. David of Posquières (1125–1198), quoted in *Shittah M'kubbeẓet, Bava Kamma* 97b, however, advances a different rationale for the 20 percent rule.

5. R. Isaac b. Jacob Alfasi (Algeria, 1013–1103), *Rif, Bava Kamma* 98a; Maimonides (Egypt, 1135–1204), *Yad, Malveh* 4:11; *Rosh*, loc. cit.; R. Jacob b. Asher (Germany, 1270–1343), *Tur, Yoreh De'ah* 165; R. Joseph Caro (Safed, 1488–1575), *Shulḥan Arukh, Yoreh De'ah* 165. A dissenting view is advanced by R. Abraham b. David. In his view no accommodation is made for the lender in case of currency depreciation.

6. Tosafot, *Bava Kamma* 97a; *Rosh*, op. cit.; *Tur, Ḥoshen Mishpat* 74:9; R. Mosheh Isserles (Poland, 1525–1572), *Rema, Sh. Ar., Ḥoshen Mishpat* 74:7; R. Jeḥiel Michel Epstein (Belorussia, 1829–1908), *Arukh ha-Shulḥan, Ḥoshen Mishpat* 74:8. R. Solomon b. Isaac (*Rashi, Bava Kamma* 97a), however, draws a distinction between the legal treatment of a monetary loan and a credit sale. It is only in the former case, in his view, that nonstipulation allows the debtor to discharge his debt with the defunct original medium of exchange, though at the time of repayment it circulates nowhere in the world. R. Mordecai b. Hillel (Germany, 1240–1298), *Mordecai, Bava Kamma* 9:110) asserts that toward the end of his life, R. Solomon b. Isaac recanted this view and subscribed to Tosafot's view.

7. *Arukh ha-Shulḥan*, op. cit.; Rabbi Abraham Isaiah Karelitz (Israel, 1878–1953), *Ḥazon Ish, Bava Kamma* 17:31 and *Likkutim, siman* 19 at *Bava Kamma* 89b.

8. *Yad*, op. cit.; R. Israel of Krems (fl. mid. 14th cent.), *Haggahot Asheri, Bava Kamma* 9:11; *Tur*, op. cit. 74:9; *Sh. Ar.*, op. cit. 74:7; *Ar. HaSh.*, op. cit. 74:8.

9. Mishnah, *Bava Meẓia* 75a; *Rif* ad loc.; *Yad, Malveh* 10:3; *Rosh, Bava Meẓia* 5:75; *Tur, Yoreh De'ah* 162:1; *Sh. Ar., Yoreh De'ah* 162:1; R. Abraham Danzig, (Prague, 1748–1820), *Ḥokhmat Adam* 134:1.

10. R. Sheshet, *Bava Meẓia* 75a; *Rif* ad loc.; *Yad*, op. cit.; *Rosh*, op. cit. 5:74; *Tur*, op. cit.; *Sh. Ar.*, op. cit.; *Ḥokhmat Adam*, op. cit.

11. R. Isaac, *Bava Meẓia* 75a; *Rif* ad loc.; *Yad*, op. cit. 10:2; *Rosh*, op. cit. 5:75; *Tur*, op. cit. 162:2; *Sh. Ar.*, op. cit. 162:2; *Ḥokhmat Adam*, op. cit. 134:2.

12. *Responsa Rosh, k'lal* 108, *sief* 16; R. Yom Tov Vidal of Toloso (14th cent.), *Maggid Mishneh, Yad, Malveh* 10:2.

13. R. David b. Samuel ha-Levi (Poland, 1586–1667), *Turei Zahav, Sh. Ar. Yoreh De'ah* 162, n. 3; R. Shabbetai b. Meir ha-Kohen (Poland, 1621–1662), *Siftei Kohen, Sh. Ar., Yoreh De'ah* 162, n. 7; *B'rit Yehudah*, op. cit. p. 317, n. 37.

14. *Siftei Kohen, Sh. Ar.*, op. cit. 162, n. 11.

15. *Bava Meẓia* 72b; *Yad*, op. cit.; *Rosh, Bava Meẓia* 5:61; *Tur*, op. cit.; *Sh. Ar.*, op. cit.; *Ḥokhmat Adam* 134:5.

16. *Ḥokhmat Adam*, op. cit.

17. *Yad*, op. cit. 10:1; *Siftei Kohen*, op. cit. 162, n. 10; *Ḥokhmat Adam*, op. cit.

18. *Yad*, op. cit.

19. R. Abraham b. David of Posquières, *Rabad* at *Yad*, loc. cit.; *Rema, Sh.*

Ar., op. cit. 162:3; R. Isaac b. Sheshet Perfet (Spain, 1326–1408), *Responsa Ribash* 19.

20. *Siftei Kohen, Sh. Ar.*, op. cit., n. 11.
21. *Yad*, op. cit.
22. R. Joseph Caro, *Beit Yosef, Tur*, op. cit.
23. *Responsa Rosh*, quoted in *Beit Yosef*, loc. cit.; *B'rit Yehudah*, p. 320, n. 48.
24. *Turei Zahav, Sh. Ar.*, op. cit. 162, n. 3.
25. *Siftei Kohen, Sh. Ar.*, op. cit., n. 9.
26. R. Yonathan Eybeschuetz (Prague, 1695–1764), *Kereti-u-Feleti, Sh. Ar. Yoreh De'ah* 162.
27. R. Isaac b. Shesehet Perfet, *Responsa Ribash* 19.
28. *R. Yoḥanan, Bava Meẓia* 45a; *Rif* ad loc.; *Rosh, Bava Meẓia* 45a; *Tur*, op. cit. 162:1.
29. R. Ḥiyya Rofe (Safed, d. 1620), *Ma'aseh Ḥiyya* 17.
30. Mishnah, *Bava Meẓia* 5:8; *Rif, Bava Meẓia* 72b; *Yad*, op. cit. 9:1; *Rosh, Bava Meẓia* 5:60; *Tur*, op. cit. 175; *Sh. Ar.* op. cit. 175:1–3; *Ḥokhmat Adam* 141:1–4.
31. *Responsa Rif*, quoted in *Shittah Mekubbeẓet, Bava Meẓia* 72b.
32. R. Ḥananel b. Hushi'el (North Africa, 11th cent.) and R. Yom Tov Ishbili, quoted in *Shittah Mekubbeẓet*, op. cit.
33. *Rema, Sh. Ar.*, op. cit. 174:1.
34. *Ran, Bava Meẓia* 72a.
35. Rabbi Ezra Basri, *Dinei Mamonot* (Jerusalem: Rubin Mass, 1974), vol. 1, p. 127. Rabbi Basri's formulation is apparently identical with the *criterion* R. Yom Tov Ishbili's teachers set forth in approximately the thirteenth century. This formulation was rejected by R. Ishbili. *See Shittah Mekubbeẓet*, op. cit.
36. *Rif, Mishnah, Bava Meẓia* 5:9. R. Joseph Caro posits that this is the view of Maimonides as well (*see Beit Yosef, Tur*, op. cit. 162).
37. R. Moses Isserles, *Rema, Sh. Ar.*, op. cit. 162:1.
38. R. Isaac b. Moses of Vienna (late 13th cent.), quoted by R. Joshua Boaz b. Simeon (Italy, 16th cent.), *Shiltei Gibborim, Pesaḥim* II and by R. Moses Isserles, *Darkhei Mosheh, Oraḥ Ḥayyim* 450. *See B'rit Yehudah*, op. cit., pp. 310–311.
39. *Yad*, op. cit. 7:10; *Tur*, op. cit. 176:7; *Sh. Ar.*, op. cit. 176:7; *Ḥokhmat Adam* 136:3.
40. Mishnah, *Bava Meẓia* 5:10; *Rif* ad loc.; Yad, op. cit. 7:11; *Rosh, Bava Meẓia* 5:78; *Tur*, op. cit. 160:9; *Sh. Ar.*, op. cit. 160:9; *Ḥokhmat Adam*, loc. cit.
41. R. Joshua ha-Kohen Falk, *Perishah, Tur*, op. cit. 160, n. 14.
42. Rabbi Mordecai Dov Twersky (Hornestopol, 1840–1903), *Turei Zahav, Yoreh De'ah* 162.
43. *Tur*, op. cit. 160.
44. *Perishah, Tur*, loc. cit., n. 15.
45. R. Abraham b. David of Posquières, quoted in *Shittah Mekubbeẓet, Bava Meẓia* 75a.
46. *B'rit Yehudah*, op. cit., *pp. 208–209.*
47. *Yad, Mattenot Aniyyim* 7:5; *Tur*, op. cit. 249:1; *Sh. Ar.*, op. cit. 249:1; *Ar. haSh., Yoreh De'ah* 249:1. Rabbi Ezra Basri's survey of the responsa literature concludes that the majority of the talmudic decisors regard the 10 percent level as an obligation by rabbinical, as opposed to pentateuchal, decree. See *Basri, Dinei Mamonot*, vol. 1, p. 403.
48. For a detailed discussion of the *ma'aser* base, *see* Cyril Domb, ed., *Ma'aser Kesafim* (New York: Philipp Feldheim, 1980), pp. 41–54.

49. Rabbi Mosheh Feinstein, *Iggerot Mosheh*, vol. 5, *Yoreh De'ah* 114.
50. See Tosafot, *Ketubbot* 105a.
51. The Talmud in *Ketubbot* 105b records this formula only in respect to the publicly appointed judges of Jerusalem who preside over cases of robbery. Maimonides (*Yad, Shekalim* 4:10), however, extends the need rule to public proofreaders of holy books. Maimonides' extension, in our view, leads to the generalization of the need formula to all religious functionaries hired by the public.
52. R. Mosheh Sofer (Hungary, 1762–1839), *Responsa Ḥatam Sofer, Ḥoshen Mishpat* 166; R. Leopold Winkler (Hungary, b. 1844) *Levushei Mordecai, Ḥoshen Mishpat* 15.
53. *Tur*, op. cit. 173:21; *Sh. Ar.*, op. cit. 173:12; R. Joel Sirkes, *Baḥ, Tur*, op. cit. 161; *B'rit Yehudah*, op. cit., p. 37.
54. Leviticus 19:13.
55. Baḥ, op. cit.
56. R. Eliezer of Toul, quoted in R. Meir ha-Kohen, *Teshuvot Maimuniyyot, Sefer Mishpatim* 16; R. Meir b. Baruch of Rothenburg, quoted in R. Yeruḥam b. Meshullam, *Toledot Adam ve-Ḥavvah, n'tiv* 29, pt. 3; *Baḥ*, op. cit.; R. Mosheh Sofer, *Novellae Ḥatam Sofer, Bava Meẓia* 73a; R. Isaac Yehudah Schmelkes, *Beit Yiẓḥak, Yoreh De'ah* 11:2, *ot* 2.
57. R. Isaac b. Moses of Vienna, *Or Zaru'a, Bava Meẓia* 5:21; R. Israel of Krems, *Haggahot Asheri, Bava Meẓia* 5:21; *Beit Yosef, Tur*, op. cit. 160.
58. *Baḥ*, op. cit. For alternative rationalizations of R. Eliezer of Toul's view, see *Novellae Ḥatam Sofer, Bava Meẓia* 33a, and *Beit Yiẓḥak, Yoreh De'ah* 11:2, *ot* 2.
59. R. Judah Rosanes, (Turkey, 1657–1727) *Mishneh la-Melekh, Yad, Malveh* 7:11.
60. Rabbi Naḥum Rakover, "Piẓuyim al Ikkuv Kesafim," in I. Raphael, ed., *Torah she-be'al Peh* (Jerusalem: Mosad haRav Kook, 1977), p. 216.
61. *B'rit Yehudah*, p. 36.
62. *Bava Kamma* 66a; *Yad, Gezelah* 1:4; *Tur, Ḥoshen Mishpat* 360:1; *Sh. Ar., Ḥoshen Mishpat* 360:1; *Ar. haSh., Ḥoshen Mishpat* 360:1. Provided the article of theft has not been materially changed, the thief must return it intact even if doing so would involve the extraordinary inconvenience of removing it from a structure he subsequently built. Nevertheless, to encourage evildoers to make amends, the sages suspended the obligation in this instance, and instead, required the thief merely to make restitution monetarily (see Mishnah, *Gittin* 5:5).
63. *Bava Meẓia* 43a; *Rif* ad loc.; *Yad*, op. cit. 3:1; *Rosh, Bava Meẓia* 111:27; *Tur*, op. cit. 362:7; *Sh. Ar.*, op. cit. 362:10; *Ar. haSh.*, op. cit. 362:15.
64. *Bava Kamma* 65a; *Rif* ad loc.; *Yad*, op. cit. 3:2; *Rosh* loc. cit.; *Tur*, op. cit. 362:8; *Sh. Ar.*, op. cit. 362:11; *Ar. haSh.* loc. cit.
65. R. Joshua ha-Kohen Falk, *Sma, Sh. Ar.*, op. cit. 362, n. 21; *Ar. haSh.*, loc. cit.

NOTES TO CHAPTER 6

1. Harvey Leibenstein, "Allocation Efficiency vs. X-Efficiency," *American Economic Review* 56 (June 1966): 392–415.
2. *Shabbat* 129a.
3. *Kiddushin* 32a.

4. *Ḥullin* 7b.
5. Shabbat 67b.
6. R. Moses b. Jacob of Coucy (France, early 13th cent.), *Sefer Mizvot Gadol, lavin* 229; R. Isaac b. Joseph of Corbeil (France, d. 1280), *Sefer Mizvot Katan, siman* 175; R. Jeroḥam b. Meshullam (France, 1280–1350), *Meisharim, n'tiv* 31; R. Eliezer b. Samuel of Metz (ca. 1175), *Yere'im [ha-Shalem]* 382; *Tosafot, Bava Mezia* 32b; *Sefer ha-Ḥinnukh* 529; Maimonides (Egypt, 1135–1204), *Yad, Melakhim* 6:10, however, regards the extensions as prohibited only by dint of rabbinical decree. This view is shared by R. Ezekiel b. Judah ha-Levi Landau, *Noda bi-Yhudah, Mahadura Tinyana, ḥelek Yoreh De'ah,* no. 10.
7. Maimonides, *Yad,* op. cit. 6:8.
8. *Bava Kamma* 91b; *Yad,* op. cit. 6:9; R. Asher b. Jeḥiel (Germany, 1250–1327); *Rosh, Bava Kamma* 8:15.
9. Leibenstein, op. cit., p. 415.
10. R. Menaḥem b. Solomon Meiri, *Beit ha-Beḥirah, Bava Kamma* 91b; Gaon, quoted by R. Bezalel Ashkenazi in *Shittah Mekubbezet, Bava Kamma* 91b.
11. R. Yehonatan of Lunel (Provence, ca. 1150–1215); R. Ḥananel b. Hushi'el (Tunisia, ca. 1055); R. Abraham b. David of Posquières (ca. 1120–1197), quoted in *Shittah Mekubbezet,* loc. cit.
12. Tosafot, *Kiddushin* 32a; R. Shneur Zalman of Lyady (1745–1813), *Shulḥan Arukh ha-Rav, Hilkhot Shemirat ha-Guf ve-Nefesh, sief* 14.
13. *Rosh,* op. cit.
14. R. David b. Samuel ha-Levi (Poland, 1586–1667), *Turei Zahav, Sh. Ar. Yoreh De'ah* 116, n. 6.
15. R. Jacob Emden (Germany, 1697–1776), Responsa *She'elat Yavetz,* no. 71.
16. Rabbi Naphtali Zevi Judah Berlin (Russia, 1817–1893), *Meshiv Davar* 10; *See* Rabbi Yosef Pinḥat Levinson, "Be-Din Kezizat Ilan Ma'akhal," *HaPardes* 34, no. 5 (Shevat 1960): 10–12.
17. Rabbi Eliezer Mosheh Horowitz (Pinsk, 19th cent.), *Haggahot ve-Ḥidushin Shabbat* 129a.
18. R. Ḥananel b. Hushi'el, *Shabbat* 129a; R. Nissim b. Reuben Gerondi (Spain, ca. 1290–1375), *Ran, Shabbat* 129a.
19. R. Ḥananel b. Hushi'el, loc. cit.; *Ran,* loc. cit.
20. *Ta'anit* 20b; R. Abraham Abele b. Ḥayyim ha-Levi Gombiner (Poland, ca. 1637–1683), *Magen Avraham, Sh. Ar. Oraḥ Ḥayyim* 171, n. 1.
21. *Rashi, Ta'anit* 20b.
22. *Magen Avraham,* op. cit.
23. Ibid.; *Ar. haSh., Oraḥ Ḥayyim* 171:2.
24. R. Menaḥem b. Solomon Meiri, *Beit ha-Beḥirah, Ta'anit* 20b.
25. Halakhically, to retain its identity as a fruit tree, the tree according to *Sefer ha-Ḥinnukh,* must yield sufficient fruit to make its maintenance profitable. An application of this principle is provided by the minimum annual yields given at *Bava Kamma* 91b for the palm and olive trees. These annual yields are a *kab* (approx. 549 cc.) and a quarter of a *kab,* respectively. *See Sefer ha-Ḥinnukh* 529.
26. R. Solomon b. Isaac, *Rashi, Bava Kamma* 91b.
27. *Bava Kamma* 91b.
28. R. Mosheh Sofer, *Responsa Ḥatam Sofer, Yoreh De'ah* 102.
29. Ibid.
30. Maimonides, *Yad, Mekhirah* 18:4; R. Jacob b. Asher (Germany 1275–1340), *Tur, Ḥoshen Mishpat* 228:16; R. Joseph Caro (1488–1575), *Shulḥan Arukh,*

Ḥoshen Mishpat 228:18; R. Jeḥiel Michel Epstein (Belorussia, 1829–1908), *Arukh ha-Shulḥan, Ḥoshen Mishpat* 228:14.

31. R. Solomon b. Isaac, *Rashi, Sanhedrin* 64b.

32. Mishnah, *Bava Meẓia* 11:13; R. Isaac b. Jacob Alfasi (Algeria, 1013–1103), *Rif, Bava Meẓia* 33a; *Yad, Gezalah* 12:1; *Rosh, Bava Meẓia* 11:30; *Tur,* op. cit. 264:1; *Sh. Ar.* op. cit. 264:1; *Ar. haSh.* 264:1.

33. R. Judah, *Bava Meẓia* 33a and *Rashi* ad loc; *Ar. haSh.*, loc. cit.

34. *Rif, Bava Batra* 21b; *Tosafot, Bava Batra* 21b; Yad, *Shekhenim* 6:18; *Rosh, Bava Batra* 2:12; *Tur,* op. cit. 156:10; *Sh. Ar.*, op. cit. 156:5; *Ar. haSh.*, op. cit. 156:6.

35. *Piskei Din shel Botei ha-Din ha-Rabbaniyim bi-Yisrael* 6, no. 3 (Jerusalem, 1965): 90; see Naḥum Rakover, *Halikhut ba-Misḥar,* no. 42 (Misrad ha-Mishpatim, 1976), p. 12.

36. For a full discussion of these rulings, see Aaron Levine, *Free Enterprise and Jewish Law* (New York: KTAV Publishing House and Yeshiva University Press, 1980), pp. 24–26.

37. R. Mosheh Sofer, *Responsa Ḥatam Sofer, Ḥoshen Mishpat* 78.

38. Rabbi Mosheh Feinstein, *Iggerot Mosheh, Ḥoshen Mishpat* 38.

39. Dr. Shillem Warhaftig, *Hassagot Gevul ve-Tovat ha-Ẓebur,* no. 38 (Jerusalem: Misrad ha-Mishpatim, 1975), pp. 19–20.

40. R. Ḥayyim Sofer, *Maḥaneh Ḥayyim, Ḥoshen Mishpat* 2:46.

41. R. Isaac Aaron Ettinger, *Mahari ha-Levi,* vol. 2, no. 130.

42. Rabbi Mordecai Yaakov Breisch, Responsa *Ḥelkat Yaakov* 2:65.

43. R. Joseph Caro, *Beit Yosef, Tur, Ḥoshen Mishpat* 156:12; *Ar. haSh.*, op. cit. 156:11.

44. R. Ephraim Zalmon Margoliot (1762–1828), *Beit Ephraim, Ḥoshen Mishpat* 26; Ḥelkat Yaakov, op. cit.; Rabbi Isaac Arieli, *Enayim le Mishpat, Bava Batra* 21b.

45. Piskei Din Rabbaniyim, vol. 6, p. 90; see Naḥum Rakover, *Halikhut ha-Misḥar,* no. 41 (Jerusalem: Misrad ha-Mishpatim, 1976), pp. 1–27.

46. R. Shneur Zalman of Lyady, *Shulḥan Arukh ha-Rav, Hilkhot Shemirat ha-Guf ve-Nefesh,* par. 14.

47. R. Ezekiel b. Judah ha-Levi Landau, Responsa *Noda bi-Yhudah, Mahadura Tinyana, Yoreh De'ah,* no. 10.

48. *Yad, Sekhirut* 13:7; *Tur,* op. cit. 337:20; *Sh. Ar.*, op. cit. 337:20; *Ar. haSh.*, op. cit. 337:26.

49. *Baraita, Kiddushin* 33a; *Rif* ad loc.; *Yad, Talmud Torah* 6:2; *Rosh, Kiddushin* 1:53; *Tur, Yoreh De'ah* 244:5; *Sh. Ar., Yoreh De'ah* 244:5; *Ar. haSh., Yoreh De'ah* 244:7.

50. *Ta'anit* 23a.

51. *Berakhot* 16a.

52. R. Meir ha-Kohen (Germany, fl. 13th cent.), *Haggahot Maimuniyyot, Yad, Berakhot* 1; *Sh. Ar., Oraḥ Ḥayyim* 110:2, 191:2; *Ar. haSh., Oraḥ Ḥayyim* 110:7, 191:4.

53. *Ar. haSh.*, loc. cit.

54. Dr. Shillem Warhaftig, *Dinei Avodah ba-Mishpat ha-Ivri,* vol. 1 (Jerusalem: Moreshet, 1968), p. 324.

55. R. Isaac b. Moses of Vienna, *Or Zaru'a,* vol. 3, *Bava Meẓia* 77a, *piskah* 242. For the legal distinction between the *po'el* and the *kabbelan,* see also *Rashi, Bava Meqia* 112a; *Beit ha-Beḥirah, Bava Meẓia* 112a; R. Meir b. Baruch of Rothenburg (Germany, ca. 1370–ca. 1390) *Responsa R. Meir b. Baruch* 477; R. Joshua ha-Kohen Falk, *Sma, Sh. Ar., Ḥoshen Mishpat* 333, n. 16.

56. *Yad, Sekhirut* 13:7; *Tur, Ḥoshen Mishpat* 337:20; *Sh. Ar., Ḥoshen Mishpat* 337:20; *Ar. haSh., Ḥoshen Mishpat* 337:26.

57. Tosefta, *Bava Meẓia* 8:2; Talmud Jerusalem, *Demai* 8:3; *Rif, Bava Meẓia* 90b; *Yad,* op. cit. 13:6; *Rosh, Bava Meẓia* 7:3; *Tur,* op. cit. 337:19; *Sh. Ar.* op. cit. 337:19; *Ar. haSh.* op. cit. 337:25.

58. T. J., *Demai,* loc. cit.; *Rif,* loc. cit., *Sh. Ar.,* loc. cit.; *Ar. haSh.,* loc. cit.

59. R. Mordecai b. Hillel (Germany, ca. 1240–ca. 1298), *Mordecai, Bava Meẓia* 6:343.

60. *Yad,* loc. cit.; *Tur,* loc. cit.; *Sh. Ar.,* loc. cit.; *Ar. haSh.,* loc. cit.

61. *Ar. haSh.,* loc. cit.

62. *Dinei Avodah,* p. 331.

63. *Responsa R. Gershom Me'or ha-Golah* 72.

64. *Torat Kohanim,* at Leviticus 25:43.

65. *Sefer ha-Ḥinukh* 346. The authorship of this work is unknown. Some authorities attribute its authorship to R. Aaron ha-Levi of Barcelona (1235–1300).

NOTES TO CHAPTER 7

1. Exodus 22:24; Leviticus 25:36; Deuteronomy 23:20; see R. Joseph Caro (Safed, 1488–1575), *Shulḥan Arukh, Yoreh De'ah* 159–177.

2. R. Joseph Saul ha-Levi Nathanson (Lemberg, 1810–1875), Responsa *Shoe'l u-Meshiv, mahadura kamma,* pt. 3:31; R. Joseph Raphael b. Ḥayyim Joseph Ḥazzan (Jerusalem, 1741–1820), *Ḥikrei Lev, Yoreh De'ah* 17; R. Isaac Schmelkes (Galicia, 1828–1906), Responsa *Beit Yiẓhak, Yoreh De'ah* 2:32, *kuntras aḥaron.*

3. Manuscript of R. Shimon Greenfeld, published by courtesy of Rabbi M. Lemberger in *No'am,* 1960, pp. 244–250; Rabbi Mosheh Feinstein (New York, 1895–1986), *Iggerot Mosheh, Yoreh De'ah* 2:62, 63.

4. Rabbi Isaac Jacob Weiss (Jerusalem, 1902–), *Minḥat Yiẓhak* 3:1; R. Mordecai Jacob Breisch (Israel, 1896–), Responsa *Ḥelkat Yaakov* 3:190.

5. Mishnah, *Bava Meẓa* 5:5; R. Isaac b. Jacob Alfasi (Algeria, 1013–1103) and R. Mosheh b. Jacob of Coucy (13th cent.), quoted by R. Joseph Caro (*Beit Yosef, Tur, Yoreh Deah* 177); R. Moses Isserles (Poland, 1525–1572), *Rema, Sh. Ar.,* op. cit. 177:3; R. Abraham Danzig (Vilna, 1748–1820), *Ḥokhmat Adam* 142:5; Rabbi Ezra Basri, *Dinei Mamonot,* vol. 1 (Jerusalem: Reuben Mass, 1974), pp. 146–147.

6. Mishnah, *Bava Meẓia* 5:5; *Rif* ad loc.; Maimonides (Egypt, 1135–1204), *Yad, Sheluḥin* 6:2; R. Asher b. Jeḥiel (Germany, 1250–1327), *Rosh, Bava Meẓia* 5:39; R. Jacob b. Asher (Toledo, 1270?–1340), *Tur, Yoreh, De'ah* 177:1–2; *Sh. Ar.,* op. cit. 177:2; *Ḥokhmat Adam* 142:2.

7. R. David b. Samuel ha-Levi (Poland, 1586–1667), *Turei Zahav, Sh. Ar.,* op. cit. 177, n. 5; R. Shabbetai b. Meir ha-Kohen (Lithuania, 1621–1662), *Siftei Kohen, Sh. Ar.,* op. cit. 177, n. 9; *Ḥokhmat Adam,* loc. cit. For the monetary requirement of the nominal fee, see *Dinei Mamonot,* vol. 1, pp. 144–145.

8. R. Solomon b. Isaac (France, 1040–1105), commentary at Mishnah 5:5; *Yad,* op. cit.; *Ḥokhmat Adam,* op. cit.

9. *Bava Meẓia* 70a; *Rif* ad loc.; *Yad, Malveh* 5:8; *Rosh,* op. cit. 5:50; *Tur,* op. cit. 177:1; *Sh. Ar.,* op. cit. 177:1; *Ḥokhmat Adam* 131:4, 142:1.

10. Tosafot, *Bava Kamma* 102a; R. Baruch (ca. 1150–1221), quoted in *Morde-*

cai, Bava Kamma 9:122; *Tur,* op. cit. 177:14; *Sh. Ar.,* op. cit. 177:5; *Rema,* op. cit. 177:5; *Ḥokhmat Adam* 142:26. Limiting the protective force of the devolvement clause, R. Abraham Y. Karelitz (1878–1953), *Ḥazon Ish, Yoreh De'ah* 76:1, posits that the *iska* agreement may only call for B to assume full responsibility for loss when the losses occur as a result of B's failure to adhere to A's conditions. Should the realized loss be unrelated to B's departure from A's conditions, the loss must be divided according to the profit-loss stipulation of the *iska* agreement. R. Shneur Zalman of Lyady (1745–1813), *Shulḥan Arukh of the Rav, Hilkhot Ribbit, seif* 44, however, validates the devolvement clause even for losses not caused by B's departure from A's conditions.

11. R. Abraham b. Mordecai ha-Levi (late 17th cent.), *Ginnat Veradim, Yoreh De'ah* 6:9.

12. *Ḥazon Ish,* op. cit.

13. *Rema,* loc. cit.; *Ḥokhmat Adam* 142:6.

14. R. Israel b. Petaḥiah Isserlein (Germany, 1390–1460), quoted in *Turei Zahav, Sh. Ar.,* op. cit. 167, n. 1, and in *Siftei Kohen, Sh. Ar.,* op. cit. 167, n. 1; *Ḥokhmat Adam,* loc. cit.

15. *Turei Zahav,* loc. cit.

16. Ibid.; *Siftei Kohen,* loc. cit.; *Ḥokhmat Adam,* loc. cit.

17. R. Moses Isserles, *Responsa Rema,* no. 80; R. Meir b. Gedaliah Lublin (1558–1616), *Responsa Maharam Lublin* 135; *Ḥokhmat Adam* 142:7.

18. R. Moses b. Joseph Trani (Safed, 1500–1580), *Responsa Ma Bit* 43; *Ginnat Veradim, Yoreh De'ah* 6:8–9; *Sho'el u-Meshiv,* vol. 3, pt. 1:137; R. Shalom Mordecai Schwadron (Galicia, 1835–1911), *Responsa Maharsham* 2:215.

19. *Turei Zahav,* op. cit. 167, n. 1.

20. *Responsa Ḥelkat Yaakov* 3:207; Rabbi Jacob Blau, *B'rit Yehudah* (Jerusalem, 1976), p. 593.

21. R. Solomon Leib Tabak (Hungary, 1832–1908), *Teshurot Shai 1:3; R. Meir Eisenstadt (Poland, 1670–1744), Panim Meirot* 2:3; R. Ḥayyim Halberstamm (Poland, 1793–1876), *Divrei Ḥayyim* II, *hashmattot,* no. 16; *Iggerot Mosheh, Yoreh De'ah* 62, 63.

22. Rabbi Meir Arak (Poland, ca. 1925), *Imrei Yosher* 1:108.

23. Rabbi Shiloh Raphael, *Torah she-be'al Peh,* 5737.

24. *Tur,* op. cit. 160:12; *Sh. Ar.,* op. cit. 160:7; *Ḥokhmat Adam* 131:10.

25. For a development of talmudic and rishonic sources dealing with both the *gemirat da'at* and the *semikhat da'at* conditions, see Shalom Albeck, *Dinei Mamonot be-Talmud* (Tel Aviv: Dvir, 1976), pp. 112–143.

26. *Bava Batra* 168a; *Rif* ad loc.; *Yad, Mekhirah* 11; *Rosh, Bava Batra* 10:19; *Tur, Ḥoshen Mishpat* 207:12; *Sh. Ar., Ḥoshen Mishpat* 207:9–13; R. Jeḥiel Miche̩l Epstein (Belorussia, 1829–1908), *Arukh ha-Shulḥan, Ḥoshen Mishpat* 207:22–53.

27. R. Solomon b. Isaac, *Rashi, Sanhedrin* 24b.

28. Ibid.; Tosafot, *Bava Meẓia* 74b; Naḥmanides (Spain, 1194–1270), *Ramban, Bava Batra* 168a; *Rema, Sh. Ar., Ḥoshen Mishpat* 207:13.

29. *Bava Meẓia* 104b.

30. *Rashi,* loc. cit. Though Rishonim generally take the position, along with *Rashi,* that a game of chance is not *asmakhta,* a gambling debt is by no means treated as an ordinary debt in Jewish law. The winner of a game of chance, according to one view, is not entitled to the pot unless both players *put down cash* in the pot before the game started. Should the game have been played on the good faith of the players, the winner is not entitled to his winnings. Expressing an even stricter ruling in this matter, another view would not confer title to the pot on the winner unless, prior to the game, the

bets were placed on a surface belonging to both players. What the latter condition accomplishes is to allow the winner to aquire *immediate* title to his winnings by dint of *kinyan ḥazar*. In the absence of this condition, the gambling debt is uncollectable (see *Rema*, op. cit. 207:13).

31. R. Isaac b. Sheshet Perfet (Spain, 1326–1408), *Responsa Ribash* 308.

32. *Talmedei haRashba*, quoted in *Beit Yosef, Tur*, op. cit. 308.

33. *Ramban* and *Ran* on interpretation of R. Joseph Caro, loc. cit.

34. R. Jacob Tam, quoted in *Tosafot, Bava Meẓia* 74a and in *Tosafot, Sanhedrin* 25a.

35. R. Solomon b. Abraham Adret (Spain, ca. 1235–ca. 1310), quoted in *Shittah Mekubbeẓet, Bava Batra* 168a.

36. R. Joseph Caro, *Kesef Mishneh, Yad, Edut* 10:4.

37. *Yad, Mekhirah* 11:2, 7.

38. *Yad*, op. cit. 11:13–14.

39. Rishonim have advanced various opinions as to what constitutes a *bet din ḥashuv*. Three individuals having expertise in the laws of *asmakhta* satisfy the criterion of *bet din ḥashuv*, according to R. Asher b. Jeḥiel (*Responsa Rosh, K'lal* 72, *sieff* 5). R. Mordecai b. Hillel (Germany, 1240?–1298), however, defines *bet din ḥashuv* as the most distinguished local court. (*Mordecai, Bava Batra* 5:323). Finally, R. Vidal Yom Tov of Toloso (Spain, 2d half of 14th cent.) regards a publicly appointed judge, even if not ordained, as meeting the definition of *bet din ḥashuv* (*Maggid Mishneh, Yad, Mekhirah* 11:13).

40. "From now" *alone*, however, counteracts *asmakhta* according to R. Tam and others in the loan-mortgage case discussed in *Bava Meẓia* 66a: A lends money to B on his field and stipulates, "If you do not repay me within three years the field is forfeit to me." B's failure to repay the loan within the stipulated time does not normally confer A with title to the field, as it constitutes an *asmakhta* undertaking. Nonetheless, inclusion of a "from now" clause makes the stipulation fully valid. Why a "from now" clause alone sufficies to remove the *asmakhta* problem in this instance is explained in various ways: (1) this loan-mortgage undertaking is very much akin to a sale, as B transfers the property to A immediately as a mortgage; (2) since the loan is a favor, we presume that B agrees to unreservedly transfer the property to A if he does not repay it (see *Ar. haSh.*, op. cit. 207:43).

41. R. Jacob Tam, quoted in *Tosafot, Bava Meẓia* 66a; R. Nissim b. Reuben Gerondi (Spain, 1310–?1375), *Ran, Nedarim* 27b; *Rosh, Bava Meẓia* 5:29; *Mordecai, Bava Meẓia* 5:321. This school of thought is quoted in *Rema, Sh. Ar.*, op. cit. 207:14.

42. *Yad*, op. cit. 11:18; *Tur*, op. cit. 207:16, *Sh. Ar.*, op. cit. 207:16; *Sh. Ar.*, op. cit. 207:20; *Ar. haSh.*, op. cit. 207:47.

43. Mishnah, *Bava Meẓia* 75a; *Rif* ad loc.; *Yad, Malveh* 10:3; *Rosh, Bava Meẓia* 5:75; *Tur, Yoreh De'ah* 162:1; *Sh. Ar., Yoreh De'ah* 162:1; *Ḥokhmat Adam* 134:1.

44. R. Sheshet, *Bava Meẓia* 75a; *Rif* ad loc.; *Yad*, op. cit.; *Rosh*, op. cit. 5:74; *Tur*, op. cit.; *Sh. Ar.*, op. cit.; *Ḥokhmat Adam*, op. cit.

45. *Bava Meẓia* 72b; *Yad*, op. cit. 10:1; *Rosh, Bava Meẓia* 5:61; *Tur*, op. cit.; *Sh. Ar.*, op. cit. 162:3; *Ḥokhmat Adam* 134:5.

46. *Yad*, op. cit. 10:1; *Siftei Kohen*, op. cit. 162, n. 10; *Ḥokhmat Adam*, op. cit.

47. *Yad*, op. cit. 10:2.

48. *Beit Yosef, Tur*, op. cit.

49. See *Responsa Rosh, k'lal* 108, *siman* 15.

50. *Turei Zahav*, op. cit. 162, n. 3.

51. R. Yonathan Eybeschuetz (Poland, 1690/95–1764), *Kereti-u-Feleti, Sh. Ar., Yoreh De'ah* 162.

52. *Siftei Kohen, Sh. Ar.*, op. cit., n. 9.

53. Mishnah, *Bava Meẓia* 5:8; *Rif, Bava Meẓia* 72b; *Yad*, op. cit. 9:1; *Rosh, Bava Meẓia* 5:60; *Tur*, op. cit. 175; *Sh. Ar.* op. cit. 175:1–3; *Ḥokhmat Adam* 141:1–4.

54. *Responsa Rif*, quoted in *Shittah Mekubbeẓet, Bava Meẓia* 72b.

55. R. Ḥananel b. Hushi'el (North Africa, 11th cent.) and R. Yom Tov Ishbili, quoted in *Shittah Mekubbeẓet*, op. cit.

56. *Rema, Sh. Ar.*, op. cit. 174:1.

57. *Ran, Bava Meẓia* 72a.

58. *Dinei Mamonot*, vol. 1, p. 127. Rabbi Basri's formulation is apparently identical with the *criterion* R. Yom Tov Isbili's teachers set forth in approximately the thirteenth century; this formulation was rejected by R. Ishbili. See *Shittah Mekubbeẓet*, op. cit.

59. R. Isaac, *Bava Meẓia* 75a; *Rif* ad loc.; *Yad*, op. cit. 10:2; *Rosh*, op. cit. 5:75; *Tur*, op. cit. 162:2; *Sh. Ar.*, op. cit. 162:2; *Ḥokhmat Adam*, op. cit. 134:2.

60. *Responsa Rosh, k'lal*, 108, *sieff* 16; *Maggid Mishneh, Yad, Malveh* 10:2.

61. *Turei Zahav*, op. cit. 162, n. 38; *Siftei Kohen*, op. cit. 162, n. 7; *B'rit Yehudah*, p. 317, n. 37.

62. *Bava Batra* 90b; *Rif* ad loc.; *Yad, Mekhirah* 14:5–6; *Tur, Ḥoshen Mishpat* 231:29; *Sh. Ar., Ḥoshen Mishpat* 231:34; *Ar. haSh., Ḥoshen Mishpat* 231:24. For an interesting glimpse into how the sages viewed the effect of hoarding on market price, see *Bava Batra* 90b.

63. *Bava Batra* 90b.

64. Ibid.; *Rif* ad loc.; *Yad*, loc. cit; *Tur*, loc. cit.; *Sh. Ar.*, loc. cit.; *Ar. haSh.*, loc. cit.

65. See Marcus Arkin, *Aspects of Jewish Economic History* (Philadelphia: Jewish Publication Society, 1975), pp. 22–33.

66. *Ar. haSh.*, op. cit. 231:23.

67. *Bava Batra* 91a; *Rif* ad loc.; *Yad*, op. cit. 14:4; *Sh. Ar.*, op. cit. 231:23; *Ar. haSh.*, loc. cit.

68. *Rosh, Bava Meẓia* 3:16; *Tur*, op. cit. 231:26; *Sh. Ar.*, op. cit. 231:20: *Ar. haSh.*, op. cit., 231:20.

The base against which the 20% profit rate is calculated is a matter of dispute. One opinion (*Meiri, Bava Meẓia* 40b; *Rosh, Bava Meẓia* 3:16; *Tur, Ḥoshen Mishpat* 231:26) puts all selling costs, including the retailer's implicit wage, in the base. The implicit-wage element of the cost base is presumably limited to the competitive rate for the type of work performed. Including a return for labor services in the cost base effectively allows the vendor to earn the allowable 20% profit rate on his invested capital and on his labor services as well.

Another opinion (*Rashbam, Bava Batra* 90a; *Rabbeinu Shimshon* quoted in *Haggahot Maimuniyyot, Mekhirah* 12:1; Maimonides on view of *Baḥ* (*Baḥ, Tur*, loc. cit.) views the 20% profit rate as a return the vendor earns for the labor services he provides in the process of selling his product. No allowance for a return on invested capital is called for, according to this view. Consequently, when continuous labor services are not rendered in the process of selling the product, the product must be sold at its cost price, i.e., at a zero profit margin.

69. T. J., *Nedarim* 5:4; R. Solomon b. Abraham Adret (Spain, ca. 1235–ca.

1310), *Responsa Rashba* 1:755; R. David b. Solomon ibn Abi Zimra; (Egypt 1479–1573), *Responsa Radbaz*, pt. 1:214; R. Samuel b. Moses Medina (Salonica, 1506–1589), *Responsa Maharashdam*, *Yoreh De'ah* 84.

70. *Rashi*, *Sanhedrin* 24b.

71. Mishnah, *Sanhedrin* 3:3; *Rif* ad loc.; *Yad*, Edut 10:4; *Rosh*, *Sanhedrin* 3:7; *Tur*, op. cit. 34:16; *Sh. Ar.*, op. cit. 34:16; *Ar. haSh.*, op. cit. 34:18.

72. *Yad*, loc. cit.; *Tur*, loc. cit.; *Sh. Ar.*, loc. cit., *Rema*, *Ḥoshen Mishpat* 370:3; *Ar. haSh.*, loc. cit.

73. R. Sheshet, *Sanhedrin* 24b; *Rif* ad loc.; *Yad*, loc. cit.; *Rosh*, loc. cit.; *Tur*, loc. cit.; *Rema* loc. cit.; *Ar. haSh.*, loc. cit.

74. Lester G. Telser, "Why There Are Organized Future Markets," *Journal of Law and Economics* 24 (April 1981): 1–22.

75. Holbrook Working, "Futures Trading and Hedging," *American Economic Review* 43 (June 1953): 314–343.

Subject Index

Above suspicion, 16–17
Abutter, *See Maẓranut*
Advertising
  bait and switch case, 45–46
  comparative merit stratagem, 49–51
  discount sales, 47–49
  disparagement of a competitor's product, 49
  inciting envy, 62–63
  puffery, 51–57
  testimonial technique, 57–59
  weasel word stratagem, 46–47
Airline Deregulation Act, 77
Arbitrage, 210, 212
Asmakhta
  and *Ḥin Ẓedek*, 7
  counteracting of, 189–200
  defined, 194
  maintainance of margin and, 197–198
  remedy for, 199–200
  selling short and, 198–199
Automatic stabilizers, 128
Avak, Ribbit
  and commodity loans, 147–150
  and delinquency in payment of wages, 154–155
  and denominating loans in foreign currency, 150–151
  and margin agreements, 191–194
  and preferred stocks, 185–188
  and reciprocal labor agreements, 152–153
  and selling short, 200–205
  and small commodity loans from a neighbor, 151–152

Bait and switch, 45
Bal Tashḥit
  and allocational efficiency, 169–171
  and current market value, 169–171
  and recycling, 161
  and subsidizing farm income, 167–168
  and the worker, 177–178
  and X-efficiency, 161–167
  biblical source, 160
  defined, 160
Bilateral monopoly, 20–21
Bluffing, 21–22
Bizzuy Okhelim, 168

Certification as an alternative to regulation, 79, 94–96
Charity
  and the Jewish public sector, 125–133
  eligibility for private assistance, 124–125
  eligibility for public assistance, 118–122
  Maimonides' ranking of, 115–116
  obligation and inflation, 153–154
  obligation of recipient, 133–135
  priorities in, 117–118
  rate limitations of, 116–117, 135
Collective bargaining, 21
Comparative merit statagem
  defined, 49–50
  disparagement of a competitor's product, 49–50
  exclusivity claim, 51
  superiority claim, 51
Consumer price index, 141

Dei Maḥsoro
  and eligibility criterion, 118–122
  and obligations of recipient, 133–135
  as a collective responsibility, 116
  defined, 116
  priority schedule, 117–118
  rate limitations of, 116–117, 135

Disclosure obligation, 89–91, 94
Discount sales, 47–49
Disparagement of a competitors' product, 49–51
Dissuasion of a customer, 63–71
Distributive justice in Jewish law, 135–137

Economic incentives
  and the humane impulse, 86–87
  dissapproval of maximum work effort in Jewish law, 83–86
  examples in rabbinic literature, 81–83, 87
Economic regulation of the marketplace and Jewish law, 87–103
Efficiency
  allocational efficiency, 159
  and halakhic obligations on a businessman, 171–172
  and halakhic obligations on a worker, 177–178
  and labor productivity, 178–182
  in Jewish law, 160–167, 169–171
  X-efficiency, 159–167
Effluent fee, 79–80, 100–101
Endowment scheme, 3–4
Escalator clause, 154

Federal reserve
  and monetary expansion, 146
  fractional reserve system, 146
Federal Trade Commission Act, 77
Forward contract, 208–209
Free rider motive, 130
Futures contract, 208
Futures market, 208–213

Garme, 27
Genevat Da'at
  and Jewish charity law, 114–115
  and the disclosure obligation, 89–91
  concealing the primary motive, 12–14, 48–49
  defined, 11
  in counteracting unwarranted bias, 24–26
  in gift case, 12
  in passive case, 14–16
  in puffery, 55, 57
  in self-assessment case, 23–24
  in self-deception case, 22
  in seller's testing obligation, 92–93
  in the testimonial technique, 57–59
  in undeserved good will, 12, 47–49

Hedging, 208–209, 210–213
Hetter Iska
  and corporate bonds, 189–191
  and margin stock purchase, 192–194
  and preferred stock, 189
  defined, 188–189
Ḥin Ẓedek
  and bait and switch, 45
  and bluffing, 22
  and the conditional contract, 7
  and the standard contract, 7
  defined, 6
Hoarding, 205–207

Idealized market conduct in Jewish law, 9–11
Idleness in Halakha, 87, 122
Ill-defined property rights
  defined, 79
  effluent fee, 79–80
  in economic theory, 79–80
  in Jewish law, 97–101
Imitatio Dei principle, 114
Income redistribution, 135–137
Inflation
  and delinquency in the payment of wages, 154–155
  and religious functionaries, 154
  and *Ribbit* law, 141–153
  and the charity obligation, 153–154
  and theft liability, 155–156
Installment plans, 59–62
Interest rate, *See Ribbit*
Integrity
  as personified in Jacob's character, 9–11
  authentic and false, 11
Iska
  defined, 185
  regulation of in Jewish law, 186

Judicial code of conduct, 57–58

Kabbelan, 179
Kofin al Midat Sedom, 36–41

Labor productivity and Halakha, 178–182
Lifnei Ivver
and the dissuasion responsibility, 64, 68–69
and the *Efes* caveat, 71
and the premarketing testing obligation, 9
in counseling, 8
in persuasion, 62
prohibition of, 8
Li-Fenim mi-Shurat ha-Din, 26–31
Lo Ta'amod, 64, 69–71
Loss leader pricing stratagem
and *Genevat Da'at*, 47–49
and *Me'ulah beDamim* criterion, 163–164
defined, 47

Mazranut, 31–36
Medical fees, 136–137
Me'ulah beDamim
and allocational efficiency, 169–171
and the least cost caveat, 162
and the "loss leader" stratagem, 163–164
and subsidizing farm income, 167–168
and the worker, 177
as subject of rishonic dispute, 161–167
Multiplier effect, 110

Natural monopoly
and economic theory, 80
and Jewish law, 102–103
defined, 80
Nedrei Zeirizin, 54–55
Negative externality
effluent fee, 78–80, 100–101
legislation against, 98–101
reciprocal nature of, 97–98
treatment in Jewish law, 97–101

Ona'ah
and financial ruination, 68
and *Mazranut*, 35
and opportunity cost, 88–89
and *Sefer Torah* case, 21
and shadow prices, 67–68
first degree, 64, 88
homogeneous product case, 64
non-standardized product case, 64
second degree, 64, 88
third degree, 64–67, 88
Ona'at Devarim
and limits on the employer's productivity standard, 182
cases, 8–9, 45–46
defined, 8
Openness responsibility
and entrepeneurial intent, 17–20
and identity disclosure, 17
Opportunity cost
and the disparagement of a competitor's product, 51
rationale for the *Ona'ah* claim, 88–89

Perekh, 181–182
Pilot testing, 47, 57, 59, 92–93
Po'el
accepting outside work, 179–181
idling on employer's time, 178–179
in work stoppage case, 22
Poverty
criterion, 122–123
halakhic definition of subsistence, 122–124
prevention vs. relief, 114–116, 127–130
Premarketing testing, 92–94
Preferred stock
advantages, 186–187
and *Hetter Iska*, 190–191
and the *Efes* caveat, 71
defined, 185
Price mechanism, 4–5
Product defect case
forthright disclosure, 90–91
seller's rights, 91–92
Product safety
defined, 78
in Jewish law, 94–97
in supply side economics, 78–79
Profit regulation in the necessity sector, 136
Progressive tax, 128, 136
Public assistance
eligibility criterion in talmudic times, 118–119
eligibility criterion today, 119–122
Public sector

and the obligation to create a humane environment, 132–133
and the obligation to uphold the dignity of the poor, 131
Puffery
defined, 51
treatment of in American law, 55–57
treatment of in Jewish law, 51–55
Pure Food and Drug Act, 77
Pure public good, 124

Reciprocal labor agreements, 152–153
Recision right, 91–92
Rent control, 136
Ribbit
and commodity loans, 147–150
and corporate bonds, 185
and credit sales, 60
and *Hetter Iska*, 188–191
and the real vs. nominal interest rate issue, 141–147
selling short and, 200–202

Se'ah be'Se'ah law
and reciprocal work agreements, 152–153
as legitimized by *Yaẓa ha-Sha'ar*, 148–149, 150–151
as legitimized by *Yesh Lo*, 148, 150
as violating *Avak Ribbit*, 147
defined, 147
involving small commodity loans, 151–152
Self-interest motive
and efficiency in the marketplace, 3–5
in Jewish law, 5–6
Severance pay, 31
Shadow prices, 67–68, 69, 164
Shoḥad, See Judicial code of conduct
Short sale against the box, 204
Social welfare, 107–137
Speculative activity
and gambling, 207–213
and prohibition against hoarding in Jewish law, 205–207
in agricultural sector, 205–207
Spontaneous harmony, 3
Stock and bond markets, 207–208
Stock index futures, 210–212
Stock index options, 212
Sumptuary laws, 63
Supply side economics
and Jewish law, 80–103
and tax policy, 75
and regulation of the marketplace, 75–80

Technological innovation and Jewish law, 172–177
Testimonial technique, 57–59
Theft liability and price changes, 155–156

Umbrella pricing protection, 174–177
Undeserved good will
cases, 12, 47–49
defined, 12
Useless work, 181–182

Veyoreta me'Elokekha, 7–9

Water pollution, 94
Weasel word stratagem, 46–47

Yaẓa ha-Sha'ar
and futures contracts, 203–204
and loans denominated in a foreign currency, 150–151
and small commodity loans, 151–152
defined, 148, 202
validating *Se'ah be'Se'ah*, 148–149, 202–204
Yesh Lo
defined, 148, 204
validating *Se'ah be'Se'ah*, 148, 204–205

Name Index

Abraham b. David of Posquières, 148, 153, 228 n.79, 231 n.145, 243 n.4, n.5, n.19, 244 n.45, 246 n. 11
Abraham Ibn Ezra, 19, 226 n.37
Abraham b. Maimonides, 228 n.76
Abraham b. Mordecai ha-Levi, 249 n.11, n.18
Abramsky, Yeḥezkel, 236 n.78
Abulafia, Meir, 97, 228 n.84, 229 n.90, 236 n.79
Adler, Binyamin, 240 n.68
Adret, Solomon b. Abraham, 39, 81, 99, 130, 131, 137, 196, 197, 226 n.27, 229 n.98, 231 n.134, 234 n.10, 236 n.78, 237 n.84, n.85, n.86, n.88, n.92, 241 n.83, n.87, n.92, 242 n.115, 243 n.3, 250 n.35, 251 n.69
Albeck, Shalom, 249 n.25
Alfasi, Isaac b. Jacob, 98, 150, 151, 203, 225 n.11, 226 n.22, n.26, n.27, 227 n.42, n.43, n.44, n.55, n.56, 229 n.87, n.88, n.90, n.92, n.97, n.101, 230 n.103, n.114, n.115, n.117, n.118, n.123, n.133, 231 n.13, 232 n.23, 233 n.33, n.34, n.35, n.37, n.40, n.41, n.42, n.43, 234 n.57, 235 n.34, n.35, n.36, n.37, n.38, n.45, 236 n.69, n.72, n.77, 237 n.86, 238 n.14, n.17, n.23, 239 n.39, n.46, 240 n.57, n.62, n.63, n.64, n.65, n.66, 241, n.79, n.82, 242 n.102, n.107, 243 n.5, n.9, n.10, n.11, 244 n.28, n.30, n.31, n.36, n.40, 245 n.63, n.64, 247 n.32, n.34, n.49, 248 n.57, n.58, n.5, n.6, n.9, 249 n.26, 250 n.43, n.44, 251 n.53, n.54, 251 n.59, n.62, n.64, n.67, 252 n.71, n.73
Algazi, Ḥayyim Isaac, 234 n. 15
ha'Amek Davar, See Berlin, Naphtali Ẓevi Judah
Arak, Meir, 192, 249 n.22
Arieli, Isaac, 247 n.44
Arkin, Marcus, 251 n.65
Arukh ha-Shulḥan, See Epstein, Jeḥiel Michel
Aryeh Judah b. Akiba, 23, 25, 49, 227 n.48
Asher b. Jeḥiel, 33, 40, 65, 81, 91, 97, 149, 164, 202, 225 n.11, 226 n.21, n.22, n.26, n.27, 227 n.42, n.43, n.46, n.55, n.56, 228 n.71, n.76, n.82, n.84, 229 n.87, n.88, n.90, n.91, n.92, n.93, n.96, n.97, n.100, n.101, n.102, 230 n.112, n.114, n.115, n.117, n.118, n.123, n.129, n.132, n.133, 231 n.135, n.136, n.144, n.13, 232 n.23, 233 n.37, n.40, n.41, n.42, n.45, 234 n.57, n.7, n.8, 235 n.34, n.35, n.36, n.37, n.45, 236 n.57, n.69, n.72, n.77, n.80, 237 n.85, 238 n.14, n.17, n.23, 239 n.39, 240 n.54, n.57, n.62, n.63, n.65, n.66, n.67, n.73, 241 n.77, n.79, n.82, 242 n.102, n.107, n.111, 243 n.3, n.4, n.5, n.6, n.9, n.10, n.11, n.12, n.15, 244 n.23, n.28, n.30, n.40, 245 n.63, n.64, 246 n.8, n.13, 247 n.32, n.34, n.49, 248 n.57, n.6, n.9, 249 n.26, 250 n.39, n.41, n.43, n.44, n.45, n.49, 251, n.53, n.59, n.60, n.68, 252 n.71, n.73
Ashkenazi, Beẓalel, 229 n.102, 236 n.78, 241 n.76, 244 n.31, n.32, n.45, 246 n.10, 250 n.35, 251 n.54, n.55, n.58
Auerbach, Solomon Z., 119, 122, 240 n.53

Babad, Joseph b. Moses, 233 n.32
Bachrach, Ya'ir Ḥayyim, 239 n.25
Baḥ, *See* Sirkes, Joel
Banet, Mordecai, 102, 237 n.96
Rabbeinu Baruch, 248 n.10
Basri, Ezra, 116, 151, 204, 236 n.59, 238 n.21, 239 n.24, 244 n.35, n.47, 248 n.5, n.7, 251 n.58
Baumol, William J., 234 n.6
Beit ha-Beḥira, See Meiri, Menaḥem b. Solomon
Beit Ephraim, See Margoliot, Ephraim Zalman
Beit Yiẓḥak, See Schmelkes, Isaac Yehudah
Beit Yosef, See Caro, Joseph
Benveniste, Ḥayyim b. Israel, 32, 36, 229 n.85, 230 n.107, n.127, 236 n.56
Berlin, Naphtali Ẓevi Judah, 225 n.15, 246 n.16
Bertinoro, Ovadiah Yarei, 239 n.44
Bina le'Itim, See Figo, Azaria
Binyan Ẓion, See Ettlinger, Jacob
Blau, Jacob, 153, 155, 243 n.1, n.13, 244 n.23, n.38, n.46, 245 n.53, n.61, 249 n.20, 251 n.61
Bleich, J. David, 95, 236 n.74, 237 n.97, 242 n.113
Bonello, Frank J., 234 n.1
Bonfils, Joseph b. Samuel, 237 n.85, n.86
Breisch, Mordecai Jacob, 69, 175, 234 n.55, 247 n.42, n.44, 248 n.4, 249 n.20
B'rit Yehudah, See Blau, Jacob

Caro, Joseph, 36, 65, 83, 90, 119, 152, 176, 225 n.11, 226 n.21, n.22, n.26, n.33, 227 n.42, n.43, n.44, n.46, n.55, n.56, 228 n.71, n.78, n.79, n.80, n.81, n.82, n.84, 229 n.86, n.87, n.88, n.90, n.91, n.92, n.97, n.98, n.101, 230 n.114, n.115, n.117, n.118, n.123, n.126, n.129, n.133, 231 n.135, n.144, n.10, n.13, 232 n.15, n.18, n.20, n.23, n.25, 233 n.34, n.37, n.40, n.41, n.42, n.43, n.48, 234 n.57, n.10, n.13, n.14, 235 n.33, n.34, n.35, n.36, n.37, n.38, n.40, n.42, n.45, n.47, n.48, n.51, n.52, 236 n.54, n.55, n.57, n.58, n.69, n.72, n.77, 238 n.11, n.14, n.17, n.22, n.23, 239 n.38, n.39, n.40, n.45, n.46, n.47, n.48, 240 n.49, n.50, n.51, n.52, n.55, n.56, n.57, n.61, n.62, n.63, n.64, n.75, 241 n.79, n.84, n.87, n.88, n.92, n.98, 242 n.102, n.107, 243 n.5, n.8, n.9, n.10, n.11, n.15, 244 n.22, n.30, n.36, n.39, n.40, n.47, 245 n.53, n.57, n.62, n.63, n.64, 246 n.30, 247 n.32, n.34, n.43, n.48, n.49, n.52, 248 n.56, n.57, n.58, n.60, n.1, n.5, n.6, n.7, n.9, 249 n.10, n.24, n.26, 250 n.32, n.36, n.42, n.43, n.44, n.45, n.48, 251 n.53, n.59, n.62, n.64, n.67, n.68, 252 n.71, n.72
Coase, Ronald H., 237 n.83
Cohen, Alfred S., 231 n.4, 233 n.52
Cohen, Shear-yashuv, 243 n.2
Colon, Joseph, 99, 237 n.87
Cordovero, Moses, 237 n.1
Culi, Jacob, 226 n.34

Da'at Tevunot, See Luzzato, Mosheh Ḥayyim
Da'at Zekenim mi'ba'alei haTosafot, 226 n.35, 227 n.41
Danzig, Abraham, 243 n.9, n.10, n.11, n.15, n.16, n.17, 244 n.30, n.39, n.40, 248 n.5, n.6, n.7, n.8, n.9, n.10, n.13, n.14, n.16, n.17, 249 n.24, 250 n.43, n.44, n.45, n.46, 251 n.53, n.59
Darkei Mosheh, See Isserles, Moses
David b. Moses, 30, 228 n.73
David b. Samuel ha-Levi, 149, 188, 202, 230 n.122, n.125, n.129, 240 n.58, 243 n.13, 244 n.24, 246 n.14, 248 n.7, n.14, n.15, 249 n.19, 250 n.50, 251 n.61
David Ibn Zimra, 38, 230 n.130, 252 n.69
DeFina, Robert, 78
Derekh Eẓ ha-Ḥayyim, See Alzagi, Hayyim Isaac
Derisha, See Falk, Joshua ha-Kohen
Dessler, Eliyahu Eliezer, 132, 225 n.4, 241, n.95

Dinei Avodah ba-Mishpat ha-Ivri, See Warhaftig, Shillem
Dinei Mamonot, See Basri, Ezra
Dinei Mamonot be-Talmud, See Albeck, Shalom
Divrei Ḥayyim, See Halberstamm, Ḥayyim
Dolan, Edwin G., 234 n.4, 236 n.76
Domb, Cyril, 233 n.20, 239 n.25, n.26, n.27, n.28, 240 n.53, 244 n.48
Duran, Simeon b. Ẓemaḥ, 237 n.84
Duran, Ẓemaḥ b. Solomon, 237 n.85

Edels, Samuel Eliezer b. Judah ha-Levi, 13, 50, 84, 85, 226 n.29, 228 n.61, 231 n.7, 234 n.18, 235 n.26
Rabbeinu Efraim, 240 n.50
Eger, Akiva, 228 n.82
Eisenstadt, Meir, 249 n.21
Eliezer of Toul, 91, 155, 236 n.56, 245 n.56
Eliezer b. Isaac of Böhman, 81, 82, 234 n.12
Eliezer b. Joel ha-Levi, 237 n.86
Eliezer b. Nathan, 30, 228 n.72
Eliezer b. Samuel of Metz, 241 n.88, 246 n.6
Eliyahu b. Ḥayyim, 85, 230 n.107, 235 n.27, 240 n.68
Emden, Jacob, 164, 246 n.15
Enayim le Mishpat, See Arieli, Isaac
Ephraim Solomon b. Aaron of Lenczycza, 20, 133, 134, 226 n.40, 241 n.99
Epstein, Jeḥiel Michel, 66, 94, 117, 118, 144, 178, 180, 225 n.11, 226 n.21, n.22, n.25, n.26,n.33, 227 n.43, n.44, n.45, n.46, n.55, n.56, n.57, 228 n.71, n.77, n.78, n.79, n.80, n.81, n.82, n.84, 229 n.86, n.87, n.88, n.90, n.92, n.97, n.100, n.101, 230 n.112, n.113, n.114, n.115, n.116, n.117, n.118, n.123, n.133, 231 n.135, n.136, n.10, 232 n.18, n.20, n.22, n.23, n.25, n.26, 233 n.33, n.34, n.35, n.37, n.40, n.41, n.42, n.43, n.44, n.50, 234 n.57, n.58, n.14, 235 n.33, n.34, n.35, n.36, n.37, n.38, n.40, n.41, n.42, n.43, n.45, n.47, n.48, n.49, n.51, 236 n.53, n.54, n.55, n.58, n.69, n.71, n.72, n.77, 238 n.11, n.14, n.17, n.22, n.23, 239 n.30, n.31, n.32, n.34, n.36, n.38, n.39, n.40, n.42, n.45, n.47, n.48, 240 n.51, n.55, n.56, n.57, n.58, n.60, n.61, n.62, n.65, n.64, n.75, 241 n.78, n.79, n.81, n.84, n.85, n.89, n.98, 242 n.101, n.102, n.107, 243 n.6, n.7, n.8, 244 n.47, 245 n.62, n.63, n.64, n.65, 246 n.23, 247 n.30, n.32, n.33, n.34, n.43, n.48, n.49, n.52, n.53, 248 n.56, n.57, n.58, n.60, n.61, 249 n.26, 250 n.40, n.42, 251 n.62, n.64, n.66, n.67, n.68, 252 n.71, n.72, n.73
Epstein, Joseph D., 12, 226 n.28
Epstein, Mosheh Mordecai, 25, 227 n.49
Ettinger, Isaac Aaron, 174, 247 n.41
Ettinger, Jacob, 95, 236 n.73
Even ha-Ezel, See Meltzer, Isser Zalman
Eybeschuetz, Yonathan, 149, 202, 244 n.26, 251 n.51

Falk, Joshua ha-Kohen, 34, 35, 90, 136, 153, 228 n.77, n.83, 229 n.89, n.95, 230 n.104, n.106, n.109, n.111, n.113, n.119, n.122, n.123, n.129, 231 n.137, 232 n.22, 233 n.39, 234 n.54, 235 n.43, n.44, n.49, 236 n.53, 242 n.106, n.108, 244 n.41, n.44, 245 n.65, 247 n.55
Feinstein, Mosheh, 25, 118, 154, 173, 227 n.51, 231 n.146, 237 n.93, 239 n.29, n.33, n.43, 245 n.49, 247 n.38, 248 n.3, 249 n.21
Figo, Azaria, 29, 228 n.68
Findeling, Mosheh, 228 n.74
Fleckeles, Eliezer, 137, 242 n.114

Gerondi, Jonah b. Abraham, 12, 226 n.24
Gerondi, Nissim b. Reuben, 151, 203, 232 n.13, 242 n.104, 244 n.34, 246 n.18, n.19, 250 n.33, n.41, 251 n.57

Rabbeinu Gershom b. Judah Me'Or ha-Golah, 180, 237 n.85, 248 n.63
Ginnat Veradim, See Abraham b. Mordecai ha-Levi
Glickman, Isaac, 242 n.1
Gombiner, Abraham Abele b. Ḥayiim ha-Levi, 240 n.66, 246 n.20, n.21, n.22
Goodman, John C., 234 n.4, 236 n.76
Greenfeld, Shimon, 248 n.3

Ḥabib, Joseph, 229 n.98
Ḥafeẓ Ḥayyim, See Kagan, Israel Meir ha-Kohen
Haggahot Asheri, See Israel of Krems
Haggahot ve-Ḥiddushin, See Horowitz, Eliezer Mosheh
Haggahot Maimuniyyot, See Meir ha-Kohen
Rabbeinu Hai b. Sherira of Pumbedita, 227 n.42
Hailstones, Thomas J., 75, 234 n.2, n.3
Halakhot Gedolot, 236 n.61
Halakhot ve-Halikhot Bar-Mizvah, See Adler, Binyamin
Halikhut ha-Misḥar, See Rakover, Naḥum
Halberstamm, Ḥayyim, 237 n.87, 249 n.21
Halikhut Yehudah, See Kagan, Yehudah L.
Ḥananel b. Ḥushi'el, 30, 150, 203, 228 n.71, 229 n.93, 244 n.32, 246 n.11, n.18, n.19, 251 n.55
Harkavi, Shelomo, 238 n.13
Hassagot Gevul ve-Tovat ha-Ẓebur, See Warhaftig, Shillem
Ḥayyim (Eliezer) b. Isaac, 237 n.86
Ḥayyim Ibn Attar, 226 n.35
Ḥayyim l'Olam, See Modai, Ḥayyim
Ḥazon Ish, See Karelitz, Abraham Isaiah
Ḥazon Yehezkel, See Abramsky, Yeḥezkel
Ḥazzan, Joseph Raphael b. Ḥayyim Joseph, 248 n.2
Ḥikrei Ya'akov, See Breisch, Mordecai Jacob
Ḥikrei Lev, See Ḥazzan, Joseph Raphael b. Ḥayyim Joseph

Hirsch, Samson Raphael, 126, 226 n.16, 241 n.86
Ḥokhmat Adam, See Danzig, Abraham
Horowitz, Eliezer Mosheh, 246 n.17
Horowitz, Pinḥas ha-Levi, 117, 239 n.41
Ḥukat Avodah, See Findeling, Mosheh
Ḥukat Mishpat, See Rabinowitz-Teumim, Binyamin

Iggerot Mosheh, See Feinstein, Mosheh
Imrei Shefer, See Eliyahu b. Ḥayyim
m'Imrei Shelomo, See Harkavi, Shelomo
Imrei Yosher, See Arak, Meir
Isaac b. Joseph of Corbeil, 246 n.6
Isaac b. Moses of Vienna, 155, 179, 234 n.12, 240 n.50, n.58, 241 n.80, n.82, 244 n.38, 245 n.57, 247 n.55
Isaac of Dampierre, 128, 241 n.91
Ishbili, Yom Tov, 12, 15, 16, 151, 203, 226 n.23, n.31, 228 n.71, 232 n.14, 244 n.32, n.35, 251 n.55, n.58
Israel of Krems, 33, 228 n.84, 229 n.93, n.94, 231 n.136, 243 n.8, 245 n.57
Isserlein, Israel b. Petaḥiah, 249 n.14
Isserles, Moses, 58, 68, 92, 116, 137, 151, 152, 203, 227 n.55, 229 n.98, 230 n.105, n.108, n.110, n.112, n.115, n.132, 231 n.136, 232 n.13, 233 n.27, n.33, n.51, 236 n.57, n.58, n.72, 237 n.92, 238 n.18, n.23, 239 n.30, n.31, n.32, n.34, n.36, n.37, n.46, 241 n.78, n.81, n.82, n.89, n.92, 243 n.6, n.19, 244 n.33, n.37, n.38, 248 n.5, 249 n.10, n.13, n.17, n.28, 250 n.30, n.41, 251 n.56, 252 n.72, n.73

Jacob b. Asher, 23, 24, 65, 90, 153, 225 n.11, 226 n.21, n.22, n.26, n.33, 227 n.42, n.43, n.44, n.46, n.55, n.56, n.61, 228 n.63, n.78, n.79, n.80, n.81, n.82, n.84, 229 n.86, n.87, n.88, n.90, n.92, n.97, n.100, n.101, 230 n.112, n.113, n.115, n.117, n.118, n.123, n.126, n.132, 231 n.135, n.10, n.13, 232 n.15, n.18, n.20, n.23, n.25, 233 n.34, n.35, n.37, n.39, n.40, n.41, n.42, n.43, n.47, 234 n.57, n.14, 235 n.33, n.34, n.35, n.36, n.37, n.38, n.40, n.42, n.45, n.47, n.48, n.51, 236 n.54, n.55, n.57, n.69, n.77, 238 n.11, n.14, n.17, n.22, n.23, 239 n.30, n.31, n.34, n.37, n.39, n.40, n.45, n.46, n.47, n.48, 240 n.49, n.51, n.55, n.56, n.57, n.61, n.62, n.63, n.64, n.65, n.75, 241 n.79, n.82, n.84, n.98, 242 n.102, n.107, 243 n.5, n.6, n.8, n.9, n.10, n.11, n.15, 244 n.28, n.30, n.39, n.40, n.43, n.47, 245 n.53, n.62, n.63, n.64, 246 n.30, 247 n.32, n.34, n.48, n.49, 248 n.56, n.57, n.60, n.6, n.9, 249 n.10, n.24, n.26, 250 n.42, n.43, n.44, n.45, 251 n.53, n.59, n.62, n.64, n.68, 252 n.71, n.72, n.73

Jeroḥam b. Meshullam, 245 n.56, 246 n.6

Joseph of Corbeil, 119, 120, 240 n.51

Joshua Boaz b. Simeon, 244 n.38

Judah b. Samuel he-Ḥasid, 21, 227 n.41

Judah Loew b. Beẓalei, 52, 86, 231 n.11, 235 n.30

Kagan, Israel Meir ha-Kohen, 70, 234 n.56

Kagan, Yehudah L., 238 n.2

Kanievsky, Jacob, 237 n.82

Karelitz, Abraham Isaiah, 188, 243 n.7, 249 n.10, n.12

Keli Yakar, See Ephraim Solomon b. Aaron of Lenczycza

Kenneset ha-Gedolah, See Benveniste, Ḥayyim b. Israel

Kareti-u-Feleti, See Eybeschuetz, Yonathan

Kesef Mishneh, See Caro, Joseph

K'hilot Yaakov, See Kanievsky, Jacob

Kimḥi, David, 226 n.19, n.20

Kimḥi, Joseph, 226 n.19

Kirschenbaum, Aaron, 133, 241 n.96, n.97

Kiryat Sefer, See Trani, Moses b. Joseph

Kotler, Aaron, 236 n.78

Kozak, Andrew F., 234 n.1

Krochmal, Menaḥem Mendel, 228 n.63

Lamm, Norman, 238 n.1, 242 n.112

Landau, Beẓalel, 233 n.36

Landau, Ezekiel b. Juda ha-Levi, 177, 237 n.93, n.94, 246 n.6, 247 n.47

Lander, Daniel, 241 n.90

Leibenstein, Harvey, 161, 245 n.1, 246 n.9

Lemberger, M., 248 n.3

Lev Aryeh, See Aryeh Judah b. Akiba

Levine, Aaron, 227 n.43, 231 n.4, 233 n.29, n.38, 235 n.39, 236 n.78, 240 n.74, 242 n.109, 247 n.36

Levinson, Yosef Pinḥat, 246 n.16

Levush Mordecai, See Epstein, Mosheh Mordecai

Levushei Mordecai, See Winkler, Leopold

Lichtenstein, Aaron, 134, 242 n.103

Lorberbaum, Jacob Moses, 230 n.119, 236 n.58

Lublin, Meir b. Gedaliah, 249 n.17

Luria, Solomon b. Jeḥiel, 226 n.27

Luzzato, Mosheh Ḥayyim, 114, 238 n.13

Ma'aseh Ḥiyya, See Rofe, Ḥiyya

Masser Kesafim, See Cyril Domb

Magen Avraham, See Gombiner, Abraham Abele b. Ḥayyim ha-Levi

Maggid Mishneh, See Vidal Yom Tov of Tolosa

Maḥaneh Ḥayyim, See Sofer, Ḥayyim

Maharam of Rothenburg, *See* Meir b. Baruch

Maharal, *See* Judah Loew b. Beẓalel

Mahari ha-Levi, *See* Ettlinger, Isaac b. Aaron

Maharsha, See Edels, Samuel Eliezer b. Judah ha-Levi

Maimonides, 23, 24, 28, 29, 33, 65, 69, 90, 93, 94, 109, 114, 115, 134, 136, 148, 149, 160, 169, 197, 199, 202, 225 n.8, n.10, n.11, n.14, 226 n.21, n.22, n.26, n.27, n.33, 227 n.42, n.43, n.44, n.45, n.55, n.56, 228 n.64, n.65, n.80, n.81, 229 n.86, n.87, n.90, n.92, n.93, n.97, n.100, n.101, 230 n.114, n.115, n.117, n.118, n.123, n.129, n.133, 231 n.135, n.13, 232 n.15, n.18, n.20, n.23, n.25, 233 n.30, n.33, n.34, n.35, n.37, n.40, n.41, n.42,n.43, n.46, n.53, 234 n.57, n.14, 235 n.33, n.34, n.35, n.36, n.37, n.38, n.40, n.42, n.45, n.47, n.48, n.50, n.52, 236 n.54, n.55, n.60, n.62, n.67, n.69, n.70, n.72, n.77, 237 n.82, 238 n.2, n.11, n.12, n.14, n.16, n.17, n.22, n.23, 239 n.30, n.37, n.39, n.40, n.45, n.46, n.47, 240 n.49, n.54, n.55, n.56, n.57, n.62, n.63, n.64, n.65, n.75, 241 n.79, n.82, n.84, n.98, 242 n.100, n.102, n.107, n.111, 243 n.5, n.8, n.9, n.10, n.11, n.15, n.17, n.18, 244 n.21, n.30, n.36, n.39, n.40, n.47, 245 n.51, n.62, n.63, n.64, 246 n.6, n.7, n.8, n.30, 247 n.32,n.34,n.48, n.52, 248 n.56, n.57, n.60, n.6, n.8, n.9, 249 n.26, 250 n.37, n.38, n.42, n.44, n.45, n.46, n.47, 251 n.53, n.59, n.62, n.64, n.67, n.68, 252 n.71, n.72, n.73

Margoliot, Ephraim Zalman, 247 n.44

Massa Ḥayyim, See Palaggi, Ḥayyim

Mastrianna, Frank V., 75, 234 n.2, n.3

Medini, Ḥayyim Ḥezekiah, 51, 231 n.8, 233 n.51, 234 n.59

Meir ha-Kohen, 245 n.56, 247 n.52, 251 n.68

Meir b. Baruch of Rothenburg, 99, 228 n.72, 237 n.85, n.86, n.89, 245 n.56, 247 n.55

Meiri, Menaḥem b. Solomon, 134, 161, 162, 165, 166, 167, 168, 225 n.12, 246 n.10, n.24, 247 n.55, 251 n.68

Meisharim, See Jeroḥam b. Meshullam

Meltzer, Isser Zalman, 136, 242 n.109

ha-Me'or, See Preil, Eliezer Meir

Meshiv Davar, See Berlin, Naphtali Ẓevi Judah

Mikhtav m'Eliyahu, See Dessler, Eliyahu Eliezer

Minḥat Ḥinnukh, See Babad, Joseph b. Moses

Minḥat Yizḥak, See Weiss, Isaac Jacob

Mishnat Rabbi Aaron, See Kotler, Aaron

Mishneh la-Melekh, See Rosanes, Judah

Mishpetei Uzzie'l, See Ouziel, Ben Ẓion Meir

Mizraḥi, See Mizraḥi, Eliyahu

Mizraḥi, Eliyahu, 226 n.20

Mizvat ha-Shalom, See Epstein, Joseph David

Modai, Ḥayyim, 234 n.15, n.16

Mordecai, See Mordecai, b. Hillel ha-Kohen

Mordecai b. Hillel ha-Kohen, 30 228 n.69, 237 n.86, 240 n.59, 241 n.80, 243 n.6, 248 n.59, n.10, 250 n.39, n.41

Moreh Nevukhim, See Maimonides

Moses b. Jacob of Coucy, 226 n.27, 246 n.6, 248 n.5

Naḥmanides, 19, 29, 30, 33, 41, 136, 196, 226 n.20, n.36, n.38, 228 n.67, 230 n.103, 231 n.145, 233 n.49, 237 n.82, n.86, 241 n.94, 242 n.110, n.111, 249 n.23, 250 n.33

Nathanson, Joseph Saul ha-Levi, 248 n.2, 249 n.18

Neuwirth, Yehoshu'a Yesha'yah, 234 n.15

Nimmukei Yosef, See Ḥabib, Joseph

Noda bi-Yhuda, See Landau, Ezekiel b. Judah ha-Levi

N'tivot Mishpat, See Lorberbaum, Jacob Moses

N'tivot Olam, See Loew, Judah b. Bezalel

Oliver, Richard L., 56, 57, 232 n.17

Or ha-Ḥayyim, See Ḥayyim Ibn Attar

Or Zaru'a, See Isaac b. Moses of Vienna

Ouziel, Ben Ẓion Meir, 31, 94, 228 n.74, 236 n.68

Palaggi, Ḥayyim, 242 n.105

Panim Meirot, See Eisenstadt, Meir
Panzar, John C., 234 n.6
Perashat Mordecai, See Banet, Mordecai
Perfet, Isaac b. Sheshet, 149, 195, 244 n.19, n.27, 250 n.31
Perishah, See Falk, Joshua ha-Kohen
Perla, Jeroḥam Fishel, 83, 236 n.61, n.62, n.66, n.67
Preil, Eliezer Meir, 25, 227 n.50
Preston, Ivan L., 55, 57, 232 n.16

Rabad, See Abraham b. David of Posquières
Rabinowitz-Teumim, Binyamin, 229 n.91, 230 n.120, 235 n.41, 236 n.55
Radak, See Kimḥi, David
Rakover, Naḥum, 155, 245 n.60, 247 n.35, n.45
Ramah, See Abulafia, Meir
Ramat Raḥel, See Waldenberg, Eliezer
Raman, See Naḥmanides
Ran, See Gerondi, Nissim b. Reuben
Raphael, Shiloh, 193, 249 n.23
Rashbam, See Samuel b. Meir
Rashi, See Solomon b. Isaac
Reagan, Ronald, 75
Rema, See Isserles, Moses
Responsa Ḥatam Sofer, See Sofer, Moses
Responsa Ḥavot Ya'ir, See Bachrach Ya'ir Ḥayyim
Responsa Ḥayyim Or Zaru's, See Ḥayyim (Eliezer) b. Isaac
Responsa Mabit, See Trani, Moses b. Joseph
Responsa Maharam Lublin, See Lublin, Meir b. Gedaliah
Responsa Maharashdam, See Shmuel de Medina
Responsa Maharik, See Colon, Joseph
Responsa Maharsham, See Schwadron, Shalom Mordecai
Responsa Maharyu, See Weil, Jacob b. Judah
Responsa Minḥat Yiẓḥak, See Weiss, Isaac Jacob
Responsa Or Za'rua, See Isaac b. Moses of Vienna
Responsa Radbaz, See David Ibn Zimra
Responsa Rashba, See Adret, Solomon b. Abraham
Responsa She'elat Yavetz, See Emden, Jacob
Responsa Shoe'l u-Meshiv, See Nathanson, Joseph Saul ha-Levi
Responsa Torat Emet, See Sasson, Aaron
Responsa Yakhin u-Vo'az, See Duran, Ẓemaḥ b. Solomon
Ribash, See Perfet, Isaac b. Sheshet
Rif, See Alfasi, Isaac b. Jacob
Ritva, See Ishbili, Yom Tov
Rofe, Ḥiyya, 244 n.29
Rosanes, Judah, 69, 155, 234 n.54, 245 n.59
Rosh, See Asher b. Jeḥiel
Rosner, Fred, 236 n.75
Ruff, Larry E., 234 n.5

Samuel b. Meir, 89, 225 n.12, 235 n.46, 241 n.94, 251 n.68
Sardi, Samuel b. Isaac, 243 n.3
Sasson, Aaron, 231 n.138, n.140
Schmelkes, Isaac Yehudah, 245 n.56, n.58, 248 n.2
Schwadron, Shalom Mordecai, 231 n.139, 249 n.18
Sedei Ḥemed, See Medini, Ḥayyim Ḥezekiah
Sefer ha-Ḥinnukh, 233 n.32, 246 n.6, n.25, 248 n.65
Sefer ha-Miẓvot, See Maimonides
Sefer Miẓvot Gadol, See Moses b. Jacob of Coucy
Sefer Miẓvot Katan, See Isaac b. Joseph of Corbeil
Sefer ha-terumot, See Sardi, Samuel b. Isaac
Sefer ha-Yashar, See Tam, Jacob
Sha'ar Mishpat, See Wolf, Israel Isser b. Ze'ev
Sha'arei Teshuvah, See Gerondi, Jonah b. Abraham
Shabbetai b. Meir ha-Kohen, 148, 149, 202, 228 n.71, n.82, 239 n.33, n.40, 243 n.13, n.14, n.17, 244 n.20, n.25, 248 n.7, n.14, n.16, 250 n.46, 251 n.52, n.61
Shakh, See Shabbetai b. Meir ha-Kohen

Shilo, Shmuel, 29, 228 n.66, 230 n.128
Shiltei Gibborim, See Joshua Boaz b. Simeon
Rabbeinu Shimshon, 251 n.68
Shittah Mekubbeẓet, See Ashkenazi, Beẓalel
Shmirat Shabbat ki-Hilkhata, See Neuwirth, Yehoshu'a Yesha'yah
Shmuel de Medina, 231 n.138, n.140, n.141, 252 n.69
Shneur Zalman of Lyady, 177, 246 n.12, 247 n.46, 249 n.10
Shulḥan Arukh, See Caro, Joseph
Shulḥan Arukh ha-rav, See Shneur Zalman of Lyady
Siftei Kohen, See Shabbetai b. Meir ha-Kohen
Sirkes, Joel, 85, 155, 226 n.27, 228 n.63, n.70, 230 n.114, 232 n.13, n.23, n.24, 235 n.20, 242 n.101, 245 n.53, n.55, n.56, n.58, 251 n.68
Sma, See Falk, Joshua ha-Kohen
Smith, Adam, 3, 225 n.1, n.2
Sofer, Ḥayyim, 174, 247 n.40
Sofer, Mosheh, 58, 68, 71, 102, 169, 170, 173, 174, 233 n.28, n.52, 237 n.95, 239 n.41, 245 n.52, n.56, n.58, 246 n.28, n.29, 247 n.37
Solomon b. Isaac, 19, 28, 31, 81, 169, 170, 171, 172, 195, 196, 197, 225 n.9, n.13, 226 n.35, n.39, 227 n.59, n.61, 228 n.63, n.77, 231 n.145, 233 n.40, 234 n.58, n.7, n.9, 235 n.24, n.35, 240 n.71, 242 n.110, 243 n.6, 246 n.21, n.26, 247 n.31, n.33, n.55, 248 n.8, 249 n.27, n.28, n.30, 252 n.70
Soloveichik, Ḥayyim, 127, 241 n.30
Soloveichik, Joseph B., 241 n.90
Spero, Mosheh haLevi, 233 n.52
Swartz, Thomas R., 234 n.1

Tabak, Solomon Leib, 249 n.21
Talmedai haRashba, 250 n.32
Tam, Jacob, 40, 41, 196, 197, 198, 199, 200, 226 n.27, 231 n.143, 237 n.80, 250 n.34, n.40, n.41
Tashbeẓ, See Duran, Simeon b. Ẓemaḥ
Teitelbaum, Mosheh, 228 n.63
Telser, Lester G., 208, 209, 210, 252 n.74
Teshurot Shai, See Tabak, Solomon Leib
Tashuvat me-Ahavah, See Fleckeles, Eliezer
Teshuvot Maimuniyyot, See Meir ha-Kohen
Toledot Adam ve-Ḥavvah, See Yeruḥam b. Meshullam
Tomer Deborah, See Cordovero, Moses
Torat ha-Adam, See Naḥmanides
Tosafot, 23, 26, 27, 28, 54, 84, 226 n.27, 227 n.47, n.54, n.58, n.60, n.61, 228 n.62, 230 n.129, 231 n.136, 232 n.14, 236 n.78, 240 n.58, 241 n.84, n.91, 243 n.6, 245 n.50, 246 n.6, n.12, 247 n.34, 248 n.10, 249 n.28, 250 n.34, n.41
Tosafot Rid, See Yehshayah of Trani I ha-Zaken
Tosafot ha-Rosh, See Asher b. Jeḥiel
Trani, Moses b. Joseph, 99, 100, 236 n.80, 237 n.90, n.91, 249 n.18
Tur, See Jacob b. Asher
Turei Zahav, See David b. Samuel ha-Levi
Turei Zahav, See Twersky, Mordecai Dov
Twersky, Mordecai Dov, 152, 244 n.42

Vidal Yom Tov of Tolosa, 229 n.99, 243 n.12, 250 n.39, 251 n.60

Waldenberg, Eliezer, 137, 242 n.116
Warhaftig, Shillem, 174, 180, 147 n.39, n.54, 248 n.62
Weidenbaum, Murray, 78
Weil, Jacob b. Judah, 34, 230 n.106
Weiss, Isaac Jacob, 242 n.1, 248 n.4
Willig, Robert D., 234 n.6
Winkler, Leopold, 245 n.52
Wolf, Israel Isser b. Ze'ev, 230 n.121
Working, Holbrook, 252 n.75
Wrighter, Carl P., 46, 231 n.1

Yad, See Maimonides
Yehonatan of Lunel, 162, 164, 166, 167, 246 n.11
Yere'im, See Eliezer b. Samuel of Metz
Yeshayah of Trani I ha-Zaken, 242 n.111